# ENLISTING WOMEN FOR THE CAUSE: WOMEN, LABOUR, AND THE LEFT IN CANADA, 1890–1920

In *Enlisting Women for the Cause*, Linda Kealey re-creates the experiences of Canadian women on the left in the late nineteenth and early twentieth centuries, a crucial period when women became more prominent in the work force, in labour unions, and in politics, where they fought for, and ultimately won, the vote.

The book examines discourse on women's work and on attempts to regulate it; labour activism, including formal membership in unions and parties as well as women's auxiliaries and organizations such as the Women's Labor League; and women's militancy during the First World War and the troubled postwar period. The author argues that while women helped mount an opposition to the inequalities inherent in industrial capitalism, they also had to struggle to move beyond the supporting role they were forced to play in the very movements to which they belonged.

Kealey explores what the left thought about women's participation in politics and in left-wing organizations across the country, and also looks at the nature of that participation itself. The scope of her book puts it in the forefront of its field.

LINDA KEALEY is a professor in the Department of History at Memorial University of Newfoundland. She is the co-editor, with Joan Sangster, of *Beyond the Vote: Canadian Women and Politics*.

LINDA KEALEY

# Enlisting Women for the Cause: Women, Labour, and the Left in Canada, 1890–1920

UNIVERSITY OF TORONTO PRESS
Toronto Buffalo London

© University of Toronto Press Incorporated 1998
Toronto Buffalo London

Printed in Canada

ISBN 0-8020-2874-8 (cloth)
ISBN 0-8020-7378-6 (paper)

Printed on acid-free paper

---

**Canadian Cataloguing in Publication Data**

Kealey, Linda, 1947–
Enlisting women for the cause: women, labour, and the left
in Canada, 1890–1920

(Studies in gender and history)
Includes bibliographical references and index.
ISBN 0-8020-2874-8 (bound)     ISBN 0-8020-7378-6 (pbk.)

1. Women in the labor movement – Canada – History.
2. Women – Employment – Canada – History.   3. Women
and socialism – Canada – History.   I. Title.   II. Series.

HD6099.K4 1998       331.4'78'0971       C97-932553-6

---

University of Toronto Press acknowledges the financial assistance to its
publishing program of the Canada Council for the Arts and the Ontario Arts
Council.

This book has been published with the help of a grant from the Humanities
and Social Sciences Federation of Canada, using funds provided by the Social
Sciences and Humanities Research Council of Canada.

# Contents

vi Contents

# Acknowledgments

This book was made possible by the support of many institutions and individuals. The initial stages were funded by a Vice-President's Research Grant at Memorial University of Newfoundland, which allowed me to apply to the Social Sciences and Humanities Research Council's Women and Work Strategic Grant Program in 1983. Without these grants this manuscript would not have been finished. Over the years, smaller summer student grants also proved invaluable.

Various individuals carried out research for the project, and none more competently than Jessie Chisholm. Translation and research were also provided by Mauri A. Jalava (Finnish), Samuel Trachtenberg (Yiddish), and Bohdana Dutka (Ukrainian). Others who assisted with translation work are Eeva Rose, Varpu Lindström (who also shared her own research with me), and Orest Martynovych.

As always, Gregory Kealey provided critical and helpful responses to various drafts, and he has supported this project from its inception. Other colleagues too numerous to mention provided research suggestions or read various drafts of papers that were incorporated into chapters. Colleagues – both faculty and students – at Memorial University of Newfoundland heard variations of draft chapters as well, and I thank them for their contributions. I owe an especially large debt to University of Toronto Press editor Gerry Hallowell for his thorough read of an earlier draft; I will be forever grateful for his unabashed criticisms and suggestions for revision. To Irene Whitfield, I extend my thanks for the seemingly endless revisions she made to the manuscript in its many versions. Thanks also go to my daughter, Caitlin, who helped in finalizing the bibliography. Finally, my thanks to all the archivists and librarians across the country who assisted me with this project.

Permission to reprint the following material is gratefully acknowledged: part of chapter 4 appeared as 'Canadian Socialism and the Woman Question, 1900–1914,' *Labour/Le Travail* 13 (Spring 1984): 77–100; part of chapter 5 appeared as 'Women and Labour during World War I: Women Workers and the Minimum Wage in Manitoba,' in *First Days, Fighting Days: Women in Manitoba History,* ed. Mary Kinnear (Regina: Canadian Plains Research Center, 1987), reproduced courtesy of the Canadian Plains Research Center; part of chapter 7 appeared as '"No Special Protection – No Sympathy": Women's Activism in the Canadian Labour Revolt of 1919,' in *Class, Community, and the Labour Movement: Wales and Canada, 1850–1930,* ed. Deian R. Hopkin and Gregory S. Kealey (Aberystwyth, 1989), 134–59.

# Abbreviations

ACWA      Amalgamated Clothing Workers of America
ALU       American Labor Union
BCWSL     British Columbia Women's Suffrage League
BLFE      Brotherhood of Locomotive Firemen and Enginemen
BRT       Brotherhood of Railway Trainmen
CCF       Cooperative Commonwealth Federation
CPC       Communist Party of Canada
CSA       Canadian Suffrage Association
CSL       Canadian Socialist League
DLP       Dominion Labor Party
FLP       Federated Labor Party
FLU       Federal Labour Union
FSOC      Finnish Socialist Organization of Canada
FUSD      Federation of Ukrainian Social Democrats
IAM       International Association of Machinists
IBEW      International Brotherhood of Electrical Workers
ILGWU     International Ladies' Garment Workers' Union
ILP       Independent Labor Party
IMB       Imperial Munitions Board
IODE      Imperial Order Daughters of the Empire
ITU       International Typographical Union
IWW       Industrial Workers of the World
JTU       Journeymen Tailors' Union of America
LCW       Local Council of Women
LEA       Labor Educational Association
LWC       Labour Women's Council
MWB       Minimum Wage Board

| | |
|---|---|
| NCWC | National Council of Women of Canada |
| NEFU | National Equal Franchise Union |
| NPL | Non-Partisan League |
| OBU | One Big Union |
| OSL | Ontario Socialist League |
| PEL | Political Equality League |
| RCMP | Royal Canadian Mounted Police |
| RTLC | Regina Trades and Labour Council |
| SDP | Social Democratic Party |
| SLP | Socialist Labor Party |
| SPA | Socialist Party of America |
| SPBC | Socialist Party of British Columbia |
| SPC | Socialist Party of Canada |
| SPD | German Social Democratic Party |
| SPGB | Socialist Party of Great Britain |
| SPNA | Socialist Party of North America |
| SYG | Socialist Youth Guard |
| TLC | Trades and Labor Congress |
| TTLC | Toronto Trades and Labor Council (also known as Toronto District Labor Council) |
| UFWA | United Farm Women of Alberta |
| UGWA | United Garment Workers of America |
| VTLC | Vancouver Trades and Labor Council |
| WCG | Women's Cooperative Guild |
| WCTU | Woman's Christian Temperance Union |
| WEL | Women's Employment League |
| WFM | Western Federation of Miners |
| WGGA | Women Grain Growers' Association (Saskatchewan) |
| WILPF | Women's International League for Peace and Freedom |
| WIULL | Women's International Union Label League |
| WLL | Women's Labor League |
| WPU | Women's Protective Union (also known as Working Women's Protective Association) |
| WSDL | Women's Social Democratic League |
| YWCA | Young Women's Christian Association |

# ENLISTING WOMEN FOR THE CAUSE

# Introduction

Until recently, the history of the Canadian labour and socialist movements has been gender-blind and has failed to acknowledge the roles played by women. This volume aims to rectify the lack of attention paid to labour and socialist women. It presents not only critical and analytical perspectives on these movements, but also argues that they benefited from the invaluable input of women, particularly working-class women, whose activities ranged from fundraising in the back rooms to taking on public leadership and organizational roles.

While most of the women active in these movements between 1890 and 1920 played supportive roles in women's auxiliaries, in strike support, and in socialist party back rooms, a number of interesting characters played more prominent parts as labour organizers, journalists, and soapbox orators. Women activists often viewed themselves as working not only for the movement, but specifically to increase the participation and power of women within these groups.

Marie Joussaye, labour organizer and poet, was an early activist who worked on behalf of her working-class sisters. Closely associated with the pioneering Working Women's Protective Association in Toronto, Joussaye emerged from obscurity as a domestic in small-town Ontario to become a committed organizer of women workers and a poet who celebrated the 'honest working girl' of the late nineteenth century.

Bertha Merrill Burns, journalist, socialist, and feminist, took a public role in the early twentieth century, writing columns for several socialist newspapers, organizing women into socialist groups, and, with her husband, leading a breakaway group from the Socialist Party of Canada. The press became a vehicle for Merrill Burns's alternative views, and for those of other women journalists on the left, such as Francis Beynon, Mary Cotton Wisdom, and Gertrude Richardson.

Laura Hughes embraced labour politics, suffrage, and the peace movement in the years surrounding the First World War. As a suffragist and pacifist, she participated in a network of like-minded women, which included Manitobans Beynon and Richardson, Saskatchewan's Violet McNaughton, and other activist women from Hughes's own province of Ontario. Not all of these colleagues, however, shared her commitment to the labour movement.

Perhaps the most outspoken of all the English-speaking activists of the period, Winnipeg's Helen Armstrong became a women's labour organizer in the years leading up to the First World War, a role that intensified during the war itself. The most prominent woman in the Winnipeg General Strike, Armstrong was purely an activist rather than a theoretician or journalist. For many years she was closely associated with the Women's Labor League and the western labour movement in general.

Sophie Mushkat was a socialist organizer and immigrant radical who came to Canada in the early part of the twentieth century and spent her life working for one socialist group or another. A political maverick who often quarrelled with party policies, she nevertheless provided a rare example of a woman political organizer.

Such women activists must be understood in the context of class and gender role expectations of the period. Working-class ideals for women included some contribution to the family economy before marriage, usually from a respectable occupation that did not expose young women to unhealthy, morally suspect working conditions. Ultimately, marriage and motherhood were expected to occupy women full-time, although pressing needs for extra income in slow seasons or in times of hardship occasioned by unemployment or the death of the breadwinner could draw married women back into the labour market. Although a powerful ideal, the family wage was often illusory, and most families depended on multiple wage earners, including children of both sexes.

By the 1890s public discourse increasingly fastened on the problem of the working woman or girl whose wages were extremely low and whose morals might easily be corrupted by the industrial system. Thus, while urging the elimination of child and female labour, male unionists (as well as middle-class reformers) simultaneously faced the elusiveness of the family wage and the increasing appetite of capital for cheaper labour. In this context the working woman became a focus, a scapegoat for much that was wrong in the industrial world. Not only did she threaten men's jobs by supplying cheap labour, she also threatened to upset the Victorian sense of moral and social order by her very presence in the labour market.

As Carolyn Strange has pointed out in *Toronto's Girl Problem*, late-nineteenth-century observers agreed that 'the further from domesticity and family women workers seemed to drift, the more dear – and dangerous – seemed the cost of urban industrial capitalism.' Despite the fact that fewer than 20 per cent of female wage earners lived independently of their families in the 1880s, investigators for the 1889 Royal Commission on Labor and Capital stressed the weaknesses and the vulnerability of young women workers and contributed to the image of the 'woman adrift' to justify interventions into working-class women's lives. According to Strange, by the twentieth century investigations of women's work 'dropped an explicitly moral approach and took on a social-scientific tone.' In keeping with the trend towards educated, middle-class women's insistence on roles that usefully employed them, some young women turned towards the professions, including social work, which stressed the study of social problems and the need for investigation and intervention. State-sponsored investigations acknowledged some of the problems confronted by women workers, such as poor and unhealthy working conditions, long hours, and low pay, but the chief concern was protection for future mothers and the coming generations of workers.[1]

Well into the twentieth century, the labour movement generally accepted the premise that working women posed a problem and a potential threat. The official labour position until the First World War featured a call to keep women out of the factories and shops, and to end child labour. While labour was resistant to the idea of women working in male-defined jobs during the war, the extreme labour shortages often meant that employers hired women, at least temporarily, to work on streetcars, in welding shops, and in munitions factories, as well as to fill the jobs more closely defined as women's work. At the end of the war, it was difficult to insist on removing women from the labour market, and in the 1920s it became more acceptable for even young, middle-class women to spend time working before marriage and motherhood. Although the family headed by a male breadwinner earning a family wage remained an ideal vision of working-class life for many, the exigencies of daily life continued to prevent its realization for most people.[2]

As the socialist movement grew from its early roots in the 1890s it promised to put in place an alternative vision of the economy, politics, and society. Part of that new vision included equality of the sexes, political and legal rights for women, equal pay, and a new basis for marriage and motherhood. As women in the socialist movement discovered, however, actual policies seldom matched the admirable rhetoric. 'Equality' within the movement was difficult to insist on, and women were most often assigned secondary status. A few achieved leadership positions, but often at great personal cost. Many more provided the social, financial, and organizational skills that kept socialist groups solvent and successful.

Until recently, such work in the party's back rooms or in union auxiliaries was dismissed as unimportant, thus obscuring the value of the work these women accomplished. As much of the more recent North American literature suggests, political activism among women has taken many forms. Labour historians have discovered that moving their focus away from the workplace and into the community enlarges their understanding of working-class activism and illustrates the ties between the workplace and the community, as well as the gendered dimensions of each. Historians Susan Levine and Sylvie Murray, for example, have both argued that 'women's auxiliaries' have played vital roles in the lives of both working-class women and men. They have provided a place for non-wage-earning women to come together for social and educational reasons and have tied their domestic lives to the world of wage labour.[3]

Dana Frank's 1994 study of the Seattle working class in the decade after the First World War also moves away from the realm of paid work to examine women's prominent roles as consumers. Frank's study suggests that the organization of cooperatives, union label campaigns, and boycotts of non-union goods and services provides a meeting point between productive and reproductive labour, and that women assumed a large role in politicizing consumption. Union label campaigns, for instance, involved the intensification of women's work as housewives and continued the work of the trade unions within the domestic arena. Thus, like Levine and Murray, Frank complicates the picture of women's contributions to the labour movement by demonstrating that non-waged women might engage in a variety of activities that supported the movement but also addressed issues of concern to women.[4]

Ardis Cameron's *Radicals of the Worst Sort* sketches the importance of women's use of community and neighbourhood ties and spaces to assist the Lawrence, Massachusetts, strikers in their battles against the textile mills in 1882 and again in 1912. Women's networks conveyed strike information, devised strategies for picketing, and warned of police movements. Neighbourhoods filled with women and children served as meeting places and parade routes and provided resources to strikers and their families. Groups of women mobbed police vans and participated in parades and pickets. Individual women were sometimes successful spies gathering information. Such actions were echoed in several Canadian strikes, most notably the 1912 Eaton's strike, a 1917 Jewish women's boycott of bakers, and the Winnipeg General Strike of 1919. In these moments working-class women mobilized to challenge class and gender hierarchies, thus fashioning their own political consciousness and establishing their own agency.[5]

A recent study of Cape Breton coal towns in the 1920s underlines the role of working-class women in bitter labour disputes in which the military was often called upon to protect the interests of the corporation. Steven Penfold documents that the soldiers sent to guard the mines were heckled and belittled by women who challenged their masculinity and their patriotism. In addition, the gendered language of male strikers and labour activists reveals the association of true manhood or masculinity with mining and working-class acts of solidarity. Conversely, class enemies were portrayed in feminine terms. 'Femininity' was even associated with potential threats to class solidarity since women as a category were typed as either passive victims or natural conservatives.[6]

Penfold's study underlines the ways in which women contested such assumptions about their sex. Viewing strikes as centres of 'community mobilizations,' Penfold maps the various ways in which women used their own resources and community networks to aid the striking miners. Women's ability to 'make ends meet' was an important contribution to labour militancy, albeit less dramatic than their participation in looting company stores. Miners recognized that their wives were the 'best financiers in the world,' according to union leader J.B. McLachlan; since miners seldom earned a living wage, their wives were charged with stretching the family's income as far as possible, especially in times of a strike. Women also banded together in small groups to defend their communities and to lend support to strikers. Women's Labor Leagues appeared in Cape Breton in the 1920s. While WLL branches were usually tied to the Communist Party, earlier versions of these groups had preceded the emergence of the CPC. Winnipeg's WLL, founded in 1917 under Helen Armstrong's leadership, combined fundraising, education, relief work, strike support, and other political interventions just as it

provided testimony that working-class women were far from conservative or passive.[7]

Why was so much women's activism assigned secondary status or rendered invisible within the labour and socialist movements of the time?
Why was difference emphasized over the similarity or complementarity
of interests between women and men? Part of the answer lies in the
period's cultural and scientific assumptions about men and women.

A persistent assumption of female conservatism runs through the discourse on women no matter what their class background. This assumption that women were *by nature* more conservative and more resistant to
change than men appears to be universal in Western culture. Women
were seen as unique, and this uniqueness, rooted in biology, explained
women's conservatism. As the sex responsible for bearing and rearing
children, women invested more in nurturing and preserving life and
thus were less willing to take risks and were less able to be independent
and autonomous. Labour and socialist supporters wielded these arguments to suggest that women were less militant, less likely to support
strikes, and less committed to socialism.

Nineteenth-century science, particularly its Lamarckian and Darwin-
ian versions, offered support for this view of gender difference. Evolutionary science tended to view certain groups – non-whites, immigrants,
and women – as genetically inferior and subordinate. Like the other two
categories, women were often compared to children or less-evolved
creatures. The conclusion was that a woman's capabilities were suited to
her unique domestic and private responsibilities, while a man's talents
were defined as universal and appropriate to the public sphere. Sometimes genetic explanations were combined uneasily with environmental
factors, suggesting that custom and social practice reinforced heredity.
Canadian socialists subscribed to these very ideas, sending confusing
messages to women in the movement. Women were praised for their
contributions, particularly on the basis of their role in the family, and
were urged to join the socialist movement; at the same time, they were
assessed as weaker and more easily led and thus as incapable of participating in the real work of organizing and fighting for a new social, political, and economic order.[8]

Other 'differences' also proved divisive. Ethnic stereotypes fostered
by Anglo-Saxon superiority threatened both the labour and socialist
movements, which accepted pseudo-scientific perspectives on racial
hierarchies reminiscent of the acceptance of gender differentials.
Assumptions of Anglo-Saxon superiority depended upon accompany-

ing devaluations of Asian, eastern European, Jewish, and non-white groups. Anti-Chinese sentiment flourished on the West Coast of North America in the 1870s and 1880s and spread to other parts of Canada by the turn of the century. The press deplored Asian immigration, associating the Chinese, for example, not only with cheap labour but also with corruption, vice, and immorality. Ironically, while the press constructed Chinese men as predators on white women, the dominant imagery undercut their masculinity and stressed their feminine characteristics. Strong anti-Chinese sentiment made it difficult, if not impossible, for the labour movement to achieve solidarity across ethnic lines.[9]

Anti-Semitism also disrupted working-class and international solidarities. Despite sharing working-class identities, Jews and non-Jews lived in separate neighbourhoods, belonged to separate fraternal groups, and often belonged to separate union locals. Other divisions, such as those of skill level, also kept Jew and Gentile apart as well as pitting men against women in many cases. Furthermore, as Ruth Frager and Gerald Tulchinsky have identified, class often divided members of the Jewish community between workers and businessmen, thus fracturing ethnic solidarity. Although there were many cultural ties shared between worker and boss that may have dampened class conflict, there were also many documented cases of Jewish manufacturers squaring off against their employees, especially in times of militant strike action, such as the major offensive by the garment unions in 1919.[10]

Gender combined with ethnicity in some cases to pit Gentile women against Jewish women and men during labour disputes. One example of non-Jewish women breaking a strike by Jewish women and men occurred in Toronto in 1911. When forty-five cloakmakers and skirtmakers went on strike to protest wage cuts and discrimination against their union, the socialist newspaper *Cotton's Weekly* noted that the strikebreakers were not Chinese, blacks, or other foreigners but 'WHITE GIRLS AND MEN OF BRITISH BIRTH ... CANADIAN GIRLS ARE HANDED WORK THAT JEWISH GIRLS REFUSE TO DO.'[11]

Even socialist publications like *Cotton's Weekly* demonstrated negative attitudes towards non-whites and immigrants, as the quote above demonstrates. Reflecting dominant groups' views of non-whites, the labour and socialist movements by and large accepted the inferiority of blacks in the evolutionary scheme and did not contest their assignment to the lowest-paying jobs. Nova Scotian–born blacks as well as Caribbean immigrants were relegated to the lowest-level jobs: for women this meant domestic work; for men, agricultural and heavy industrial labour.

Small numbers of black men were recruited from the Caribbean to work in Nova Scotia's mines and steel mills especially around the First World War, and a similar scheme brought one hundred Guadeloupean domestics to Quebec in 1910–11. Most of their employers reported satisfaction with their performance, but the Caribbean Domestic Scheme was shelved out of fears of 'immorality' among the women. Despite shortages of domestics, especially during the war, immigration officials rejected pleas for more immigrants from the Caribbean. In 1922, Order-in-Council PC 717 effectively limited immigration to certain categories of workers and to British subjects from white, English-speaking countries.[12]

Ethnic divisions and racist attitudes pervaded the socialist movement in Canada in the first two decades of the twentieth century. With some notable exceptions, the leadership of the main socialist groups – the Socialist Party of Canada and the Social Democratic Party – tended to be born in either Britain or North America. Language and cultural differences complicated the task of organizing locals and running meetings – hence, the adoption of 'language locals,' which brought together members of the same ethnic group. Although such a strategy may have encouraged growth in the socialist movement, it also reinforced feelings of difference among the various immigrant groups. Difference was also emphasized among women of diverse ethnic groups, at least in the press. The *Western Clarion*, for example, unfavourably compared English-speaking women comrades to their Jewish and Finnish counterparts who took active and outspoken roles at gatherings. By contrast, the English-speaking women were retiring and reluctant to speak out, according to the newspaper.[13]

Despite divisions and differences that spanned class, gender, race, and ethnicity, labour and socialist women in Canada have left us evidence that they did not always acquiesce to attempts to deprive them of their own identities, agendas, and activism. This study builds on some of the previous literature in Canada, the United States, and elsewhere that suggests that a wider perspective on what constitutes women's activism yields a new appreciation for what women did in fact accomplish. This wider view, in turn, demands a rejection of any narrow definition of what is judged as 'political.' Older descriptions associate the political with public-arena activism, usually in the form of a party, lobbying group, or union. By widening the focus to encompass women's activities in the home, the neighbourhood, and the community, as well as in the union, the party, or the workplace, much more becomes visible that previously was hidden or ignored.[14]

By taking a national and cross-regional perspective, this book focuses on the wide sweep of women's activism across the country while maintaining an eye on regional differences. Different levels of economic and political development clearly had an impact on the nature of the labour market and the union movement, and on political possibilities. These same structural factors shaped the lives of women and men in their neighbourhoods and communities; as this book suggests, however, cultural background and ideological proclivities are integrally related to daily life and the possibility of challenging the status quo. Recognition of the power of structural and ideological pressures does not rule out the potential for contestation, for human agency.

The time period chosen for the study reflects the lacunae in previous writing on Canadian labour and the left, which tended, until very recently, to pay more attention to the period before the 1890s or after the First World War. Since this project began, Janice Newton completed her PhD on a similar topic and has recently published a revised version of her thesis. Her work concentrates on the English-speaking socialist women in three left-wing groups between 1900 and 1918 and addresses what socialist men and women thought and wrote about the 'woman question.' In contrast, this volume attempts to provide a wider framework and more than a history of discourse. Part of this framework encompasses the overlapping interests and realms of labour and socialist women and the tensions between progressive, middle-class women and their working-class sisters.[15]

It became increasingly clear in the course of research that labour and left-wing women's activities intersected and overlapped. Often women were involved in several organizations. Some of these groups were more directly related to labour's concerns with women's work as wage earners or as working-class wives and mothers; others were more avowedly left-wing political groups whose agendas included fundamental transformation of the economic and political framework of industrial capitalism. While not all labour women subscribed to a socialist view of the world, women identifying with the socialist movements of the period often addressed themselves to issues related to women's work, either paid or unpaid. Despite socialist ambivalence or outright hostility to gender issues, some socialist women (and a few men) persistently raised women's concerns within these movements and organizations, arguing that such issues had to be addressed in order to strengthen and expand socialism itself. Within the labour movement, women activists had to make similar arguments. In doing so, these women were fighting the widely held perception that feminism was of necessity a middle-class movement with little to offer working-class women whose major problems seemed to stem from the unequal division of wealth and power inherent in capitalism. The discourse of working-class feminism, while muted, was shared by labour and socialist women who attempted to bring women's issues to the forefront, albeit within different but overlapping contexts.

The organization of this book reflects the dual focus on labour and the left in Canada. Chapters 1, 2, and 5 directly address women workers and their struggles in the workplace. Chapter 1 provides a context for contemporary views on women workers who, according to social reformers, government officials, and union men, appeared to pose a threat to Canadian society. As this chapter makes clear, the stereotype of the easily victimized 'working girl' was countered by the alternative view of 'honest womanhood.' Chapter 2 addresses women's labour activism from the 1890s through to the First World War, with particular emphasis on labour disputes involving women; the last section of the chapter moves beyond the workplace to women's auxiliaries and label leagues, which most often involved married working-class women in community-based activities allied to the labour movement. Chapter 5 examines the war period, highlighting the impact of the war boom on women's work, attempts to regulate and organize female labour, and the record of women's wartime strike militancy, particularly in the late stages of the war. Chapters 3, 4, and 6 specifically address the role of women in the various socialist groupings of the period – from early socialist leagues through the Socialist Party of Canada and the Social Democratic Party of Canada – as well as evidence of separate women's organizations. While chapters 3 and 4 deal with women's activism before 1914, chapter 6 details the experience of women socialists during the war, including the difficult choices women pacifists made during this profoundly disturbing period. Finally, chapter 7, which includes discussion of the Winnipeg General Strike and its aftermath, focuses on postwar militancy and politics as they affected labour and socialist women.

Every historical study is shaped by the nature of the available sources. This book has relied heavily on the press of the period, particularly labour and left-wing newspapers. Personal papers were scarce, and key organizational records were not always extant. While historians of more recent decades might turn to oral history, most of the fascinating women uncovered in the research died long ago, leaving few traces. Government-generated records, such as the Department of Labour's

Strikes and Lockouts files, or the various commissions appointed by those in power, served particular purposes that are not necessarily compatible with the questions asked by historical researchers. Nevertheless, these sources have been of considerable value, especially in conjunction with surviving union records, in trying to understand women's work and labour activism in the period. Similarly, socialist women's activities have been ferreted out of movement sources that often played down or were suspicious of gender-conscious women's activism, or out of government-generated sources that, particularly during the First World War, aimed at surveillance, usually of radicals, who were considered especially dangerous. Selective destruction of RCMP files in the past and the state's focus on those later associated with the Communist Party have meant that records on lesser-known activists, or those not associated with communist activities, were not collected or were destroyed.[16]

As a writer and historian, I bring to this work my own world-view, which has been strongly influenced by involvement in the oppositional culture of the 1960s and 1970s, including the student movement, the anti–Vietnam War movement, and the rediscovery of feminism. Shaped also by graduate-school training and the exciting discovery of social history in the 1970s, my work reflects some of the tensions and many of the possibilities opened up by these currents. As a socialist-feminist historian I had initially hoped and expected to find labour and socialist women activists who provided clear leadership for working-class women within these movements, much as the men did – in public, at demonstrations, strikes, and meetings. It became clear, however, that only a vocal minority were able to do so, because of the different nature of women's lives, which were bounded by family and community responsibilities and subject to particular standards of appropriate gendered behaviour. These competing demands made it more difficult for women to assume public roles similar to those of labour and socialist men. Such a distinctive positioning often meant that the women looked at issues differently than the men.

As Barbara Taylor stresses in *Eve and the New Jerusalem*, there is a value in trying to re-create the past experiences of women on the left. Their experiences and struggles remind us that women's left-wing activism is not a product of the recent past alone, that other women confronted barriers of class, gender, ethnicity, and race. There is a tendency to forget or erase the radical past or to identify such experiences with more recent, and now much changed, movements such as the Communist Party or perhaps the social democracy of the Cooperative Commonwealth Federation, now the New Democratic Party. This book, then, is intended to remind us that women in the late nineteenth and early twentieth centuries also mounted an opposition to the inequalities inherent in industrial capitalism and, sometimes, to the inequalities in the very movements they so closely identified with.[17]

For indeed, the recurring themes of this book revolve around the consistent assignment of separate, supportive, and often less valued roles to women in the labour and socialist movements. Women in these movements experienced a gendered division of labour much as they did in the labour market. In both the movement and the market, working-class women were to be protected and assisted. Some women might not need this protection and assistance and might demonstrate aptitudes for organization and activism; most women, however, were expected to stay in the back room or play roles associated with appropriate domestic support of the union or party.

Labour and socialist women had to contend with the expectations and the real material constraints surrounding the meaning of working-class womanhood in the late nineteenth and early twentieth centuries. These expectations and constraints varied according to culture and marital status but centred around the clear premise that women's primary allegiances had to be to their families and working-class communities. Even though class and ethnic loyalty was expected, such loyalty was filtered through the lens of family and community, with their specific gendered divisions of labour.

The material conditions of women's lives and the prevailing gender, class, and ethnic ideologies reinforced such a division of labour within the labour and socialist movements. As the following chapters demonstrate, however, women were not always content to play supportive or less public roles. Women workers could subscribe to the self-respecting notion of 'honest womanhood,' which proclaimed the value of waged labour and the dignity of the 'working girl.' Working women might vote with their feet by leaving an exploitative job or, in the right circumstances, might strike as a collective method of redressing grievances. In assessing their own needs as members of ethnic, labour, or socialist groups, women could and did develop their own organizational forms of struggle, most often at the local level. Despite pressures to remain within prescribed limits, and widespread distrust of 'bourgeois feminism,' labour and socialist women activists challenged the boundaries and participated in the initial stages of a working-class feminist project.

# 1

# 'Only a Working Girl': Women's Work and Regulation, 1890–1914

I belong to the 'lower classes':
That's a phrase we often meet.
There are some who sneer at working girls;
As they pass us on the street,
They stare at us in proud disdain
And their lips in scorn will curl,
And oftentimes we hear them say:
'She's only a working girl ...'

So when you meet with scornful sneers,
Just lift your heads in pride;
The shield of honest womanhood
Can turn such sneers aside,
And some day they will realize
That the purest, fairest pearls
'Mid the gems of noble womankind
Are 'only working girls.'

Marie Joussaye, 'Only a Working Girl'

By 1891 one out of every eight Canadian workers was a woman or a girl. Marie Joussaye, the author of 'Only a Working Girl,' was one of thousands of young women who had to earn their daily bread in the context of a maturing industrial capitalism. Born in Belleville around 1864 and growing up in a fatherless family of five children, Joussaye had experiences in the paid labour force that were not uncommon. Like many other young women in similar circumstances, she had little formal education, and at the age of eleven she began to earn her living as a servant in her hometown. Also like other women, she was attracted to a larger urban area – in this case Toronto – where presumably she sought employment. But in other ways Joussaye was unique: she became an organizer for servant girls and a labour poet.[1]

By the late nineteenth century, women who needed to earn a wage faced a wider array of employment possibilities than had Joussaye. Depending on region and the local economy, women workers might seek employment in the mills, shops, and factories of Ontario, Quebec, and the Maritimes, or they might find work as seamstresses in the growing sweated trades of urban Montreal, Toronto, Hamilton, Halifax, or Winnipeg. In the far West with a more agricultural and resource-based economy, women found work as domestics or in the service sector more often than in manufacturing. Servants remained in great demand in both rural and urban areas at the turn of the century, and service occupations employed a far greater proportion of women than factory work well into the twentieth century.

Choice of occupation was structured not only by region and level of economic development, but also by marital or family status and by cultural norms and constraints. In the contemporary mind and in the official census returns, the typical working woman was young, single, and in the labour force only until marriage or family responsibilities precluded further wage work. It was assumed that most working women would become wives and mothers, busy with innumerable domestic chores; it was also assumed that a male wage would provide the family's main support. Until then, young working-class women engaged in paid labour as a necessary evil, to support themselves and perhaps contribute to the family while living at home. Because women workers were young, unskilled, and low-paid, many reformers sought some kind of protection for them from the extremes of exploitation, if only as a means to protect them from immorality and possible future risks to their unborn children.

To social reformers, male workers, and to many working women themselves, the expectation of eventual marriage and motherhood was central to their views on paid labour for women. This expectation made it possible to justify lower wages for women, for example, or particular kinds of work most suited to their future status as wives and mothers. Unpaid domestic labour was the lot of all but the wealthiest women; it was assumed to be part and parcel of the married woman's role and, to a lesser extent, that of unmarried, dependent female relatives. Such labour was not referred to as 'work,' unless performed by a servant for remuneration. Domestic labour performed by wives or other female household members remained private, invisible, and 'natural,' as opposed to the public, paid, and problematic work of women in the labour market.

Recent studies of women's work in Canada suggest that the emphasis on young single women working only before marriage and motherhood is at best a partial view. The death or illness of a spouse, chronic underemployment or unemployment, and seasonality in male work patterns often meant that widowed or married women and their older children also had to contribute to the family economy. The form that contribution took depended on geography, the local economy, and cultural norms and constraints. Widows in nineteenth-century Montreal and twentieth-century Paris, Ontario, for example, found a number of ways of contributing to the family economy. They might take in boarders, clean by the day, run small shops, or take on other employments that fit with household duties. Married women might also explore these and other options such as sewing at home for clothing manufacturers. Much of this work was hidden from the census takers and thus not recorded as paid labour. In addition, married women's work was considered to be detrimental to the welfare of families because it disturbed women's focus on the care of home, husband, and children, whose needs were viewed as primary.[2]

Ethnic or racial origins also shaped the kind of work women could do. African–Nova Scotian women were relegated to particular forms of wage employment such as peddling in the Halifax market and domestic service. Jewish women in urban centres such as Toronto were heavily concentrated in the garment industry, constituting 60 per cent of the industry's workers in 1911. Homework by women, men, and children in cramped unsanitary conditions was common in the industry, driving down prices paid for garments. In contrast, Finnish women immigrants often preferred domestic work, in which they took considerable pride.[3]

The increasing prominence of women's work, exposés of the exploitation of female and child labour, and concerns for the health and morality of a rapidly urbanizing Canadian society fuelled fears that the trend towards women's increasing labour force participation would fundamentally damage the bedrock of Canadian society – the family. Allied to these fears about the security and stability of the normative family – that is, one headed by a male breadwinner – were concerns that women's

work potentially competed with men's and thus threatened to undermine men's employment and wages. Fear of immorality also pervaded
the debates about women's and girls' work. Participation in paid work
in public spaces might expose female workers to moral dangers in the
shape of exploitative foremen or bosses, and their low wages might
tempt them to a life of prostitution, which offered, in the minds of many,
financial inducements higher than the wages commonly paid to women
and young girls.

Women's work at the turn of the century presented a dilemma that
demanded discussion and action. For the labour movement the answer
lay in campaigns to eliminate women's work as well as child labour. Up
to the beginning of the First World War, the national labour umbrella
organization, the Trades and Labor Congress of Canada (TLC), advocated the elimination of such work, but working women such as Joussaye, who felt the daily pressure to earn a living, did not have the option
of leaving paid employment. Instead, working women insisted on the
value of wage earning and proclaimed that there was no shame in being
a 'working girl' as long as wages were earned in honest employment. It
was possible to earn a living and remain a 'respectable' member of the
working class. After all, Christ himself, as Joussaye reminded her readers, had earned his daily bread as a humble carpenter. Working women
could take pride in their strength and skill while earning wages to support themselves and their families, thus demonstrating their 'honest
womanhood.'

Critics warned that wages might also be spent selfishly or unwisely
on dress or amusements. Such spending demonstrated an unseemly
autonomy from family, or, even worse, a taste for a lifestyle beyond
the means of most working women. While dressing neatly and presenting a clean, well-groomed appearance was a mark of a respectable
working woman, either a sloppy appearance or a penchant for finery
threatened to undermine her character and place her in the 'promiscuous' category. Thus, working women had to walk a fine line between
respectability and promiscuity. Their dress, deportment, and spending
habits were closely observed and much commented upon, particularly
by those among the middle and upper classes who concerned themselves with the 'problem' of the working girl in need of guidance and
protection.[4]

While working-class women insisted on the value of honest womanhood, social reformers from the middle or upper class looked to voluntary groups and, later, to governments, to regulate working-class life,

including employment. Social agencies, often inspired by religious and moral concerns, provided counselling, education, and material assistance to those most in need, but for many reformers this was not sufficient. Activist, Christian social reformers and progressive intellectuals also argued that women and young girls employed at paid labour should be protected, most often through legislation that limited hours of work, provided better pay, and specified working conditions conducive to health and safety. Women and young girls were more vulnerable than men: they were weaker in physical strength as well as in moral character and thus ought to be protected from potential abuse.[5]

While women workers constituted a separate group, their interests were often perceived as parallel to those of children, with whom they shared certain disabilities. Just as social reformers argued for public health measures such as visiting nurses and pure milk depots to help working-class children, they also advocated stronger factory and shop legislation, better sanitary conditions in workshops, the elimination of sweated labour, and the appointment of women factory inspectors to benefit women workers. Clearly, reformers thought the state ought to act through its legislative and regulatory powers to ensure the protection of women workers, just as it supposedly acted in the interests of protecting children.

In the context of late Victorian Canada, women and children were often viewed in contradictory ways – on the one hand as weaker members of society, and thus in need of protection; on the other hand as a pool of cheap labour that threatened to undermine the pre-eminent position of the male worker. At the same time, as Constance Backhouse and many others have pointed out, the underlying concern for the protection of women stemmed from anxiety over their reproductive health and ultimately that of future offspring. Concerns for children centred around the possibility of improper socialization through lax education and religious instruction.[6]

It would take pressure on government to achieve increased state intervention, however, and voluntary organizations often undertook the necessary first steps to demonstrate the need and feasibility for such intervention. Women's organizations, churches, and secular progressive reformers worked to convince various levels of government of the necessity for action. Economic and political mobilization of the skilled working class in the last third of the nineteenth century also resulted in support for some regulation of the workplace, although the labour movement per se remained ambivalent on the question. Even when action was taken, such as the passage of factory acts regulating the hours of labour for women and children, voluntary groups continued to press for their enforcement, for wider coverage, and for attention to the needs of women workers through the appointment of woman inspectors. While the state found advantages in setting up special departments to handle labour questions and favored the appointment of numerous commissions to investigate difficult labour problems and disputes, the appearance of state agencies and commissions by no means guaranteed impartial handling of labour questions. In most instances, these bodies featured the appointments of men (and a few women) from the upper levels of society or from the skilled working class; rarely did they include representatives closer to the everyday realities of working-class life. Consequently, they generally failed to examine the condition of working women closely and sympathetically. Factory and shop legislation itself was often the product of compromise between employer interests, social reformers' concerns, and organized labour's pressure.[7]

In the absence of a systematic, empirically based study of Canadian women's work in the period, this discussion draws on the secondary literature and various social investigations commissioned during the period to provide a perspective and a context for the problem of women's work in the late nineteenth and early twentieth centuries. While official reports and investigations offer only a partial view of working women, they do reveal something of the way in which such women were perceived by reformers, politicians, and bureaucrats, the latter category covering both middle-class and working-class functionaries. Case studies carried out by historians provide a useful counterpoint to the findings of public investigations. In addition, it is crucial to try to understand, even partially, how working women viewed themselves whether in songs, verse, letters to the editor, strikes, or membership in labour, ethnic, or socialist organizations. Although the concept of women's culture has recently been subjected to several critical reappraisals, the notion of a variable women's work culture remains useful here, especially in conjunction with official viewpoints and attempts to regulate the conditions of working women's lives. In some circumstances, working women used various means to contest attempts to define them as weak, exploitable, and insignificant. This chapter is largely concerned with exploring the 'official' views of working women promulgated by governments and reformers. The voices of women workers were often muted, especially in official realms, yet even here we can find some evidence of their search for dignity and respect.

I

In late-ninteenth-century Canada, the problem of women's paid labour was addressed through a number of studies and commissions initiated by governments and voluntary agencies in central and eastern Canada, where industrial development was most advanced. Toronto and Montreal in particular became centres of industrial production by the last third of the century. In 1891 two-thirds of Toronto's industrial labour force were men; the remaining third was composed of women and children. Montreal's industrial labour force was even more feminized, with women and young girls constituting 39 per cent of the labour force in 1881. Women's labour was highly visible in the sewing and shoemaking trades of both cities during the late nineteenth century. This heightened visibility of women's industrial work combined with fears for the future of the family, concerns about the erosion of women's domestic roles, and anxieties about competition between the sexes to produce heated debate about the nature of industrial Canada.[8]

What do these investigations reveal about public perceptions of women's paid labour? A number of themes emerge from these late-nineteenth-century studies: exploitation, deep ambivalence towards women's work, the potential for promiscuity, the need for protective measures, the respectability of white-collar work, and the near impossibility of independent living. The Royal Commission on the Relations of Labor and Capital (1889) reflected only minor concern with women workers' problems. Relatively few women testified, and many of these witnesses would not give evidence of their complaints to the commissioners unless they were no longer employed or could testify anonymously. Nonetheless, the commission did provide some evidence of actual conditions and wages for women engaged in factory work. Hours varied from nine to eleven per day, and wages differed according to age and skill. Work was seasonal in many industries, and the evidence attests to the uncertainty of employment and the reduction of already small wages through fines. Independent living remained out of the question for many women workers who remained at home and contributed to the family economy. These young women could not afford to live in boarding houses.[9]

Given the reticence of female witnesses, much of the information on women workers in the commission's report comes from the men who testified before the commission as well as from the commissioners themselves. Testimony from male employers underlined the profitability of women's labour, given its lower wages. Male workers who commented on women's employment demonstrated ambivalence towards female competition. The commissioners themselves were eager to pursue the question of immorality occasioned by men and women working in the same factory. Despite the lack of evidence of immoral behaviour, the commissioners pursued this area of questioning with a wide variety of witnesses, underlining the class and gender expectations surrounding working-class women. Such discourse indicated that working-class women were presumed to be vulnerable to the weakness of their sex and moral downfall.[10]

Exploitation of women workers was also documented in the low wages uncovered by Jean Scott in her 1892 study published under the auspices of the University of Toronto. The sexual division of labour meant lower wages for women, who were assigned less skilled work. In glove factories, for example, she noted that 'skilled' male cutters earned much more than the average of four or five dollars per week earned by 'unskilled' women stitchers or embroiderers. While Scott conceded that men and women generally performed different jobs, she also noted that in some trades women threatened men's jobs, particularly in cigar-making, tailoring, retail sales, office work, telegraphy, and teaching. Although conceding the need for equal pay for equal work, Scott clearly felt that women were physically less able to perform certain types of work that could destroy their health. Furthermore, she wrote:

What does the displacing of men by the competition of women at lower wages mean if not that the former often find employment more difficult to obtain or less profitable than formerly, and are less able to provide means of maintenance for a family? Man was intended by nature to be the breadwinner of the family; and if family life is to be maintained such he must remain: so that the persistent usurpation of his place by unfair competition must mean eventually a danger to the continuance of the home.

Even a critic such as Scott was enmeshed in prevailing assumptions about women's physical inferiority and secondary status within the family. Nevertheless, her insistence on equal pay for women who contested these assumptions is striking.[11]

While domestic service and unpaid household work by wives, daughters, and sisters consumed most of the waking hours of female servants and family members, no concerted campaign was waged to eliminate or reduce these forms of exploitation of female labour. According to social commentators and reformers, domestic service provided a suitable occupation for young working-class or rural women who would eventually become wives and mothers responsible for their own households.

In contrast, by the 1890s sweated labour in the needle trades became a focus of critics of women's paid work as labour organizations and government functionaries drew attention to the phenomenon in an industry where women and girls accounted for 70 to 80 per cent of the workers. Sweated labour, whether performed at home by predominantly female labour or in a subcontractor's shop employing both men and women, represented a clear threat at several levels. As Robert McIntosh notes, at one level sweated labour was inoffensive to patriarchal norms and expectations, but it came to be viewed as undermining men's incomes. Sweated labour threatened domestic life and women's abilities to care for children while also exploiting child labour in unhealthy, disease-ridden surroundings. Low wages and unhealthy conditions also portended the possibility that desperate seamstresses might turn to prostitution, thereby compounding the public health problem. Thus, sweated labour encapsulated several strands of anxiety that permeated Canadian life at the end of the century: it threatened working-class family life, morality, and gender relations as well as posing a threat to the health and morals of society at large.[12]

Such misgivings, as well as annual requests from the Trades and Labor Congress for the prevailing (union) rates on all public contracts, helped sway the dominion government to appoint a royal commission in 1895 to investigate sweated labour in Canada. This investigation followed similar efforts in the United Kingdom and in the United States in the late 1880s and early 1890s. The one-man commission of A.W. Wright – labour reformer, former Knights of Labor leader, and Tory supporter – resulted in the 1896 publication of the *Report upon the Sweating System in Canada*. While Wright carefully distinguished Canadian conditions from what he saw as a much worse situation in the United States and England, he made a number of recommendations for stronger laws and penalties that he felt would limit or eliminate some abuses in the clothing trades. His recommendations included an alien labour law, expanded factory acts, and legal penalties for those employers who paid very low wages or no wages at all to beginners. Wright wanted manufacturers and contractors to be required to provide a list of persons working for them, and he favoured penalties where clothing was manufactured in unsanitary, disease-ridden homes. The report included verbatim transcripts of two meetings called by Wright to which he invited a committee of the Toronto Trades and Labor Council (TTLC), the three Ontario factory inspectors, and clothing contractors. From these conversations one can glean some idea of how the system affected women workers.[13]

As the report noted, the sweating system depended on a large pool of mostly female labour willing to work for very low wages. While many contemporaries blamed the contractors and subcontractors for grinding down their workers to poverty levels, a few recognized that the manufacturers encouraged this system because it left them with little responsibility for those who actually performed the work and shifted the responsibility for negotiating payment to the contractors who engaged hands to sew for them either in a shop or at home. Payment might be by the week or by the piece, with piecework predominating in cases where sewing was done at home. For a manufacturer and retailer like Eaton's, contracting and subcontracting eliminated the company's direct responsibility for workers, particularly in the cheaper ready-made line of clothing, in children's and ladies' wear, and in some types of men's clothing. While contractors sometimes set up their own shops, they also could send out particular items for sewing. Either way, garments were made in stages, and the individual worker usually learned to do limited operations on the piece of clothing. As a result, few workers could assemble a garment from start to finish. The division of labour into many different operations undercut the ability of the worker to bargain, especially with the widespread use of contracting and subcontracting. When an individual woman received bundles from a manufacturer or contractor to sew at home, her bargaining power was slight: she faced the employer alone and usually had to accept the price offered. If her work was returned with faults, she had to redo it or accept fines. As factory inspector James R. Brown noted, sometimes the wives of workingmen agreed to prices below those a contractor would ask, thus compounding the competition. For the manufacturer, contracting and homework pitted workers against one another. This competition helped to obscure the actual source of the exploitation as well as making it extremely difficult for workers in the trade to organize.[14]

Testimony from Louis Gurofsky of the Toronto Journeymen Tailors' Union (JTU) underlined deteriorating conditions for both men and women in the garment trade during the recession of the 1890s. Skilled male workers were particularly hard hit. Pressers who once made two dollars per day and handled the entire garment now made only three to five dollars per week and were responsible for pressing only parts of each garment. Gurofsky reported average wages of twelve dollars for men and four dollars for women in early 1896, noting that in shops where both men and women worked, women's wages tended to be higher than in those shops that employed only women. In Gurofsky's shop, the women started work at 7:30 instead of 7:00 AM, perhaps to avoid contact with male co-workers, and quit at 6:00. Saturday was a half-day. While some of the contractors argued that women were better off in contract shops than they were in taking bundles home directly from the manufacturer, Gurofsky asserted that women (and men) received better pay and working conditions when working directly in the manufacturer's shop; contractors acted as middlemen and reaped the profits that might be better used to pay workers decent wages. While the contractors defended the sweating system, Gurofsky consistently challenged them, citing lower wages, fines, and health risks.[15]

Sweated labour also occurred in the custom trade and led to a strike in Toronto in 1896, at the same time as Wright conducted his investigation. A strike by 140 men and 50 women pitted the JTU against employers seeking control over custom work on pants and vests. One commission witness noted that nineteen employers were paying from sixty-eight cents to a dollar per pair for custom pants instead of the usual two dollars per pair, and he feared that the situation would worsen.

We have struck to support these people because the contractors are just grinding them down. We want as a union to control this labour and to aid the girls in the pant and vest departments. The employers said we will pay $1.50 and $1.25 for vests and you not interfere, but if we did not interfere these girls would soon be doing the work for fifty cents. We will fight this thing. The only way to prevent it is to make the employers of labour do away with back shops and employ without contract ... These men would not care if the women prostituted their bodies at night to make a living wage ... These contractors are all sweaters.

The strikers were unsuccessful, and the strike became a lockout spreading to approximately five hundred workers, who remained out from January to early April. The employers fought the union and opposed the JTU's attempt to organize non-union workers, including the women.[16]

Sweated labour remained a thorn in the side of the labour movement well into the twentieth century. Occasional references in the press noted examples of sweated labour, particularly among women, into the First World War. In the Quebec garment trades, where labour was cheaper than in the rest of the country, subcontracting and homework remained a prominent feature into the 1930s.[17]

## II

Revelations about sweated labour, with its long hours and low wages, accompanied by perceptions of promiscuity among working women and fears for the health of future generations of workers, provoked debate on the measures that ought to be taken to correct the most glaring abuses of the industrial system. The most commonly proposed solutions entailed protective legislation and an enforcement mechanism. Other solutions included training more women for domestic service or, alternatively, for white-collar occupations. A few critics suggested that working women should organize into self-help societies that would equip them for 'self-government' and 'independence,' characteristics that would help them 'learn how they can best promote their own interest and those of their fellow workers.' This same writer argued that trade unions, such as the Knights of Labor and a few others, held little appeal for women who 'lacked the training necessary to carry on such unions,' who do not remain long in employment, and who lack the 'class spirit' more common among working men. Ignoring the unique premises upon which the Knights had built a considerable following among women workers in the 1880s – the importance of organizing the unorganized, deliberate appeals to women homemakers as well as wage workers, and the commitment to equal pay for equal work – this writer concluded by recommending revisions to the legislation governing women's employment to extend protection to those who must work in factories and shops.[18]

Factory and shop acts were passed in Ontario and Quebec in the 1880s. Jean Scott's 1892 study discussed and criticized the Ontario Factory Act, which was passed in 1884, proclaimed in 1886, and amended in 1889. Generally critical of loopholes in the legislation, which applied only to manufacturing establishments with at least six employees, Scott complained about inadequate lunch breaks as well as exemptions permitting more than ten hours labour per day as long as the total hours worked in a week did not exceed sixty. Night work for women and children was not clearly addressed in the Factory Act, allowing women and children to work night shifts. Furthermore, the Shops' Regulation Act (1888) made no provisions for limiting hours of girls over age sixteen, and no inspection was mandated. Thus, young women in smaller stores often worked very long hours, especially on Saturdays when small shops remained open until the late evening. Telephone operators' hours varied in a complex shift system, which included employment on Sundays, and the work involved constant nervous strain and physical danger from electrical shocks. Nurses also worked long hours and were expected to be on duty for twelve hours, with some breaks.[19]

In the area of sanitation and health, Scott noted some improvements, but she also pointed out the ineffectiveness of introducing regulations without adequate means for inspection. The lack of inspection under the Shops' Act, for example, undercut the stated regulation of seats for sales clerks not engaged with customers. Even under the Factory Act, there were too few inspectors. But the problem was not just one of an inadequate number of inspectors: On the basis of American evidence, as well as her own experience, Scott suggested that women inspectors would be more successful than men in obtaining information from women workers.[20]

The National Council of Women of Canada (NCWC), whose members were largely drawn from the middle to upper-middle class, also supported some protective measures for women factory workers, although they much preferred encouraging and training women to become domestics in bourgeois homes. A resolution to petition provincial governments to appoint women inspectors passed without much dissension at NCWC meetings in both 1894 and 1895. The 1894 meeting also discussed the cooperation of women workers for protective purposes in the recently formed Working Women's Protective Association. The Toronto-based organization, associated with Marie Joussaye, affiliated with the Toronto Local Council of Women (LCW) and provided them with information on the conditions of women's work.[21]

A far more divisive issue arose in 1895 when a resolution on the nine-hour day for women and children was proposed by Kingston author and Christian social activist Agnes Maule Machar. Citing the frustration of Kingston's YWCA in trying to provide evening lectures and classes for exhausted factory operatives, Machar supported the shorter work day as a means of preventing mental and moral deterioration among the factory women. 'I think our girls are of more consequence than webs of cotton or wheels,' she stated, adding that the very strength of the nation depended to a significant degree on healthy mothers. Montreal's Local Council of Women led the opposition, with Lady Julia Drummond claiming that 'hardship comes oftener from slack work than from overwork.' Other Montreal representatives argued that women would bear the brunt of starvation if their hours were limited and that such legislation would undermine the natural laws of competition. McGill botany professor Carrie Derick also strongly opposed protective legislation, arguing that it would disadvantage women workers, a position that also reflected her own status as a single professional woman. Miss Hepburn of the Women's Protective Union defended her sister workers but waffled on the specificity of nine hours, pointing out that employers tended to examine the amounts of money women workers were able to earn, often cutting the rates on the basis of the productivity of the quickest workers. Limiting hours of work, therefore, would not necessarily prevent exploitation. The issue was not resolved in 1895, and at the 1896 meeting Montreal women redoubled their opposition, arguing that the differential treatment of women workers contradicted the plea for equal capacity and treatment: 'We must bear in mind that every protection or privilege which is accorded to her womanhood is also an injury and a disability to her as a worker and wage earner.' Instead the opposition argued that men and women must be treated equally and that expanded legislation should apply to both sexes. Despite support from some of the other local councils, the nine-hour resolution went down to defeat. Notwithstanding the national defeat, local councils continued to agitate for amendments to provincial legislation to extend protections to women and children under shop regulation acts and factory legislation.[22]

As Jean Scott had suggested, enforcement of legislation was key to curbing abuses of women workers. By the 1890s both Ontario and Quebec had appointed female factory inspectors, but as late as 1913 each of these provinces had only two female inspectors. Women in factories still worked between fifty-five and sixty hours per week, with overtime in rush seasons adding a further ten to fifteen hours. Ontario's first female inspector was Margaret Carlyle, a Scottish emigrant, suffragist, and business woman. Appointed in 1895 and serving in that capacity until at least 1914, she had complete jurisdiction over factories employing women and children (excepting fire safety and machine fencing) and joint jurisdiction in factories employing men, women, and/or children. In 1902 she reported that full sixty-hour weeks were common only in textile factories, but she also noted that in a number of factories employees worked more than ten-hour days in order to have Saturday afternoons off; employees, she asserted, preferred this schedule and urged her to overlook the infractions. The following year Carlyle noted the existence of illegal overtime in the clothing trade; homework after hours was imposed on employees, a practice Carlyle found difficult to control. Piecework also became more common in the first decade of the twentieth century, as Carlyle noted in her 1902 report. While factory inspectors worried that intense labour on the piecework system spelled health and safety dangers, businessmen – particularly in the clothing trades, which depended heavily on cheap female labour – had other views. As one clothing manufacturer who advocated piecework revealed, 'I don't treat the men bad but I even up by taking advantage of the women.'[23]

While Ontario and Quebec featured some of the earliest investigations and legislation dealing with female and child labour, the Maritime provinces also began to tackle these issues by the early part of the twentieth century. Industrialization occurred later in that region than in central Canada. From its beginning in the 1880s, eastern industrial development was uneven, with Nova Scotia experiencing the greatest transformation. Even within Nova Scotia, there were large differences between communities, as Del Muise's study of female labour in Yarmouth, Amherst, and Sydney Mines illustrates. For instance, while the latter community, a steel-making town, offered little except clerical or service employment for a few women wage earners, Yarmouth's turn towards manufacturing in the 1880s meant gainful employment in sailcloth production, woollens, and shoes. With the increasing employment of women and children in these new industries, the pressure to legislate protective measures grew. Nova Scotia passed a Factory Act in 1901, but, without the appointment of a factory inspector, it remained a dead letter for many years. In New Brunswick, agitation for a Factory Act commenced in the early part of the century under the joint initiative of the Saint John Trades and Labor Council and the Fabian League. The latter was modelled after the British Fabian Society, which advocated gradual change rather than violent upheaval. The campaign for the Factory Act in New Brunswick provides a case study of the inherent contradictions arising from such reform activities.[24]

The campaign for the Factory Act began in earnest in March 1903 with the Fabian League's discussion of a paper by labour leader P.C. Sharkey, who argued for factory legislation modelled on a New Zealand statute. In addition to suggesting licensing, age limits, minimum wages, and an inspector, Sharkey proposed an eight-hour day and the abolition of sweated labour. A subsequent meeting of the league resulted in a decision to send several members to visit factories in Saint John and report on conditions. League members R.G. Murray and W.F. Hatheway visited several establishments including laundries, tobacco works, and a paper box factory, although an unnamed cotton factory refused Sharkey permission to enter, probably because it employed young children for eleven and one-quarter hours a day. The visitors discovered that the majority of workers in the city's laundries were young women. Employees worked ten hours per day for wages of $2.50 to $12 per week, the higher wages earned by the men. In the paper box factory, female employees worked nine-hour days for wages of $3 to $3.50 per week, while the men, who accounted for about 20 per cent of the factory workforce, put in ten-hour days for wages up to $14 per week. Two tobacco factories visited by Hatheway caused him some concern. In one such establishment, dust, overcrowding, and the doors opening inward to several flights of stairs suggested unhealthy and unsafe conditions for the sixty female and twenty male employees. Most of the establishments visited needed to improve their safety provisions around machinery or their fire escape routes, and a number had inadequate toilet facilities. Largely uncommented on were the wages and conditions of women workers. Much of the subsequent discussion about proposed legislation emphasized the elimination of child labour and the protection of young workers, more than the protection of women.[25]

Discussion of the proposed legislation in the provincial legislature in March 1904 raised objections to various facets of the act: mandated holidays, fees, enforcement provisions, and the definition of a factory. When some objected to the hours limitations, Attorney General Pugsley replied patronizingly that the legislation aimed to protect women and children 'against their own willingness to work long hours.' At hearings on the bill, employer Charles Brown objected to fire escape and door regulations as well as restrictions on homework, perhaps partly because visitors to his paper box factory had noted the absence of a fire escape. Delegations from the Board of Trade, the Fabian League, the TLC, and women's groups visited the premier in Fredericton to present their views; while the Board of Trade urged caution in proceeding, Hatheway for the Fabian League and Sharkey for the TLC urged that the bill remain as drafted. Mrs Emma Fiske, suffragist and former president of the Women's Enfranchisement Association, and Mrs W.C. Matthews urged a woman inspector and stronger measures to protect women and children. A newspaper noted that Fiske was better versed than the premier on the bill, which may explain her subsequent presence on the commission set up by government to sift through the conflicting advice and make recommendations on the legislation.[26]

The commissioners' report of 1 March 1905 noted that their visits to major towns and cities around the province had convinced them that some establishments needed improvement, especially in the areas of health and safety. They noted that 'the weight of the testimony was that while there was no objection to a Factory Act, no absolute necessity existed for it at the present time.' Furthermore, they found no complaints from employees, who 'all seemed well satisfied with their treatment.' Fragmentary testimony of the witnesses reported in the newspapers made it clear that the commissioners mainly interviewed employers; where employees testified, they did so in front of their employers. One community newspaper condemned the procedures of the commission, pointing out that no employee would publicly complain about conditions for fear of losing employment. Large manufacturers had advised that it would be unwise to pass legislation that might interfere with investment in manufacturing because 'these industries are in their infancy and should be encouraged, rather than impeded,' a comment that echoed arguments made in Ontario twenty years earlier. A draft act provided for protection of employees in the areas of fire escapes, dangerous machinery, and sanitation and regulated the hours and types of work young persons and women might do. It forbade the employment of children under fourteen, unless the inspector authorized such employment. Hours of work were limited for young girls and women to ten hours per day or sixty hours per week, unless a different arrangement was agreed to in order to obtain the Saturday half-holiday, and limits were placed on overtime work. The draft legislation suggested, but did not require, the appointment of a female as well as a male inspector. It also provided fines and penalties for non-compliance, including a fine for parents who knowingly allowed their underage children to work.[27]

The final legislation, based on the commission's report and the government's earlier proposals, was a far cry from the original suggestions of the Fabian League and the TLC. As these groups became involved in the process of devising the act, they backtracked on their earlier positions, which had included a shorter working day, minimum wages, and abolishing sweated labour. Moreover, the government's 1905 legislative agenda was subject to pressure from business. The amended legislation allowed thirteen-and-a-half hour days (eighty-one-hour weeks) in trade emergencies, thanks to the objections of the candy manufacturer Ganong Brothers. Fish and food processors whose businesses were located outside urban areas were exempted from the act. Furthermore, the act was amended to define a factory as an establishment employing a minimum of ten, rather than six, persons. Opposition to the long hours worked by women operatives in the cotton mills was answered with the argument that employees favoured eleven-hour days in order to have a Saturday half-holiday and that New Brunswick needed to retain long hours to be competitive with Quebec's mills.[28]

Despite the recommendation for a female inspector, the government appointed John McMulkin as the first factory inspector for the province. During his varied career, McMulkin had been an alderman, a sawmill operator, a steamboat captain, and a deck hand; at the time of his appointment, he was a grocer. He was a strong Liberal Party supporter, and his appointment clearly reflected patronage from the provincial government, who bypassed seven other men including labour leader P.C. Sharkey. The Local Council of Women reiterated their request for a female inspector in 1910, but they were ignored. Even as late as 1918, the LCW unsuccessfully suggested a nominee for the 'proposed position of female assistant factory inspector.' While child labour clearly continued to concern the government, the conditions of women workers in the province had a much lower profile.[29]

Similar problems occurred in Nova Scotia. It was not until 1908, seven years after the passage of the Factory Act, that the first factory inspector, Philip Ring, was appointed. Even then the government ignored the repeated requests of women's groups to designate a female inspector. The Halifax LCW, which had requested the appointment of a woman in 1899 and 1906, channelled their efforts towards undermining the attractiveness of factory work by attempting to elevate the status of the domestic servant and encouraging the offering of domestic science courses at the Technical College. From 1909 on, the LCW ran a hostel for immigrant maids. The hostel opened its doors to all working women once the war slowed down immigration.[30]

Nova Scotia's 1901 act prohibited children under fourteen from working, except from July to October in fruit and vegetable picking and processing. Women's work hours were not directly specified, although they could not occur before 6 AM or after 9 PM, except for a limited period during the fruit- and vegetable-processing season. In 1909, amendments to this act, and to the Shop Closing Act of 1900, provided a limit of eight hours on weekdays (four on Saturdays) for young persons under sixteen and a nine-hour limit under the Factory Act for women workers. The following year, under pressure from cotton manufacturers, the government attempted to repeal the child labour clauses of the Factory Act without discussing the changes with child welfare organizations. A concerted opposition from the unions and welfare groups pointed out the hardships for the thirty-eight boys and sixty-four girls who worked long hours in hot temperatures in the Halifax cotton factory. Speakers against the proposed measure accused the government of favouring slavery and of robbing children of their childhood. While male workers were now campaigning for the eight-hour day for themselves, children would be subjected to ten or eleven hours. One writer posed the dilemma in terms of children's well-being versus dividends: 'Those who prefer high dividends to healthy citizens are Not Without Precedence.' This concerted campaign against repeal of the child labour clauses worked; instead, the government removed the nine-hour restriction on women's factory labour, a move that elicited little protest.[31]

Nova Scotia's factory inspector noted the worrisome presence of underage children in some factories in his first report in 1909. Perhaps because Philip Ring had been the president of the Halifax Coopers' Union, he was sensitive to workers' concerns with health and safety and child labour. On the latter question, Ring used his powers to prosecute employers who hired underage workers. Candy manufacturer William Moirs and car manufacturer Clarence Silliker both appeared in police court to answer charges. An editorial in the Halifax *Herald* wondered why Ring concentrated on prosecuting manufacturers for hiring underage workers when so many other violations were not prosecuted.[32]

To his credit, Ring also provided some statistics on women workers in his reports and pushed for laundries to be included under the act because they were just as dangerous as factories, a point he underlined in his 1909 report with the case of a fifteen-year-old girl who had lost her hand in a laundry mangle. In his 1910 report, Ring noted that his workload had expanded to the point where he could visit only the larger towns and cities. He also noted the difficulty of eliciting complaints from women workers, but reported that he found it helpful to keep in touch with female factory inspectors elsewhere. In his 1914 report he ventured a mild criticism of the 1910 act, which had removed the nine-hour limit from women's work; nearly all the large employers of women and girls reported labour shortages and the need for longer hours. In order to get Saturday half-holidays, the women were working eleven hours a day, which Ring felt was too long. Even by 1920, when the Nova Scotia government received the report of its commission on women's wages, hours, and conditions, many women workers reported fifty to fifty-five hours as their normal working week.[33]

If central Canada and the eastern provinces provided a modicum of industrial employment for women workers, such was not the case in the West. Thus it is not surprising that protective legislation geared towards women in industry lagged behind that in central Canada in particular. While Western cities attracted immigrants (including women) in the era before the First World War, manufacturing jobs for women were scarce in a resource-based economy. Such a labour market presented fewer opportunities for women's paid work than in the East. In 1901, for example, women workers accounted for only 6 per cent of the labour force in British Columbia, rising to 14 per cent in 1931. In the Prairie province of Saskatchewan women constituted 6.4 per cent of the labour force in 1911 and 11 per cent in 1931. Many women worked as unpaid housewives or farmers, of course, but the census did not take into account family labourers or unpaid domestic workers.[34]

In the absence of a significant manufacturing sector, western women were disproportionately employed in domestic and personal service. Christine Smillie found that, in 1911, 54 per cent of Saskatchewan women workers were classed as domestics, waitresses, or employees of hotels or boarding houses, compared with a national figure of 38 per cent. Forty-two per cent of Vancouver's female labour force in 1911 was engaged in paid domestic work, a figure also higher than the national average. In comparison, Winnipeg was more highly industrialized in the early twentieth century, and its factories, mills, and shops already employed a significant number of children and women.[35]

Manitoba's factory and shop legislation was enacted in 1900 and 1901, respectively. Although the Factories Act provided for the appointment of both male and female inspectors, the government initially appointed only a man, architect D.A. Smith, who served until 1912. Smith's tenure as inspector was less than effective since he continued to work full time at his profession. Not until June 1914, one month before a provincial election, did the Roblin government take action, appointing Ida Bauslaugh and former Winnipeg Trades and Labor Council member Ed McGrath as inspectors. Subsequent scandals revolving around the construction of public buildings in Winnipeg spelled the downfall of the Conservative government in 1915. The new Liberal government of T.C. Norris, under pressure from reform and labour organizations, carried out its program of social reform, which included the expansion of the Bureau of Labor, as well as temperance and women's suffrage legislation. During the war the Factories Act was amended to include shops employing three or more persons (instead of five) and to include Chinese laundries, which had earlier been exempted.[36]

Despite the more favourable political climate for labour and reform, Ida Bauslaugh, like other female factory inspectors, found her job an uphill battle. Her attempts to provide emergency first aid stations, lunch rooms, and other improvements often met with unsympathetic responses. Nevertheless, combined labour and reform pressure succeeded in 1916 in accomplishing some legislative change: the Bureau of Labor was charged with the enforcement of the revised Shops Regulation Act, Factories Act, and other relevant labour laws. Although reformers pressed for raising the minimum ages of employment for boys and girls, they were not successful. They did, however, succeed in limiting factory overtime. A bid for a regular working week limit of forty-eight hours for women and young persons was defeated, leaving the limit at fifty-four hours in the factories. In stores, young persons and women could work up to fourteen hours a day, with a sixty-hour limit per week, except in emergencies allowed by the inspector. The law allowed the employment of children under age fourteen for forty-eight hours per week, if the school authorities and the Bureau of Labor agreed that it was necessary, thus undercutting the compulsory schooling law for destitute working-class and immigrant children helping to support their families. Organized labour also pressed for the prohibition of employment of white women by 'orientals,' a stand also taken by labour in other western provinces. Such legislation reflected widespread race, gender, and class anxieties about Asian workers, who, it was alleged, undercut white labour and corrupted white women.[37]

In a province largely agricultural in its economic base, Saskatchewan's government demonstrated little concern with women's employment until the passage of the Factory Act in 1909, which provided for health and safety measures and an inspector, much the same as in other Canadian jurisdictions. The labour movement, backed by social reform interests, initiated the pressure for passage of the act. Amendments in 1910–11 defined factories as places employing three or more, rather than the original five persons, and set a forty-eight-hour limit on women's work, with the usual provision for extended hours during trade exigencies. Despite evidence of the high cost of housing and other necessities in Regina, J.S. Woodsworth, reporting to the Methodist Church in 1913 and the province's Bureau of Labor in 1914, found little cause for concern about the wage-earning women of that city, with the notable exception of laundry workers, who earned as little as one dollar per day. Not until the end of the war did the province, along with a number of other jurisdictions, legislate a minimum wage for women workers.[38]

The only other province to pass factory legislation before 1914 was British Columbia, which did so in 1908. Alberta's factory legislation was not enacted until 1917. British Columbia's legislation differed from that of most provinces in that hours for women and young persons were limited to forty-eight per week and eight hours per day. Like other provinces, however, British Columbia was slow to appoint its first inspector and ignored requests for women inspectors. The province's Shops Regulation Act of 1900–1 had little effect: enforcement by municipalities was non-existent and a source of complaint from the organized labour movement as well as from women's organizations. The Factory Act itself was not strictly enforced, according to the 1914 royal commission report on all aspects of labour in the province. This commission, appointed in late 1912, visited 62 communities and held 127 sessions, hearing from 419 witnesses. Prior to the commission's report, the Vancouver Trades and Labor Council had requested the City of Vancouver to investigate women's work, a request that the city had turned down, despite estimates by the YWCA that over six thousand Vancouver women were wage earners.[39]

Evidence collected during the course of the royal commission hearings centred on several themes relating to women's employment: stricter enforcement of existing legislation, such as shop and factory acts; collection of data on actual working conditions and wages of women workers, with particular stress on poor wages and conditions for shop clerks; and the desirability and level of minimum wage scales. A number of witnesses and, ultimately, the summary report tied stricter enforcement of legislation to the need for women inspectors, who could more easily gather information and complaints from female workers. Both the Vancouver Trades and Labor Council and the Vancouver LCW favored such a step, with the LCW approaching the attorney general, unsuccessfully, as it turned out, in the fall of 1914. A number of witnesses and the final report of the commission also noted that many stores ignored legislation by not providing seats for shopgirls or by refusing to let them sit down while unoccupied (a recurrent theme in other provinces as well). The LCW's presentation to the commission also underlined the plight of women who worked in stores for long hours at low pay and with little chance of organizing into unions. Research into conditions and wages in stores suggested that Vancouver clerks earned, on average, seven to nine dollars a week, but that a significant number earned five or six dollars, and sometimes less, which did not constitute a living wage for independent women. As numerous witnesses noted, employers expected their female clerks to live at home and, indeed, attempted to screen out those who did not. A few employers deliberately hired young girls, sometimes under the age of fourteen, to work at 'learner's wages,' only to fire them when they acquired experience. The LCW tended to apportion the blame for the exploitation of young girls between employers and parents, blaming the latter's desire to keep daughters occupied and off the streets while contributing to the family economy.[40]

Other evidence gathered by the commission suggested that in the larger Vancouver department stores young women earned more than in the stores catering to cheaper goods, such as Woolworth's and the Fifteen Cent Store. The manager of the Fifteen Cent Store testified that he paid, on average, wages of five to six dollars a week to young women, but that the youngest earned only four dollars. The latter were living at home and were too young to earn a living wage, he asserted. This testimony prompted one of the commissioners to state that 'you are the most disgraceful corporation we ever heard of,' noting that the Hudson's Bay Company paid wages at least double those of the Fifteen Cent Store. Evidence of low wages in stores and other occupations generated some discussion of a minimum wage for women workers but little action was taken until the latter stages of the First World War.[41]

## III

In the early twentieth century, protective legislation provided limited benefits for women in factories and shops and depended on inadequate enforcement mechanisms. Other alternatives appealed to the middle- and upper-class women whose organizations grappled with the 'problem' of the working woman. Although Local Councils of Women did press for factory legislation, women inspectors, and other ameliorative changes before 1914, they also felt that factory work was degrading, and they pushed domestic service as a more 'respectable' occupation. Some reformers turned to other escape routes, urging training in white collar or technical fields for women. For working-class women, clerical or sales work represented a step up from the factory. Despite the low wages paid, especially to sales clerks, middle-class observers considered the work 'cleaner' than factory work, although it was also considered dangerous because the combination of poor pay and temptations to acquire finery might lead young women astray.

In the burgeoning offices of insurance companies, banks, governments, and other businesses in the early twentieth century, clerical work was transformed from a male-dominated occupation to an increasingly female task. As Graham Lowe remarks, 'No other major occupation has undergone such a dramatic shift in sex composition, from exclusively male to predominantly female.' Between 1900 and the Depression the modern office emerged, with its concomitant fragmentation, mechanization, and routinization of tasks. Increasingly, these tasks were assigned to women, who formed a growing pool of cheap clerical labour.[42]

Like clerical work, sales promised working women a higher status, white-collar occupation. Saleswork did not require as high a level of education as clerical work, but it did demand neatness of appearance. Wages were usually low, making it very difficult for women to live up to the standards of dress required by the department stores that hired them. By 1896, Toronto department stores employed over two thousand female shop clerks. They were closely supervised to prevent flirtations with male customers and to extract the most work out of them. Moreover, a few minutes' tardiness often resulted in loss of half a day's pay.[43]

Investigations conducted in British Columbia and Manitoba on the eve of First World War revealed that the low pay and poor working conditions of female sales clerks continued to be a cause for concern, although the Manitoba study was flawed by lack of access to wage records. The report of a University Women's Club study of clerks in four different Winnipeg stores, including Eaton's and Hudson's Bay, focused on the benefits of vocational education and of low-cost housing for working women. The stores were only mildly chastised for inadequate ventilation and failing to provide seats for overworked sales clerks.

Vocational and technical training as a solution to low-paying and exploitive work for women (and youths) seemed to offer a solution, and several commissions in the 1910s examined the issue. The Manitoba government appointed a royal commission in 1910 to examine this question, with commissioners representing the fields of education, labour, business, social services, and women's organizations. Prominent Winnipeg trade unionist R.S. Ward joined J.S. Woodsworth of the All Peoples' Mission, Mrs A.W. Puttee of the Women's Labor League, five other trade unionists, one businessman, four education representatives, and two government ministers on the commission, which reported in 1912. Surviving testimony from women witnesses from the WLL, YWCA, the All Peoples' Mission, a domestic servants' emigration society, the hospital, and Eaton's, as well as from one garment worker, provide some perspective on women's employment and the employment of female children in Winnipeg.[44]

While women witnesses were generally favourable towards the idea of technical training for women, some expressed the view that few women would take advantage of the opportunity. Eaton's chief dressmaker, Helen Dixon Rue, testified that young women preferred office work or clerking to learning the finer points of dressmaking. In her business she employed women with some knowledge of sewing and had no time to take apprentices. While she approved of night school courses in dressmaking, she was not confident that many young women would take such courses. Young women pressed by economic necessity found piecework in the garment trade more attractive than skilled dressmaking, since the former was done on machines and required only a short learning period. Yet, as garment worker Margaret Tweedy noted, piecework did not afford women opportunities for advancement. Six months of employment would make a woman a proficient worker who could earn better wages on the piecework system without necessarily acquiring a wider variety of skills.[45]

Women workers at the All Peoples' Mission, located in the immigrant and working-class North End of Winnipeg, also favoured technical education, but pointed out that their clientele of immigrants often sent their young children, especially girls, out to work to support the family, thus effectively preventing the girls from attending technical classes. Girls could find employment, particularly in domestic work, at younger ages than boys. Mission workers also noted that they had to go out and bring children and young people into the mission rather than relying on them to come forward. The older girls who worked in factories would rather spend their evenings in the dance halls and theatres, commented one mission worker. Given that most of the classes for girls and young women focused on cooking, sewing, and other domestic skills, reluctance to participate in the mission's 'uplifting' work is perhaps not surprising. As one worker at All Peoples' Mission explained, her work was necessary because 'it will help the individual and from the individual it will help the family, and in helping the family it helps the state.'[46]

In partial contrast to the moral uplift perspective of some of these witnesses was the testimony of WLL representative Mrs Ada Muir. Her background teaching dressmaking and millinery to working women in London, England, and her connection with feminist issues such as suffrage and dower law reform in Manitoba gave her a perspective that was less paternalistic towards the working class. Muir proposed that technical education should be carried out as part of community life in general, with the same stature as public schooling. Technical education should not be a matter of charity: it should be equally available to all and should proceed from people's needs. Envisioning a radically democratic and efficient system of technical education, Muir proposed that government should provide the funds for adequate facilities. Students could either pay fees or work them off; Muir suggested that women would benefit particularly from the latter. Some types of study – office work, photography, chemistry, hygiene, and first aid – should be open to both men and women, but Muir expected that women and men would gravitate towards specialized studies suited for each sex.[47]

Three years after the Manitoba commission, the dominion government appointed the Royal Commission on Industrial Training and Technical Education. Several of the women who gave testimony presented the views of the middle-class women who belonged to Local Councils of Women. Consequently, while some submissions stressed vocational and technical training as a high priority for young women, the most consistent request was for training in domestic science. Many submissions lamented working-class girls' distaste for domestic service and urged the provision of such courses to raise the reputation and attractiveness of this field, not only as a source of employment, but also as training for homemaking. May Sexton of the Halifax LCW (the wife of F.W. Sexton, president of the Technical College in that city) took an interest in women's work and training. She recognized that many women of necessity had to earn wages both before and after marriage. Unlike some witnesses she urged the availability of more domestic science education in public schools, high schools, and colleges as well as evening courses for those young women and girls who had to drop out of school to earn a living. While domestic science was necessary, Sexton also felt that needlework offered about the only skilled work available to women. Sexton specified that the ideal industries for a woman worker 'must be clean and sanitary; must have no injurious physical or moral influences or lead her away from her ultimate work of home-making; and they must offer living wages and afford hope for her advancement and development.' How Sexton envisioned needlework as fitting in with her ideal is not clear. She recognized that increasing mechanization of sewing had reduced the amount of skilled hand-sewing work available to women, but she apparently did not see the problem in continuing to recommend needlework to women.[48]

Carrie Derick, president of the Montreal LCW and professor of botany at McGill, asserted in her brief that 'A woman's work is to her the same source of strength and pleasure as to a man; self-respect is deepened by economic independence and her true womanliness is only fully revealed when every power is given opportunity of exercise.' As a single professional woman herself, Derick had an understanding of the value of women's economic independence. Derick suggested that better training and the opening of opportunities for women would improve their economic position. Derick's survey of Montreal women's work touched on clerical, sales, and factory employment. Skilled, well-paid work eluded women in most fields, particularly in factory work where most women earned much less than a living wage and had to live at home. While skilled work in dressmaking was much in demand, according to Derick, the lack of training was a distinct obstacle for women. Clerical work in clean, pleasant surroundings was an option for women with business training, but most women had to rely on short courses given by private business schools, which did not prepare women adequately. Sales jobs contrasted favourably in some ways with domestic service, but poor working conditions and wages suggested to Derick the need for inexpensive boarding houses for women employed in this field. Her overall recommendations stressed further training opportunities for women to allow them to acquire the technical and commercial education beyond public schooling thus equipping them with specific skills in demand in the market place. Stress on technical and commercial training for independent working women clearly differentiated Derick's approach from the usual assumption that domestic work was the best option for women who needed to earn wages.[49]

## IV

The character of the 'working girl' was a much-discussed aspect of working women's lives from the late nineteenth century through to the First World War. While social reformers worried that employment at low wages and for long hours severely tried the moral fibre of individual working-class women, the women themselves sometimes responded with an affirmation of honest womanhood, based on a realization of their own strengths and skills. Such convictions helped to sustain working women's sense of pride and self-respect. Solidarity and self-respect among working women could be expressed in a number of ways: voting with their feet to leave exploitive employers; protesting employer practices; organizing themselves into associations and unions; participating in boycotts and strikes; and using public forums, including the media, to challenge false representations of working women.[50]

A letter to the editor of a Halifax daily in late 1912 sparked a controversy in the press about attitudes towards, and the conditions facing, factory women. The author of the letter aroused the indignation of several respondents, who challenged the assertion that factory women were poorly paid, lived less than respectable lives, and spent their money on finery they could ill afford. A correspondent who signed her letter 'Experience' claimed that factory girls received good wages and lived decently and furthermore ought to be able to buy finery if they wished. A young employee at Clayton's, a clothing manufacturer, was interviewed by the newspaper and objected to the original letter, saying that factory girls' morals had been unfairly slurred on false assumptions. Her position was backed up by her employer, W.J. Clayton, who explained that of the thousands of young women he had employed over the years, only three had opted for an immoral life; his employees had too much self-respect to tolerate working with women of low morals. While another correspondent wondered if it were true that women in downtown Halifax worked for as little as $1.25 to $1.50 a week in stores, one working woman wrote in to explain her situation, denying that women in the city were paid enough to maintain respectability. 'A Working Girl' noted that, although she had to work three nights until 11 PM, she made only $3.50 per week, a sum that had to cover board, laundry, clothes, and other necessities. She argued that she could not look respectable on that amount and she could not afford a respectable street for lodging. Her fatherless family needed her support, and she could not risk losing her job by asking for a raise after two years of employment at the same rate. The writer rejected the suggestion that working women were content with their wages. It was time, she noted, for the businessmen of Halifax to do more for their employees, so that they could make enough to look respectable.[51]

Similarly, 'Unemployed Working Girl' wrote to the *Garment Worker*, a union newspaper, to protest a system of low-waged exploitation that rewarded young women workers in Toronto with wages as low as four dollars a week in 1914: 'There are people in this city who give their time and energy rescuing girls from the streets and the vile dens they get lured to. Is it any wonder that girls go wrong?' she asked. This writer was particularly angered that the manufacturers made huge profits off women who 'must strain every nerve in their bodies and receive in return the magnificent sum of $4 per week.'[52]

Thus, some 'working girls' articulated a notion of honest womanhood and respectability, but their voices were often muted in comparison with those of social reformers, labour leaders, and government bureaucrats who sought solutions to the difficulties raised both by child labour and female labour. Government response was limited to the passage of legislation and the appointment of investigatory and advisory bodies to study problem areas. Reluctantly, the provincial governments appointed inspectors or created bureaucracies to deal with conditions, hours, and wages of 'problem' groups in the labour market. Socially conscious reformers in the churches, the labour movement, and women's groups adopted the premise that the state had an obligation to intervene once the socio-economic system became imbalanced – that is, when it became excessively profit-oriented and exploitative of weaker groups. These reformers urged more direct intervention by government, usually at the provincial or local level, to tackle the exploitation of those least able to protect themselves. While men were viewed as largely capable of dealing with market forces, women and children were not and needed assistance. Men might organize into unions or change employment, options that were less likely for women or children. While not closely questioning the fundamentals of the socio-economic system of industrial capitalism, social reformers clearly questioned the excesses this system created. Overt exploitation was condemned, but the sexual division of labour, the family wage, and the place of women at the centre of family and community life remained part of the framework of Canadian society, a framework that would be severely tested in the years after 1914, particularly during the labour upsurge of 1917 to 1919.

# 2

# Gender Divisions: Women in
# Labour Organizations, 1890–1914

Unionize the Printery and Bindery workers.
Unionize the Fur Stitchers and Finishers.
Unionize the Laundry Workers.
Unionize the Stitchers and Sewers of all kinds.
Unionize the Women Clerks and every kind of Shop and Factory Labor
    where females are employed.

'Field for Organization,' *Voice*, 6 June 1902

This call to action appeared in a Winnipeg labour paper that recounted
the events of the previous few weeks surrounding the lockout of some
forty women workers at Paulin-Chambers confectionery company. The
Winnipeg Trades and Labor Council had organized a meeting to demonstrate public support for the striking women, who had refused to accept
a wage cut when their hours were shortened to conform to the eight-
hour limit mandated by the new Factory Act. Seeking assistance from
the council, the women had had the temerity to join the bakers' union.
In response, the manager had presented the women with the alternatives – return to work without the union or leave. The women chose the
latter, and Winnipeg's trade union men rallied to the cause, trying to
intervene with management, organizing relief funds, and criticizing the
company. Vigorously denouncing the treatment of the women, who
made between three and five dollars per week, the council accused the
company of denying the women rights held by all British subjects,
namely, the right to organize and the right to bargain collectively. For
these trade unionists, however, such rights were related to their concept

of manliness. The *Voice* noted that union men 'are deeply pledged by every principle that counts for manhood and especially that principle – the right of association to defend their daughters and sisters against the designs of unprincipled profit-grinders. Pledged as individuals, pledged in their several lodge rooms, and pledged in mass meeting to defend womankind and help them also to help themselves. From this forward the labor movement in Winnipeg will be more than ever a man and woman movement; a brotherhood and sisterhood.' Using the language of kinship and protection, this newspaper clearly revealed its view that women workers were vulnerable and needed union men's assistance. If competent women workers could barely earn a subsistence wage, then 'our boasted wealth and prosperity becomes little better than organized and legalized crime, an insult to womanhood, a constant menace to her social status and morality.' Union men must respond to the insult and the potential for immorality among women who did not earn enough to live on. Pledging to fight the 'sweatshop principle,' Winnipeg's trade unionists mounted a sustained effort to aid their locked-out sisters and daughters.[1]

The situation worsened as the company brought in strikebreakers. In an effort to boost morale, Kate Robertson, president of the United Garment Workers local, was brought in to address the strikers. In her speech, Robertson expressed sympathy for her sister workers and urged them to remain united. She recalled that, like the Paulin-Chambers strikers, the garment workers had been discouraged in their strike three years earlier, but she noted that they had eventually won their battle for justice. Indeed, Robertson offered to place fifteen to twenty of the strikers at the Hoover Manufacturing Company, a unionized garment manufacturer. Also present at the strikers' meeting was one of the five women who had quit the Reid box factory where orders for Paulin-Chambers were being filled under false names. As the *Voice* noted triumphantly, these unorganized women would not scab: 'The finer sense and quicker sympathy of woman tells in cases of this kind, especially with the more intelligent and better informed; they shrink instinctively from scabbing on their sister woman in trouble, as from something odious and unnatural.' Moreover, 'such cases appeal strongly to the manliness, even the chivalry of men, especially of union men for it is their battle they are fighting.' Cross-occupational solidarity among women workers is evident here, but so too is the recurring theme of male appropriation of women's struggles for the cause of union solidarity.[2]

This evidence demonstrates the potential for women's labour organization, potential that contrasted sharply with contemporary beliefs that women were unorganizable because of their youth, transiency in employment, and ultimately because of their nature. As this example demonstrates, women workers organized under extremely adverse conditions, joined largely male unions, and fought strikes both with (and sometimes without) union support.

In some respects the Paulin-Chambers experience is representative of women's labour activism in the period. It was typical in that the women were unorganized at the box factory and only newly organized at the confectionery company. Labour organization was often sporadic and short-lived among unskilled or semi-skilled workers as compared to those workers defined as skilled. In other ways, however, the strike was atypical. First, few strikes occurred in the food sector before the war. The concerted involvement of the labour movement through the Trades and Labor Council in this struggle was also unusual. Moreover, when the union movement mobilized support for striking women, the community generally increased pressure on employers to settle, but in this case the pressure failed. Finally, the Paulin-Chambers strike was atypical in that some strikers were able to find employment at a unionized factory that, as we shall see, was itself created by workers after a bitter labour struggle in the garment trade.

As this chapter will demonstrate, women workers were willing and able to organize. While most of the prewar strikes occurred in textiles and garments, other areas of manufacturing, as well as the newly burgeoning sectors of service work (hotels and restaurants) and public utilities (telephone and telegraph), experienced female militancy. The trend towards more women in clerical and sales work, however, did not result in significant labour organization until the First World War.

Because of the pattern of Canadian industrialization, Ontario and Quebec predominated in women's strike activity in the first decade and a half of the twentieth century. British Columbia garment workers, waitresses, laundry workers, and telephone operators also struck, but most strikes were in central Canada. The Prairies and the Maritimes showed less activity, partially because of under-reporting but also because of the small number of enterprises that used women's labour. While the prairie economy depended heavily on agriculture, construction, transportation, and some mining, the Maritimes had a more developed industrial sector based on secondary manufacturing, port activity, and the development of coal and steel, although much of the region remained centred on agriculture and fishing. In the railway, metal, and coal towns in the Maritimes studied by Ian McKay, an active labour movement drew upon male workers who were often willing to strike for higher wages and better conditions in a labour-scarce, buoyant economy in the early twentieth century. With the exception of women workers in textile and garment factories, the Maritime labour market was male.[3]

The evidence of women's union organization also suggests the prevalence of gender division and differentiation within the labour movement itself. Just as work was gendered, so too was the labour movement, which was led primarily by men, most of whom belonged to craft organizations headquartered in the United States. Women workers, assumed to be difficult to organize, had to convince male trade unionists to the contrary, or initiate their own organizations. While not all women workers were convinced of the benefits of unions and many were sceptical of male unionists' commitment to organizing women, some actively pursued these options, in hopes of bettering their lives and those of their families. Such labour activism raises questions that can only be partially answered by a survey of women's strike activity and labour organization since the evidence does not always permit full appreciation of the local context. Under what conditions were women militant? What factors discouraged women's activism? Were there distinctive patterns to this activism? How important was male trade union support? Was it a help or a hindrance? Did women workers view their needs as different than men's? As the following discussion indicates, the patterns of women's labour activism were varied and complex, defying simple categorizations.

I

While social investigators and reformers studied and debated the plight of the woman worker in Canada in the late nineteenth century and occasionally bemoaned her reluctance to join with her sisters to improve her wages and working conditions, working women in the 1890s were far from passive victims, as they were often portrayed. While few belonged to unions, they exhibited a willingness to band together in labour disputes and sometimes to form their own female associations. In a number of cases in the 1890s women workers were aided by their communities in confronting the industrial system that paid them appallingly low wages for long hours worked under unsanitary conditions. On rare occasions a working woman might use the legal system to sue an employer, as Barbara McClogherty did in January 1891 when she sued for damages when her hair was caught in laundry machinery and had to be cut off; McClogherty won damages of $624 from the Gale Manufacturing Company in Toronto. For most working women, however, their best hope lay in labour organization, backed by community support. Yet even with such support there were limits on what working women could accomplish.[4]

Two 1891 disputes in Toronto demonstrate these limits. In March the Nationalist Association, modelled on the cooperative vision of Edward Bellamy's American movement, adopted a resolution that women employed in making uniforms for the city's police and firemen be paid union scale. The Trades and Labor Council took the matter up, supported by the Journeymen Tailors' Union (JTU). When an alderman later attempted to rescind the agreement, the women were again successfully supported by their union brothers. A second controversy revolving around the wages and hours of young female telephone operators, however, resulted in a defeat. The TLC noted that a proposed five-year Bell Telephone monopoly left workers with no assurance of better wages; young women earned three dollars per sixty–hour work week, and learners were paid no wages when they started. City council decided to amend the proposed agreement with the company by inserting a minimum wage clause and an eight–hour day. While the amendment passed, opposition increased and the company refused to accept the conditions, leading to the rescinding of the clause and an eventual agreement minus the protective provision. Despite the efforts of the TLC, these unorganized women operators and their allies on city council were no match for Bell and its friends.[5]

These events of 1891 led 'Sister' to write a critical letter to the *Labor Advocate* in August decrying the lack of support for reducing the hours and raising the pay of women workers, particularly those in the restaurant and confectionery businesses where women put in seventy-five hours or more each week. Her letter underlined the reality that such businesses were not governed by the Factory Acts. It also underscored the relative lack of interest among trade union men in organizing women, particularly in women's trades. Comparing the lot of women in such industries with slavery, 'Sister' asked trade unionists 'Do you ever think of your sisters and daughters?' Fear of female competition and acceptance of the family wage ideal often militated against sustained organizational activity among women workers.[6]

While labour men might condemn 'the way in which we ... allow our "lady" sisters to become wage slaves to be exploited and demoralized,' and might pass resolutions calling for the 'abolition of female labor in all branches of industrial life ... where it is brought in direct competition with manual labor,' working women faced the necessity of labour and resisted exploitation where they could. The Working Women's Protective Association was founded in Toronto in 1893 and promised 'to defend the rights and advocate the interests of working women, to foster friendship and sisterhood, and to shield from aggression the defenceless toiler.' Also known as the Women's Protective Union (WPU), the organization involved itself in at least one strike, which resulted in the creation of the Toronto Co-Partnership Manufacturing Company, a producer cooperative organized in the face of manufacturer intransigence over a gloveworkers' strike. This 1893 strike protested a twenty-five-cent charge for steam power imposed by the company on its twenty-two female and twelve male workers. Management responded by increasing the charge and refusing to deal with the strikers, who then set up the new operation. The WPU's activities appear to have been short-lived, however, for no mention is found of their activities after 1895.[7]

The 1890s witnessed severe depression and increased competition as well as corporate consolidation involving the centralization of capital. Despite inauspicious times and, in many cases, women workers' lack of organization, labour disputes involving women demonstrate the spirit of honest womanhood at work. In the 1890s women workers were involved in over forty strikes or lockouts, most of which occurred in the textile and garment factories of Toronto and Hamilton (see Table 2.1, p. 56). The highly competitive garment trade witnessed continued attempts by manufacturers to erode price scales. Hence many of the garment strikes of this period were fought by workers seeking to maintain or improve price scales for piecework and to combat sweated labour. In a number of cases employers also tried to block worker organization or at least to weaken unions by dismissing individuals prominent in these organizations. Attempts to cut rates were sometimes accompanied by the introduction of new machinery, as was the case in a Berlin, Ontario, shirt factory in 1896 when a new starching machine occasioned a reduction in wages.[8]

In textiles, the depression of 1893–7 led employers to try to reduce costs by cutting prices for piecework and by reducing wages generally, and most textile strikes that involved women in the 1890s were fought against wage cuts. By the end of the decade as conditions improved, workers attempted to secure increases to compensate for past reductions in the industry, which was concentrated in Ontario, Quebec, and the

Maritimes. At the Merchants Cotton Factory in St Henri, a ward of Montreal, in May 1899, approximately one hundred young women workers earning between $3.00 and $3.50 per week initiated a strike for a 10 per cent increase in wages. The manufacturer offered, and the strikers eventually accepted, an increase of 6.5 per cent.[9]

Several cotton mills in the Maritimes experienced strikes in the mid-1890s over wage reductions. In Saint John, for example, twenty female carders led eighty other employees in an unsuccessful month-long strike in 1894 against reductions of $1.50 to $2.00 per week at the cotton mill in Courtenay Bay. Another mill in Saint John as well as the St Croix Cotton Mill in Milltown also experienced wage reductions and unsuccessful strikes in the same year. Undaunted, the Courtenay Bay mill workers, male and female, staged another unsuccessful strike in 1895 to regain lost wages, asking for a 10 per cent increase.[10]

Strikes were also fought in Ontario mills against wage cuts. At Rosamond Woolen Mills in Almonte over three hundred weavers, most of whom were women, struck at the end of January 1898 against reduced rates and the elimination of a bonus. A union was organized among three hundred female textile workers at Hamilton's Eagle Knitting Mills in November 1899 during a week-long strike. New machinery, the women claimed, reduced their earnings and accounted for the strike.[11]

The garment trades also faced discouraging prospects during the depressed 1890s, and few of the strikes in this industry resulted in clear-cut victories. A large Toronto strike in 1899 involved five hundred women and men in a struggle that lasted from the beginning of January to early April. The employing master tailors attempted to prevent the Journeymen Tailors' Union from organizing non-union men and women, precipitating a strike followed by a general lockout. The length of the strike and united employer resistance spelled disaster for the JTU. Divisions between Jewish and non-Jewish workers in the trade, which were frequently noted after the turn of the century, may have played a role as well. Another Toronto JTU strike in fall 1899 was more successful. Over two hundred men and women employed in shops along King, Queen, and Yonge Streets united to demand a uniform scale of wages and use of the union label. Strongly backed by their international, the tailors fought a successful campaign, organized most of the tailors in the city, and won a minimum scale.[12]

Two sizeable garment strikes involving women workers in Winnipeg demonstrate common traits: worker resistance to wage cuts countered by employer organization and accompanied by community support of the strike. While Winnipeg newspapers claimed that the garment workers' strike of 1899 was the first strike by women workers in the city, a Journeymen Tailors' Union's strike in February 1893 had involved seventy-five men and women in a fight against rate reductions. Fourteen firms had banded together to form a merchant tailors' association to resist the strike and had imported strikebreakers from Toronto and Montreal. The dispute had dragged on into April when the union went back at the old rate of wages.[13]

The 1899 strike differed in that all the strikers were women. The dispute, which started in mid-January at the Emerson and Hague Overall Company over wage reductions, was settled in favour of the strikers, temporarily. In February the women garment workers decided to ask the Winnipeg Trades and Labor Council to help them form a union, and they became Local 35 of the United Garment Workers of America. The following week, when three women were dismissed for union activity, all the women walked out, launching a strike that involved many of Winnipeg's unions and received considerable support within the community. The council organized public support meetings for the approximately thirty-five strikers, including one meeting that featured prominent unionists and E. Cora Hind, agricultural writer and later prominent member of the suffrage movement in Manitoba. The Woman's Christian Temperance Union also met with a delegation of union men and commended the labour movement for its support of the garment workers. Public contributions enabled the Trades and Labor Council to disburse strike pay. The new union publicized news of the dispute and urged young women not to break the strike. Many unions pledged financial support and adopted resolutions urging members to buy only union overalls. Because of the strike, women garment workers began to attend meetings of the TLC for the first time. Strikers wrote letters to the local papers detailing their conditions and wages, which were less than a dollar a day. One striker wrote of short pay, constant harassment by the foreman, and of being constantly switched from job to job, which made it difficult to earn decent wages. Still, Emerson and Hague refused to settle or arbitrate. In March a new company was organized, the Hoover Manufacturing Company, which paid union rates and shared 10 per cent of its profits with its employees. By 1902 the Hoover Company employed over one hundred hands and occupied two locations, paying wages of six to nine dollars for a forty-eight-hour week. Despite the intransigence of Emerson and Hague, community support and the creation of a union shop assisted these women garment workers in the long run.[14]

Extensive discussion in the *Voice* during the strike revealed the labour movement's positive views on women workers, but also its concern with respectability and the reproductive capacities of women workers as future mothers. A writer in the *Voice* carefully pointed out that the women strikers were 'all highly respectable and intelligent women, a credit to our city and citizens.' Noting that the strikers were dependent on their own exertions for making a living, the paper also drew attention to the fact that 'many of them are breadwinners of a household.' Contrasting Winnipeg to older cities in the dominion, the writer asked 'Will Winnipeg stand by and see the worst features of eastern cities thrust upon us in the West. Remember that it is not alone the cause of these 35 women that is in jeopardy, but it is the cause of all women workers that is being imperiled.' In contrast to the positive comments about the striking women as workers, the newspaper felt called upon to note that 'These women are among those who will be the mothers of the coming generation ... We want a strong and vigorous race in the West, our climate and our development demand it.'[15]

Community support proved important in other strikes involving women in the 1890s. Peterborough's electrical workers struck in April 1895 to resist deductions for rejected piecework. Some 280 men and women at Canadian General Electric succeeded because of public support. Although press reports indicated that most of the strikers were skilled and thus probably men, women were present among the strikers. Similarly, community support helped Victoria's postal workers win partial success in an 1894 strike of two women and twenty-nine men.[16]

Strikes and lockouts also provide evidence of women workers' willingness to take radical action. In 1892 a dozen waitresses at Kingston's Thousand Island House struck when they found themselves locked out of their residence after returning from a night concert. Other evidence of militancy occurred in strikes in cotton mills when women workers objected to new foremen, particularly abusive ones. Objecting to a tyrannical forewoman, fifteen women walked out of a London, Ontario, shoe factory in April 1899; more than twenty men followed, in sympathy. While they lost the strike, they organized a local of the International Boot and Shoe Workers' Union. In rare cases women workers were arrested in the course of a strike. An 1894 dispute at Toronto's J.D. King Company led to the arrest and trial of seven women and one man for intimidation of two female shoeworkers outside the factory.[17]

The strike at J.D. King's also illustrates women's autonomous organization and limited cooperation between women and men workers. The women belonged to the Women Shoe Fitters' Association, which met separately to discuss the proposed wage reductions of 10 to 50 per cent. Issuing their own press release, the women asserted that the employer had reduced wages the previous November by 15 per cent and now proposed further cuts through changes in work classifications. These cuts were too much to bear for the women who earned only one to four dollars per week. Meeting separately on 13 January, the 'girls' decided not to return to work until satisfactory prices had been arranged. They also requested a meeting with J.D. King, but received their only answer in the press: a denial of the earlier cuts and a list of the proposed reductions. Responding in kind, the women reasserted that cuts had been made in November, but emphasized that their concern was with the current reductions. The subsequent arrest of women picketers galvanized local unions such as the stonecutters, brassworkers, and others to pledge financial and moral support. Assistance was also forthcoming from the Women's Protective Union, which entertained the strikers. While the men's differences with the company were nearly adjusted by the third week of February, the company's refusal to deal with the women prompted male shoeworkers to hold out until 'an understanding is arrived at with the girls.' Settlement on 27 February, however, left the women shoeworkers awaiting recall to the factory, as business permitted. Solidarity between men and women workers was shortlived. While the arrests of women workers offended masculine pride, failure to settle with the women strikers apparently did not. Despite the stated support from male shoeworkers and the solidarity from other unions, the women bore the brunt of the company's anger in the aftermath of the dispute.[18]

Women's labour activism in the 1890s appeared sporadically, sometimes in strike situations and sometimes in the formation of rare groups such as the Working Women's Protective Association. In the depression of the 1890s it was difficult for workers, whether male or female, to resist widespread wage cuts, to improve their working conditions, or to fight for union recognition. For women workers there were additional problems related to gender: viewed as secondary wage earners, temporary workers, and competitors for men's jobs, women faced hostility and distrust. Yet in times of crisis, they were occasionally able to forge links with male co-workers who defended their interests as part of a larger class interest. While community support could tip the balance in strike situations, large corporations, such as Bell Telephone, or effective employers' associations, such as the master tailors, were too often more powerful than the opposition. Sometimes, however, the combination of well-organized labour support and community pressure produced favourable strike settlements or, in several cases, new factories paying better wages.

## II

With the turn of the century, women workers remained largely unorganized yet continued to play important roles in workplace struggles, particularly in the textile and garment industries in central Canada. Strikes involving women workers in the decade and a half before the First World War demonstrate the involvement of women in workplace efforts to improve wages and conditions and at the same time suggest the limits of such efforts in the relatively small numbers of strikes. While women's activism was not limited to strikes, these strikes provide its clearest evidence.[19]

Working women's potential for labour radicalism was shaped by a variety of circumstances and contingencies. Structural factors (which include the nature of the labour process, the size and location of work groups, the degree of gender segregation, and the technology used) were influential in shaping opportunities for, and attitudes towards, workplace confrontations. A sense of community based on region, ethnicity, class, or gender could reinforce a willingness to engage in workplace confrontation as well. On the other hand, the gendered division of labour entrenched the notion that women were suited only for unskilled or semi-skilled work, usually as a prelude to marriage, thus discouraging militancy or cross-gender cooperation in a labour dispute. Similarly, prevailing gender stereotypes usually reinforced the idea that women were more conservative than men and less likely to engage in collective action.

As Table 2.2 (p. 57) indicates, women workers participated in more than 160 strikes during the period 1900–14. The distribution of strikes by year in Tables 2.1 and 2.2 indicates that periods of higher strike activity occurred at the turn of the century (1899–1900), in 1907, and in 1910–13. These trends are somewhat different from those of general strike activity in Canada. While the five-year period from 1899 to 1903 witnessed a general strike wave in Canada, involving the metal trades, transportation, mining, construction, and manufacturing, women's strikes occurred only in the latter sector in textiles, garments, and boot and shoe manufacturing; the other sectors were entirely male-dominated. The year 1907 stands out as a peak for women strikers, more so than for general strike activity, because of the large number of garment and textile strikes in that year in Ontario and Quebec, a phenomenon repeated in 1912–13, and also evident in 1910–11. The predominance of garment and textile sector strikes for women workers is clear in this decade and a half, as it had been in the 1890s.

Where women went on strike in the first fifteen years of this century, they did so most often over wages, usually for increases, but also, in about one-quarter of the cases, against reductions. In textiles, the most frequent reason for a strike was to achieve higher wages; in garments, higher wages, control over working conditions, and union recognition were often tied together, particularly in those years when the garment workers' unions launched campaigns to organize previously unorganized workers, including women and British/Canadian workers, who were a minority within Jewish-dominated garment unions. In early 1911, the *Ladies' Garment Worker*, for example, noted the increasing interest in unions among Toronto and Montreal garment workers, partially as a result of previous victories in New York City. The paper also noted the divisions among the garment workers, many of whom adhered to socialist principles and eschewed ties with the American Federation of Labor's bread-and-butter unionism. As the garment unions reached out to previously unorganized sectors and implemented industrial union strategies, reluctance to organize diminished. Nevertheless, union organizers commented on the timidity of Canadian women in joining organizations such as the United Garment Workers of America. American organizer Margaret Daley, who frequently visited Canada to recruit members, said in an interview that the 'greatest difficulty we have is to put fight into the Canadian women. They are by nature and because of their customs more timid than American women. The employer takes advantage of that ... But we are gradually making the women understand that behind the union must be the moral force of its members and that they must stand for their rights if we are to help them.' By 1911, observers noted that the main obstacle to further organization was not the Jewish workers but the Gentiles, who were reluctant to join with their Jewish co-workers. Ethnic friction as well as political differences between Jews and non-Jews remained a formidable obstacle to organization and union solidarity.[20]

The other major area of women's strike activity outside the garment

TABLE 2.1
Strikes Involving Women, 1890–1899 (by Industry)

| Year | Garment | Textile | Boot & Shoe | Tobacco | Service | Printing | Other | Total |
|---|---|---|---|---|---|---|---|---|
| 1890 | 1 | 1 | – | – | – | – | – | 2 |
| 1891 | – | 1 | – | – | – | – | – | 1 |
| 1892 | – | – | – | – | 2 | 1 (1*) | – | 2 |
| 1893 | 4 | 1 | – | – | 1 | – | – | 7 |
| 1894 | 1 | 3 | 1 | 1 | – | – | – | 6 |
| 1895 | – | 1 | 1 | – | – | – | 1 | 3 |
| 1896 | 2 | 1 | – | – | – | 1* (1**) | – | 5 (1**) |
| 1897 | 1* | 1 | – | – | 2 | – | – | 3 |
| 1898 | 1 | – | – | – | – | – | – | 2 |
| 1899 | 5 | 3 | 1 | 1* | – | – | – | 10 |
| Total | 15 | 12 | 3 | 2 | 5 | 4 | 1 | 42 |

*Objection to women in trade or threat to use women as replacements for men

**Strike details unclear on women

Source: G. Kealey and D. Cruickshank, data for Plate 39, *Historical Atlas of Canada*, vol. 3, *Addressing the Twentieth Century* (Toronto: University of Toronto Press, 1990).

TABLE 2.2
Strikes Involving Women, 1900–1914 (by Industry)

| Year | Garment | Textile | Boot & Shoe | Tobacco | Service | Communication | Print | Food | Other* | Total |
|---|---|---|---|---|---|---|---|---|---|---|
| 1900 | 1 | 6 (1) | 1 | 1 | 1 | – | – | – | 1 | 12 |
| 1901 | 1 | (1) | – | 1 | – | – | – | – | 1 | 4 |
| 1902 | 1 | 2 (1) | – | – | 2 | 1 | 1 | 1 | 1 | 10 |
| 1903 | 1 (2) | 1 | – | 1 | 1 | – | 1 | – | 1 | 8 |
| 1904 | 3 | 1 | – | – | 1 | 1 | 1 | 1 | – | 8 |
| 1905 | 3 | 1 | – | – | 1 | 1 | 1 | – | 1 | 8 |
| 1906 | 7 | 1 | – | – | – | 1 | – | 1 | 2 | 11 |
| 1907 | 7 | 7 | 3 | – | – | 3 | – | – | – | 21 |
| 1908 | 1 | 2 | – | – | 1 | 1 | – | – | 2 | 6 |
| 1909 | 6 | 2 | – | – | – | 1 | – | – | – | 9 |
| 1910 | 7 (1) | 2 (1) | 1 | 3 | – | – | – | 1 | 1 | 16 |
| 1911 | 6 (1) | 3 | 1 | 1 | – | 1 | 1 | – | 1 | 14 |
| 1912 | 15 | 1 | 1 | 1 | – | – | – | – | 1 | 20 |
| 1913 | 9 (1) | 2 | 2 | – | 1 | – | – | – | 2 | 17 |
| 1914 | 3 | – | – | – | – | – | – | – | – | 3 |
| Total | 71 (5) | 31 (4) | 9 | 8 | 8 | 9 | 5 | 3 | 14 | 167 |

*Other: paper mill – 2; boxer and machine workers; paperbox – 2; carriage works; matches – 2; rubber; tin works; hairmaking; metal mfg – 2; musicians

( ) means strike details on women unclear

Source: *Labour Gazette*; Strikes and Lockouts Files (Department of Labour); newspapers.

trade occurred in cotton textile production, where women constituted almost half the workforce in the period 1900–14. Approximately half of all cotton mill workers laboured in Quebec and the rest in Ontario and the Maritimes. Quebec's larger mills employed fewer women than mills in other provinces; the female portion of the workforce in Quebec's mills was around 40 per cent. Two large firms, the Montreal Cotton Company (established 1888) and the Dominion Textile Company (established 1905), dominated Quebec's cotton industry. Both companies experienced significant strike activity before the First World War, especially in 1900 and again in 1907–8. The latter strikes led to a federal royal commission, under the aegis of William Lyon Mackenzie King of the Department of Labour, which reported in January 1909. On balance, the report was more critical of labour leaders than of employers, although it criticized the long hours worked by women and children, recommended revision of the Factory Act and stricter enforcement of child labour laws, and chastised employers for their rather abrupt reduction of wages without consultations with employees. The commission also recommended the adoption of joint agreements, one-month's notice of changes in wages and conditions, and a permanent board of conciliation. Overall, the commission blamed the worldwide recession of 1908 for the necessity of the most recent 10 per cent reduction in wages in the industry. The commission examined all strikes and lockouts in the trade after 1900 and noted that the majority were fought over wages. In 65 per cent of all disputes in the mills, the employers won, indicating that strikes in this industry were less successful for workers than was generally the case in Canadian industrial disputes.[21]

*Textile Strikes*

A number of strikes in the large cotton mills of Quebec in 1900, 1908, and 1909–13 will be examined for strike activity among women textile workers. Not all textile strikes occurred in Quebec, of course; several Ontario strikes and one large 1903 strike in New Brunswick will also be examined. These strikes most often involved women and men, but in some cases the women precipitated the strikes within largely female-defined occupations. A number of strikes refute the premise that women were reluctant to engage in militant job actions.

Valleyfield was the site of four separate strikes in 1900 at the Montreal Cotton Mills, while two smaller strikes against the Dominion Textile Company occurred at Magog and Montmorency Falls. In Valleyfield the first strike began on 29 January over a demand for increased wages for seventy-five female bobbin winders; the strike affected fifteen hundred male and female workers, some of whom belonged to the Knights of Labor. While the week-long labour stoppage failed to produce any wage increases, a second larger strike on 21 February, lasting until 3 March, resulted in a compromise and a 5 per cent raise for a small number of workers. Most of the twenty-five hundred workers involved in the second strike were women. Weavers at Valleyfield struck the mill again between 12 and 17 July, objecting to the 'employment of certain persons.' A settlement led to the replacing of some of the five hundred weavers who had gone on strike, and others left to find other work. Weaving was a process dominated by women in this instance, while spinning employed mostly men.[22]

The final and largest labour stoppage in Valleyfield occurred from 26 to 30 October, when most of the workforce of three thousand – about two-thirds of whom were women or children – engaged in a sympathy strike to aid labourers building a new mill site. The walkout was prompted by the mobilization of the militia to protect company property during the labourers' strike. Mill hands objected to the presence of the troops, and workers demonstrated their opposition by throwing rocks at the troops and striking on 26–7 October. When the company dismissed some employees for striking, three hundred spinners and weavers refused to return to work even after, owing to the intervention of Mackenzie King, most of the other workers had gone back. The remaining strikers agreed to return as long as the troops were removed and the dismissed workers were rehired. The troops left, but the workers had to apply individually for reinstatement. Construction ceased a few weeks early as the company wished to defuse a tense situation.[23]

The Montmorency Falls strike of 589 men, women, and children erupted shortly after the company served notice on 210 employees that their services would no longer be required after 27 August 1900. The company then proceeded to dismiss some employees even earlier than the specified date. On 15 August, a meeting of the recently organized Knights of Labor Assembly agreed to strike, charging certain foremen and other workers with objectionable behaviour and demanding their dismissal. According to the company, trouble arose when a female employee quit after being refused a wage increase. When she was replaced by another woman, the Knights disputed the replacement's assignment and ordered her to give up the position or face expulsion from the organization. She resigned from the Knights, and others refused to work with her, stopping work and closing the mill. The company clearly hoped to break the Knights' organization and brought in scabs from the Lac St-Jean region to try to reopen the mill in early September. By late September half of the strikers had returned, some agreeing to sign a pledge not to join any labour organization. Approximately one-fifth of the strikers left Montmorency Falls to find work elsewhere, leaving less than one-third of the original strikers still out. The outcome was the destruction of the Knights' organization, and the incident dampened labour activity for years to follow.[24]

Mill communities in the Maritimes also experienced strikes. Milltown, New Brunswick, was the home of the St Croix Cotton Mill (established in 1882), which was owned by Canadian Colored Cotton Mills. Drawing on a local labour force that included nearby Calais, Maine, the mill was an important source of employment for eight hundred men and women. In March 1903 three hundred weavers struck for a 15 per cent wage increase to compensate for reduced earnings occasioned by an inferior grade of raw material. The decision to seek an increase had been taken in January. The delay in strike action on wages may have been occasioned by another controversy brewing at the mill. In January, a new American superintendent of the mill had fired some Milltown employees, replacing them with American workers. By February, town pressure and protest to management in Montreal had forced the superintendent to resign in favour of a New Brunswick man. That issue resolved, the employees went out on strike, successfully shutting down the mill to enforce their earlier demands for a wage increase. An abortive attempt to reopen the mill failed when only thirty weavers, mostly women, showed up for work. Mackenzie King's intervention on 7 April resulted in an agreement to call off the strike.[25]

In Ontario, small towns situated on rivers provided good locations for textile mills producing both cotton and woollen products. Manufacturers of fabric, sweaters, underwear, and knitted goods set up mills in small towns like Almonte and Paris, or sometimes in larger towns like Kingston, which had a steam-powered cotton mill, or, less frequently, in cities like Hamilton, where Canadian Cottons provided employment in its large factory. Small towns like Paris, where Penmans manufactured knit goods, often faced labour shortages, particularly of experienced female mill workers. Penmans responded by recruiting experienced women workers from the knit-goods industry in Britain, which was experiencing slack times at the end of the first decade of the twentieth century. Before the recruitment drives produced any volume of emigrants, Penmans faced labour troubles in 1907 when 850 women and 150 men struck for the continuance of the Saturday half-holiday throughout the year rather than just from April to October. The *Labour Gazette* correspondent J.C. Watt noted the active participation of two single women, Kate Thomas and Frances Bertram, as leaders in the dispute. The ten-day strike at the unorganized mill resulted in a partial victory for the workers, who obtained the half-holiday, but only after a specified date.[26]

A strike at the Penmans mill in St Hyacinthe, Quebec, in June 1907 pitted 259 women and 224 men against the company over wages and dismissals, as well as union recognition for the recently organized local of the textile workers union. Intervention by the Quebec Conciliation Bureau resulted in a compromise on the question of wage increases and reinstatement of those fired, but a refusal to recognize the union. Intervention also came from several politicians and the president of the Confederated Textile Workers of Canada. Unlike the Paris strike, where women predominated, this strike involved more equal numbers of men and women, with men taking the leadership. A year later, the St Hyacinthe mill experienced a small, unsuccessful strike by twelve female stocking knitters for higher wages.

Where women textile workers dominated numerically and developed some leadership and solidarity, they proved willing to take action. Even in small numbers women could be militant, especially where they worked at the same jobs in a department, as was the case when twenty-five finishers in one department of the Almonte Knitting Company went on strike three times in as many weeks in November 1909 over dismissals of young women workers and then of the female strike leaders.[27]

The strike wave of 1907–8 in Quebec's mills, spurred by a 10 per cent wage reduction, reverberated for several years in the industry. In Magog, for example, strikes were fought in 1909 and 1911 to restore full wages and against discriminatory treatment of union members. In May 1909, 368 women and 540 men went out in a spirited strike that featured daily meetings in the Opera House and outdoors. At one of these gatherings, 'une ancienne employée de la filature de Magog,' Mme Ludger Vezina, who herself had been blacklisted by the company, urged the workers not to give in until their demands were won. Despite such enthusiasm, the strike was unsuccessful. The 1911 strike of spinners and printers involved two hundred women and three hundred men in another bid to restore the lost 10 per cent. Earlier the mill workers had joined the textile workers union as part of a campaign to meet with management to press for restoration of wages. Dominion Textiles refused the increase and posted notices warning of outside labour agitators. Although management eventually agreed to meet with a committee of three, they spurned the representatives and indicated that they preferred to meet directly with their employees. The textile workers' committee endeavoured to put pressure on the company by publishing wage comparisons with other companies, which paid wages 15–20 per cent higher, but the strike failed.[28]

Wage reductions affected cotton textile workers in other provinces as well. In Hamilton, the Imperial Cotton Company faced a strike of 150 women and 125 men, all unorganized workers, in May 1910 for restoration of the 1908 wage cut. The dispute dragged on until July with the company closing the mill until the workers conceded. An attempt to form a union met with no success. In all provinces, the attempts by women and men textile workers to reverse the wage cuts of 1908 met united employer resistance, which spelled failure for the textile operatives.[29]

The pattern after 1908 then was one of the rare successes for textile workers. There were few textile strikes in 1913 – all employer victories – and none in 1914. At Montmorency Falls, in March 1913, forty cardroom employees, nearly all women, tied up the mill's spinners, weavers, and other operatives who could not carry out their work without the carders. Despite their importance in the early stages of the textile work process, these workers were defeated when the company quickly found replacements. Unlike skilled garment workers, textile workers were more easily replaced and their unions more difficult to maintain. While some women textile workers were active and militant, consistent management strategy and the overall character of the industry, with large mills and, at least in bigger towns and cities, a ready supply of replacement workers, spelled defeat.[30]

*Garment Strikes*

The clothing industry was the most important sector of women's strike activity in the early twentieth century. The industry ranked third in size among all manufacturing industries in 1900. The total number of women in the needle trades was large: women outnumbered men in the early part of the century in factory garment production, and they also did homework and were employed in small dressmaking and tailoring shops. For our purposes, the discussion will focus on women involved in factory clothing production in urban areas. Montreal, Toronto, and Winnipeg dominated the clothing industry in this period, and the first two cities were the scene of most of the strikes involving women workers.[31]

The clothing trades were divided by type of product, skill, and union. The men's clothing trade was distinct from that of women (and children) and developed a labour process more complex than that in the women's trade. In men's clothing skilled labour such as cutting and pressing was reserved for men, while women performed supposedly less skilled tasks such as basic sewing, finishing, and buttonhole making. In the women's clothing sector, the cloak and suit operations were similar to the production of men's coats and suits: the cutting and pressing was done by men while women sewed vests, linings, and other items. With the development of the shirtwaist and the ready-made dress, women's clothing was produced by women operators using sewing machines or, particularly in the custom trade, by hand sewing. While both men and women might be paid by the item, piecework was largely associated with women's work. Male tailors fought the imposition of piecework, although not always with success. While piecework was usually associated with homework or the sweating system, it was also part of women's factory experience. In general, women's work in the clothing trades was labelled unskilled or less skilled than men's, and the sexual division of labour was reinforced by low wages. Both men and women in the trade faced seasonal layoffs, alternating with intense periods of production to gear up for the spring and fall seasons.

Four major unions were involved in organizing the industry, three of them important before 1914. The earliest, the Journeymen Tailor's Union, originated in the 1880s and by the turn of the century had thirty-eight locals in Canada, most in Ontario. Conceived as a union of craftsmen, the JTU gradually adapted to the presence of women in the industry, admitting them to membership. Far more important were the United Garment Workers of America (UGWA) in the men's industry and the International Ladies' Garment Workers' Union (ILGWU) in the women's clothing trade. The UGWA first organized in Canada in 1894; in 1899 the first women's local was formed in Winnipeg. Later, in 1914–15, the UGWA was eclipsed by a breakaway union, the Amalgamated Clothing Workers of America, which eschewed the conservative approach of the earlier union. The ILGWU first appeared in Canada in Montreal in 1904. A Toronto local established two years later quickly disappeared. Montreal Local 28 successfully settled a strike with the Star Mantle Manufacturing Company in 1904 involving fourteen women and nineteen men, negotiating a union shop, an arbitration committee to settle the new wage scale and any disputes, and the reinstatement of the strikers. Mercedes Steedman notes that by 1914 the ILGWU claimed four thousand Canadian members, but such auspicious numbers were accompanied by instability, as locals often disappeared between seasons only to reappear the next season to fight another strike for better wages, hours, and conditions.[32]

Almost half the strikes appearing in Table 2.2 occurred in the garment industry, with peaks in 1906–7 and 1912–13. While strikes in men's clothing tended to predominate, strikes also occurred in the women's clothing sector even though it was slower to organize. The largest strikes occurred in Toronto and Montreal, particularly in the years just prior to the First World War. The most famous was the 1912 Eaton's strike, although strikes in smaller shops were more common than large-scale actions. While, according to different estimates, the Eaton's strike involved six hundred to one thousand workers, most other strikes involved fewer than two hundred workers. In 1905 and 1906 in Toronto, for example, the Lowndes Company experienced two strikes among its men's clothing trade workers. These strikes involved 200 workers in 1905–6 and 145 in 1906–7, with women constituting 60 per cent of the former and 30 per cent of the latter.[33]

In Montreal in August 1907, twenty-five women and twenty-seven men went on strike over the reinstatement of a discharged foreman and in an unsuccessful attempt to force union recognition at H. Vineberg and Company. The failure to gain the closed shop in this small firm was not unusual. The workers apparently also struck for the choice of piecework versus weekly rates, which the company ultimately agreed should be at the discretion of its employees. Almost simultaneously with the Vineberg strike, four other Montreal firms faced a strike of 90 women and 276 men who wanted to abolish piecework, removing the work from contractors. Eventually at least eight large firms and eight hundred workers were affected. This strike also included a demand for shorter work weeks – a fifty-five hour maximum for men, and fifty-one for women. By early September the firms had agreed to reduce work weeks to fifty-two hours for women and fifty-five for men, to accept the Saturday half-holiday, and, significantly, to stagger work times for women and men. The men began a half-hour before the women and quit five minutes later. Two new garment workers' locals were formed as a result of the dispute, one of them a women's local with over three hundred charter members. Two hundred of these women took part in the Montreal Labour Day parade to celebrate their new local. The larger question of piecework and contracting out was not part of the settlement. Press reports indicate that the contractors threatened to lock out more employees in order to put pressure on the clothing companies to increase the prices paid to the contractors so they in turn might pay their workers better, but no reports of increases were found. The Montreal strikes demonstrate several common occurrences in garment strikes: the uneven organization among garment workers; the welcoming of women into the union; the positive impact of a strike in galvanizing new locals among garment workers; and the continuing struggle over piecework and the role of contractors in the industry. For some employees, the piecework system was preferred but, in general, workers in the industry opposed it.[34]

In a number of strikes, companies were challenged by unorganized workers. In Toronto in February 1910, fifty-eight women at the Braime Company struck to challenge deductions for thread, a practice that had fallen into disuse in most garment firms, but, according to Mr Braime, remained in place in his company to discourage waste. He defended this practice and claimed that his net profits the previous year were only 9.5 per cent on his capital. He also denied that his business was a sweatshop and claimed that the women averaged seven dollars a week after deductions. The women, however, declared that their wages were between five and seven dollars. Sam Landers of the UGWA stepped in to advise the strikers and to organize the strike meetings, which occurred twice daily at the Labour Temple. The women also picketed the factory in five shifts. After the strike, Landers's efforts were gratefully acknowledged when twenty former strikers presented him with an engraved ring as a token of their appreciation. Women operatives in UGWA Local 202 invited the strikers to be their guests at a meeting, probably in the hope of furthering organization among the women overall and shirt operatives. The strike lasted into the spring, and the strikers had to raise funds from the city's unions. Despite these efforts and donations from unions and from the Canadian Suffrage Association, the strikers found themselves without employment at the Braime Company in the spring, although Sam Landers helped to place some of the strikers in union shops. The involvement of the suffrage organization was described by the Winnipeg *Voice* as the first instance where women seeking political reform offered assistance to their working-class sisters fighting for 'industrial emancipation.'[35]

Simultaneously a small strike erupted at Continental Costume, which manufactured women's ready-to-wear garments. *Labour Gazette* reporter

Tom Banton wrote that 'many of the strikers are of the foreign element, Jews and others.' Twenty-two women joined forty-eight men in the strike over recognition of the Independent Cloakmakers' Union of Toronto, formed in September 1909 by Abraham Kirzner and about fifteen other Russian and Polish Jews. The union embraced not only the cutters and pressers, but the operators and finishers as well and was reported to have five hundred members in the city. Continental Costume owner W.M. McCausland refused to recognize the union, which involved almost all the employees, but he agreed to put clear price tags on the garments at the insistence of the strikers. When the strike ended on 30 March, the workers claimed a minor gain, although not union recognition.[36]

These 1910 garment strikes were the beginning of a strike wave in the industry, which lasted until 1913 and included about forty stoppages (see Table 2.2). Fuelled by successes in the United States, garment workers in Canada engaged in similar organizing and strike activity in the years just prior to the First World War.

The most famous strike among clothing workers took place in Toronto in February 1912, with a smaller sympathetic strike in Montreal. The Eaton's strike occurred in the context not only of previous labour strife in Toronto's garment sector, but also significant victories in the trade in the eastern United States. The strike was precipitated when Eaton's management insisted that sixty-five male cloakmakers machine-finish the sewing of linings into women's cloaks, a task previously done by women hand sewers. When the cloakmakers refused, and sat idle for ten days at their machines before being thrown out of the factory by the police, a lockout ensued followed by the walkout of approximately one thousand other Eaton's employees. Most of the workers were Jewish, and a third of them were women employed in clothing production. Although not employed in a 'union shop,' the Eaton's workers were members of the ILGWU and the UGWA, and the latter workers struck in sympathy.[37]

The cloakmakers, whose actions started what would turn into a four-month struggle, refused to take bread from their sisters' mouths, but they also were refusing to do extra work without any increase in the price they were paid for each garment. While some writers have tended to downplay the cloakmakers' concern for the elimination of their sister workers' employment, others have emphasized the rare solidarity presented by the initial refusal of the cloakmakers to take over the women finishers' work. Although the cloakmakers might have been able to argue for a higher price for doing the extra work, Frager argues that they chose to stand by the women finishers. While the cloakmakers' motivation remains difficult to prove, the strike at Eaton's was a significant demonstration that gender divisions could be blurred in a crisis. Yet, as Frager has noted, the cloakmakers' refusal to do women's work paradoxically reinforced the gender division of labour. Nonetheless, the contemporaneous strike of the Toronto's Journeyman Tailors' Union in March, which included a demand for equal rates for equal work for its women members, suggests that at least some men were conscious of the exploitation of women workers and committed to changing the wage scale.[38]

The Eaton's strike illuminates a number of other factors pertinent to the clothing trade and its workers. First, the strike mobilized a significant sector of the union movement, which contributed its moral and financial support to the strikers and their families. The Toronto District Labor Council took an active role in publicizing the strike among its members and across the country, soliciting funds as well as strike support and organizing a boycott of Eaton's. The boycott was especially effective within the Jewish community, where women punished the company. Anti-Semitism and lack of concern for immigrant workers undercut the boycott outside the Jewish community, although women's auxiliaries of some of the major Toronto unions, such as the International Typographical Union's, pledged their support.[39]

Second, the dispute drew the attention of the central offices of the ILGWU and the UGWA. Two women organizers as well as Abraham Rosenberg, the international president of the ILGWU, visited Toronto during the strike to aid in the struggle. Women organizers from the United States came to help the strikers generally and also to meet specifically with the women strikers. Josephine Casey arrived on 20 February and spoke at several mass meetings with Rosenberg. Later Gertrude Barnum came to Toronto from Chicago. She played an active role in the strike during March, speaking to meetings such as one called by the auxiliaries of seven unions. Barnum urged neighbourhood organization to boycott Eaton's and warned of the dangers that violence would bring to the strikers' cause: 'The slugging of one thousand helpless working people by cold and hunger for five weeks elicits no comments from the press, pulpit or platform, yet the impulsive act of some hot-heads will bring instant unsavory notoriety to sufferers.' Barnum helped to organize parades held on 23 March and a meeting at Massey Hall where she spoke to urge a women's boycott. The morning parade of some three hundred children of the cloakmakers and garment workers publicized the meeting, as did the larger afternoon parade of two thousand people, the majority of whom were women and children carrying banners and wearing badges supporting the strikers.[40]

Third, the strike illustrated the limits of gender solidarity among the women of Toronto. Class and ethnic differences proved insurmountable barriers in the strike. Middle- and upper-middle-class Anglo-Saxon women apparently could not relate their struggle for the franchise to Jewish immigrant women's fight for work and decent wages. Alice Chown and Estelle Kerr of the Equal Franchise League attempted to interest suffrage supporters in the women strikers' cause, but without much success. Chown's semi-autobiographical novel, *The Stairway* (1921), revealed her frustration with the lack of sympathy among the various women's clubs, 'unless I had some tale of hardship to tell.' When Chown presided over a suffrage meeting featuring one of the American women organizers, she commented: 'I did not expect an audience who had never considered that justice to working people was a higher virtue than charity, to respond any more cordially than they did.' The meeting aroused 'a great deal of hard feeling among the zealous suffragists, who were afraid that their pet cause would be hurt through being linked with an unpopular one.'[41]

Fourth, the strike demonstrated the power of Eaton family. The company proved difficult to meet, let alone to negotiate with, despite the attempts of local community leaders to arrange meetings. The strikers' own committee had to utilize the services of third parties to negotiate with Eaton's, and the company gave no ground, insisting that, in addition to accepting the originally contentious system of production, the strikers should deny union and Labor Council statements made about the dispute and apologize for the damage to the reputation of company president J.C. Eaton. Toronto newspaper coverage of the strike was scant and was castigated by the labour movement. Rumours of a settlement in mid-April proved to be false when it became apparent to strike leaders that the company was backing out of the tentative agreement, which included reinstatement for all the strikers. The powerful Eaton's empire also brought in strikebreakers from Yorkshire – one hundred young women who had not been informed of the strike. Despite union protests, the Department of Immigration refused to act, insisting that there was nothing in the Immigration Act to prevent this type of emigration. All the department could do was inform its agents in England as to the strike situation at Eaton's. As the strike dragged on, financial hardship increased, and many strikers found work in other shops. Attempts to raise more funds from the Toronto public were hampered by an anti-begging by-law, which the police chose to strictly enforce despite the fact that they had often turned a blind eye to street-corner collections for the Salvation Army and for various fundraising tag days. Thus, the authorities at all levels decided to keep clear of the Eaton's empire and offered no assistance to the strikers in resolving the dispute.[42]

Finally, the dispute revealed the overwhelmingly male leadership of the strike and exposed ethnic tensions within the labour movement. While Casey and Barnum represented the international union and appealed to women to support the strike and boycott, the Toronto leadership lacked women. In addition, the strikers were unable to forge strong links with non-Jewish workers in the trade. In Montreal, the sympathy strike pitted Jewish men and women against French-Canadian women who refused to strike. In Toronto, non-Jewish clothing trade workers also were reluctant or unwilling to strike, thus reinforcing ethnic divisions and perceptions that the strike involved only 'foreigners.' The strike eventually disintegrated in the summer of 1912. Its length, the strength of company resistance, as well as anti-Semitism were key factors in the final outcome.[43]

A shorter strike of the JTU by 550 employees, 200 of them women, was more successful. Within days of the 4 March 1912 strike, a few of the twenty-one firms affected had already settled, and by mid-April a majority of the workers had returned under an agreement that provided for a union shop, a forty-nine-hour work week, time and a half for overtime, and wage increases of 12.5 to 15 per cent. The union insisted that changes had to be made in the scale for pieceworkers and that women workers should get the same terms as men. Minimum scales for women who performed different jobs than men, however, were about half of what the union demanded for men. Employer attempts to split the union's ranks by appealing separately to the women misfired. As one leader of the JTU noted, the employers found that the women were 'even stronger in their objections to the old conditions of things.' A year later, *Labour Gazette* correspondent Edith Elwood reported that twenty-five women were still on strike.[44]

While the ILGWU in Toronto suffered a setback from the unsuccessful Eaton's strike, the UGWA waged a successful strike affecting more than twenty large and small firms, involving perhaps two thousand women and men in the spring of 1913. The strike began on 18 March against six firms, but it affected a large number of businesses indirectly since the result would set the standard in other shops. Eighty women and 120 men in the six shops demanded overtime pay, better sanitary conditions,

and wage increases of 20 per cent for cutters and 10 per cent for operators. Four of the six firms settled within five days, agreeing to the
increases. Edith Elwood noted that 'Conditions among the Gentile girls
[are] said to be very good. Among Jewish girls not so good, owing to the
fact that a large number of Jewish girls are employed in outside contract
shops, also that there is a subcontracting system.' Reverberations of the
Toronto strike were felt in Montreal where garment workers anticipated
that one thousand workers would benefit from the settlement. In addition, cloak and skirt operators threatened a large walkout if better wages
and conditions were not forthcoming.[45]

Other large strikes in the trade also provide evidence of women's
labour activism in 1912–13. An estimated forty-five hundred garment
workers in Montreal, many of them members of the UGWA, struck on
10 June 1912 for shorter hours, overtime pay, abolition of subcontracting, and other demands. One-third of the strikers were women who
joined their male co-workers in the forty-eight-day strike. Amid considerable strife, which included a number of arrests and court cases alleging assault of strikebreakers and obstruction (for flashing mirrors to
annoy and frighten workers in one of the dozen factories affected), hundreds of women and some young men conducted a tag day outside
downtown office buildings to raise strike funds. The press also reported
two hundred 'girls' wearing red sashes taking to the streets to distribute
copies of the socialist newspaper Cotton's Weekly in return for a strike
donation. Editor W.U. Cotton threatened to sell the paper himself if the
police interfered. While the editor was assured there was no problem,
the strikers continued to complain to the police about intimidation by
plainclothes officers. Fuel was added to the fire by allegations that, just
before striking, workers at Friedman Brothers had deliberately damaged
goods and cut up thousands of dollars worth of cloth. Leaders of the
strike denied giving any such orders. This militant and bitter strike
demonstrated deep divisions between workers and wealthy manufacturers, both of whom belonged to Montreal's Jewish community. It also
illustrated the importance of the left-wing Jewish workers' movement,
which was 'battling not just for improved wages and working conditions, but for social justice and recognition of the dignity of labour.' In
the end, union recognition was blocked, but the strikers obtained at least
one of their key demands – the reduction of the work week from fifty-
five to fifty-two hours until November and thereafter to forty-nine, with
a compensatory increase in piece rates.[46]

Garment workers in Hamilton struck in the spring of 1913 when a wage increase was refused by the large garment manufacturers and over forty contract shops. Three weeks before the 15 April strike of pressers, operators, and tailors, the pressers had unsuccessfully approached their employers for an increase. The pressers then asked the operators and tailors for support. The latter agreed, also asking for a 20 per cent increase for themselves. Aided by the recently revived district council of the garment workers and by the decision of the cutters and trimmers to join the strike, fifteen hundred women and five hundred men struck. Most of them returned to work on 28 April with a compromise settlement – parity with Toronto scales. As the *Spectator* pointed out, the cutters' decision to strike was critical because the manufacturers could not easily replace them. The Hamilton strikers were also aided by walkouts in Toronto, where workers protested that they would not do the strikers' work. The UGWA sent in Toronto's Sam Landers and Margaret Daley of the executive board in New York and successfully turned back strikebreakers from New York.[47]

Issues specific to women workers figured prominently in the strike. Exploitation of women in the shops was discussed in the press, which noted that some of the women made only $4 a week and had to pay $3.50 for room and board. A.H. Carroll, general organizer for Canada, commented that 'we contend that this kind of thing tends to very undesirable social and moral conditions.' In support of this assertion, he noted a court case pending against a foreman who allegedly discharged a worker earning four dollars a week because she refused his offer of more money if she consented to 'become his personal friend.' The strike also mobilized women garment workers to meet separately from their male counterparts and added numbers to the union. When management allegedly attempted to meet with the women separately from the strike committee, they refused. Despite these positive signs of activism and solidarity, union organization in these shops did not outlive the crisis of the strike.[48]

Subcontracting remained a formidable problem for garment workers, who found that their wages were cut under competition, especially by women outside the major centres of garment production. A large strike, which involved one thousand garment workers, half of them women, erupted over this question in Montreal in September 1913. Two firms, Vineberg and Elkin, were struck, and a third firm's workers went out later in sympathy. The workers objected to the practice of sending experienced garment workers to Joliette, a small town north of Montreal, to train young women who were paid much less than Montreal workers and who worked fifty-five or sixty hours a week instead of the forty-nine worked in Montreal shops. The union responded not only with a strike of Montreal workers, but also organized the Joliette women, who later walked off the job. While both men and women struck, clearly the men felt threatened by the country women who could potentially take away their jobs. Despite the solidarity of the country women with their Montreal counterparts, the strike failed as some returned to work without any resolution by the end of October. Elkin's settled with some of its workers at the end of November, but 350 strikers from Vineberg's remained out. In December 1913 several hundred strikers gathered outside Vineberg's to confront scabs and policemen, resulting in a scuffle, one injury, and five arrests. An arbitration settlement worked out in mid-January faltered when Mr Vineberg refused to dismiss those taken on after the strike commenced and insisted on an open shop. Vineberg had also fought his workers over the closed shop in 1907, and he had no intention of giving in now. His antipathy towards the union frustrated the strikers, particularly since both the employer and many of the strikers were Jewish. In the end, no settlement was reached with Vineberg's, and the workers found employment elsewhere.[49]

While garment workers' strikes were sometimes successful, major problems remained in the industry and union organization often faltered. Nonetheless, these prewar strikes reveal that women garment workers played an active role in labour disputes. Divided by gender and ethnicity, as well as by the labour process, working-class women and men in the garment trades were occasionally able to overcome differences and band together to improve their working conditions and wages and to defend their organizations against employer intransigence. Fundamentally, however, women workers waged an uphill battle in the context of gender divisions in the workplace and in the labour movement. Generally, working-class women's solidarity was expressed most clearly in separate women's organizations within the movement, sometimes in the form of women's locals within the garment unions or through separate women's meetings. As a number of these strikes indicate, women stuck together despite attempts by management to divide them from male co-workers. Unorganized women whose sense of justice was offended could also pull together to confront employers. Yet female solidarity across class and ethnic lines was problematic, particularly in the case of the Eaton's strike. While some middle-class women's organizations supported women strikers in labour disputes, this was a relatively rare occurrence. Finally, the labour movement in general, and specific unions engaged in strikes, worried about women workers as competition, as potentially undercutting union labour. While men and women might cooperate to obtain better wages and conditions in the garment trades, women's work posed particular dilemmas. Women's moral and reproductive vulnerability because of low wages and poor working conditions was never far from the minds of trade unionists, who used these fears to appeal for support for striking women workers, thus reinforcing gender divisions.

*Boot and Shoe Strikes*

Unlike the textile and garment sectors, boot and shoe work did not readily lend itself to labour militancy among women in the early twentieth century. Jacques Ferland has argued that in Quebec, the pre-eminent centre of the Canadian shoe industry, women shoe workers found little voice in the male-dominated unions. In addition, unlike the situation in textile production, the physical segregation of women's labour, the technological links between women and sewing machines, and the malleability of women's labour processes in the women's department, all countered cross-gender solidarities in labour disputes. The cotton mills of Quebec fostered a tradition of militancy that was facilitated by homogeneous work groups and more independent labour processes. Shoe work, unlike textile production, was carried out in small or medium-sized shops in a decentralized and competitive industry.[50]

In examining the boot and shoe strikes of 1900–14, it is evident that fewer than a dozen strikes involved women workers. In the 1890s, there were a few instances of independent women's organizing, especially in the 1894 strike at Toronto's J.D. King Company, where women in the Women Shoe Fitters' Association took an active role, assisted by the Working Women's Protective Association. After the turn of the century, however, independent initiatives from women shoe workers do not appear to have existed, at least not before the First World War. Large-scale work stoppages occurred in Quebec at the beginning and end of the period, and smaller strikes took place in Ontario, mainly in Toronto, involving women shoe workers who most often performed stitching and finishing tasks.

Massive work stoppages in boot and shoe manufacturing occurred in Quebec in the early twentieth century. One of the important results of the October 1900 strike at twenty-one factories was the eventual involvement of the Catholic Church, first in mediating the dispute and eventually in creating confessional unions, although they appear to have represented only male workers. A large strike in 1903 over piece-work is similarly difficult to read for women workers' roles. Several of the women involved were alleged to have written a supplicating letter to the manufacturers, imploring them as husbands, fathers, and citizens to take action in the dispute 'so that the poverty-stricken will bless you ... and the gratefulness of our people will always be with your endeav-ours.' For a decade relations between employers and shoe workers in the province remained calm. An employer offensive launched in 1913 against thousands of Quebec shoe workers primarily affected men since women were not members of the union.[51]

Between 1907 and 1913, Ontario shoe workers waged a number of strikes, all of them at single shops. As in Quebec, the evidence does not always indicate what role women workers took in the work stoppages. In Toronto in 1907 at the Victoria Shoe Company, for example, twenty women and ten girls may have been part of a work stoppage over a rumoured 10 per cent wage reduction and a dispute over cutting certain styles of shoes. Whether the women belonged to the Boot and Shoe Workers' Union, Local 232, is unclear. The contract provided for arbitra-tion on changes not mutually agreed to, but the company claimed that new machinery would increase earning power by 20 per cent. In the end the company agreed to restore former piece rates.[52]

Gender solidarity rarely appeared as a contributing factor in work stoppages in the trade, but in Toronto in 1912 a strike erupted at the unionized Adams Boot and Shoe Company over the reduction of wages affecting a number of 'girl operators.' While the firm claimed that read-justments in piecework prices would not penalize the women, *Labour Gazette* reporter Tom Banton noted that the women would lose between $1.00 and $1.50 per week. The strike dragged on for over two months (from 26 October 1912 to 1 January 1913) and resulted in a satisfactory solution, with rates restored and most of the strikers reinstated.[53]

Labour activism among women in the boot and shoe trade, while apparently virtually absent in Quebec, appeared in Ontario to have con-tributed to winning at least a few disputes, particularly between 1907 and 1913. Piecework prices were usually the centre of the conflict, although in one case the issue at stake was a company rule about length of notice required for leaving employment. Boot and shoe disputes occa-sionally revealed solidarity between women and men workers, but they also uncovered the underlying notions of what work was appropriate for 'girls,' as opposed to men.

*Twentieth-Century Departures: Communications*

In addition to the well-established manufacturing sectors for women's work, new areas of women's wage labour oriented towards consumer and public services began to emerge by the turn of the century. By the last decade of the nineteenth century women operators had replaced boys in the telephone industry, and commercial telegraphy offered a small number of women a skilled trade. In the latter field, women worked with men in the same offices, while telephone operators worked almost exclusively with other young women in gender-segregated offices. At the turn of the century most operators in the telephone and telegraph business were employed in one-person offices in towns and villages; it was only in the larger urban centres that women worked in offices with fellow employees. Union organization and labour disputes were more common in these urban offices, not only because of the numbers of workers, but also because of the introduction of new equipment.

A number of studies have dealt with women telephone operators and some of the significant strikes they waged in the decade and a half before the First World War. Previous research has highlighted the Vancouver strikes of 1902 and 1906 and the Toronto strike of 1907. The 1902 strike had caught the New Westminister and Burrard Inlet Telephone Company by surprise and had garnered community support. By contrast, the 1906 strike found the company, by then the British Columbia Telephone Company, already armed with strikebreakers, and the strike dragged on for months, never actually reaching a formal resolution. While the operators had formed a women's auxiliary of Local 213 of the International Brotherhood of Electrical Workers (IBEW) in 1902, by 1906 a new agreement failed to include them, and the women's 'auxiliary' no longer covered most operators. Local 213's insistence on a closed shop and the company's refusal to recognize the operators' local led to the February walkout of thirty-four operators and twenty linemen. By the third week of the strike, the company was operating normally with strikebreakers, little disruption in service had occurred, and the business community, which had supported the operators in 1902, was largely uninvolved and unaffected by the strike.[54]

A large strike of four hundred operators in Toronto in February 1907 was unsuccessful despite the militancy of the women operators. The women were unorganized but were highly motivated in resisting the Bell Telephone Company's move to increase efficiency by extending the workday from five to eight hours. Although the company claimed it would raise wages at the same time as increasing hours, the operators realized that their hourly rate would decline by 25 per cent under the proposed scheme. Public sympathy was with the strikers as evidenced by the daily press and by public harassment of strikebreakers outside the exchange and over the telephone lines. A number of prominent individuals, including several dozen physicians who testified that the work was nerve-wracking and might jeopardize telephone workers' ability to have children, took up the women's cause, but to no avail. When a royal commission was proposed by Mackenzie King of the federal Department of Labour, the operators were pressured to return to work under the new conditions. What appeared as a victory for the strikers became a setback when the company refused to abide by the commission's findings, granting only a few concessions for the sake of public relations. (Ironically, the commission's report proved influential in American federal and state investigations of telephone workers' conditions.) While the operators were in favour of unionizing, and agreed to affiliate with the IBEW, it was not until 1918 that Toronto operators organized under that union's auspices. After the strike of 1907, the Ontario labour press continued to comment critically on the wages and conditions, at least until Bell raised wages by two dollars a week just before the war.[55]

Labour unrest was not confined to large cities. In the decade and a half before the war some telephone workers in smaller centres also demonstrated their discontent with working conditions and wages. Three women walked out in Galt, Ontario, in October 1905 to protest the lengthening of the workday at the central exchange. In Fort William, Ontario, eight of fourteen operators at the Board of Water and Light walked out in August 1907 to protest the appointment of a chief operator from the United States, a move that bypassed the senior operators employed by the board. Discontent with their male supervisor also played a role in the walkout. Press clippings reveal that the local ratepayers held a public meeting to discuss the hiring not only of the chief operator, but also of the chief lineman, who also had come from the United States, and both individuals were sent back as a result. Whether the operators who walked out got their jobs back is unclear. Northern Ontario communities under the Temiskaming Telephone Company faced a strike in 1909 when women operators in Haileybury and New Liskeard were joined by operators in Cobalt striking in sympathy with the demand for an increase in wages. The Haileybury women worked twelve hours a day, seven days a week for only twenty-five dollars a month.[56]

Operators' resistance to low wages, long hours, and minute supervision was made difficult by the telephone companies' sustained opposition to unions and efforts to control operators' discontent through welfare schemes. As one labour newspaper noted, the BC Telephone Company had instituted welfare schemes for the 'purpose of maintaining absolute control of the girls in and out of service.' In addition to welfare schemes, telephone companies posted detailed rules about behaviour and appearance in order to maintain control over the primarily young, single women they employed. Such rules sparked a walkout in Chilliwack, British Columbia, in September 1911. The operators found these posted notices 'so offensive in the public gaze regarding what they might or might not do that they demanded a withdrawal,' which was refused by the company. The women were replaced and service maintained with the 'assistance ... of good subservient jelly backs of the male persuasion,' one newspaper noted.[57]

By the early twentieth century telephone operating was stereotyped as a female occupation, but telegraphy demonstrated a mixed gender pattern. Women as well as men became telegraphers, and the trade was one of few skilled occupations women could enter. Yet 'skill' was defined differently for male and female telegraphers, even when they performed the same job in the larger urban offices. The question of how to define skill became a pressing issue during the war as the union fought to control the effects of automation. In the prewar period, labour troubles disrupted telegraph services several times, once in a sympathy strike with American operators in 1907 and earlier, in 1904, when operators at the Great Northwestern Telegraph Company went out to demand higher wages and to protest firings of union members. Press coverage noted that the scale of wages for women generally ranged from fifteen to thirty dollars a month, while male operators might earn as much as seventy dollars. Both women and men telegraphers objected to the well-known anti-union stance of the company superintendent, who placed a spy in a Toronto union meeting, resulting in five men and women losing their jobs. The telegraphers defended their freedom as well as their union and underlined the role of their organization in initiating and educating young telegraphers and in fostering temperance. In addition to resisting the company's anti-unionism, they objected to low wages and extra shifts, as well as the company's practice of keeping them on call. A contributor to the *Toiler* who signed herself 'Woman' noted the loyalty of the women strikers to the cause: 'Why should not the women stand as firm as their brothers in every labor question, for they suffer quite as much as the men do.'[58]

While women workers might 'suffer quite as much as the men' in a strike, the situation for women strikers was not the same, by any means. While the local support of the labour movement might rally male workers to the cause in particular instances, the overall emphasis on unionizing skilled male workers to defend their turf from the less-skilled, usually female or child workers militated against successful organization and struggle. For male workers and trade unionists the strike was inherently a gendered strategy most appropriately utilized by male workers. Similarly and more fundamentally, waged work was masculine: the male worker represented the universal while women workers presented a problem, an exception to the rule. While women, particularly when young and single, might engage in paid labour to supplement inadequate family incomes, women workers were not permanent members of the labour force. They were primarily wives, mothers, daughters, and sisters caught up in an industrial system that undermined working-class families' abilities to maintain themselves and their values. These values included the expectation that men would provide for and protect women and children. Thus women's work and women's labour activism called up profound contradictions for working-class men.[59]

Working-class femininity could also send mixed signals. Women were dependants as female kin within the household and also as supplementary wage earners in the labour market. Yet some working-class women also proclaimed their honest womanhood and the value of paid labour for women, fostering an alternative, more positive reading of women's work and labour activism that not only challenged working-class women's dependence in the family and workplace but also questioned accepted notions of femininity. Working-class femininity was tied to expectations of marriage and raising a family, as Lise Vogel and others have argued. Marriage meant leaving the paid labour force after a number of years of waged labour. While transiency in the world of waged labour and expectations of unpaid labour in the home may have discouraged working women's activism, harsh material conditions and the realization that waged work was a necessity in working-class families even after marriage might also provide the impetus for women workers to contest wage reductions and arbitrary employer practices and to seek better pay and conditions. Involvement in labour disputes and unionization initiatives provides some evidence that working women found a measure of hope in honest work and womanhood. For those who were not waged labourers, more traditional avenues existed in which working-class women could play an active role in labour's struggle. As members of working-class families and communities, these women played important roles in women's auxiliaries, union label leagues, and cooperatives that stressed the supportive and complementary functions of working-class women in strengthening the labour movement.

## III

More so than for men, women's activism extended into the larger community where their daily lives intersected with a wide range of institutions, such as local businesses and schools. As part of the labour movement working-class wives, mothers, sisters, and daughters participated in women's auxiliaries and union label leagues, which performed a wide variety of tasks of benefit to the male-dominated labour movement. While such activism might challenge the division of labour between men and women, most often women's participation in auxiliaries and label leagues proceeded from an acceptance of that division. Women usually performed stereotypically female tasks within their auxiliaries and leagues unless a crisis, such as a strike, arose. Union men also revealed their concern that women's organizations stick with typically 'women's work' so as not to challenge their own pre-eminent roles or masculine authority. Auxiliaries have, therefore, often been dismissed as unimportant within the labour movement and the result, with few exceptions, has been a lack of research into these organizations.[60]

*Women as Supporters of Trade Unions*

In Canada, women's auxiliaries were a phenomenon of the early twentieth century. Between 1900 and 1920 most women's auxiliaries appeared among those craft unions whose members were better paid and better organized. The printers, machinists, and railroad running trades provide evidence of the strongest auxiliary organizations. One exception to this pattern is the existence of a women's auxiliary among the miners belonging to the Western Federation of Miners (WFM) in the first decade of the century. The WFM in Rossland, British Columbia, organized the first Canadian local of the union in the mid-1890s. By 1908, the women's auxiliary was sponsoring a lecture course called 'Working Women and the Ballot,' as well as providing the usual entertainments for miners and their families. In 1911, Helen Chenoweth, the auxiliary's organizer in the province, wrote to the local at Sandon asking whether it was prepared to fulfil a promise from the last District 6 convention where miners promised to assist in creating women's auxiliaries. Chenoweth remarked that it was time the province got moving, pointing out that 'you will find that the women will be such a help to you in more than one way.' She offered to visit and to initiate activity, which would be carried on by local women, and suggested that the expenses involved could be easily defrayed by a social event. 'Have your wives help you,' she advised. Correspondence from the district office that same year indicated that delegates from the women's auxiliaries were to receive expense money to attend meetings, the same as a representative from a local union.[61]

Whether the auxiliary movement among the miners experienced any growth is unclear. Sporadic references to auxiliaries within the United Mineworkers of America provide little information on this period. Miners' wives, however, were noted for their militancy, as was seen in the Springhill, Nova Scotia, strike of 1909–11 and the Vancouver Island strikes of 1912–14. The latter led to the formation of the Miners' Liberation League and a women's auxiliary that played a vital role in the strike.[62]

Auxiliaries to the various railroad trades appeared in the early part of the twentieth century in major rail towns and cities. Toronto boasted auxiliaries of the railroad conductors, railway trainmen, and locomotive engineers by 1905; a ladies' auxiliary to the Toronto street railway union was reported by 1910. Small railway centres such as St Thomas and Stratford, Ontario, also boasted women's auxiliaries, which were offshoots of the various railway unions. Cities in the Maritimes as well as in the West reported very active auxiliaries. Calgary's Brotherhood of Railway Trainmen (BRT), for example, featured a ladies' auxiliary from 1905 on, as well as an auxiliary to the Brotherhood of Locomotive Firemen (later, the Brotherhood of Locomotive Firemen and Enginemen [BLFE]). The women involved in the BRT auxiliary and the BLFE organization in Calgary were active in providing social events and attending joint meetings with the brothers of the union. In addition, both auxiliaries featured access to insurance schemes that provided sickness and death benefits in an age in which no government or employment-related benefits were required. A register of such policies for the women's auxiliary of the BRT in Calgary shows that approximately eighty-five women between 1905 and 1920 took out insurance; almost all were listed as wives or housewives and, where age was provided, most were in their twenties or thirties when they took out the policy. Death notices in the magazine of the BLFE reveal that women's auxiliary members took advantage of insurance policies worth between two hundred and five hundred dollars. With over ten thousand members in the United States and Canada, the Ladies' Society of the BLFE possessed a large membership base that made such schemes feasible.[63]

Canadian women were prominent in the leadership of some of the international auxiliaries. Mrs Maude E. Moore of Stratford, Ontario, retained the presidency of the Ladies' Society of the BLFE from at least 1913 until 1920 when she became 'editress' of the women's section of the union's magazine. In 1913, seven Canadian women delegates, including Moore, attended the Eleventh Annual (First Triennial) Convention of the Ladies' Society in Washington, DC, representing Toronto, St Thomas, Chapleau, Sault Ste Marie, and North Bay, Ontario as well as Montreal and Winnipeg. Moore's presidential report showed that total membership of the international auxiliary had passed the ten thousand mark and that most members subscribed to the insurance plan. By the time of the 1919 convention in Denver, Moore was accompanied by a dozen Canadian women; half of these delegates came from Ontario while the rest ranged from Montreal to Medicine Hat. Moore's presidential report revealed that she had travelled nearly forty thousand miles in the previous three years, visiting lodges, particularly those in need of assistance. She noted the difficulties facing women officers of the organization's lodges, the majority of whom were tied down by domestic responsibilities. Moore reported that her own household duties were few, but that in her absence the office work and correspondence piled up to appalling levels. Her report and her longevity in office demonstrate her commitment to the women's auxiliary movement, a commitment no doubt facilitated by her relatively light domestic duties.[64]

Like the auxiliaries of the railroad running trades, the women's auxiliary of the International Typographical Union (ITU) tended to accept the division of labour between men and women in the union movement. For many years after the founding of the first auxiliary in Toronto in 1905, that city had the only active Canadian auxiliary. In 1910 a Mrs MacDougall wrote to the editor of the *Typographical Journal* complaining that the 'unions do not realize the usefulness of women in organizational bodies, yet the time is not far distant when all trades will have auxiliaries ... Is not woman the spending power and the home educator? Let the women become imbued with the true spirit of unionism ... for the betterment of the family.' These sentiments were undoubtedly shared by most women in auxiliaries, whose prime purpose was to support union men through their buying power and their fundraising and educational activities. In the case of the printers, women supporters could help boost the union label, an option not open to all trades.[65]

The label question in the printing trades brought the women's auxiliary movement into some conflict with the National Council of Women during the First World War. The NCWC's 1917 convention took place in Winnipeg, where western members of ITU auxiliaries pushed the council to adopt the union label on all its printed work. The agitation was led by Mrs B.W. Bellamy of Medicine Hat, who was a vice-president of the ITU's Women's Auxiliary and a major figure in the Western auxiliary movement. As a delegate from Medicine Hat's Local Council of Women, Bellamy raised the label issue, which caused division at the convention and led to the striking of a special committee to investigate the relationship between organized labour and the NCWC. The following year representatives of the Ontario ITU's women's auxiliary attended the NCWC meeting in Brantford, Ontario, at which the report of the special committee was presented. Unfortunately, the chair alienated the labour representatives by giving her report without allowing the delegation to speak. By 1919, however, the NCWC finally decided to use the union label on its stationery and in its yearbook, thus resolving the specific issue, although by no means dispelling the tensions between working-class women and their middle-class counterparts.[66]

The war years were particularly active ones for the ITU auxiliaries in the West. With the dynamic leadership of Bellamy, new auxiliaries appeared in Winnipeg and Moose Jaw. The Winnipeg group plunged into various activities. In addition to the usual social gatherings, war work was complemented by more political activities, such as sending out speakers to organize new groups, boost the label, and support the Winnipeg Cooperative Society. The auxiliary also supported the Trades and Labor Council and the Women's Labor League (WLL) in their agitation for a minimum wage for women workers. The Winnipeg group initiated a request for more pages for auxiliary news in the *Typographical Journal*, a request that the international officers turned down, although not without presenting the auxiliary with a number of compliments, no doubt in a rather condescending attempt to ward off discontent. The 1918 meeting of the Western Canadian Conference of typographical unions produced a request to the editor of the *Journal* to use the term 'women's auxiliary' instead of referring to the 'ladies' – a request that was accepted, after some years of refusing to do so. By 1918, representatives from women's auxiliaries could attend the Alberta Federation of

Labor conventions as delegates, and Bellamy became the first woman delegate to participate officially in a federation convention.[67]

Like the railroad and the printing unions, the International Association of Machinists (IAM) also boasted an active auxiliary movement in Canada. Toronto again featured the first women's group, organized in late 1902 under the leadership of Minnie Singer, a powerful figure whose contributions extended far beyond the auxiliary movement. The aims of the IAM auxiliaries were the same as those of other groups: sociability, upholding unionism, union label support, education of women in trade unionism, funeral benefits, and the achievement of a higher standard of living. The international movement claimed two thousand members in the United States and Canada in 1914, making this auxiliary movement considerably smaller than that of the railroad trades. In Canada the most active centres were in Toronto and Winnipeg, with other groups appearing in Stratford, Calgary, Moncton, and Hamilton by 1914; later auxiliaries appeared in Saskatoon, Transcona (Winnipeg), and Vancouver.[68]

At the forefront of the machinists' auxiliary movement, Minnie Singer of Toronto provided key leadership from its inception in Canada. Like Maude Moore of the BLFE and Mrs Bellamy of the ITU, Singer directed the movement in Canada and assumed a prominent role in the international organization as vice-president for several decades. An eloquent orator, she spoke frequently on behalf of the auxiliary movement and organized new auxiliaries. Without much financial support this was a difficult task, requiring persistent exchanges of correspondence with IAM locals. Where possible, Singer visited personally to deliver her message. In her speeches she appealed to the wives of machinists to join an auxiliary, always careful to caution them not to neglect the home, while also stressing the importance for women of having activities beyond the domestic sphere. Auxiliary work would benefit children, she suggested, as well as the mothers themselves. Her consistent message stressed the need for women to stand together with their class, albeit within limitations. The auxiliary had no intention of interfering with IAM business but rather sought to support the men, educate the women, visit the sick, provide sociability, and raise standards of living. Described by one Winnipeg colleague as an effective platform speaker 'without any suggestion of militant suffragism,' Singer appeared to combine the best qualities of working-class womanhood, devotion to the union cause, leadership abilities, and acceptance of women's complementary role within the working-class struggle.[69]

In addition to whist parties, picnics, and other social events, the women of the IAM auxiliaries also raised funds for organizing drives and strikes and, during the war, aided returned soldiers and their families. They were preoccupied with increasing the membership, and contests were developed to stimulate the interest of potential new members. Unlike the railroad workers' and printers' auxiliaries, the IAM women's auxiliaries took less of a role in international conventions, at least during the war. Mrs W.H. Logan of Winnipeg, later a prominent member of the Women's Labor League and supporter of the One Big Union, reported that, aside from Minnie Singer, she was the only Canadian auxiliary member at the Baltimore international convention in 1916. Compared to the much larger auxiliary movement among the railroad running trades and their keener interest in conventions, the machinists' auxiliary may well have had fewer resources available to them.[70]

The women of the IAM took a more direct interest in their single working sisters than did women in other auxiliaries, particularly during the war. The Toronto IAM auxiliary invited American textile workers' organizer, Miss McKelleher, to speak to them in April 1917 while she was on an organizing tour. The Winnipeg group participated in the WLL and invited Helen Armstrong to address them on the wages and conditions of working women. Later in 1917, factory inspector Ida Bauslaugh provided a lantern-slide show relating to women's work. Women in the auxiliary faced male hostility to their work and to the threat of competition from women working in machine shops during the war. In the union's bulletin, R.B. Russell reported on the Angus shops in Montreal where women had been hired to do jobs usually performed by men. Machinists in the West clearly opposed the hiring of women and threatened to strike if the women were not removed. Women were also employed in Calgary at the Ogden shops, causing concern for a writer in the IAM *Bulletin*: 'We have the beautiful spectacle of women working on the triple valve bench, unloading cars of lumber and sweeping up the shop. To us that have been exiled from the old sod through economic pressure this is nothing new, but who ever thought this rotten business would be introduced in this glorious land of freedom.' The men were forced to accept the women as a war measure only, with the understanding that any reorganization would not adversely affect them and that the women would receive equal pay for equal work, thus protecting wage rates. While the women's auxiliaries recorded no comment on this development, tensions over this question must have touched the lives of machinists and their families.[71]

Of all the auxiliaries active in the early part of the twentieth century, the IAM auxiliary under Singer's leadership was the most politically active. Closely involved in the Labor Educational Association (LEA) and the Independent Labor Party in Ontario, Singer hoped to rally women under the banner of the LEA in the spring of 1919 by starting a women-controlled organization that united women from all labour groups under one umbrella. Singer's vision encompassed working women and working-class wives, unions and labour political groups, in one organization led by women with similar interests. For most women's auxiliaries, however, the main tasks were defined within the limits of women's social and educational roles.

*Women as Consumers*

While various trades in the late nineteenth century had taken up the idea of promoting union-made goods to encourage the working class to buy items made under union conditions, label campaigns increasingly became defined as women's work in the early twentieth century. As more emphasis was placed on women as consumers and buyers in the working-class family, union men began to view label work as part of women's contribution to unionism. Women too came to adopt the view that label work was an area in which they might do important work. While many trades and labour councils assigned members to committee work to promote the union label, in some cases the work fell more and more to women supporters. In the early part of the century Toronto provided a case in point when a branch of the Women's International Union Label League (WIULL) was formed in 1902, under the leadership of the Toronto Trades and Labour Council (TTLC). While formally initiated by the TTLC, the league's most important leadership came from a group of trade union wives led by socialist activist May Darwin. The connection between union labour and union buying power was made by a male TTLC delegate at the founding meeting when he noted that it was useless for the men to organize unless their wives spent earned wages on label goods. Castigating the men for neglecting to inform the women of the existence of the league, Darwin nevertheless welcomed the formation of the group as a forward step and became one of its chief spokespersons. The league held separate meetings from the TTLC, but its existence also provided an opportunity for the group to be represented at TTLC meetings beginning in June 1903 when three women, including Darwin, represented the label league. In addition to promoting the union label, social events such as picnics and dances were a staple part of the league's activities. The label committee of the TTLC welcomed a representative of the WIULL to its meeting in September 1903. This arrangement was formalized by the executive at its December meeting. Evidently, the women of the WIULL also were important in raising funds for the building of the Labour Temple, a task that also involved the Ladies' Auxiliary of the IAM.[72]

Women who participated in label work might also get involved in other areas of inquiry for the TTLC. For example, Mrs Huddlestone of the TTLC's label league sat on the house rents committee appointed by the TTLC in 1904 to investigate high rents in the city. By the fall of 1905 a second branch of the WIULL had been organized in the city. Despite a growing membership and evidence of success, Darwin and two other women members of the WIULL had to threaten resignation from the TTLC label committee to demonstrate their concern with the failure of male TTLC delegates to attend the meetings of the committee. Ultimately, the women remained on the committee and continued to work for the union label. In addition to these activities, Darwin attended the meeting of the executive council of the WIULL in Chicago in February of 1906 and helped to organize a Hamilton branch of the league in January. Evidently these successes did not make it much easier to get union men to attend meetings, as the reports of the Toronto label committee indicate.[73]

The emphasis on women as consumers, as supporters of unionism, and as educators of future generations also contributed to the creation of a special role for women within the Winnipeg Cooperative Society. The idea of a cooperative society and store attracted two hundred men and women to the first meeting in January 1914 where a Ladies' Social and Educational Committee, modelled on the British Women's Cooperative Guild, was formed. Mrs R.A. Rigg acted as the first president of the group, which was renamed the Women's Cooperative Guild (WCG). Noting in her remarks to the official gathering to launch the Guild in November 1914 that Winnipeg lacked an organization that provided a social home for workers, she said that the WCG stood for 'the progress and power of working women' and intended to provide educational as well as social opportunities. Vice-president Mrs Iveson, also a member of the Women's Cooperative Guild in England, stressed the WCG as a 'democracy of working women' who possessed the 'basket power' of consumers and aspired to national citizenship. For Iveson, the idea of citizenship encompassed both the women who worked for pay and the even larger number of 'married women who as home makers contribute by their unpaid labor just as directly as wage earners in the support of family life.' Working women were a new force in national life, with public responsibilities as citizens and office holders. Women should not only exercise their power as consumers but should also take their places in public life. By 1915, the Winnipeg WCG supported the enfranchisement of women and an activist perspective for working women.[74]

Women's auxiliaries, label leagues, and cooperative societies were premised on a division of labour between men and women. This division accentuated men's roles in the workplace and women's roles as supporters of trade unionism through their social and educational activities as wives, mothers, and consumers. This neat division of roles and responsibilities, however, was undercut by the increasing presence of women in the paid labour force and the refusal of married working-class women to separate themselves entirely from other working women. The appeal to women as workers, whether paid or unpaid, and to women's potential as activists in the cause of working-class improvement led to a blurring of the lines between the separate spheres. While working-class women's organizations in theory toed the line, remaining adjuncts to men, periods of crisis and strong leadership extended their perspectives and challenged them to act and to take matters beyond the expected.

## IV

Compared to their status in 1890, women workers and their organizations had a more visible presence in public life at the start of the First World War. While organized labour could call for the abolition of women's paid labour in the late 1890s, by 1914 such a call had been abandoned as it had become all too clear that women's paid work was integral to Canadian life. Women workers organized associations, although such groups were often short-lived and lacked formal support. At other times they joined sometimes equally evanescent union locals. Women strikers, as we have noted, predominated in certain trades, such as garments and textiles, during the period 1890–1914. Solidarity between men and women workers was precarious, often further undermined by the competitive system that pitted workers against one another on the basis of skill differentials or ethnic diversity. Gender solidarity across class lines was also extremely rare. While middle-class reformers undoubtedly were concerned with women workers' plight, their organizations by and large were preoccupied with political reform and sometimes viewed involvement in strikes as detrimental to their cause.

The male-dominated labour movement tended to treat the primarily young and single women workers as 'other' – that is, women's concerns were often couched in language that emphasized their vulnerability to exploitation, their need for male protection, or their future roles as wives and mothers. Since male unionists tended to view women as the weaker sex, evidence of women's militancy appeared to surprise observers, who pointedly commented on incidents of women's solidarity in labour disputes. While women's militancy was unexpected, the labour movement at some junctures attempted to reach out to women workers engaged in labour disputes. Too often, such help consisted of male guidance, protection, and support using the language of chivalry and manliness, which stemmed from an acceptance of gender divisions imbedded not only in work but also in the labour movement itself.

These gender divisions also permeated other areas of women's labour organization. Label leagues and women's auxiliaries offered women relatives of union men a supportive yet subordinate role. As consumers, working-class women could assist the movement by buying, and by educating others on the importance of buying, union label goods. As wives, mothers, daughters, and sisters, working-class women provided the social connections, strike support, access to insurance benefits and education that was beneficial to the labour movement generally. By engaging in these activities, working-class women sometimes found themselves questioning gender boundaries, boundaries that would be tested during the war years.

# 3

# 'A Socialist Movement Which Does Not Attract the Women Cannot Live': Women in the Early Socialist Movement

The socialist movement in Vancouver has been a men's movement in the past but the gentler sex will have to be reckoned with in the future – and a socialist movement which does not attract the women cannot live.

*Canadian Socialist*, 30 August 1902

Riding on a euphoric crest of socialist success in the early twentieth century, the writer who described the first socialist picnic in Vancouver in 1902 envisioned a socialist movement that combined the interests and enthusiasm of women with those of male comrades. Describing the Vancouver picnic as a 'socialist revival meeting,' the author noted the presence of several women who played a role in the early British Columbia socialist movement. At their convention a month later, Ontario socialists passed a resolution stating that, 'in the opinion of this convention very much may be done in the propaganda for socialism by a special effort among women in Canada; and be it further resolved that the executive committee be instructed to pay special attention during the coming year to work along this line.' Thus, the two provinces with the strongest socialist organizations declared their intent to cultivate the potential harvest among women at the beginning of the twentieth century.[1]

This chapter examines women's experiences in the early socialist movement, before the emergence of the Socialist Party of Canada in 1904. The early socialist movement, characterized by a strong attachment to Christian or ethical socialism, provided a fertile field for women, especially those women concerned with broad social change, whether labour reform, temperance, or, more broadly, women's rights.

While not all women socialists in this early period were attracted by ethical or Christian socialism, many of the leadership figures were deeply committed to a form of socialism that was based on Christianity and principles of Christian social justice. The tenets of brotherhood, peace, and spiritual equality, when combined with social justice concerns such as decent wages and working conditions, temperance, and the amelioration of poverty, attracted progressive-minded women to a form of socialism that promised to put these principles into practice. Furthermore, Christian socialism envisioned a more equal relationship between women and men. While early socialist organizations encouraged women's participation in the movement, they could not entirely overcome the deeply engrained gender divisions prevalent in Canadian society at large. Most women thus played supportive roles, but a number worked visibly and actively to shape the movement and increase its appeal to women.

I

Common to the movement and to many of the women and men involved in early socialist circles was a belief in a collective moral, social, and economic system loosely based on Christian principles and practices. Unlike later streams of socialist thought, ethical or Christian socialism was not premised upon antagonism between the spiritual and the material realms, or between social classes, but rather accepted complementary relations between them.

Early socialist organizations first developed in the late nineteenth and early twentieth centuries in Ontario and British Columbia. These provinces also had well-developed progressive reform organizations concerned with labour, women's rights, temperance, and other issues. Progressive groups sometimes interacted with and provided recruits for the emerging socialist organizations of this period. In addition, these provinces spawned the first newpapers that addressed many of the issues central to the emerging socialist movement.[2]

As Ramsay Cook has demonstrated, social criticism of various types flourished in late Victorian Canada. Free thought, theosophy, spiritualism, Bellamyite nationalism, single tax, the social gospel, and socialism found expression in the myriad of reform organizations in English Canada. Men and women who participated in these groups might well espouse several philosophies and belong to a number of organizations. For most, a critical stance towards Christianity as practised in the late nineteenth century was part of their willingness to challenge the status quo. Some identified with the social gospel's insistence that Christian churches had to become involved in solving contemporary social, economic, and political problems; others were attracted to theosophy or spiritualism. Theosophy rejected Christian theology but 'claimed to combine the best elements of the world's main religions and to reconcile or transcend the gulf between science and religion by adapting evolutionary thought to religious faith.' Whether one adopted a Christian social gospel perspective or preferred theosophy, or even a more materialist approach, those concerned with the pressing issues of the day at least agreed that the solution involved the transformation of an individualist and capitalist society into a cooperative commonwealth.[3]

The idea of a cooperative commonwealth suggested a system that accepted sharing rather than competition and rejected a social system that accepted extremes of wealth and poverty. Many liberal Protestants identified with a social gospel that stressed the moral responsibilities of employers to provide decent wages and working conditions for their employees. Within the social gospel tradition, however, there were divergences of opinion on how the cooperative commonwealth could be achieved. Christian socialists pushed this idea furthest, insisting that the economic underpinnings of nineteenth-century society had to be radically altered to accommodate the needed changes. Christian socialism stood for the 'brotherhood of man,' sharing of resources, eradication of social, economic, and political inequalities, and the use of educational means as well as the ballot to remedy perceived inequity. Such an approach might restore Christianity to its original aims; after all, was not Christ a workman and an upholder of social justice? Christian socialists differed from other social gospellers in their willingness to place the labour question at the centre, accepting the notion that labour was the source of all value. Such beliefs stood in stark contrast with the industrial conditions prevailing in Canada in the late nineteenth and early twentieth centuries.

Christian socialism was the starting point for many who became adherents of the socialist cause. Initially inspired by the works of Englishman Robert Blatchford, author of *Merrie England*, or by *Looking Backward*, the utopian novel of American Edward Bellamy, the early socialists found in these writers much that expressed their critical views of industrial society as well as suggestions for what a transformed collectively oriented society might look like. While Blatchford himself was agnostic and hostile to organized religion, he 'appealed directly to the moral sentiments nurtured in the churches and chapels,' taking his inspiration from nineteenth-century British socialist and artist William Morris. In Bellamy's immensely popular novel, readers found a blue-print for a society with collectivized production and distribution achieved without bloodshed. In addition, this society exhibited little class or gender hierarchy, and women played a prominent part with full political rights. The state provided many of the necessary services for the reproduction of daily life, including creches, maternity benefits, and other social supports.[4]

Canadian socialists also embraced continental and British streams of socialism. Drawing on the works of Marx and Engels, as well as other writers, Canadian socialists in the early period absorbed such notions as the primacy of class struggle based on irreconcilable differences between the bourgeoisie and the proletariat. The struggle between Capital and Labour, which was building to a climax, overshadowed all other considerations. Other contradictory features of capitalist society were subsumed in the primary struggle to transform an exploitative system based on class. While this tradition raised the question of women's roles in industrial capitalist society, it placed less emphasis on the exploitation of women than on the exploitation of the working class as a whole. The 'woman question' was discussed in the writings of Marx, Engels, and Bebel, especially the latter two. They recognized that women were subordinate in nineteenth-century society and found the origin of this inequality at that point in history when private property and the monogamous family appeared and 'mother right' ended. The emancipation of women thus depended on the destruction of private property and the disappearance of traditional marriage and the family, which could only happen through socialist revolution. Socialist opinion, however, divided on the question of equal rights for women and the desirability of separate women's organizations, usually associating them with the 'bourgeois' women's movement. These debates occurred within the international socialist movement and within the Canadian context as well.[5]

Despite such influences, the early Canadian socialists of the period 1890–1904 often emerged from groups with decidedly Christian leanings. Christian socialism did not disappear in mid-decade, but it was increasingly challenged by more materialist interpretations. As one early commentator on the socialist movement in Toronto noted, religion was often a prickly subject among socialists, particularly for the socialist parties that emerged in the early twentieth century. Even before the existence of these parties one can find examples of emerging socialists who rejected the potential link between the church and socialism. Former labour reformer and journalist Phillips Thompson, for example, severely criticized the churches for their lack of interest in social problems and expected little from them in terms of practical responses to pressing social ills. Like a number of socialists, Thompson found theosophy more congenial to his socialism.[6]

Christian socialism had other drawbacks, especially for women interested in righting not only the injustices of the class system but also the inequalities in gender relations. Appeals to brotherhood and invocations to Christ as the model socialist suggest the limitations inherent in this perspective. The very language used to appeal to progressives indicated a world view that presumed that women could be subsumed into a largely male-defined grouping. The 'brotherhood of man' might imply the potential transformation of the socio-economic order through co-operation, education, and political activism, but it did not and could not address issues of gender inequality.

## II

Christian socialism emerged from the milieu of late-nineteenth-century reform, drawing on the ferment evident in the myriad social reform groups of the period. Christian socialist groups appeared in the 1890s in Toronto, in small-town Ontario, and in both large and small centres in British Columbia. Prominent among these early groups was the Canadian Socialist League (CSL), which had its beginnings in Toronto and Montreal and soon spread to British Columbia. Prior to the existence of the CSL, Ontario also was home to various small socialist clubs and organizations in towns such as Galt, St Thomas, Guelph, and Collingwood, as well as in the larger cities of Toronto and Ottawa. Toronto boasted a number of reform/socialist groups in the 1890s: the Direct Legislation League, the Single Tax Association, the Henry George Club, the Proportional Representation League, and the Social Reform League. A small branch of the DeLeonite Socialist Labor Party also existed in Toronto and several other Canadian locations in the 1890s. Although it never achieved much prominence in Canada, it continued to exist throughout much of the twentieth century.[7]

The Canadian Socialist League eclipsed other groups after its founding in the summer of 1899. A constitution and declaration of principles were adopted in August at a Toronto meeting, a national founding convention was held in 1901, and by 1902 the organization had grown to its peak of sixty-eight locals. The CSL was motivated by the belief, as expressed by the league's Toronto newspaper editor, George Wrigley, that 'Modern civilization is crushing the life and soul out of the people.' In response the CSL advocated the need for a Christian socialist organization that stood for the brotherhood of man, best achieved through education, agitation, and electoral politics aimed at removing social inequalities. Close study of political economy and strong ties to the labour movement complemented these tactics. Local 2 of the CSL in Toronto, for example, worked with the Toronto Trades and Labor Council in 1900 when the two groups sent a joint delegation to government on the question of the eight-hour day on government contracts. By 1902, when the CSL had changed its name to the Ontario Socialist League (OSL), to distinguish itself from the leagues in other provinces, its approach had shifted somewhat to represent a more class-conscious view. While the CSL in 1900 had affirmed that its approach was to man as 'man,' not as 'capitalist' or 'wage slave,' the OSL program of 1902 recognized 'the existing system founded on class distinction, under which the possession or control of the means of production, including land, capital and machinery enabled the capitalist to practically enslave the workers.' The OSL platform of public ownership, reduction of hours of labour, increases in wages, progressive income tax policies, and other political reforms, including equal suffrage for women and men, was a far cry from the loose CSL groupings of 1899–1900, which had rejected a constitution or platform as too divisive.[8]

The CSL stressed brotherhood and cooperation with other social reformers and it attracted a variety of supporters from the reform community. Ministers, journalists, skilled workers, proprietors of small business, professionals, some working women, and women involved in reform groups such as the Woman's Christian Temperance Union and the Single Tax Association, participated in the newly founded CSL. A number of CSL supporters had recently emigrated from Great Britain where they had belonged to such groups as the Fabian Society, the Labour Church, or one of the British socialist groups. Despite his criticisms of Christianity, Phillips Thompson became a prominent activist for the CSL and its successors, becoming secretary of the Ontario group in 1902.[9]

In the early days of the CSL, a number of women participated actively in its work and held office. Nonetheless, gender roles tended to define the activities open to women. Sarah Wrigley, for example, edited a short-lived column for *Citizen and Country*, the CSL newspaper edited by her husband, George. The Kingdom of the Home appeared several times in the spring of 1900 and reflected Sarah's commitment both to prohibition and the wider cause of social reform. As superintendent of temperance in Sunday schools for Ontario, she appealed to women readers to follow the example of Frances Willard, Christian socialist and founder of the Woman's Christian Temperance Union in the United States. The title of her column signified the central role Sarah Wrigley assigned to home and family as the basis of a reformed nation, a theme developed by some later women socialists. 'The Kingdom of the Home,' she wrote, was based on love and collective responsibility; the nation and its leaders ought to reflect the purity of temperate home life and should foster values conducive to peace, harmony, and freedom. While prohibition of alcohol was 'most earnestly to be desired,' she noted that the success of prohibition depended on cooperation with other social reformers. Furthermore, she told her readers:

The writer of these lines undertakes the responsibility of conducting this department only upon the understanding that she, with others, must be regarded as a willing student of the all-important economic and social problems that make for good in every community. She will aim to present to readers the best thought of the most advanced teachers of sociology in all lands, rather than to burden the people with conclusions she herself has reached. She will stand behind the curtain and present before it the living master of reform, chief among whom was Christ, the Model Socialist.

As the first appearance of the column indicated, women in social reform groups, and especially the Canadian WCTU, were targeted as a special audience for *Citizen and Country*. Sample copies were sent to WCTU women throughout the dominion in the hope of bringing them into the Christian socialist arena. Apparently this attempt failed because the newspaper refused to drop its tobacco ads, which offended the temperance union. The paper argued that church and WCTU support could not replace advertising revenues and noted that not all its readers were abstainers.[10]

The Wrigley family was deeply enmeshed in Toronto's social reform and socialist circles. Sarah and George's son, George Weston Wrigley, played a major role as an organizer for the CSL in Ontario and later in British Columbia. The younger Wrigley also wrote columns for the newspaper as well as several reports on socialism in Canada for the

*International Socialist Review*. In the summer of 1902, George Weston Wrigley married Edith Robinson, former secretary of CSL Branch 2 and daughter of active Christian socialists in Toronto. George Weston and Edith moved west in 1902, settling in Victoria for some years while George Weston organized for the American Labor Union and the Socialist Party of British Columbia. The couple participated in Victoria's socialist circles, serving on the music committee of the local branch of the CSL in early 1903. By 1905 George Weston was back working for the movement in Toronto; three years later, Edith and George Weston both participated in an acrimonious debate over whether there should be a women's column in the *Western Clarion*, the newspaper of the Socialist Party of Canada. Both argued for the initiative, especially Edith, who was outraged by male insensitivity to the needs of women socialists.[11]

In addition to those in the Robinson and Wrigley families, other women also contributed to early socialist activism in Toronto. Frequent financial contributors to the socialist cause included Mrs Agnes Murphy and Miss M.E. Youmans, whose name had appeared in the 1890s as secretary of a Socialist League of Canada. In 1902 Youmans wrote to the *Western Socialist* complimenting the paper for its content; she added that she was not surprised that women were becoming interested in socialism since it promised them emancipation from wage slavery and recognized them as equal to men and entitled to the vote.[12]

Local 2 in Toronto also utilized the talents of Mrs J.W. King as treasurer in 1900. In September of that year, King and her husband were present at the independent political action convention initiated by trade unionists and leaders of the CSL. The Kings were joined by Toronto delegates Mr and Mrs John Carroll and by Mrs McCoy of Wallaceburg. McCoy seconded an adult suffrage plank, but it failed to get a two-thirds majority. By 1902, however, equal suffrage was included in the platform of the OSL. Equal suffrage was one of a series of reforms proposed by Christian socialists to combat social inequalities, and the female vote was promoted as a means of protecting the interests of women and children. Still, the most common role for women was a supportive one, particularly in general fundraising and helping to finance *Citizen and Country* and successive socialist newspapers. An organizer for the league commented in August 1902 on social activities sponsored in Toronto by the organization where they gained 'ten lady comrades' to the fold; he noted that these women frequently spoke out and were invaluable at organizing social events.[13]

With its support for equal suffrage, turn-of-the-century Christian socialism promised women a wider political role. Several Toronto women in the league played prominent parts in the Ontario provincial election of 1902. In doing so, they claimed a niche for women in politics that extended beyond the right to vote, and for women in socialist politics that transcended traditional supportive activities. Margaret Haile became the first woman candidate for the provincial legislature, running as a candidate in North Toronto on the OSL platform. Described as an expert stenographer, Haile was a Canadian with wide experience in the New England states, where she had served as Socialist Labor Party state secretary for Connecticut and later in a similar position in Massachusetts for the Socialist Party of America. During the Ontario election campaign she proclaimed that socialism knew no lines regarding colour, creed, sex, or nationality. Haile's election meetings were supported by prominent female reformers and suffragists. Her candidacy received support from 'Dr Emily Stowe-Gullen' (probably Augusta Stowe-Gullen, Emily Stowe's daughter), who 'gave an interesting address in support of the principles of socialism and the enfranchisement of women.' In response to Stowe-Gullen, Haile made it clear that she was running as a socialist rather than as a woman suffrage candidate. She agreed that women should have the franchise, but only as a step towards the ultimate goal of socialism. Other middle-class women reformers spoke for Haile, including Mrs Dr Gordon, a woman suffrage supporter, Jean Grant of the University of Toronto, and Clara Brett Martin, the first woman lawyer in Canada. Their presence suggests the common ground sometimes shared by feminists and socialists.[14]

Present throughout Haile's campaign was May Darwin, who chaired or spoke at many of the candidate's meetings. Darwin's activities as a socialist were noted as early as November 1901 in the daily press when she spoke on 'Women and the Social Problem' at a CSL meeting. In her speech, Darwin argued that women and children were the greatest sufferers from the competitive system and she urged women to join the socialist movement. Women were drawn to the work of socialist propaganda because the movement advocated the brotherhood of man and the equality of the sexes, she noted. In 1902 after the Ontario Socialist convention, Darwin was put in charge of the Toronto committee to organize socialist propaganda work, and she herself gave occasional lectures in 1902–3.[15]

Darwin's activities demonstrated the links between socialism, the woman question, and the labour movement. Not only was she secretary and treasurer of the CSL, she also wrote a women's column for the labour newspaper the *Tribune*, and she served as chair of the local labour council's education committee. Later she ran for office on the socialist platform. Her connections to the labour movement were reinforced by family ties and through her activities in the union label campaign between 1902 and 1905. While Darwin, like Haile, may be considered unusual for her public roles, these activities did not provide complete redefinitions of female roles within a socialist organization that tended to accept a sexual division of labour. That division of labour assigned women supportive roles, particularly focused on social and educational tasks. Indeed, Darwin presided at the daily 'drawing room reception' at the socialist tent at the exhibition ground in Toronto and reported it a great success. While Darwin and others undoubtedly used these roles to encourage more women to participate in socialist activities, clearly a sexual division of labour was common in socialist circles, much as it was in the labour movement and labour market.[16]

## III

Christian social reform and socialism provided a base for organization on the West Coast as well in the last decade of the nineteenth century. The CSL's influence rapidly spread to British Columbia in 1899, partly because of *Citizen and Country* and its Christian socialism, but also because of editor George Wrigley's contacts and a visit he made to Western Canada in the summer, during which he noted a readiness in the region to engage in the struggle for greater social freedom. By the spring of 1900, *Citizen and Country* reported that Local 6 had been established at Port Moody near the site of the collapsed Ruskin Colony, which had been established in 1896 by an Ontario-based group, the Canadian Cooperative Commonwealth. The new local at Port Moody reported O.L. Charlton as secretary and J.M. Cameron as organizer. Both men had been involved in the cooperative venture (which had included a saw mill, shingle mill, and dairy and vegetable farm) that went bankrupt in 1899, and both were active in the socialist movement in the province in the early part of the twentieth century.[17]

The Ruskin Colony had also attracted Annie Chapman, born in Ontario and later transplanted to Victoria by her parents. An ailing Chapman had gone to the colony to stay with friends to regain her health. There she met Charlton, whom she married in 1899. While at the colony, Annie was introduced to socialism through her reading. In her brief reminiscences she described her discovery of the American socialist newspaper *Appeal to Reason*, and her commitment to Christian social-ism: 'Socialism deals with the materialistic side of life and Christianity deals with the spiritual and neither need clash with the other.' Her read-ings and discussions helped to crystallize a long-standing discontent and questioning of the status quo, which she attributed to her childhood experiences of poverty on a Northern Ontario farm. She wrote, 'I think I was a little rebel at the age of nine,' having watched her father struggle to make a living farming in the summer and logging in the winter, only to be cheated of half his logging wages. Times were hard, and Chapman remembered having to leave school for a year at age nine to help out at home caring for her baby sister 'while my mother wore herself out with other home tasks and struggled to clothe the family with made-over garments.' At seventeen, she read Bellamy's *Looking Backward*. The book 'appeared ... just a beautiful dream,' until five years later when she went to Ruskin and learned about the cooperative movement and socialism. Subsequent to her marriage, Chapman's name rarely appeared in the socialist press, perhaps because of her growing family of one son and three daughters. Nevertheless, her reminiscences indicate that she remained active in other socialist groups until her death in 1940. The Charltons left the SPC and became members of the Social Democratic Party in 1911. After the war they joined the Federated Labor Party and later the Cooperative Commonwealth Federation.[18]

While not much is known about some of the other women active in the early stages of the Christian socialist movement in British Columbia, the press provides occasional glimpses of their activities. Mrs John M. Cameron was referred to in the press as an 'active worker in the socialist movement' in early 1903, yet we know little of her activities, except that she occasionally participated in social gatherings and she ran a news-stand that sold socialist literature on Westminster Avenue in Vancouver. The socialist press provided a sketch of her husband, John, that illus-trates at least one common trajectory for early male socialists. Born in Ontario of Scottish parents, John Cameron learned his father's trade of carpentry in his planing mill before becoming active in Toronto in the Knights of Labor. An accident disabled him for five years, but he resumed his trade in British Columbia, where he linked up with the CSL and later the Socialist Party of British Columbia and the Socialist Party of Canada. Cameron's work with the Christian Commonwealth took him to Ladner, British Columbia, where he wrote that he had difficulty finding any Christian socialists until he met the local minister and the president of the WCTU. Cameron organized for the CSL in the province between 1898 and 1900. He then turned up in Manitoba, assisting in the organization of a local in Winnipeg in 1902, before returning to Vancouver. Cameron's path from Ontario and his skilled labour background, including experience in the Knights of Labor, were common among the early socialists, who often shared some previous experience with labour or socialist groups.[19]

Another socialist activist, Ada E. Clayton of Victoria, described as an 'active lady comrade' by Citizen and Country in 1902, wrote to the paper to send in the subscriptions she had solicited to help raise funds for the cause. She noted that she was pleased to see that four socialists had run in Toronto during the provincial election. Clayton also occasionally spoke in public, as in 1903 when she gave a talk, 'Why Women Should Be Socialists,' to Victoria's socialists. Clayton joined the Socialist Party of Canada (SPC) when it was formed and acted as secretary for the Victoria Local until its failure in 1906. A few months later, Clayton appeared as the secretary of the newly formed Victoria International Socialist Club. By 1907 the SPC local had been re-established: Clayton reported eighteen members, with equal numbers of women and men. As we shall see in the next chapter on the SPC and the Social Democratic Party, Clayton took part in a significant debate within the SPC on the 'woman question' and defended the needs of women within the party.[20]

British Columbia in the late 1890s and early 1900s proved to be fertile ground for a variety of socialist groups. Not only did the CSL prove attractive to those interested in the 'social question,' but the province spawned other groups with more Marxist ideological stances. The DeLeonite SLP established its presence in the province in the latter part of the 1890s but, as in the East, it never represented a major force. Two events were much more important to the development of socialism in British Columbia: the creation in the fall of 1901 of a provincial Socialist Party under the leadership of the Vancouver CSL, and, a year later, the merging of socialist organizations to form the Socialist Party of British Columbia (SPBC). The latter adopted a platform of revolutionary socialism as reform socialists joined with more militant and class-conscious workers in the aftermath of considerable labour tension, particularly in the mining districts.[21]

The emergence of the SPBC brought to the fore the question of leadership. Among those nominated for positions on the executive were Ada Clayton, Bertha Merrill (later Burns) of Nelson, and Dora F. Kerr of Phoenix. Merrill deserves consideration here as one of the most prominent women involved in the early provincial movement. A talented writer, Merrill contributed a column to the *Canadian Socialist* (later known as the *Western Socialist* and the *Western Clarion*) especially for women – 'We Women' ran from July 1902 to October 1903. Her nomination to the executive of the SPBC was successful: the results of the vote showed her in second place, just three votes behind the powerful E.T. Kingsley, spokesperson for the Nanaimo socialists. Her presence in Nelson may have related to her connection with the American Labor Union (ALU), an organization that challenged the American Federation of Labor's dominance in the West and that linked socialism and industrial unionism. By 1903 she was assisting R.P. Pettipiece in running the *Western Clarion*. Later that year she married fellow socialist Ernest Burns, who also sat on the executive of the SPBC and served as treasurer for that organization. Burns was on the board of directors of the *Western Socialist*. Both Merrill and Burns would remain important, if controversial, figures in socialist circles in the province, where they would lead a breakaway group from the SPC in 1907.[22]

The We Women columns and the correspondence to the early socialist newspapers from women readers offer an opportunity to observe what women within the movement were thinking about. Certainly many women, Bertha Merrill Burns included, expressed Christian socialist views. In a column that appeared in early 1903, Burns (who wrote her columns under the pen name Dorothy Drew) indicated her adherence to Christian socialism: 'It may not smack of "scientific socialism" to say so, but I believe more men and women are attracted to socialism by the divine reaching-out-for-others spirit that is its basic principle than come to it from any other motive of self-help or expediency.' Clearly Burns was familiar with the scientific socialism of Engels and other writers, yet her own background and formative experiences may well have convinced her of the efficacy of the Christian socialist approach.[23]

The We Women column addressed the women readers of the socialist newspaper and, as such, dealt with topics close to women's experiences as wives and mothers. Burns also touched on women's political roles and urged women to use their concerns and talents as wives and mothers to further a socialist consciousness among women. Her column did not address only women. In her first column she castigated her male comrades in Toronto for not giving Margaret Haile their votes in the 1902 provincial election, and in subsequent weeks she discussed general issues of relevance to the working class as a whole.[24]

Burns's readers were most likely wives and mothers, with a smaller proportion of women wage workers. Homemakers were particularly in need of the socialist message, not only because family life encouraged individualist rather than collectivist thinking, but also because the housewife represented a potentially positive influence over her family. Thus a number of Burns's columns responded to the problems married women and mothers faced in daily life. As wives, Burns noted, women faced difficult situations within marriage when they had to cope with a husband's unemployment, illness, or even death. Economic hardship often meant marital strife, while widowhood could mean great suffering for families suddenly deprived of their breadwinner, a situation not uncommon in British Columbia's coal mines.

Many of the women who wrote letters to 'Dorothy Drew' posed questions relating to motherhood and childraising. When a woman wrote to ask advice about her adopted seventeen-year-old daughter's promiscuous behaviour, Burns invited her readers to respond to the woman, who stated that she had provided a good home and proper environment. The columnist's own response suggested a belief in collective action overcoming inherited tendencies: 'Socialists think it is about time the fathers – and mothers, too – quit sinning so as to lift the burden, of the collective sin of generations past, off the shoulders of children of the future.' May Darwin also expressed pessimism in this case, based on 'the laws of heredity.' She added, however, that 'socialism can do much for future generations, I do believe. When conditions are made such that woman can live the pure healthy life that God intended man and woman to live, the children, too, will be pure and good.' Where prostitution resulted from economic causes, socialism could make a difference. A Victoria correspondent echoed these same sentiments, that socialism would remove poverty and the necessity for women to sell themselves. Expressing a belief in environmental triumph over heredity, Burns herself quoted Engels's view that, once capitalism was destroyed, a fundamental change would be possible in the social relations of the sexes.[25]

Children's access to information about sex concerned another writer to the women's column, who requested information on books for children. Noting the lack of material written for young people, Burns advocated complete parental openness with children on these questions, attributing her conviction to a Winnipeg lecture given by Amelia H. Yeomans, a suffrage and temperance supporter. Perhaps more revealingly, in this same column the sex education debate brought into focus the tension between women's concerns and socialism's program, as Burns viewed it: 'This is not socialism, perhaps some will say. No, but it is not less important than socialism. The only reason I put socialism first is because I believe that until we have an economic and social system based on justice and brotherhood, we can never have an ideal mother-hood and a race towering Godward in its onward march. So long as we look upon the origin of life – the fusion of sex force – with contempt and shame, so long will life itself be held the cheapest and lowest commod-ity in the universe.' While promising openness in matters like sex educa-tion, socialism meant that women would have more control over their lives, that they would bear children without anxiety and with dignity.[26]

The Dorothy Drew column also addressed the question of women's paid work and their unionization. A working woman herself, Bertha Burns credited her own experience working on a newspaper with her eventual adoption of socialism. Her indignation at the treatment of some young women at this newspaper led her to investigate the general conditions of women's work and drew her to socialism. Burns's views on women in the labour force included a commitment to equal pay for equal work. Writing about a newspaper article on two women working for an American railroad line, Burns not only expressed the hope that their pay match that of their male counterparts, she also commented that if the women were married, their husbands ought to perform domestic labour to assist them. A correspondent from Morrisburg, Ontario, wrote to Dorothy Drew about her rage that women teachers in rural areas received lower pay than those in urban centres. As a high school teacher and university graduate, 'Fides' compared women rural teachers' salaries with those of saleswomen and asked why women did not rise up to demand their rights. Burns's sympathies were clearly with equal pay and recognition. She also urged working women not to turn their noses up at other working women, encouraging them to become class-conscious and thus command dignity and respect. Whether women were single and in the labour force or married and responsible for home and children, Burns's columns encouraged them to take an active role in all that affected them.[27]

An early column reflected on Mother Jones, the feisty American champion of the miners, who was then in jail for her support of the coal miners and 'the little slave children' of the south. Burns compared her to Joan of Arc and to Harriet Beecher Stowe, an American anti-slavery cru-sader, and called her the mother of strikes. Strikes, she noted, often were opposed by 'we women,' yet she asked why the 'mother hearts of the world do not rise up in rebellion against the murderous system' that makes the exploitation of children and coal miners lawful. The potential of women's collective power was enormous, and Burns particularly emphasized the role women might play, based on their strong maternal responsibilities, in mobilizing other women to put an end to exploitation. Because the economic system threatened the very children women bore and raised, they should be interested in socialism. Unfortunately, according to Burns, women often could not perceive the connections between the home and the wider world. Thus in the women's column she constantly pushed the message that women should attend socialist meetings, become involved in politics, particularly at the local level on school boards, and generally become well-informed.[28]

On the issue of woman suffrage, Burns noted that socialists supported woman suffrage as a matter of justice, but she wondered whether working-class women would support their class, as leisure-class women did. This note of ambivalence permeated socialist thinking on suffrage generally. Burns, however, supported suffrage for women as part of her larger vision of a politically active sisterhood.[29]

Integral to Burns's vision of women's potential within the socialist movement was her conviction that men could not be trusted to secure women's freedom. While marriage and motherhood was the common lot of women and gave them the vantage point necessary to connect individual experiences within the home and family with the broader political, social, and economic changes envisioned by socialism, Burns worried that socialist women were not vigilant enough in securing their own share of the socialist future. In October 1902 she noted that not one woman was a delegate to the British Columbia convention of socialists: 'We are way behind our California sisters who were visible at the state socialist convention last month in San Francisco.' In a 1904 lecture given to the Vancouver and Victoria SPC locals, Burns cautioned her female audience: 'Unless you, women, secure your political and economic freedom while the battle for freedom is on, I am not sure that these men, once slaves themselves, will not seal you as slaves unto themselves forever.' Men viewed women as childbearing, cooking, washing, and scrubbing machines, Burns stated. Unless women stood up to be counted as full-fledged human beings, they ran the danger of being treated as property. Her expressed discouragement about women's willingness to act as an organized source of social change did not deny their potential, a potential based particularly on their roles as mothers. She urged women to become active socialists because 'there is so much to accomplish for the children tomorrow that only the mothers can do.'[30]

In an earlier article, 'Why Women Should Be Socialists,' Burns spoke directly to the question of why so few women were involved in the movement. 'The fault, if fault there be, does not lie directly with the women themselves but is rather the natural result of education and environment,' she insisted. Women were just as capable of identifying injustice as men, but 'they have not yet beheld this other vision – the vision of hope in the life that now is; the vision of beauty ready to unfold; the vision of happiness within their grasp; the vision of justice and love – all inviting them to move forward where these good things await them. It is for those whose eyes have already been blessed with this vision to show it to them.' The struggle to convince women of the benefits of socialism would be a long one, she realized. The problem was that 'the average woman, even in this age of the new woman, leads a sheltered home life,' protected from the 'monsters of greed and iniquity' by her husband, who provides her only contact with the world. Furthermore, Burns wrote that women have been taught to avoid politics and devote their energies to the church. If women would only throw this energy into the socialist cause, then 'in that day socialism will fling its banner of justice and equality over the whole world.'[31]

One of the reasons why women should pledge their allegiance to 'the redemption doctrines of socialism' was that the battle for socialism was being waged on behalf of women's realm in the home. Not only did women need to understand how capitalism contributed to adulterated food and drink, but they also needed to understand that socialism promised lighter workloads for women, security of housing, and benefits for children who would no longer have to toil long hours for wages and be brought up in a system that accepted class privilege for the few. As in some of her other articles, Burns stressed that socialism would assist women in having wanted and healthy children because the fear of not being able to provide would no longer exist. Parenthood would become a positive experience rather than a 'dreaded task.' In general, 'the gospel of socialism means that fear will be driven out of life,' she wrote. Without fear 'and with only a few hours of work each day, with plenty of room and fresh air, with ample opportunity for culture and enjoyment, with a natural intercourse of the sexes, every man able to marry and bring up children, every woman able to bear strong, healthy, happy children, we may expect such a development of manhood and womanhood as the world never knew,' she concluded.[32]

Burns's socialism sprang from several sources, but primarily it reflected a Christian socialist viewpoint. This stance, however, was wedded to her maternalist convictions, convictions which were shared by the mainstream women's reform movement. Motherhood united women in a common experience that gave them the potential power for social change once the connections had been made between the individual experiences of women in the family and the wider economic, social, and political environment. What is not completely evident from her writings is the extent to which she felt that cross-class cooperation was possible. Certainly Burns perceived class differences among women, yet her Christian socialism led her to admire Frances Willard's activities in the United States in trying to effect organization among all women on the great questions of the day – temperance, labour, and women's rights. For Burns, Willard's actions suggested the need for a concerted effort among women to work for the emancipation of the race from the 'thralldom' that produced intemperance. Such a position implied that working-class women might well find some allies among progressive women in other classes.[33]

Another recurring strand in Burns's writing encompassed her notion of what socialism would mean for women. Emancipation under socialism would mean not only a larger role in public affairs, but also sexual freedom. Women would be respected citizens, no longer ornaments for men. Prostitution would become a thing of the past, and women would acquire the 'right to bear her children in love' because she would not have to worry about how to feed and clothe them. Burns believed that these questions were intimately related to socialism, although she tended to accept the view that socialism dealt mainly with questions of economics and politics in the public arena. Her views on socialism and the woman question were shared by those women in the movement whose ideas are ascertainable through the press.[34]

The links between women's rights, sex reform, and socialism were muted in Bertha Merrill Burns's writing in comparison to that of Dora Forster, a socialist who, with her husband, Robert Kerr, moved to British Columbia in the 1890s. Angus McLaren describes the couple as English Fabian socialists who, because of their radical views, which tied eugenic ideas of 'race improvement' to women's rights, divorce, and birth control, 'did not go out of their way to make themselves known.' Forster's interest in these topics stemmed from her own analysis of contemporary society, which she found stifling, particularly for women. Indeed, Forster insisted that the class war was complemented by the sex war. Contemporary marriage practices, particularly monogamy, restricted women to a very narrow life with few satisfactions. Not only did she compare marriage to footbinding, she also devastatingly compared it to prostitution when she asserted that 'the honest woman like the honest politician is the one who stays bought.' Few women found their slave-like marriages satisfactory on the sexual side since men knew little about women's sexual pleasure. Thus it was little wonder, Forster commented, that women were revolting against marriage with their refusal to propagate the species. The decline in married women's fertility suggested the viability of the 'birth strike' as a tactical weapon: 'I hope the scarcity of children will go on till maternity is honored at least as much as the trials and hardships of soldiers campaigning in wartime.' Forster was concerned that control of reproduction be used constructively, particularly in turning sexuality into a positive force. Only in a society in which children learned the 'facts of life' in a natural, straightforward manner and young adult women were free to choose their first sexual partner, prior to choosing the father of her children, could women achieve any degree of freedom. Forster envisioned a series of life stages that commenced with sexual experimentation and progressed (in a woman's twenties) to childbearing, and (in her thirties) to a 'home partnership' that would not necessarily be monogamous. The result, in Forster's view, would be freely chosen motherhood, based on sexual freedom for women.[35]

The emancipation of women depended on other factors as well, including their economic and mental independence. Forster's views on women's work challenged socialist assumptions that married women ought not to work. Her comments on this subject did not appear until 1909 in the socialist newspaper *Cotton's Weekly*, where she reinforced the positions of American feminist and social critic Charlotte Perkins Gilman on the evils of female economic dependence. Economic dependence posed the danger that women would let men do their thinking for them. For Forster, who noted that women were not always incapacitated by childbearing, married women's work was not the problem. Rather the issue that needed to be addressed was overwork for all women no matter what their marital status. Nurses, who were usually single, were notoriously overworked. Should their potential motherhood not be taken into account? For Forster, while the issues of sexual freedom and women's rights were intertwined with socialism, she warned that 'No woman who is mentally worth anything will support a socialism which aims at securing systematized work and livelihood for men while leaving women in their present position of political and social slavery.' As her writings indicate, Forster developed a radical critique of women's roles based in libertarian sexual thought, rather than Christian socialism.[36]

Forster's radical sexual reform ideas formed an integral part of her socialist vision. Similar ideas became the subject of controversy at the Sointula community located on Malcolm Island in British Columbia. This utopian socialist community was founded in 1901 by the controversial Finnish nationalist and socialist Matti Kurikka. Kurikka has recently become the subject of much historical interest, partly because of the role he played in the history of the Finnish working class and socialist movement in Canada. For the purposes of this discussion, however, Kurikka's biography is relevant mainly because of his strongly held and widely promulgated views on sexuality and marriage. At Sointula in early 1904 he launched a campaign against marriage, based on his belief that love and marriage were not necessarily related. Kurikka's ideas can be traced back to Finland and his association with the prominent feminist, socialist, and suffragist writer Minna Canth, whose writings castigated the subject position of women in Finnish society. Kurikka's theosophy also contributed to his views on these questions. In contrast to the organized churches which promoted marriage and monogamy, Kurikka interpreted theosophy as a spiritual force that stressed harmony, noncoercive relationships, and the power of spiritual forces. Marriage was a coercive institution that sanctioned female slavery and oppression and denied natural sexual drives.[37]

Thus, like Forster, Kurikka separated love from marriage as well as from motherhood. Such views were not universally accepted at Sointula and led to controversy within the community. There are also suggestions that scandal surrounded Kurikka himself, who formed a close friendship with the wife of Sointula's other major leadership figure, A.B. Makela. In addition to possible personal repercussions for these two friends, the timing of the controversy over 'free love' proved unfortunate because the colony faced severe economic problems, a point Makela made in opposition to Kurikka's views. For a combination of reasons, Kurikka left Sointula in the fall of 1904, taking with him half of the colony, thus undermining the possibility of its survival as an experiment in utopian socialism. Kurikka later founded another colony in the Fraser Valley called Sammon Takojat, which was, in contrast to Sointula, favorably situated close to potential markets. Whether this colony followed Kurikka's philosophy of free love is not clear, but many settlers followed Kurikka from Sointula to the new colony.[38]

The visions of a new sexuality and an alternative moral code as espoused by Dora Forster and Matti Kurikka do not seem to have resonated elsewhere in the Canadian socialist movement. Perhaps it was only possible for such discussions and experiments to occur in 'the frank-spoken west,' as Forster called it. While such sexual radicalism formed a minor current of the early socialist movement, it is not without significance since it represents the first major challenge in a socialist framework to the position of women within Canadian society in general and within the socialist movement in particular. Such challenges would arise again, although in a different context.

## IV

Canadian socialism in its earliest days represented a challenge not only to class rule, but at times to male dominance as well. From the earliest days of the Canadian Socialist League, women were very much present in the organization, sometimes in public roles, more often in the back rooms. Male socialists of the CSL and the SPBC commented occasionally on the need for more work among the women comrades, and the press noted women's contributions. Correspondents to the press commented favorably on new female recruits to the movement and urged the movement to respond to women's needs. The commentator quoted at the top of this chapter was not alone in suggesting that women were vital to an expanding socialist movement. George Weston Wrigley made the same point at a gathering in his honour when he noted that the Vancouver local was now on a firm basis, partly because the 'women had enlisted in the work.' Similar comments were made in Victoria and in Ontario centres. Clearly some women played important roles in the early days of socialism, most of them inspired by a vision of Christian socialism that promised them, as well as their families, a world based on justice, equality, and shared plenty. To varying degrees and with different talents, these women took part in the organizing, the speaking, the writing, and, less often, the electioneering, most often addressing their efforts to women either in the movement or to those outside who might join if they understood its relevance to their own lives. Even so, their numbers were limited and, in the context of a deeply gender-differentiated society that valued women mainly as wives, mothers, daughters, and sisters, many more women played supportive roles than leadership ones.

Although the 'brotherhood of man' promised to include women, it did so mainly in the name of challenging an unequal socio-economic system. Christian socialism's main tenets remained fixed primarily on changing that system without altering the gender roles assigned to women, except in the public arena. Temperance reform and equal suffrage, for example, promised a wider public role for women but left unchanged, for the most part, their expected roles within the family. With the exception of a few sexual radicals, most early socialist women did not envision a total restructuring of gender relations but rather tried to create an expanded space within the movement for their family- and community-based political activities.[39]

While Christian socialism provided a philosophy attractive to many women, by the middle of the first decade of the twentieth century its widespread appeal was undermined by a more materialist conception of socialism that rejected religion and most forms of social reform as anti-thetical to socialism's program. George Weston Wrigley summed up the new perspective in his report on Canada in the *International Socialist Review* of 1904–5 where he proclaimed the growth of 'a revolutionary Socialist movement' based on the 'abolition of the wage system.' In discussing these developments, he referred to the earlier socialist leagues but dismissed them as 'based on sentimentalism.' The new movement would be based on 'scientific socialism.' It also would definitively subordinate women's issues to the larger task of gaining working-class political power.[40]

# 4

# 'Full of the Spirit of Revolt':
# Women in the Socialist Party of Canada
# and the Social Democratic Party

Are you going to stand by and see a woman, naturally physically less fit for the rugged work of Socialist propaganda, do the bulk of the work? Talk about chivalry, it's not common manliness.

*Western Clarion*, 29 August 1908

In every department of life socialists desire the absolute equality of the sexes. They stand for the enfranchisement of women, the abolition of all laws prejudicial to women in their relations to men, the exclusion of women from industries specially injurious to their physique for the benefit of generations yet unborn, and equal pay for the sexes for the performance of equal work.

*Cotton's Weekly,* 24 November 1910

In the decade prior to the First World War, European and North American socialist movements were forced to grapple with the 'woman question.' By the time of the 1907 International Socialist Congress held in Stuttgart, where as many as sixty women delegates attended both the main congress and a separate socialist women's conference, the question of women's equality was often posed in terms of the right to vote. Indeed the 1907 congress endorsed a resolution that obligated socialist parties in all countries 'to fight energetically for the introduction of the Universal suffrage for women.' While women's equality was endorsed and much discussed, there were significant disagreements about the roles women ought to play politically and economically. Nowhere was this more pronounced than within the Canadian movement. According to socialist organizer Wilf Gribble, women were less fit to do the hard slogging of propaganda work. Speaking as a member of the Socialist Party of Canada (SPC), Gribble reflected the party's emphasis on political action and its view that women, by and large, were unsuited for certain kinds of political activity that were defined as male.[1]

Unlike earlier Christian socialist appeals to a cooperative commonwealth, the SPC stressed the 'irrepressible conflict of interest between the capitalist and the worker ... culminating in a struggle for the possession of the reins of government.' Political action, whether on the soap box or at the ballot box, was paramount. With few exceptions, both lay outside of women's realm. Socialist orators and voters were men who understood that the party stood for the 'transformation of capitalist property into the collective property of the working class,' management of industry by workers, and production for use rather than profit. Socialist men who ran for office understood that the SPC pledged its officeholders to support only legislation that benefited the working class. Women were not expected or encouraged to run for office, and woman suffrage, despite the 1907 resolution, was often viewed as a diversion from the main goal of overthrowing capitalism through class-conscious propaganda. Such class-consciousness required party members to eschew 'immediate demands' such as woman suffrage, municipal ownership, or other legislative reforms in favour of strictly revolutionary goals and tactics. Dubbed 'impossibilist' because of its uncompromising revolutionary stance, the early SPC found itself challenged by discontent among the ranks, which eventually led to the creation of new socialist parties.[2]

Even the emergence of breakaway social democratic parties in 1907 in British Columbia and more broadly across Canada in 1911–12 did not signal any significant changes for women socialists. While the impossibilist SPC consistently suspected women's activism, including their suffrage campaigns, and all too frequently made derogatory statements about women in the press, the rival Social Democratic Party of Canada (SDP) was committed to practical reforms to improve the conditions of working-class men and women. The SDP, therefore, supported woman suffrage and welcomed the formation of women's and youth groups alongside party activity. Its structure was more flexible, more in line with European social democratic movements and thus attractive to immigrants familiar with social democracy. Women too found more flexibility within the SDP. Nevertheless, like the SPC, the social democrats tended to view women primarily as wives, mothers, and daughters circumscribed by familial life. Women were publicly encouraged to join the movement, but male socialists' attitudes and policies towards issues of concern to women often undermined women's participation. Although individual socialist women won some respect and recognition, gender issues remained secondary. For ethnic women, language barriers and cultural expectations created further obstacles.

In the North American context, the SPC contrasted with the Socialist Party of America (SPA), which from its founding in 1901 officially endorsed equal civil and political rights for men and women. Socialists in the United States campaigned for woman suffrage at the state level in the early part of this century. This progressive public stance, however, obscured the very real debates that occurred over the 'woman question' within the SPA. As noted by Mari Jo Buhle, a strong socialist-feminist group within the party had to contend with more orthodox views that subordinated women's issues to class issues and analysis. While women socialists had a voice at the national executive level of the SPA from 1909 to 1915, intense factionalism within the party in 1912 led to the cessation of financial support for the Women's National Committee and considerable disarray among the committee's leaders. After 1915 there was no central focus or coordination for American socialist women; within the Canadian socialist movement there was no equivalent national level grouping at all for women.[3]

While estimates of female participation in the SPA, the SPC, and the SDP range from 10 to 15 per cent, the German Social Democratic Party (SPD) could claim somewhat higher proportions of 15 to 20 per cent, a figure unmatched by other European parties on the left. In 1891 the German SPD officially endorsed and supported women's emancipation through the vote and other measures to promote political equality. Beyond this move, the party also supported the organization of a socialist women's movement under the leadership of Clara Zetkin. This movement aimed at raising women's class-consciousness in order to equip them for the struggle against capitalism. Although the emancipation of women was tied in theory to the emancipation of the working class, in actual practice a struggle had to be waged against male socialists who often expressed ambivalent or hostile attitudes towards women, a problem also found in North American socialist parties. Despite the existence of an officially sanctioned socialist women's movement in Germany and internationally in the years just before the First World War, socialist women had to struggle within male-dominated party structures to maintain a presence. Even in the German case, the

SPD executive gave preference to a non-threatening woman over the outspoken Zetkin when it came to a seat on the executive, and it further undermined women's autonomy by abolishing women's conferences as well as the party's women's bureau.[4]

Canadian socialist organizations tended to relegate women to supportive roles and to assign women's issues secondary importance. A number of women socialists nevertheless refused to accept such roles and persisted in arguing for women's equality within the movement. Resisting the dismissal of woman suffrage by the SPC, for example, women socialists argued that the vote would give women recognition and a weapon with which to fight for justice. Angered by patronizing remarks in the *Western Clarion* about women's lesser commitment to socialism, occasioned by a request for a women's column, women wrote in to demand a movement that took women's needs into consideration. The existence of women's columns, study groups, and autonomous women's organizations attested to the real and perceived need for such activities among women themselves.

Within the ethnic communities, particularly among the Ukrainians, Jews, and Finns, women also actively participated in socialist organizations and created their own separate groups, both to educate themselves and to support the movement. Several women from ethnic communities became active propagandists for the movement, but at great personal cost. Like their Anglo-Canadian sisters, most ethnic women played supportive roles. Despite the evidence of women's activism in the movement, socialists were unable to overcome notions of basic biological and social differences between men and women, thus reinforcing divisions within the movement as well as in the home and workplace.

I

Originally formed in 1904, the SPC grew slowly in 1905 and 1906, but by 1907 organization campaigns began to produce results in the western coal-mining regions as well as in urban areas. By the fall of 1907, the Dominion Executive Committee (DEC) and the Provincial Executive Committee (PEC) of British Columbia established a paid secretarial position. The Ontario party, which claimed four hundred members, formed its own PEC in October. The small Socialist Party of Manitoba joined the SPC in April 1905 as did a small local in Fredericton, New Brunswick. The *Western Clarion*, the SPC's paper, boasted two thousand subscribers in late 1905. Other locals were formed in Ontario, British

Columbia, and Alberta in 1905–6 and a local was formed as far north as Dawson in the Yukon Territories.[5]

In Quebec, Montreal formed an SPC local by the end of 1905, with an initial base in a German workingmen's club. Montreal May Day celebrations in 1906 featured a parade of five thousand people, some of whom carried red flags. Harassment during Montreal's May Day celebrations the next year established a pattern of conflict between socialist activists and the authorities that was repeated several times. Moreover, in this primarily Catholic city, socialists were often hounded by the church as well as by the police. Despite the harassment, the SPC's organizational success was apparent among immigrants in Montreal as ethnic branches of the party existed among not only the English and French but the Russians, Jews, Italians, and Latvians before 1910. By 1913, Poles and Lithuanians were also represented in Montreal's socialist community, along with the Ukrainian Social Democratic Federation, the Industrial Workers of the World, and a group of Young Socialists.[6]

It was not only in Montreal where ethnic groups formed their own SPC locals. Indeed, from central Canada to the West Coast, Finnish and Ukrainian organizers were sent to settlements of their own people to try to start locals, often with considerable success. By 1910 there were locals of Finns from Toronto to British Columbia, although the Ukrainian locals tended to be located in the western provinces. Winnipeg featured a multi-ethnic socialist population with branches among the Russians, Germans, Ukrainians, Poles, Latvians, and Jews, as well as among the English-speaking population. Similarly, Toronto's socialists included English, Italian, Jewish, and Finnish members by 1907. Other major centres of the SPC were dominated by English-speaking members, although in Vancouver, which had about two hundred SPC members in 1909, the Finnish population formed a significant presence. Outside of Vancouver, British Columbia's socialist populations were more varied ethnically.[7]

By 1910, the SPC had established itself as the leading socialist party, with perhaps three thousand members in Canada. Retaining that presence, however, proved difficult, as dissension within the ranks increased. Between 1907 and 1911, several breakaway movements were launched, the first in Vancouver in 1907. The Social Democratic Party of Vancouver was created in that year after Ernest Burns was suspended from the SPC for arranging speaking engagements for Walter Thomas Mills, a 'reform socialist.' Ernest Burns, Bertha Merrill Burns, and sixty others left to form the new organization. Bertha Burns had noted rising discontent within the SPC as early as summer 1906. In a letter to Margaret MacDonald – wife of Ramsay MacDonald, one of the leaders of the Independent Labour Party in Britain – she wrote: 'Matters are going on in the same old way here, the Impossibilist element in full control, but there is a strong movement among the foreign comrades, led by the Finns, who outnumber the English speaking members of the SP of C, for a reconstruction of the constitution along more rational lines, and for a platform of Immediate Demands.' After the break, she wrote MacDonald in 1907 that the SPC had lost many of its former supporters to the new party. E.T. Kingsley, editor of the *Western Clarion*, was 'left with only a few ranters to support him – lip revolutionists but utterly incapable of any organized activity.' She also noted that the new party had 'a good per centage of women ... and we mean to so conduct it that we shall keep them there.'[8]

Toronto's Finnish socialists were also pressing for changes in the SPC. At the party's 1908 Ontario provincial convention, the Finnish branch appointed a committee to draft a broader program. The Finns wanted practical measures included to accomplish political reforms in the tradition of social democratic reform in Europe. They proposed that the program include universal suffrage without regard to sex, municipal ownership of land and utilities, municipal housing, a stand against contract work on government projects, and municipal responsibility for employing the unemployed. The convention vote split along ethnic lines, and the Finns lost by one vote.[9]

Across the country, discontent with the SPC grew over centralized control from British Columbia, the question of reform affiliation with the Second International, and the demand for greater autonomy for ethnic locals of the party. In British Columbia the Finnish comrades within the SPC had by this time set up a separate ethnic executive, which they defended as necessary to strengthen ties among their compatriots and to carry out propaganda work. By spring 1909, Port Arthur (Ontario) Finns passed a resolution aimed at securing a party referendum on affiliation to the Second International, opposed by the Dominion Executive. A similar resolution was sent by the Toronto local. Winnipeg's ethnic socialists passed resolutions regretting the DEC's unilateral decision and asked for a reconsideration and referendum of the SPC's membership to decide on the affiliation question. By the late summer of 1910, most of Winnipeg's Jewish, German, Ukrainian, and Latvian members had defected to the loosely organized SDP, a move that was echoed in Ontario. In October 1910 Port Arthur Finns and others called for another referendum, this time to organize in the SDP.[10]

Chaos and discontent also reigned among the English-speaking members in Ontario. The DEC's refusal to affiliate with the Second International and its refusal to countenance a referendum on the issue led to the eventual revocation of the charter of Local 1 and the reorganization of ethnic branches into separate locals. A new English-speaking local (number 24) emerged, which sided with the Dominion Executive and claimed jurisdiction over all English-speaking comrades in the province. The dissidents of Local 1 protested this move, the expulsion of around two hundred comrades (146 Finns, 30 Jews, 22 English, 10 Italians) from the party, and the high-handed manner in which the DEC interfered in Ontario. The ousted members appointed a committee to draft a pamphlet to explain their position, and the contents were ratified at a joint meeting of the branches on 23 December 1909. The pamphlet outlined the events of the past few months and suggested that the SPC was not growing because the most outspoken English-speaking members, now in Local 24, attacked religion, maligned the trade unions, insulted people, and talked wildly about guns. The pamphlet pointed to George Weston Wrigley as the prime culprit in such offences.[11]

In response, the Dominion Executive dissolved the Ontario PEC. The dissidents countered by organizing a convention in Toronto in May 1910 initiated by the Galt, Guelph, and Berlin members. This convention endorsed changes in the platform to instruct the national and provincial executives on when referenda must be held, and it passed another resolution asking for a vote on affiliation to the Second International. The Ontario dissidents called for a dominion convention and chose Berlin as the new provincial headquarters. If the SPC as a whole chose not to recognize this meeting, the dissidents resolved to continue to meet. At the 1911 convention of the new group, the independent socialist newspaper *Cotton's Weekly* noted the new spirit of 'hopeful enthusiasm and practical work,' which sharply contrasted with the gloomy meetings of 1910. SPC intransigence in the face of demands for change resulted in the creation of a rival national party by 1911–12 – the Social Democratic Party of Canada. The membership of the new party was dominated by the Finns, Ukrainians, Jews, and Poles who were organized in language (ethnic) locals. English-speaking members were in the minority but tended to assume leadership positions.[12]

Another breakaway group from the SPC emerged in the winter of 1910–11. The Socialist Party of North America (SPNA), three or four small locals in southern Ontario, objected to what it deemed 'reformism' among the elected representatives from the SPC, and it aligned itself with the more extreme impossibilism of the Socialist Party of Great Britain (SPGB). Despite the revolutionary program of the SPC, the SPNA felt that political leadership was lacking and that the SPC engaged in too much vote catching. Eventually the SPNA revised its opinion on trade unions and urged its members to join unions and engage in political education, thus breaking with the extreme impossibilism of the SPGB. A number of the SPNA's members participated in the founding of the Communist Party of Canada after the war.[13]

Little commented upon is the role of women's issues in these developments. Matters such as woman suffrage, women's exploitation in the labour market, and the place of women's autonomous groups within the SPC were never major preoccupations for male socialists. Yet it is through such issues that the fundamental difficulty between the SPC and the SDP – determing the place of immediate demands and practical reforms for the working class – can be examined. Each issue suggests the major ambivalence felt by male socialists towards women in the movement and helps to explain why socialist women's activities were largely confined to support activities. The careers of the small number of women agitators who rose to prominence within the socialist movement will be examined within this context to demonstrate not only the ideological obstacles posed by the socialist movement, but also the material conditions under which these women laboured for the cause.

## II

In May 1911 the *Western Clarion* printed a letter from Lena Mortimer of Vancouver commenting on a conversation overheard after an SPC meeting on the woman question. The men were heard to say that the women should remain home and leave the voting to the men. Exasperated at 'the same old yarn,' Mortimer wrote that if women were fit to be mothers and the educators of children and to occupy a variety of positions in life, then they should be able to vote. The wife of socialist tailor John Mortimer, she reiterated what many working-class women felt on the suffrage issue – that the franchise would give the working-class woman recognition and the means to affect legislation pertinent to herself as a worker, a wife, and a mother. 'The vote is only a means,' wrote E.M. Epplett, a Toronto woman socialist. Dora Forster Kerr claimed that the vote was the first step in justice for women, pointing out the absence of women in the legislature and the resulting injustices women suffered as mothers unable to obtain custody over their children.[14]

Despite these arguments, the Socialist Party of Canada remained ambivalent about the franchise for women. In 1906 and 1909 socialist MLA J.H. Hawthornthwaite introduced private member's bills in the British Columbia Legislature to extend the vote to women. Yet he warned women that the franchise would not cure all ills and that economic independence was needed for real freedom. Moreover, he observed that, while the average woman was just as qualified as a man to vote, she was 'necessarily more conservative than man,' a remark that neatly summed up socialist anxieties about women. In response to a 1911 fundraising letter from the mostly middle-class BC Political Equality League (PEL), the *Western Clarion* replied that workers knew only two kinds of people – masters and slaves, not men and women. While the paper did not oppose the enfranchisement of the PEL women, it also observed that these women would use the vote against the working class. Later in 1911, a woman member of the SPC reiterated this position after attending a PEL meeting: 'You claim that votes for women will change conditions under which women work! And yet you talk largely of upholding private property interests and dower laws ... The vote will not then seriously touch on the majority conditions of women. They, like the men, are the proletariat or property-less class ... To a Socialist there is no inequality between the sexes. Rather is the inequality in prevailing economic conditions.[15]

In contrast to socialist support for woman suffrage in the United States and Europe, the SPC's negative attitude towards woman suffrage hardened, particularly after the creation of the SDP. The latter's support for the enfranchisement of women confirmed the SPC's suspicions that the movement represented a reformist approach that would enable wealthy women to participate in a system that oppressed the working class. As for the much-touted regeneration of society through women's virtues of compassion and love, SPC spokespersons denied that the vote would change capitalism, but rather would only dress it up 'in the frills and laces of feminine sentimentality.' The suffrage movement was essentially a bourgeois movement whose aims were antithetical to socialism. Indeed, to support suffrage or any other reform was 'feminine,' in contrast to the strongly masculine focus on revolution. As one socialist writer wryly observed, supporting woman suffrage 'is probably a very gallant thing to do, and very expedient too, especially during the pairing season. But the scientific socialist, and he is the only real socialist, waives all obligations to this movement ... And so the scientific socialist tells [the socialist woman] that the suffragette movement has no

connection with the working class movement for the overthrow of capitalism.'[16]

Not all socialists agreed with this condemnation of the suffrage campaign. Within the SPC itself some members supported woman suffrage,
as did correspondents and writers to *Cotton's Weekly.* Mary Cotton Wisdom, Christian socialist and editor of the women's page in the paper,
often wrote of the need for the franchise among working-class women.
She rejected commonplace assumptions that the female franchise was
unnecessary because women influenced men's votes. Echoing the suffrage movement's vision of women cleaning up and purifying politics,
Wisdom associated the women's vote with improvements in legislation
affecting women and children. More generally, women's political clout
would assist in the repeal of legislation that condemned many to mar-
ginal existence because of laws favouring the propertied and wealthy.
As a critic of government and as a 'real suffragette,' she admired the
courage of British women militants in the movement, 'though I must
admit they express their opinions a little forcibly at times.'[17]

Ethnic women, particularly the Finns, also supported suffrage almost
as a matter of course. Having won the vote in Finland in 1906, Finnish
women were sometimes puzzled by the divided opinions on suffrage
within the Canadian socialist movement. The highly visible presence of
Finnish, Ukrainian, and Jewish women in the SDP encouraged that
organization to confirm its support for the female franchise in its platform, and active SDP women participated in suffrage meetings and
organizations across the country. Vancouver's SDP, for example, under
the leadership of Bertha Merrill Burns, sponsored meetings on the topic
in the prewar period. During the war years other SDP women also
assisted in the suffrage campaign, including Mary Norton, who also
belonged to the Pioneer Political Equality League, the Local Council of
Women, and the Women's International League for Peace and Freedom
(WILPF). The Pioneer Political Equality League in particular worked for
suffrage and drew in women of various political stripes. Norton recalled
that tensions between socialists and non-socialists in the league and
the WILPF caused some problems, and Norton herself claimed that
she never mentioned her socialism to the Pioneer Political Equality
League.[18]

Labour leader Helena Gutteridge, who edited the women's column in
the *BC Federationist*, urged working women who identified with the suffrage campaign to join the British Columbia Women's Suffrage League
(BCWSL). Gutteridge had found the PEL too conservative and had orga-

nized the BCWSL as an alternative that would also deal with issues of concern to working women. She noted that both suffrage and labour activities were 'supplementary and necessary to each other, if the economic freedom of women is to be obtained. The economic value of the ballot is one of the strongest arguments in favour of votes for women.' Despite Gutteridge's role in the labour movement and particularly in the Trades and Labor Council of Vancouver, the outbreak of war and male workers' anxieties about the threat of cheap female labour undermined the support for women's suffrage that had characterized prewar labour meetings.[19]

In other major urban centres the SDP gave support to the suffrage issue, although in cities such as Winnipeg the spokeswomen of the middle or upper middle class tended to dominate the suffrage campaign. Winnipeg's PEL, formed in 1912, took up the cudgel for the franchise with the talents of women journalists and writers such as Francis Marion Beynon and her sister Lillian Beynon Thomas. As editor of the woman's page of the *Grain Growers' Guide*, Francis Beynon utilized her column to muster support for a number of causes including woman suffrage. Beynon's Christian socialism linked her to the reform community in Winnipeg, which included moderate socialists and labour party activists such as Fred Dixon, R.A. Rigg, and Winona and Lynn Flett among others. The PEL actively supported Dixon's election campaigns for a seat in the provincial legislature as an independent progressive in 1914 and 1915 because of his pro-suffrage and reform views, which included compulsory education, efficient factory inspection and prohibition of child labour. Dixon married Winona Flett in the fall of 1914. In addition to campaigning for her husband, Flett was active in the suffrage movement and, later, supported women as political candidates in the Dominion Labor Party. Fred Dixon's arrest during the Winnipeg General Strike in 1919 also involved her in Defence Committee activities in 1919–20. Her sister Lynn became prominent in the Women's Labor League of Winnipeg in 1918 and 1919 and later served as the league's representative on the province's Minimum Wage Board, which was created in 1918.[20]

Toronto socialists in the SPC in 1909 also favoured woman suffrage, defending it as a weapon against capitalism in the hands of women workers. A resolution favouring suffrage was endorsed, and the Socialist Women's Study Club cooperated with the Canadian Suffrage Association (CSA) in lobbying the Ontario government to extend the ballot to women on the same terms as men. The dissidents from the SPC who formed the SDP passed a resolution in December 1910 advocating amending Toronto's election by-laws to include married women in the electorate and to permit any citizen, property-owner or not, to run for civic office. The former resolution echoed demands made ten years previously in the *Labor Advocate* and by the Local Council of Women, both arguing for women on school boards and for the extension of the municipal franchise to married women.[21]

By 1909, the suffrage work of Flora MacDonald Denison in Toronto, particularly through her column in the *World*, had begun to bear fruit. The labour newspaper, the *Lance*, noted with approval the increased agitation for suffrage based on arguments for justice and representation of women taxpayers. Realizing the potential benefit of good relations with labour, the Toronto suffrage movement launched a campaign to interest working women in the cause. Strong ties developed: by early 1914 labour supported the woman suffrage referendum campaign, led by Dr Margaret Gordon and Harriet Dunlop Prenter, to change the municipal by-laws to allow married women to vote. Despite a clear pro-suffrage victory in the referendum, the provincial legislature rejected a proposed bill on the topic in 1914. The labour movement continued to support the franchise issue throughout the war, sending representatives to meet with the government as well as using the pages of the *Industrial Banner* to promote labour support of woman suffrage. Labour's support for suffrage, however, was tinged with ambiguities at times. Many in the labour movement viewed women through the lens of maternalism, expecting women to clean up politics and promote industrial reforms. While touting the women's vote as a progressive force, the labour movement also viewed women workers as a threat to male workers because the women were a source of cheap labour. These fundamental ambiguities undermined the links between the groups.[22]

As for cooperation between socialists and feminists, despite the resolutions in favour of woman suffrage, socialists were not the main actors in the suffrage campaign. Yet the presence of support from the SDP and individual socialists cannot be dismissed as insignificant, particularly at the grass-roots level. Social democratic women in urban areas publicly supported woman suffrage as a basic democratic right. Toronto's Women's Social Democratic League, an autonomous organization with ties to the SDP, supported the female franchise as did the Independent Labor Party in Ontario. Montreal SDP activist Mrs R.P. Mendelssohn defended socialist support for suffrage, noting that it was unrealistic to expect economic changes without the political participation of women voters. Mendelssohn also promoted the recently established Equal Suffrage League of Montreal as a positive step. At the local level, labour and socialist women demonstrated their commitment to political as well as economic change for women.[23]

## III

Socialists were also divided on the question of separate women's organizations and activities. While the SDP accepted that various interest groups within the party would band together, the SPC treated such attempts with suspicion and hostility. In 1908 controversy over a women's column in the *Western Clarion* highlighted SPC difficulties with separate women's activities within the party. George Weston Wrigley wrote in August to suggest including a women's column in the newspaper. Editor D.G. McKenzie responded in such a way as to touch off a debate that encompassed not only the column, but also the role of women in the party itself. In his response, McKenzie wrote: 'So far as women are concerned while we have a few women comrades, some of who[m] are second to none and a leap or two ahead of most of the men, yet as a general rule, a woman who is a socialist is a socialist because some man is.' By mid-September McKenzie had retreated from the field, as women angrily wrote to denounce him. McKenzie referred the matter to of the women's column to E.T. Kingsley, former editor and a financial supporter of the paper, claiming it was his decision to make. At the same time he bluntly stated his scepticism of female abilities to produce a regular column and warned against modelling any column on the bourgeois press. Female correspondent B.O. Robinson of Toronto condemned the editor for his 'narrow-minded egotism,' warning that male opposition and intolerance would defeat the ultimate goal of socialism, 'for women with the spirit of revolt aroused in them can never be encouraged to join such an obvious man's movement.' Robinson pointed out that socialist propaganda did not appeal to women, especially women workers, and she further asserted that 'it is just as ridiculous to ignore their [women's] position as it would be, say that of the miners or any one particular line of industry.' Thereafter Robinson became involved in organizing a Socialist Women's Study Club in Toronto.[24]

Edith Wrigley of Toronto connected male socialists' indifference to women's problems to women's lack of political power. Until women could vote for socialism, she argued, the SPC would expend no energy on women. Wrigley criticized socialist men because they did not encourage their wives and daughters to participate in SPC activities; the men never took them to meetings, nor did they pay dues for them. Tackling McKenzie's assertion that women only joined the party because of their relationships with socialist men, Wrigley chided McKenzie: 'I have come in contact with women full of the spirit of revolt and very often it is not because some man is a socialist but because of some man she is working for.' She closed her letter with a plea for more equality and democracy in the socialist movement.[25]

Others wrote to the *Clarion* to protest as well. 'A Worker' suggested that socialist men stay home with the children and let their wives go to propaganda meetings. She challenged McKenzie's estimation of socialist womanhood and concluded, 'We want common sense and logical revolution but we want it to. include the working woman's field.' George Weston Wrigley wrote in again to urge a change in party attitudes towards women: men and women were needed in the party to make it 'a two-sex working class movement.' He noted that he had to recommend the United States publication, *Socialist Woman*, to the workingman's wife for lack of other alternatives. Ada Clayton of Victoria, commenting on the controversy over the women's column, wrote that she too recommended the American publication to show the part women could play in the movement. She urged women to send material to the *Clarion*, suggesting that socialism had to address not only the needs of working women, but also the position of married women who received no wages and resented dependence on husbands' wages. She criticized socialist speakers who, in promising merely that men would be able to support their wives and families under socialism, ignored the current of unrest among women. Clayton echoed sentiments similar to those espoused by Bertha Merrill Burns in her We Women columns of several years earlier.[26]

While the SPC declined to act on the agitation for a women's column, in the fall of 1908 *Cotton's Weekly* began such a column, which continued to appear for nearly a year. Published from Cowansville, Quebec, by William U. Cotton, lawyer, prohibitionist, and Christian socialist intellectual, *Cotton's Weekly* remained independent until the war, when it became the official organ of the SDP. Its women's column combined articles on domestic topics with commentaries on the roles of women at home and in the workforce and with appeals for socialism. Mary Cotton Wisdom, sister of William, wrote and edited much of the material and reprinted articles from American and European socialist newspapers. In one of her early pieces, Wisdom appealed 'To the Wives of Workingmen' to recognize the importance of understanding politics and the need for female activism if any change in women's position were to occur. Women no longer needed to follow the conservative idea that men should run their affairs. Her columns encouraged women to speak up for themselves as well as for their men, and they also documented social conditions under capitalism, which she felt might be changed if women had the vote. In May 1909 she recommended that men change places with women for a few years. If women were the only enfranchised group, they would begin government housecleaning immmediately and concentrate on issues relating to the home, children, sanitation, housing, and property. In the spirit of Christian socialist and temperance advocate Frances Willard, Mary Cotton Wisdom stressed suffrage as integral to socialist and feminist activism.[27]

The attitude of *Cotton's Weekly* towards women sharply contrasted with that of the *Western Clarion*. The debates carried on in the pages of these papers reflected the ferment over the woman question within the socialist movement. The years 1908–9 marked a crisis point for public discussion of this question. The divisions over woman suffrage and the women's column were part of a larger debate on the nature of the socialist movement. This debate was also furthered by the influx of ethnic groups into the ranks of the socialist parties. The visible participation of ethnic women in party activities raised the general issue of women's participation in socialist politics.

## IV

Women in the Jewish, Ukrainian, and Finnish communities played important, if heretofore little understood, roles in their ethnic socialist milieux. The activities of these women remain mostly undocumented, except in the Finnish case; however, their important contributions cannot be ignored. While, with few exceptions, the leadership figures of these various ethnic socialist groups were male, activism among the women took various forms: drama groups, sewing circles, ethnic organizations, trade unions, study clubs, and in the male-dominated socialist parties themselves.

### Ukrainian Women

Socialist politics among Ukrainians were dominated by men, who assumed the leadership positions. Nonetheless, there is evidence that

Ukrainian women took active roles in their communities, some urging other Ukrainian women to participate in the movement. Most Ukrainian settlement occurred in the West, and it was here that women's activities were most visible in the prewar period. The Ukrainian socialist press and organizations were centred in major Western cities, especially Winnipeg and, to a lesser extent, Edmonton, Vancouver, and Calgary, and the small mining towns of Alberta and British Columbia. Montreal also contributed to the Ukrainian socialist movement in the prewar years, as did Toronto, Hamilton, Ottawa, Welland, and the Lakehead, the movement in the smaller Ontario cities emerging just before and during the war.[28]

The Ukrainians first formed a branch of the SPC in 1907 in Winnipeg (simultaneously with branches in Portage La Prairie and Nanaimo), where the first Ukrainian socialist newspaper – *Chervonyi Prapor* (Red Flag) – appeared in November 1907. The next month, the newspaper reported on an SPC meeting of the Ukrainian Winnipeg local to deal with municipal elections. The local stood for the eight-hour day, minimum wage legislation, equal suffrage and municipal ownership of electrical power. Support for women's rights, especially suffrage, appeared from time to time in Ukrainian papers.[29]

Ukrainian women on the left took on a variety of activist roles. The arrest of members of Winnipeg's Local 2 prompted a public address by Antonia Jacks at a protest meeting in which she called on the working women of the city to help in the cause. The issue of women's work reappeared a week later, in early January 1908, when 'H. R-kivna' wrote in to rouse the Ukrainian women of Winnipeg to action, noting that about five hundred Ukrainian women were employed in factories, laundries, and restaurant kitchens at poor wages. The solution to such exploitation, she wrote, did not lie in marriage and upward mobility through English husbands, but in working with Ukrainians and abandoning scornful attitudes towards Ukrainian men. Occasionally women from small towns, like Mariyka Osadchuk from Sarto, Manitoba, wrote to urge women to join in the movement, but larger centres like Winnipeg provided more evidence of a female presence: Hanna Stechyshyn (wife of Federation of Ukrainian Social Democrats' leader, Myroslav Stechyshyn) took on responsibilites in the FUSD on committees and on the advisory council of Ukrainian Socialist Publishing Association. Hanna also carried the red flag in Winnipeg's May Day parade in 1909. As new locals of the FUSD were organized, the federation's paper, *Robochyi Narod* (Working People), often reported on the sex composition of the new local, noting with approval the presence of women. In 1911 the newspaper carried articles on prostitution, childrearing, and other issues that appealed to its female readership. The issue of minimum wage laws provided an opportunity for the discussion of what was seen as women's real work – that is, house and children. Ukrainian women were urged to join the SDP to fight for their right to a home and children. Although the lack of protection for women workers was often commented upon in the Ukrainian press, some articles also pointed out that protective laws were created by the capitalists. In the case of minimum wages, one writer noted, such laws would increase exploitation while not forcing capitalists to employ women. The obvious solution was to organize to obtain better legislation. Thus, Ukrainian women were urged to become involved in politics, particularly socialist politics, in order to change oppressive conditions for women workers and to exert greater influence over those areas that affected home life.[30]

This connection between women's domestic roles and politics appeared in the Ukrainian press on the eve of the war. A number of writers linked childrearing, cooking, and cleaning to larger political questions, such as the need for involvement in schools, municipal health, and even issues of national importance such as tariff policies, since all affected home life: 'The house isn't an island hidden away from the world, but a part of society.' Yavloha Pynduse, a Montreal Ukrainian woman, wrote *Robochyi Narod* in early 1914, stressing that the working class 'doesn't consist only of men, but of whole families ... They're all sufferers and they all need to fight for a better future.' Pynduse criticized a socialist movement without women because it lacked the rage, the emotion, and the family love that motivated the struggle for change: 'We women, we girls are those who pour the magic potion of courage into these fighters' hearts,' she wrote. Urging women to join social democratic organizations, she claimed that it was only the socialist movement that sought to free women from their social enslavement. Women who ignored the struggle became enemies of their class and of themselves. Because women 'are stamped on by the capitalists a hundred times worse than men,' their place should be in the ranks of social democracy with men. This theme of women's indifference about the struggle also informed Anna Novakovska's 1914 letter to the paper. It contained a call to women workers to recognize their servitude and the importance of their labour power as a source of strength. She urged women workers to stand on an even footing with male workers and to replace religious reading with socialist and educational works. Since women 'play an even bigger role in life than do men, ... we should prove we're really equal to men.' This, according to Novakovska, was the way to win more respect.[31]

Despite these urgings, women were not highly visible in the Ukrainian socialist movement at the leadership levels. Other activities undertaken by women remain largely invisible, although there clearly were supportive tasks performed by women. Reports of newly organized locals suggest that women's involvement varied substantially from place to place. In April 1914, women in Winnipeg participated in the founding and running of an amateur theatre circle, which presented plays on topics of working-class interest. Cultural activities were important features of ethnic working-class life and politics. Concerts, choral recitals, and theatrical performances reinforced group identity and also carried political messages to the audience. Anne Woywitka has described such cultural activities in Cardiff, Alberta, in the early war period, noting the important leadership given by Teklia Chaban, a miner's wife. Winnipeg's Ukrainian theatre no doubt served similar purposes in Ukrainian socialist circles. Other ethnic groups such as the Finns and the Jews also organized such undertakings in which women were very active participants.[32]

*Jewish Women*

According to the census, the Jewish population of Canada was somewhat larger than the Ukrainian. Despite the larger numbers and the urban concentration of the Jewish population, little research has been published on Jewish radicals, and especially on Jewish women radicals, before the 1920s when the Communist Party attracted many women. The major Jewish settlements were in Montreal, Toronto, and Winnipeg, and a majority of Jews worked in the needle trades in these cities and were active in the various garment workers' unions. While women garment workers in the United States produced a number of well-known Jewish leaders, few Canadian women rose to such prominent positions. The lack of indigenous leadership accounted for the tendency of the garment workers' unions to send American women to Canada when large strikes were waged in Canadian cities.[33]

Jewish women were active in the socialist movements of the major urban areas in which they lived. Montreal's SDP in the prewar and war years featured the active participation of Mrs R.P. Mendelssohn and Becky Buhay, among others. Buhay would become one of the major women leaders of the Communist Party of Canada after the war. Toronto's Jewish women in the prewar period are less well-known, although they are described as early as 1907 as active workers for the SPC. Organizer Wilf Gribble noted that the Jewish branch of the party, organized in late 1905, was the most active and most international in outlook; he particularly commended the women for their active work in branch affairs, and contrasted the retiring behaviour of women in the English branch with their Jewish and Finnish sisters. During the war years, Jewish women were also active in the Women's Social Democratic League, although the leaders were usually native Canadians or emigrants from the British Isles. In Toronto, as elsewhere, Jewish women established women's organizations to provide poor relief, put on plays and recitals, and provide other services. A socialist Sunday school was organized in Toronto in 1911, the first in Canada. Supported by the Jewish socialists along with their Finnish, Italian, and English comrades, the school sought to counteract the information students received in capitalist schools by teaching socialist views of economics, science, and history. Similarly, women were involved in the creation in Toronto of a Young Jewish Workers' Club in 1916, which combined physical culture and mental and moral development with debates and fundraising for strikes and political campaigns.[34]

Winnipeg's Jewish radical women were involved in similar activities – usually through the SDP, which had a women's branch. The local Jewish press of the period also indicates that some Jewish women involved themselves in the suffrage campaign and some belonged to the Women's Labor League in the city. Young women were involved in organizations like the Young Jewish Literary Association, and a number of women worked with the Young Socialist Club, founded in 1913 by Jews. The club attracted young women such as sixteen-year-old Rose Gonevitch, who chaired a meeting of a hundred young people in 1914, exhibiting 'remarkable talent' according to one observer. The club seemed to flourish, celebrating its fourth anniversary in 1917, and its success in Winnipeg's North End led to discussions of starting a similar organization among English-speaking young people.[35]

Jewish socialist women were consistently concerned with educational matters in the 1910s. Rose Alcin, later to run as a labour candidate in the 1919 Winnipeg school board elections, came from an anarchist background. She became involved on the committee to set up the Jewish Radical School, which opened in May 1914. In addition, when a major rift occurred in the school over nationalism and language in 1916, Alcin served as assistant superintendent of the SDP's socialist Sunday school, which opened in October 1916, after the more internationalist and left-wing members had abandoned the Jewish Radical School. Also involved in the Sunday school was SDP member Sara Zeimanovich, who often gave lectures to the children on subjects such as history. Others involved in this effort, largely run by the women's branch of the SDP, were Mrs Jake Penner (although not of Jewish background) and Mrs William Baum, whose husbands were prominent socialists.[36]

This brief survey indicates the important presence of women in Jewish radical circles, while also suggesting the need for closer study of these women in the three major urban centres where Jewish settlement concentrated. While Ruth Frager's work on Toronto has opened up Jewish women's history on the left, most of her evidence is richest on the 1920s and 1930s. Nevertheless, it suggests how Jewish immigrant women from Eastern Europe drew on a culture that stressed women's strengths and a commitment to fight class oppression and anti-Semitism. While this culture remained patriarchal in essence, it did not restrict women to the home, and Jewish women played important roles in the market place and in the paid labour force.[37]

*Finnish Women*

In Canada, as in the United States, immigrant women from Finland played a proportionately larger role in the socialist movement than any other ethnic group. Buhle estimates that upwards of 35 per cent of Finnish socialists in the United States were women. While national estimates for Canada's Finnish socialist population by gender do not appear in major studies to date, scattered community-level evidence suggests a similarly high involvement by Finnish women in Canada.[38]

Finnish settlement in Canada began in earnest at the turn of the century, with Finnish men and women tending to settle in Toronto, the Lakehead, Northern Ontario, parts of the prairie West, and in the small mining towns in Alberta and British Columbia. A significant colony of Finns also migrated to Vancouver Island's mining towns, in addition to those who settled in the utopian community of Sointula. Itinerant workers, who took up seasonal occupations in the woods or on the railways, accounted for a large proportion of the Finnish male population. Finnish women who emigrated to Canada to find work were employed largely as domestic servants. Many of these women came to Toronto initially and found work with the help of Finnish community contacts and the job exchange and social centre run by a Mrs Anderson. Domestic work provided employment and the opportunity to learn English, sometimes in a working-class home or boarding house or in the home of a wealthy Canadian family.[39]

Finnish women were attracted to the Finnish halls in their communities, not only for social contacts and leisure activities, but also for politics. The social democratic tradition in Finland meant that young Finnish immigrants had some familiarity with socialism. A 1910 survey among the Finnish community in Toronto revealed that more than half described themselves as socialists. Women were vocal and active members of the SPC, organizing a sub-branch that claimed thirty-eight members in Toronto in 1907. Women also joined sewing circles, some of them connected to the halls or the SPC, where the women discussed politics as well as performing the role of an auxiliary to the party. While domestic duties and male dominance often limited what women could accomplish in the socialist movement, occasionally the movement produced a woman leader willing to accept the hardships of socialist agitation work. Prominent among the Finns was the exceptional Sanna Kannasto, who became a paid organizer for the SPC in the prewar years.[40]

Finnish women's participation in the SPC extended to the smaller mining towns in Canada. A Finnish annual published at Christmas 1910 contains detailed information on one coal-mining town on Vancouver Island. Ladysmith's Finnish population of 232 included 74 men and 52 women as well as 106 children. Of these, thirty-two (including eleven women) belonged to the Finnish socialist local in 1910, down considerably from the forty-four members (twenty women) the previous year. These figures compare well with estimates made of women's participation elsewhere and suggest the importance of Finnish women to the movement. Ladysmith's socialist local sponsored family socials and outdoor festivals and plays, as well as publishing occasional issues of the 'fist press' – handwritten newspapers that were passed around the community. The fist press appeared in many Finnish communities, including Edmonton, where *Moukari* (Sledgehammer) announced the activities of the recently formed sewing circle among the women. The anonymous writer confirmed that the purpose of the circle was to aid the Socialist Party materially in the socialist cause.[41]

Finnish sewing circles demonstated the potential adaptations women could make in their own domestic culture. Sewing provided the entrance point for women into a broader socialist movement and exposed them to ideas and debate. The program of Sointula's sewing

circle, for example, included a speech, poetry, and story recital, a topic
for discussion, and singing. Between 1911 and 1915, Sointula's sewing
circle followed this program, attracting ten members to meetings; about
twenty others sewed for the sales that helped to pay for the Finnish hall
but did not participate in programs. The women discussed material in
*Toveritar* (Woman Comrade), the Finnish-American women's paper, and
elected correspondents to write to the paper. Other discussion topics
included women's rights and legal disabilities. The sewing circle in
Rossland, British Columbia, used profits to support those in need, while
hotly debating which socialist party the circle should affiliate with. The
decision to join the SPC caused much discontent. Sewing circles often
put on plays and organized women's day celebrations. Anna Lehto
wrote to *Toveritar* in 1916 that Toronto's Finnish women were celebrating
international women's day by distributing the paper free, with speeches
and songs by female performers, as well as other entertainments. In
June 1916 Laura Autio reported that the Toronto circle had made $200,
proving that women were of value. Sault Ste Marie's sewing circle discussed the possibility of putting on a play called *The Female Slave* in
order to raise money for a sick and destitute woman whose husband
was serving time for raping his step-daughter. The sewing circles thus
provided the movement with concrete monetary support and assisted
destitute or ill families in the Finnish community.[42]

The strong showing of Finnish women in radical circles may reflect
partially on the amount of research carried out by scholars in the field.
Similarly the strong social democratic tradition in Finland and the relatively early achievement of woman suffrage in that country may also
help to explain why Finnish women seem to have been more outspoken
than their Jewish or Ukrainian counterparts. A third factor is the presence of *Toveritar*, the Finnish women's newspaper in the United States,
which circulated across the border and provided Finnish women with
discussion material and a focus for debate. In this period neither the
Jews nor the Ukrainians had a woman's paper that addressed working-
class and socialist women. The presence of a women's column or of a
separate women's newspaper furthered the discussion of women's
issues within the class struggle and allowed for the questioning of
socialist positions on relevant issues. As early as 1902, Hulda Anderson,
then living on Malcolm Island at Sointula, argued for the necessity of a
woman's magazine for the enlightenment of women. Despite SPA
approval of such a newspaper in early 1909, the first issue of *Toveritar*
did not appear until two years later. It served as an invaluable forum for

Finnish women, discussing topics that varied from domestic matters to working women's concerns to controversial issues such as prostitution and birth control.[43]

## V

Between 1904 and 1914 the major role for women socialists was a supportive one involving key activities that contributed to the growth of the movement. Fundraising and soliciting subscriptions to the socialist press occupied women in every part of the country. Ethnic women's voluntary organizations often staged dramatic or musical performances as well as sponsoring sewing circles and sales of women's crafts to raise money. These techniques were also used by native-born and British women, and socialist women usually provided their organizing skills and domestic talents for social events sponsored by the local socialist community. Whether general social events such as dances, whist drives, or summer picnics, or special celebrations to commemorate May Day, Labour Day, or the anniversary of the Paris Commune, women pitched in to help. Occasionally a social event aimed at recruiting more women comrades. Visiting speakers, often from the United States, attracted both men and women, the latter responding particularly to the novelty of a woman orator. Well-known women socialists and social reformers such as Elizabeth Gurley Flynn, May Wood Simons, or Charlotte Perkins Gilman were especially effective in attracting women to meetings.[44]

Other activities initiated by women included study groups and reading circles to provide women with a basic socialist education but also to discuss the position of women, past and present. Toronto's SPC women organized a Socialist Woman's Study Club in September 1908, which continued to meet until the next summer. E.M. Epplett outlined the work of the study group, noting that in order to understand the position of women in capitalist society and their status in previous stages of development, the group began with Engels's *Origin of the Family, Private Property, and the State*, later reading other socialist works. A dozen women attended regularly once a week, contributing funds to buy books. As Epplett noted, 'as working women we have double chains to lose.' A similar undertaking occurred in Vancouver, and Toronto's Women's Social Democratic League later sponsored a reading circle for its members.[45]

Toronto's SDP women were active participants in the creation of that organization; at the 1911 Ontario convention, three of thirty-two delegates were Toronto women. Mrs Edith Bellemare, former secretary of the SPC's Toronto Local 1, had taken part in the debates of 1910 over the Dominion Executive Committee's action in expelling a large number of SPC members. Of Mrs Crawford, the second delegate, little is known. The third, Elizabeth Nesbitt, was associated with the socialist Sunday school. Other SDP women were also politically active. For example, another socialist Sunday school activist, Mrs Elizabeth Crockett, contested several elections for the SDP. In late 1912 she ran for city council on the Political Action Committee ticket, a coalition group composed of the SDP, the ILP, and the Toronto TLC. In 1914 the SDP nominated Crockett for the Board of Education in Ward 1 and Florence Fraser in Ward 5. The SDP, unlike the SPC, encouraged women to organize their own branches of the party, thus allowing women more scope to develop their own agendas. In British Columbia, women's branches of the SDP were widespread enough to require a provincial secretary. In the fall of 1913, Bertha Merrill Burns was elected provincial secretary of the women's organizations, and all locals were instructed to elect committees for women's organization. In 1914 several women held prominent positions within the SDP: Mrs Helen Christopher of Victoria was Provincial Women's Organization Secretary, Mrs Edmonds of Vancouver was provincial secretary for the Young Peoples' Socialist League, and Ada Clayton and Bertha M. Burns were secretaries of the Victoria and Vancouver locals of the SDP respectively.[46]

Toronto's Women's Social Democratic League (WSDL) was formed in September 1914 to aid in propaganda and educational work among women in the socialist and labour movements. The executive included Edith Bellemare, Mrs May Young, and Mrs Lucy MacGregor; Young later ran in Ward 4 for school trustee and MacGregor became involved in the Toronto Women's Labor League (WLL) and helped organize women workers into unions. The WSDL was officially launched in October with a speech by the Reverend W.E.S. James in which he outlined why the organization was necessary. Women were needed primarily to be the wives, mothers, and sweethearts of socialists, he claimed, but they also needed to organize to articulate working-class demands and to help realize the ideal of woman in the cooperative commonwealth. The WSDL cooperated with James's Church of the Social Revolution, using its facilities for a reading circle. The group also maintained ties with the Christian Socialist Fellowship group in Toronto. The Toronto WSDL, which began with thirty members, envisioned itself as the nucleus for similar groups 'to be extended into every town and city in Ontario.' Writing in 1916, Gertrude Mance noted that the WSDL was open to all progressive women since it was not a party branch, but an autonomous organization. Debates sponsored by the group were not open to men, although lectures, socials, and fundraising events were. WSDL efforts, nevertheless, helped to clear the SDP's debts in 1916, and a Christmas bazaar that same year provided funds for the party newspaper, the municipal election campaign fund, and for various Jewish organizations, as well as for the WSDL itself. The organization carried on a vigorous schedule of activities throughout the war and beyond.[47]

## VI

By and large, the socialist movement looked to men to perform the task of organizing new locals of the SPC or the SDP in the prewar period. Women speakers and activists were less rare than women organizers, and most large urban areas could count on some women to give lectures or speeches. Vancouver, Victoria, and Toronto in particular produced women leaders in the early days of the movement. These women remained active, and their numbers were augmented as the movement grew before the the First World War. Party organizing work proved more difficult for women, for both material and ideological reasons. The peripatetic lifestyle of a socialist organizer meant enormous difficulties for married women with children to care for and husbands who might object to their long absences from home. Because of the contested terrain of gender ideology, women faced significant prejudice not only about their abilities but also, more basically, about the desirability of their organizing for the party. Despite these difficulties, some women performed such work, some as partners of socialist organizers and some on their own.

For women who shared organizing activities with a partner, the lifestyle was not as problematic. SPC couples such as Sarah Johnston-Knight and Joe Knight and Ruth and Charles Lestor worked together at times. Ruth Lestor, a British emigrant to Canada, accompanied her organizer husband on his travels and spoke to the women comrades, a not uncommon role for the female half of couples who organized for the party. In summer 1909, speaking on 'woman's place,' Lestor argued that a woman's class position was of paramount concern because sex was not the chief factor determining women's industrial position. The capitalist hired the cheapest and most efficient worker, regardless of sex, she argued. Reiterating the position of other party speakers, Lestor observed that socialist women had to pay special attention to the housewife who had a narrower outlook than her working sister. On the suffrage issue, Lestor differed with party views, arguing that working women's political power would assist in the overthrow of capitalism. Private property was the source of female oppression, and women needed socialism even more than men because they suffered more under the capitalist system. By 1911 Ruth Lestor had become quite critical of SPC women, and was pessimistic about women in general, pointing to their cruelty, superstition, and intellectual backwardness. Such views were perhaps in reaction to the factional fighting that had led to breakaways from the SPC. Her anger reflected her increasing isolation from the women in the party: 'I rarely found one of my own sex worth talking to,' she complained. While her husband continued to organize, Ruth Lestor's own organizing career was curtailed by illness and the birth of two children. Described as 'one of the best lady speakers of the SPC,' she disappeared from the public eye after 1911. In 1915, Charles Lestor left the SPC but appears to have rejoined by 1917 when the *Western Clarion* reported him in an Alaskan jail, sentenced to a year's imprisonment for unpatriotic statements, leaving his wife and two children dependent on the movement.[48]

Two other women organizers achieved a considerable reputation within socialist ranks in the prewar period: Sophie Mushkat (later McClusky) and Sanna Kallio (later Kannasto). Both were immigrants to Canada in the first decade of the twentieth century; both began their organizing work while single; and both continued their work after marrying, although Mushkat temporarily disappeared after her marriage to homestead with her husband in Alberta. Each woman had one child; and each had close connections with the Communist Party in later life. While there are gaps in their biographies, enough information exists to trace their organizing careers for significant periods of time.[49]

Born in Vasa province in Finland in 1878, Sanna Kallio was one of seven children in a poor farming family and came to the United States in 1899 with two sisters before moving to Canada. She joined the Socialist Party in 1905 and was elected a temporary organizer for the eastern section in June 1907. Based in Port Arthur, Ontario, Kallio toured the United States and Canada for sixteen months after her election as organizer, founding Finnish socialist locals. She was a delegate to the Ontario provincial convention of the SPC in September 1908, along with two other women, Edith Wrigley and a Miss Sowini. Working under the direction of the Toronto and Port Arthur locals, Kallio spent the next few months organizing Ontario Finns. In early 1909 an illness brought her to a Finnish hospital in Michigan; on her journey home the next month, she stopped to speak in Sault Ste Marie. Kallio entered into a 'free' marriage with Finnish socialist J.V. Kannasto, and they had a son, Jussi, the birth of whom perhaps accounts for her sporadic activity in the next few years.[50]

By 1913 Sanna Kannasto again took on organizing work for the Finnish socialist cause, beginning a western organizing tour in August. According to the discussion at a Finnish Socialist Organization of Canada (FSOC) meeting in March 1914 in Port Arthur, she was the only one of the party's organizers who fulfilled the requirements of a speaker who was well-versed in Canadian conditions, with an understanding of the state and the development of industry, and a knowledge of working-class life. Her efforts in the farming communities of the West had produced a number of locals, and her next organizing tour was to cover Ontario. At the Port Arthur meeting Kannasto spoke against dividing the country into districts, claiming that the opening of new rail lines made longer trips easier to organize. Socialist organizers, she noted, had to be lecturers on a variety of topics, but the message should be the same whether the audience consisted of farmers or urban workers.[51]

Despite her assurances that train travel would be relatively easy, Kannasto's later letters to J.W. Ahlqvist, secretary of the FSOC, documented the difficulties of holding meetings because of train schedules in Northern Ontario. She also sent Ahlqvist regular reports about the audiences and the hardships of some of the journeys, as well as detailed accounts of money collected and spent. Earning three dollars a day for her organizing, Kannasto sometimes instructed that her salary be sent home to pay her mortgage. In some places the Finnish community dared not organize a meeting or provide her with accommodation because of anticipated repercussions. Writing from Worthington, Sanna explained that no one would give her a place to stay in the town and she had to stay a mile and a half away at a farm owned by 'foreigners.' After the outdoor meeting, she reported back to Ahlqvist, 'I do not know whether anyone comes to hear. The people here have become pressed down to slavery.'

The working conditions of a socialist organizer were harsh and discouraging. In June 1914 Kannasto wrote from Naughton, Ontario, complaining of the lack of cleanliness, the bedbugs, and black-flies. In November she reported that she had an eleven-mile walk from the meeting in Finland, Ontario, to her living quarters outside the town. In general she noted the difficulty of visiting such places because of travel problems, the need to find a place to stay, and the necessity of walking to various scattered communities of Finns. Even then 'one cannot expect much support because of poverty and ignorance.' During a trip to New Finland, Saskatchewan, Kannasto had to report running out of money and borrowing from the party local there. Requests for her presence in some of the smaller communities nearby were thwarted by bad roads and inconvenient train schedules. Occasionally she could not speak as planned because the local hall was booked or the organizers had forgotten about her visit. Communication problems sometimes resulted in failure of local representatives to meet her train. On more than one occasion she was left wandering in the countryside, lost, alone, and ill from lack of food and accommodation. A winter visit to Makama, Ontario, through the snow and woods meant fatigue and wet clothes: 'I am suffering from great internal pains. The cold and the rather poor food must have been their causes. The life here is miserable as most everybody is oppressed by poverty. In other respects, Socialism is now easy to spread,' she wrote to Ahlqvist in January 1915. Later that same month from Port Arthur she thanked him for a cheque because she had only one American penny to her name.[53]

Letters detailing Kannasto's organizing trips continued until the summer of 1916. Her experiences reflected the continuing hardships of the itinerant organizer, yet she detailed the dozens of meetings she spoke at and the hundreds of listeners who came from widely spread out Finnish settlements to hear her speak. Her topics included idealism and materialism in history; principles of socialism; revisionism and radicalism; realism and individualism; scientific socialism; and the theory of class struggle. Her letters almost always asked after friends and sometimes their children, with an occasional mention of her own son or brother, but rarely of her husband. Tension had existed between Sanna and her husband in earlier years over her organizing trips. The lifestyle and hardships of the itinerant organizer precluded much family life, but on this subject she said little. By 1920, however, her relationship with J.V. Kannasto was over.[54]

Sanna Kannasto continued to organize for the Finnish left until 1930 in Canada and the United States. In a letter she wrote in her eighties, she recalled that she had been a political prisoner in both countries. She was convicted of an offence in the United States that would have cost her twenty years in prison had her appeal not been successful. Her deportation to Canada led to imprisonment for ten months. She claimed that, during her incarceration, she was tortured at RCMP headquarters in Lethbridge and was left with partial paralysis in her right foot and wrist. But, as she defiantly wrote, her soul was not paralyzed. Canadian officials failed in an attempt to deport Kannasto in 1920. While not much is known about her later activities, clearly in the prewar and war period she was a committed organizer and leading spokesperson for Finnish socialism in Canada.[55]

A contemporary of Ṣanna Kannasto was Polish-Russian immigrant Sophie Mushkat. Born in Warsaw in 1887, Sophie arrived in Canada in 1903 or 1904. By 1909 she emerged as a speaker for the SPC in Moncton, where she, her father, William Mushkat, and friend Fanny Levy formed the core of the socialist movement. A visit from Roscoe Fillmore, of Albert, New Brunswick, helped to launch both the socialist movement in Moncton and Sophie Mushkat's organizing and speaking career. In August 1909, Fillmore reported that 'the lady comrades can talk plain, straight socialism without ever once mentioning ice cream, bon-bons, directoire gowns or peach-basket hats.' Described by Fillmore as 'a Russian revolutionist and true blue,' Mushkat gave speeches and assisted Wilf Gribble in his eastern organizing tour. Gribble reported that he had difficulty finding any English-speaking socialists, but found some Jewish comrades with Mushkat's help. A Labour Day celebration in Moncton gave the socialists an audience for a street meeting, but was disrupted by hecklers. The disturbance prompted the socialists to prosecute one of the perpetrators, and the resulting trial testimony featured Mushkat as one of the key witnesses. When questioned about her background and beliefs, she said that she was a proud member of the SPC, although had not been a member of any radical society in Russia before she emigrated. Mushkat continued to organize and speak throughout the fall and winter of 1909–10. When Big Bill Haywood of the Industrial Workers of the World spoke in Moncton at the end of November, Mushkat also addressed the crowd. In February 1910, she visited Newcastle, home of H.H. Stuart, socialist preacher and activist in the New Brunswick teacher's association. Speaking at Temperance Hall, she discussed temperance and prohibition from the socialist point of view, tying the drink problem to poverty and capitalism. The audience of twenty-six men and nine women were described as attentive as she explained to several ministers the flaws in profit-sharing plans and the differences between socialism, materialism, and anarchism. In his scrapbook, H.H. Stuart noted beside the newspaper clipping about the meeting that 'Miss Mushkat – [Russian-Jewish] stayed at our house one night, sat up with Eileen ($2\frac{1}{2}$) who was very ill.'

By March 1910, Mushkat was embroiled in the Springhill miners' struggles, speaking with Fillmore to large audiences, including hundreds of women, on the duty of women in the labour movement. Returning to Springhill in July, at the height of strike tensions over the use of scabs in the mines, Mushkat was harassed by a company thug who refused to let her speak to a Polish woman. Despite this intimidation, she spoke on revolutionary socialism in Springhill on the same platform as Roscoe Fillmore. Described as 'the Mother Jones of the Canadian Socialist movement,' Sophie Mushkat was admired for her uncompromising commitment to socialism and her courage in adverse circumstances.[57]

Later in 1910, for unknown reasons, Sophie moved west, where she remained for almost twenty years. She first lived in Winnipeg, where she taught English to immigrants. By 1913 she had commenced an organizing tour for Alberta's SPC, which covered the mining towns of southern Alberta and British Columbia. Between 28 April and 10 June 1913 she reported speaking at thirty-three English and ten Polish meetings. In the fall Mushkat spoke in the Fort William area in Ontario before proceeding east to New Brunswick for a visit. By early 1914 she returned to the West, touring northern and central Alberta where she visited settlements with strong Russian components as well as farming areas. She held a total of fourteen meetings, at which she spoke on the hardships of homesteading and the farmers' relationship to the working class. By the fall of 1914 Mushkat had settled in Calgary and was earning her living as a teacher and serving as provincial secretary of the SPC.[58]

At this time she became involved in an organization of the unemployed that worked in conjunction with the Calgary TLC. The Unemployed Committee in Calgary resembled similar committees formed elsewhere in the country, serving as an umbrella coalition for labour and social reform groups intent on pressuring the various levels of government to provide work. Mushkat represented the Unemployed Committee in November 1914 at a conference called to discuss the unemployment situation with business and government representatives. This conference passed resolutions that demanded public works projects and relief funds from the federal and provincial governments to be administered by the municipalities during the coming winter. Mushkat was vocal in her arguments that the federal government should levy taxes for relief, just as they were doing for the war. She noted that the government needed recruits, and asked, 'Where are you going to get them if you are going to starve them?'

Mushkat continued to work for the SPC as an organizer while teaching English to immigrants, and on her Christmas holidays she travelled between Calgary and Edmonton speaking for the SPC. This pattern continued until August 1915 when the DEC confirmed the Alberta PEC's decision to expell Mushkat for her part in the Alberta prohibition campaign. Her expulsion apparently did not slow her down because in September the *Western Clarion* reported on her activities in the Alberta mining towns of Hillcrest and Bellevue, organizing for the John Reid Defence Fund. Sophie's marriage to socialist William McClusky in January 1916 and their move to a homestead at Berry Creek, however, diminished her activities, as did the birth of daughter, Laberta. After the war, in the early 1920s, Sophie's activities for the SPC, the Workers' Party, and the unemployed brought her to the attention of the RCMP. From these and later reports it appears that Sophie remained very outspoken in her views, frequently alienating those who disagreed with her. Later she would return to the Maritimes to settle in Halifax, maintaining her old ties with socialists such as Roscoe Fillmore.[60]

These examples of women organizers in the socialist movement illustrate the very real difficulties women faced within the movement. For some, like Ruth Lestor, illness, childbirth, and domestic responsibilities hampered an organizing career. For Sanna Kallio Kannasto and Sophie Mushkat McClusky, their organizing careers overshadowed other responsibilities, although there were occasions when family and domestic duties claimed precedence. Tensions with spouses led to difficulties and conflicts. McClusky separated from her husband, yet she was not completely free to pursue her political aims. In 1931 she wrote Communist Party leader, Tim Buck, to inquire about how to offer her services to the Soviet Union. Having met the radical writer and supporter of the Soviet Union, Anna Louise Strong, in Winnipeg in 1925, she was persuaded that she could do useful work in the USSR since she spoke several languages and had experience in poultry raising, farm and small business management, and teaching. She noted, however, some opposition from her husband: 'My husband would not allow me to move the child, and I did not feel like leaving her in a position that might mean parting with my only child forever ... Now my daughter is in my custody and I feel to a degree independent of master and slave.' In a postscript she added, 'I could take my daughter with me. She is 14 very bright and healthy ... could help with english [correspondence?] between school hours if necessary.' In Sanna Kannasto's case, her son may well have been brought up by her brother's family, who lived in the Port Arthur area. Clearly, the material difficulties and dilemmas of motherhood affected both women's organizing careers and marital relationships. The male socialist model of itinerant organizing proscribed this path for the majority of socialist women.[61]

The ideology of sex differences played a more general role in the socialist movement, which displayed an ambivalent attitude towards women. On the one hand, women were encouraged to assist in the movement and use their domestic talents in the cause. On the other hand, acceptance of biological and social differences between the sexes pervaded socialist thought and action, limiting the types of roles acceptable for women to play. While some male socialists viewed the participation of women as key to success, others were forthrightly suspicious of, or hostile to, women in the movement. The misogyny of Saskatchewan socialist Alf Budden was not common. Budden wrote in 1910 that 'he holds the whole fair sex (except one) under suspicion.' He accused women of burning the *Western Clarion* before their husbands returned home and believed that women were more superstitious than men. When Ruth Lestor wrote a critical article about prairie socialists, Budden responded with threats, reiterating his suspicion of all women, adding that he might challenge her husband to a fight.[62]

Much more common in socialist writing about women was the denial that women could be equal to men because of biology. An unsigned article on 'sex equality' in 1911 insisted that there is 'no foundation in fact to the sex equality upon which the feminists insist and no reality to the sex war as some of them proclaim.' The writer stated baldly that women made slow progress not only because of their upbringing and environment, but also because of 'the deeper reason of their biological femaleness,' which condemned them to passivity and conservatism. Another writer, W.W. Lefeaux, observed that while emancipation from wage slavery would probably benefit women more than men, women, because of their upbringing and their acquiescent nature, would be slower to pursue change. Women might accept the benefits of a new social order once they understood it, but they certainly would not lead the fight for such change. These biological and evolutionary views permeated the socialist movement, affecting socialist attitudes, not only towards suffrage, women's autonomous organizations, and women as organizers, but also towards women's work in the home and in the labour force.[63]

## VII

An essential component in the attitudes and actions of the socialist movement regarding women was the socialist conception of the role of women's paid labour force activity and its relationship to the family. While an occasional writer in the socialist press thought otherwise, male and female writers on the subject usually agreed that women's paid work threatened men's jobs, a position shared by the trade union movement. The *BC Federationist*, for example, in the years immediately preceding the war, pointed to the low wages paid to women, particularly in Vancouver, and the failure of both women and unions to organize the female labour force to improve the situation for women and to eliminate competition between men and women in the labour market. The SPC's critical position on trade unions was undercut by the fact that most of its members, nevertheless, belonged to unions. The SDP espoused participation in unions and disagreed with the SPC's attitude on this question. Both parties, however, shared certain perspectives on women's work and its relationship to the family.[64]

According to the socialist view, women and children were driven from the home into the labour market because the male wage earner could not support the family. The need for several incomes to maintain the family allowed capitalists to lower wages, and women and children competed in the labour market with men. Socialists repeated this theme over and over again. In defending their beliefs against charges of 'free love,' they argued that capitalism, and not socialism, was destroying the family by making female and child labour necessary: wages were being lowered to the point where marriage for many men and women remained an impossibility.[65]

In reply to the often-asked question concerning the position of women under socialism, writers in the socialist press stressed that women would be economically independent in a socialist system and that this independence would alter the relations between men and women, thus raising women to the status of comrade and equal partner. But the socialist application of economic independence for women apparently varied according to marital status and whether or not a woman had children. Family responsibilities were pre-eminent in the case of married women, and thus the family wage ideal was key.[66]

While some socialists defended a married woman's paid work as integral to her independence, most commentators stressed the evils of the paid labour of both children and married women and accepted the family wage ideal, that is, the male breadwinner's primary responsibility to provide for all members of the family. 'Gourock,' for example, stated this position most clearly in 1908: 'Socialists don't believe in mothers working at all. They hold that under a sage industrial system wherein the worker would obtain the full value of his products, the man could earn sufficient to raise and maintain his family under proper conditions and that various exigencies which may arise, such as sickness and accident, be provided against by the community.' Another writer promised that 'your wife will no longer have to leave the baby at the creche on her way to the factory.' While some commentators allowed women a choice in the matter, the expectation was clear that married women would choose not to work. Given the conditions and wages for women workers in prewar Canada, the socialist position is understandable. Nonetheless, the emphasis on marriage, motherhood, and the family wage served to restrict female potential. Motherhood was presented as woman's true vocation, and freedom of choice as to marriage partner emerged as the socialist conception of women's future economic independence. Women need not marry for bread, as they did under capitalism. Once women were economically independent under socialism, they would marry on the basis of love and free choice and 'Let the Best Men Win!'[67]

In the socialist future, maternity would be elevated to its proper place, and the state would provide the best possible maternal care. A number of writers speculated that married women would cease to be drudges once municipal or state-run laundries, bakeries, kitchens, and kindergartens were in place. Mary Cotton Wisdom noted the double burden of working-class women: while the men were agitating for the eight-hour day, their wives often put in sixteen-hour days and had to deal with the needs of infants in the evenings. She urged men to pitch in and help their wives, and she described socialism as meaning honour for mothers and a lightening of their workload. A clerical advocate of socialism described the true home under socialism in terms of 'love ... innocent childhood ... work enough ... leisure for reading and study and recreation ... all the comforts and none of its harmful luxuries.' The ideal socialist home and family included children brought up with collective values and freed from the necessity to labour.[68]

Condemnation of child labour came from middle-class reformers as well as working-class leaders, often for different reasons. While reformers feared the effects of child labour on children and their families and the potential for crime, ignorance, and social disorder, the working-class and socialist movements stressed the harm done to working-class male breadwinners as well. In 1891, 'Workingmen Their Own Worst Enemies' commented on the blindness of workingmen to the effects of child and married women's labour on their wages and their family life. Exclusion of such low-waged workers from the labour market would give working-men a chance to fight for decent wages sufficient for the entire family. Consumer goods produced by the cheap labour of women and children cost more than the public realized because they did not consider the exploited labour that went into the product. Child labour was linked to poverty in working-class families. Class differences in access to employment and a living wage meant that the working-class child, unlike more affluent children, could not count on education or medical attention, or even adequate food and shelter. The results of such a disadvantaged environment concerned socialists. Roscoe Fillmore used the example of slum children, who could not escape from such an environment 'as they have not inherited the necessary strength from parents who were themselves degenerates and weaklings,' to argue that heredity and environment could only be overcome with a fundamental social change – socialism. Moncton socialist Fanny Levy recalled a woman and child coming into the dry goods store she ran with the Mushkats, to buy cheap rubbers. The eight-year-old girl had to stay home to do housework while her mother went out to clean to earn their bread. Like thousands of other poor children, the child could not go to school. Compulsory schooling laws, Levy noted, would not address the problem of want.[69]

More immediate solutions to the problem of child labour and poverty among working-class children were proposed by socialist and labour spokespersons. While the SPC rejected proposals to take up the work of spreading socialist ideas among children, the SDP encouraged the creation of Young Socialist groups and Sunday schools. Ameliorative measures such as pensions for poor children and improved medical provisions in schools were urged by socialist and labour groups as one way of providing working-class children with at least a minimal standard of care their parents could not afford. In the West, Francis Marion Beynon used her column in the *Grain Growers' Guide* to press for more education for rural children, disputing the wisdom of withdrawing children from school to assist with harvesting and threshing. The realities of survival on the family farm, as well as in urban working-class communities, usually prevented the realization of such goals. Still, socialists, particularly in the SDP, encouraged children and youth to become active in their own organizations or branches of the party. Children were the socialists of the future, and the early inculcation of socialist principles could not be ignored. Critical of bourgeois organizations like the Boy Scouts, socialists developed their own youth organizations to counter such groups.[70]

During the 1909–11 Springhill miners' strike in Nova Scotia, children of striking miners refused to attend school with the children of scabs, necessitating the intervention of the province's attorney general. When his efforts were to no avail, the non-union children were requested to stay home. Within a few months socialist miners had organized the Socialist Young Guard (SYG) as an alternative to mainstream children's organizations and to counteract 'the pernicious teachings the young children get.' Based on an Italian model, the ethics of the SYG stressed learning, love of justice, recognition of the role of labour, internationalism, fidelity to truth, respect for all, and the right to resist oppression. The encouragement of such values clearly represented an attempt to impose more consciously collective ideals in children. Both girls and boys were encouraged to join, signalling the possibility of equal comradeship for women and men in a socialist society.[71]

The underlying presumption that women belonged in the family, as supporters of socialist husbands and as the chief educators of socialist children, ignored the situation of single wage-earning women. Socialist men tended to perceive wage-earning women only as dependants and as future wives and mothers. The newspapers carried stories and comments on industrial conditions and wages of working women, but these discussions often turned to one of the most feared results of low wages – prostitution. While an occasional correspondent to a socialist newspaper might suggest that economic reasons were not paramount in women turning to the street, socialists, by and large, viewed the phenomenon as the result of inadequate wages. Rooting out capitalism and the profits made through the 'social evil' would enable women to earn a living without recourse to an immoral life. The future socialist society, with equal pay for equal work and consequent financial independence for working women, would cease to be troubled by women selling themselves to make a living and by the double standard in general.[72]

Although commentators in the socialist press were usually men, controversy in early 1909 over the prostitution issue prompted a writer for the woman's page of Cotton's Weekly (probably Mary Cotton Wisdom) to voice her anger on the issue. Outraged by the self-righteousness of ministers who condemned prostitution and dragged these unfortunate women into court to be sentenced to reformatories or jails, the writer asked why the prostitute's male clients were merely subject to a small fine. She further asserted the injustice of women having no say in these laws and vowed, 'from now on I will be an ardent woman suffragist.' Another column the next month repudiated the suggestion made by a

Montreal alderman that prostitution should be legalized, again referring to women's need for the ballot to prevent this 'legal degradation of women.' In another woman's page column, 'Rosa Gabriel' commented further on the Montreal controversy, noting the double standard of treatment for prostitutes and their male customers. What galled these women socialists was that the state meted out harsh punishment to women accused of prostitution, rather than addressing the motivation behind prostitution. As Newton has argued, the general socialist view accepted male working-class sexuality as 'normal' – accepting as well that, under capitalism, economic obstacles to marriage might lead such men to patronize prostitutes – while condemning upper-class men's exploitation of prostitutes. Yet some women socialists recognized that the problem went beyond economics to encompass the reality of male domination.[73]

The socialist movement tended to approach the issue of single women's work with ambivalence, convinced that most women were potential, if not actual, wives and mothers. Yet, those closest to working women, particularly women socialists and trade unionists, fought to organize and educate working women in the belief that economic and political change was paramount for women as well as for the working class in general. Labour and socialist women such as Helena Gutteridge in Vancouver, May Darwin in Toronto, Helen Armstrong in Winnipeg, Jean McWilliams in Calgary, and other less well-known figures helped to organize predominantly single working women into unions. These organizers viewed unions as one means of political education and economic protection in a larger array of potentially useful organizations. Women's Labor Leagues, political parties, labour churches, and other organizations were formed to address the needs of working women, complementing efforts at industrial organization.[74]

Helena Gutteridge was one of the prime movers behind the establishment of the 1914 Women's Employment League in Vancouver, which assisted young working women to find employment in the recession years 1913–15. As a working woman and self-described socialist, she helped to organize women laundry, garment, and domestic workers in British Columbia while also serving on the Vancouver Trades and Labor Council and the Local Council of Women, and writing columns for the *BC Federationist*. Her columns, some of which addressed the need for suffrage for working women, hammered on the question of women's work, pointing out that women worked in many dangerous and heavy industries for below subsistence wages. Her reports on the Women's

Employment League demonstrated that the majority of women workers seeking help were single women with no other recourse. Married women's work arose, she noted, because 'the wages earned by husbands and fathers are too small to keep the household going.' Women's economic inferiority, she asserted, led to a 'sickly degenerate race born of the mothers who try to fulfill the triple duty of worker, wife and mother.' Yet Gutteridge moved beyond this familiar analysis to bring her feminist insights to bear on the question of women's work. She pointed out that the woman worker had to fight on two fronts – against the employer and her male comrades: 'The history of women in industry ... is the story of struggle against not only the capitalist class who have exploited them mercilessly, but also against the men of their own class who said because they were women they must not expect to be looked upon as co-workers or receive the same pay when doing the same kind and quantity of work.' Gutteridge demonstrated the contradiction inherent in socialist and trade union attitudes to women's work, which sought to organize women only in lower-skilled jobs for less pay. Working-class men wanted to keep the highly skilled jobs for themselves. The woman worker received a confused message: 'First she shall not join the union, as in the early days, then she must, because his interests are at stake, then finding that does not keep him top dog, she must leave the trade entirely alone – it belongs by divine right to him. Oh, Chivalry, thy name is man!'[75]

Women socialists and trade unionists such as Gutteridge linked their socialism to a consciousness of women's inferior position and the need for trade union and allied activism. As we have seen, these connections appeared rarely in the socialist movement in general; some women, however, understood both the class and gender parameters of working-class women's lives, recognizing the double burden these imposed. The same cannot be said of the movement in general. Acceptance of the primacy of wifehood and motherhood, distrust of women workers as competitors and potential strikebreakers, and the ideal of the family wage reinforced structural inequalities within the movement, as well as within the labour market. Advocacy of equal pay stood side by side with, and in contradiction to, the family wage ideal and comments on the deterioration of the family – the increasing impossibility of working-class marriage, high infant mortality rates among working-class families arising from the need for married women's work, and the growth of prostitution. While a few decried the pitfalls of female economic dependence on men and noted that women were not always engaged in domestic duties, by and large socialists of both sexes subscribed to the prevailing notion of woman's role in the home and stressed the social and educational roles of women socialists in supporting their husbands and bringing up the next generation of socialists.

## VIII

Socialist women 'full of the spirit of revolt' expressed their commitment in many forms, most often through gender-specific activities that included educational, social, and fundraising tasks, but also through campaigns that aimed at increasing the visibility and participation of women in the movement. Across the country small groups of women contested the limited roles assigned to them by party structures, organizing for woman suffrage, separate women's activities and groups, and for the general recognition that women were integral to the movement. Although this activism in some respects continued the efforts of earlier women, the context in which it occurred had changed with the founding of the SPC in 1904. The party single-mindedly attempted to focus on the transformation of a capitalist system into a socialist one through explicitly political means. By defining the revolution in masculine terms and by adhering to a model of political class-consciousness among 'wage slaves,' the SPC delimited gender-specific roles in which women were expected to take on secondary and supportive functions in the struggle. By defining other forms of social change as diversionary and 'sentimental,' SPC activists identified immediate demands with a more 'feminine' approach and equated true revolution with manliness and masculine strength.

The SDP, on the other hand, identified itself with British and European social democracy, familiar to many of its members through first-hand experience, and constructed a platform and party structure more favourable to the inclusion of issues such as woman suffrage, trade unionism, legislative change, and other ameliorative reforms. The SDP's structure allowed for some input from special interest groups – whether that of ethnic groups, youth, or women – but the SDP, like the SPC, placed more emphasis on the overthrow of capitalism. Although the SDP allowed more scope for women's autonomous groups and opinions, women's issues were subordinate to the larger struggle, rather than integral to it. Thus, while both major socialist parties could boast of outspoken women orators and organizers, the material and ideological paradigm within which women operated provided limited support for their activities and underutilized their potential. Still, some women drew attention to the necessity of making socialist organizations responsive to the needs of women, with varying degrees of success. They did so not only to advance women's cause, but also because they appreciated the need for a 'two-sex movement.' They realized that a socialist movement that ignored the problems and potentials of women was at best a flawed socialism.

# 5

# 'Wanted – Women to Take the Place of Men': Organizing Working Women in the Era of War and Reconstruction

I was put to work inspecting garments, the pay being five cents a dozen. I worked as fast as I could all day, and even through the noon hour, and only inspected fourteen dozen. Once when the lacers were slow I laced a dozen for which I received one and one-half cents.

Laura Hughes, quoted in *Telegram* (Toronto), 19 November 1915

Concerned about the reported sweating of women workers in war industries, suffragist, labour supporter, and pacifist Laura Hughes spent two weeks working in several factories, among them the Joseph Simpson Knitting Mill, which was filling a militia contract at the time of her investigation. There, 'on her first day she worked from eight till six with only fifteen minutes for dinner and only earned 71 and a half cents.' In the tradition of progressive social reformers and at the behest of the Toronto Trades and Labor Council (TTLC), Hughes learned first-hand of the conditions and wages working women could expect. What she saw convinced her that manufacturers were short-sighted and indeed ignorant about actual conditions. Citing long overtime hours, wage cuts, and noxious fumes and dust, Hughes's report reached Ottawa, resulting in an inspection and a guaranteed minimum wage of one dollar a day. The inspector, however, appeared to have been satisfied with the conditions if not the wages, as was a reporter from the Toronto *Star*.[1]

While this particular manufacturer and the knitting industry in general were kept busy with war orders in the early stages of the conflict, conditions in other industries were much different. In general, the early war years continued to witness uncertain employment, short-time for those who were employed, and high levels of unemployment in many industries. By 1916, the economy began to pick up and, because of labour shortages, government officials increased their efforts to recruit women to work in war-related industries, including munitions production. Organized labour, however, was suspicious of the introduction of women into 'men's work.' As one labour commentator sarcastically remarked: 'Wanted, women to take the places of men – banks and financial houses lead the way – others to follow. Sure this is a good move to reduce the wages of the men, and if they don't like it fire them – starve them to enlist. Businessmen, get wise to a good thing – this is the way to reduce your expenses, and when the men return from the war, why the game is in your hands.[2]

Through the last two years of the war, an economic boom was in full swing, and as more men enlisted, or were conscripted, women's labour became increasingly necessary and more extensive, despite the reluctance of employers and unions. Under conditions of relative economic expansion and labour scarcity, women obtained employment in some areas previously defined as men's work and, perhaps just as importantly, expanded the labour force in more traditional areas of women's work, such as the manufacture of clothing. Clerical work was dramatically transformed and reshaped as women's work between 1911 and 1921, but women also continued to fill jobs in manufacturing, hotels and restaurants, and laundries and stores, among other more traditional areas. Expanding numbers and pressure from voluntary groups concerned with the effects of women's employment paved the way for investigations like that of Laura Hughes, and for campaigns for minimum wage acts and other protective legislation. The wartime boom also enabled unions and women's labour groups to organize previously non-unionized sectors and to strengthen existing groups. As a result strike activity among women workers also proliferated in 1917–20, with the peak in 1919.

Thus, the war years were important ones for women workers and women's labour organization and activism. While wage-earning women continued to present problems for organized labour and the state, the pressing need for their labour in the wartime emergency ultimately gave women some leverage to expand their occupational horizons, to earn higher wages, and to organize. The conditions of the late war years presented an unprecedented opportunity, providing favourable circumstances for women's militancy, which suggests the untapped potential working women possessed.

For the state, women's labour provided an answer to the shortage of men in industry, yet politicians and government officials did not always see eye to eye on the substitution of women for men – termed the 'dilution of labour' – nor did they always adopt a consistent approach to the organization of women's labour. Government officials' correspondence revealed many of the anxieties and assumptions about women's labour and demonstrated the widespread protectionist discourse also evident in concurrent debates about the minimum wage legislation that was enacted late in the war and in postwar period.

Unions were often reluctant participants in government schemes to employ women, fearing the replacement of men by women, the deskilling of jobs, and the lowering of wages. This reluctance to accept the 'dilution of labour' was partially offset by organized labour's adoption of the demand for equal pay for equal work in areas where women's labour threatened men's jobs. In practice, however, equal pay demands were only intermittently raised in wartime disputes. Nevertheless, the exigencies of war gave women labour activists like Helena Gutteridge the opportunity to argue that women workers were taking their places beside men as comrades and equals and thus deserved equal remuneration.[3]

I

Declaration of war in August 1914 did not immediately affect general economic conditions, which had been depressed since the middle of 1913. Commentators on the employment situation for women had noted high levels of unemployment in the summer of 1913. The women correspondents of the *Labour Gazette* reported slack factories in Toronto and a general depression in business in Vancouver during that summer; the Winnipeg correspondent noted in December that the stenography trade was very slow with many experienced women unable to find jobs. As the winter of 1913–14 wore on, municipal and volunteer employment bureaux began to report on the numbers of unemployed looking for work, including some married women in search of domestic work to tide their families over because of the unemployment, illness, or death of a spouse.[4]

Within a month or two of the beginning of the war it became clear that the conflict was having a downward effect on employment and wages. Many sectors reported paralysis: in the garment trade in Toronto, hundreds were laid off, and in some garment factories married women were

discharged to give work to the 'needy.' By November the TTLC estimated that seventeen thousand people were out of work, a figure that
increased by a thousand the next month. Stenographers, office workers,
waitresses, laundry workers, and even domestics found employment
difficult to come by in Vancouver, Winnipeg, Toronto, and Montreal, the
cities reporting specifically on women's work.[5]

The tough times of fall 1914 prompted many cities to establish or support employment bureaux, a number of them begun by voluntary
groups that later demanded full municipal support for these services.
Such was the case in Vancouver in September 1914 when the Local
Council of Women (LCW), in cooperation with the city, the Board of
Trade, the Trades and Labor Council, and women's groups, held a special meeting to discuss the problem of unemployed women. The president of the LCW, Mrs Unsworth, was also an executive member of the
Civic Relief Committee, which had been discussing the great need
among unemployed women in Vancouver. Helena Gutteridge, active in
the trade union movement and a LCW member, explained to the special
meeting that 'it was not charity that was asked for at this time but help
to tide over an unusual situation brought about by the war.' Gutteridge
estimated that there were at least 100 waitresses, 100 to 200 domestics,
60 tailoresses, and 250 stenographers, as well as an unspecified number
of unskilled workers, out of work. Moreover, in many cases those still
employed worked only half-time. J.L. McVety, president of the Vancouver TLC, complimented Gutteridge for opening up the topic, but suggested that the numbers out of work might be even larger. In his view
the problem of unemployment was more serious among women than
among men. McVety's comment notwithstanding, most voluntary or
municipal bodies tended to downplay women's unemployment and
concentrated on finding work for men.[6]

The result of the special meeting was a decision to set up the Women's
Employment League (WEL), which conducted its founding meeting on
30 September with representatives from a wide variety of women's
groups and the support of the Vancouver TLC. While the organization
was independent of the LCW, Gutteridge and Unsworth retained prominent roles in both organizations. The WEL passed a resolution calling
on the provincial government to provide employment for women and
offered to manage a business that would provide such employment. At
the same time a resolution was sent to Ottawa asking for contracts to
manufacture uniforms for the army. Neither request produced results,
and in October the WEL met with the finance committee of city council

and then with council itself to convince the city to provide a grant of $2,000 so that a toy manufacturing business and cooperative home could be set up. Work and lodgings for a hundred women working three days per week would eventually be financed by the sale of the toys, supplemented by donations. As Helena Gutteridge pointed out in her weekly column in the BC *Federationist*, many more women needed help: the group had received applications from nearly 300 single women and over 100 married women in the first three weeks of its existence. By November, over 700 women had registered with the WEL, and toy manufacturing, as well as sewing orders, kept over 100 women employed part-time. In early December Gutteridge reported that 882 women had registered (of whom 132 were married): 150 were making toys, 140 had found domestic positions, and others had been given occasional assistance. She reminded her readers, however, that many hundreds could not be helped and that the federal and provincial governments had not yet done their part. The numbers of unemployed women continued to climb during the winter, and in February 1915 the league reported total registration figures of 1,189 women. Realizing that the need for a women's employment bureau was a permanent one, the WEL approached city council in June requesting that the city take it over and make the WEL part of its Civic Relief Department, which council agreed to do.[7]

In comparison to the public attention given to the problem in Vancouver, most cities tended to ignore or downplay the plight of unemployed women. A toy-manufacturing project in Toronto, supported by a number of trades, employed only men while promising to add women later. In Winnipeg, the editor of the *Voice* asserted in December 1914 that the city's employment bureau had registered eight thousand men and no women. These numbers are somewhat counterbalanced by the fact that the Winnipeg LCW had earlier opened a similar bureau for women, perhaps in recognition of the shortcomings of the city's own bureau. Journalist Francis Beynon reported on the Bureau of Work for Women in September 1914, noting the large number of women thrown out of work by the financial panic that accompanied the war. Evidence from other Canadian cities, such as Calgary, Edmonton, and Moose Jaw, suggests that officials and politicians discussed unemployment primarily as a male phenomenon and were concerned with giving married men with families priority on city relief projects.[8]

War and unemployment, not surprisingly, had a noticeable impact on labour activism and strikes. Both 1914 (after the war's start) and 1915 witnessed relatively small numbers of strikes. When economic conditions improved and the labour shortage began to be felt during 1916, strike activity increased.

## II

Beginning in 1916, women correspondents to the *Labour Gazette* began to note that previously laid-off women were gradually filling the men's places in stores, offices, and banks. By summer, the women correspondents reported shortages of women in some areas and little unemployment. In many sectors, wages went up as the demand for workers increased. Domestics' wages in Vancouver were reported as twenty dollars per month in July 1916, as compared with a low of twelve dollars during 1913–15. Work previously done by men in nearly all-male domains was reassigned. In Toronto, for example, street and steam railway officials were reported as employing women and Chinese to clean passenger coaches. Street railway workers in Vancouver at the end of 1916 publicly asserted that they would not oppose the introduction of women conductors, as long as they became union members and were given equal pay for equal work. Discussions of the dilution of labour assumed more prominence as the armed forces absorbed more men. Perhaps one of the most striking examples of this discussion occurred in the production of munitions. While munitions manufacture was tied directly to war and was therefore of limited duration, this sector represented a non-traditional employment area for women that occasioned much debate and some conflict. Taken as a case study, the production of munitions illustrates government and labour attitudes towards women workers, exposes the tensions within the labour movement over competition from women, and suggests to a limited extent the obstacles women faced, as well as their responses.[9]

While no comprehensive study of women munitions workers exists in Canada, it is possible to make some observations, based on contemporary studies, government records, and the labour press. Women's work in munitions was concentrated in Ontario and Quebec where an estimated thirty-five thousand women produced war *matériel*, primarily shells. Some munitions production involving women also occurred in Vancouver, Victoria, and Winnipeg, as well as Nova Scotia. The front page of the *BC Federationist* of 26 January 1917 proclaimed 'Women Employed in Local Munition Plants,' referring to twenty women who began work that week at the Vancouver Engineering Company. Virtually accusing Mark Irish, the director of the Imperial Munitions Board's Labour Department, of lying, the newspaper drew attention to the failure of this company to rehire laid-off men and to their stated new policy of hiring women to work on the shells formerly made by men. This dilution of labour was strongly resented by the labour movement and regarded with suspicion by many employers as well. Within the federal government ambivalence was also pronounced. Women, however, sought out such employment, especially when it paid better wages than most female-stereotyped, unskilled or semi-skilled labour.[10]

Organized labour, under the umbrella of the Trades and Labor Congress (TLC), felt that the conditions of work in war-related industries created problems severe enough to warrant a conference of all eighty international and national unions representing workers in Canada. In his official circular of 7 May 1917 calling for the conference in Ottawa, TLC president James Watters cited the non-cooperative attitude of Sir Joseph Flavelle, chair of the Imperial Munitions Board (IMB). A list of grievances compiled from the conference included elimination of the eight-hour day, unnecessary dilution of labour by the introduction of women before available skilled manpower had been exhausted, and failure to pay the same standard of wages to women as had been paid to men. The conference was concerned that excessive hours of labour were tolerated for women, citing evidence of work weeks of seventy-two hours or more at the Verdun plant in Montreal. Furthermore, the conference castigated the 'indiscriminate use of female labor without any consultation with labor representatives or others who were in a position to provide the necessary skilled male help.' Organized labour clearly felt threatened by the presence of women and the potential for replacing men and lowering wages in jobs performed by men. Gender self-interest was mixed with a realization that government and business were using largely unorganized female labour as a lever against organized labour, threatening to extinguish the earlier gains in wages, hours, and conditions. While some sectors of the labour movement realized that the best protection for workers was to organize the women, many trade unionists resisted such a move or gave it very low priority.[11]

The question of women munitions' workers exercised the Toronto Trades and Labor Council when reports of exploitation of women were voiced at a May 1916 meeting where one delegate stated that he knew of fifty women receiving ten to fifteen cents an hour while men who normally earned higher wages were being laid off in munitions plants. The TTLC proceeded to write the federal Department of Labour as well as the executive of the Trades and Labor Congress. In a subsequent meeting in June, after an unsatisfactory answer from the Minister of Labour, the TTLC decided to get in touch with local women's groups recruiting women for munitions work, to discuss the importance of equal pay. As an editorial in the *Industrial Banner* noted, Canada lacked regulations such as those enforced in Britain mandating a standard wage scale, thus opening the door for employers who viewed women as cheaper labour.[12]

In the early stages of munitions production, employers were reluctant to accept women in the plants, viewing the dilution of labour as a last resort. As the labour shortage became more acute, initial reluctance was overcome, and the savings in wages no doubt helped to convince some contractors to employ women. The IMB steadfastly refused to accede to labour's demands for wage standards and hours limitations, arguing that it could not interfere in its contractors' employment practices. The IMB did, however, appoint Ontario MPP and insurance broker, Mark Irish, to head the department in charge of organizing women's labour in munitions plants. Irish's job was not only to marshall women's labour power, but also to convince employers to use their labour. To accomplish the latter he sometimes sent circulars to all contractors, warning of labour shortages and advertising his department's expertise on women's labour, and he occasionally conducted personal investigations, such as a visit to Winnipeg in March 1917. Surviving correspondence between Irish and the chair of the IMB reveals some of the difficulties and frustrations Irish encountered in his post and also provides some perspective on government attitudes towards women workers.[13]

In one of Irish's first letters, he gently chides Flavelle for his reluctance to use publicity, remarking that the public feels 'peculiarly concerned' about the labour shortages and recommending the cultivation of sentiment in favour of the IMB's efforts for the war. Promising not to embarrass Flavelle, Irish outlined his first steps in encouraging the public acceptance of women's labour in munitions, which included the preparation of an illustrated book, moving pictures, badges recognizing service, and the equipment of an entire factory in St Catharines with facilities for women. The latter was to provide 'housing, canteens and everything that goes with the scheme in its fullest' so that Irish would 'have a point of demonstration that cannot be denied.' He also promised that a thousand women would be placed in one Toronto plant within a month, observing that there were 'indications that the manufacturer is coming round.' Yet not all was positive: Irish admitted there were rebuffs as well as encouragement in the labour dilution scheme.[14]

A few days later, Irish again wrote his chief to describe his reactions to a lunch meeting with Prime Minister Borden and R.B. Bennett, director general of the National Service Board. Reserving his critical remarks for Bennett, Irish bemoaned the latter's 'peculiar' attitudes towards female labour. Bennett expressed deep-seated anxiety about creating a female army of labour with lower wages, and worried that women would never voluntarily give up factory work, thus setting the scene for a clash with returned soldiers. Irish's disappointment and frustration with Bennett was reinforced in February 1917 after a National Service Conference held in Ottawa. Complaining about the lack of any definite action resulting from this meeting, Irish underlined Bennett's failure to understand that more women could be employed in war-related industries if there were enough resources to reconstruct plants to adapt them to women's labour. He also dismissed Bennett's statement that women who did not need the work should leave it for those who did. Irish pointed out that it was not in the best interests of munitions production to urge women to leave their positions once they had already been trained. Too much valuable time and training would be wasted if women were to leave munitions production under some kind of misguided philanthropy, he stated.[15]

Irish's frustration at the lack of a unified policy on women's labour was compounded by his open criticism of government bureaucratic practices supposedly aimed at economy in the war effort. Writing to Flavelle in April 1917 on the decision to issue badges costing two dollars each to women munitions inspectors, Irish fulminated against this decision, in the light of government efforts to cut the wages of these women: 'One marvels at the mental gymnastics performed in the name of economy. By all means cut the wages so a woman lives on something over one dollar per day but let us spare no expense in the decoration of the Golden Fleece.'[16]

While Irish was convinced that women's labour was key to freeing men for the war effort, his approach to the employment of women workers reflected clear assumptions about gender. Women were suited for particular types of munitions work, Irish felt, and should not be be placed in certain dangerous occupations. Writing to Flavelle in January 1918, Irish was of the opinion that women should be a last resort in the explosives plants at Trenton and Nobel, Ontario. Citing health and humane reasons, Irish was loathe to expose women to disability and possible disfigurement resulting from accidents in these plants. No such sentiments applied to men working under dangerous conditions. In addition, he reiterated his consistent belief that the introduction of female labour required the construction of a women's colony with services tailored to women's needs. Irish's protective stance towards women workers delineated a division of labour between men and women grounded in perceived gender differences that implied that women were not skilled enough, or strong enough, for certain jobs and that women's physical appearance was more valued than men's.[17]

Moral questions also preoccupied the director of the IMB's Labour Department. In September 1918, Irish wrote to Flavelle regarding the Royal Air Force's proposal to second Irish's assistant, Mrs Mary Fenton, to help the RAF introduce women into the service. Fenton was the frontline worker with the women in munitions plants, and both Irish and Flavelle were reluctant to see her go. Upon reflection, however, Irish decided that he should release her to help the air force, primarily because he thought her appointment might help to reduce the possibilities for public scandal within the RAF 'cesspool.' Irish felt that Fenton's reassignment was the most efficient choice, noting that he had been guided by the principle of the greatest good for the greatest numbers.[18]

Labour unrest in war-related industries and in industries affecting war production became an increasing concern during 1917–18. The reduction of wages for women inspectors threatened to tie up the munitions industry in Hamilton in spring 1917, for example. The women held a meeting on 28 March over wage reductions rumoured to take place on 1 April. With the advice of the Hamilton Trades and Labor Council, the women wrote to Joseph Flavelle, through the services of TLC secretary, Walter Rollo, asking for an explanation. Shortly after, women munitions inspectors in Montreal, who were also employees working under the Canadian Inspection and Testing Laboratories, met to protest any change in wages and working conditions by sending Flavelle a resolution to that effect, signed by eight women. The company responded to the crisis, which they feared might turn into a strike, by assuring the director of inspection, Colonel W.E. Edwards, that the new schedule of wages would apply only to newly hired women inspectors and not to those engaged originally by Mark Irish at higher rates of pay. Irish had hired women under certain conditions, namely that they have a high school education, that they learn the work at their own expense, that they agree to transfers, and that they work a minimum of six months. These women earned twenty-five cents an hour, plus overtime, which one official calculated as approximately $690 per year for each of the four hundred women examiners. The new proposal lowered the hourly rate to an average of twenty cents, thus saving $150 per year per woman. Since no strike ensued, it would appear that the women were satisfied with the guarantee that their rates would not change. New regulations meant that all further hiring was to occur through Ontario government hiring bureaux, rather than through the Department of Labour of the IMB. From the correspondence, it is clear that Mark Irish was a participant in these decisions, thus suggesting the limits of his concern for the well-being of women munitions workers. This change of policy accorded with the general practices adopted by Flavelle of distancing the IMB from the question of wages paid by contractors to their workers. No discussion ensued in the correspondence regarding whether women workers could live adequately on these wages.[19]

Clearly Irish and others in government recognized the advantage of using female labour to replace men. This option, however, entailed special considerations: employers, the public, and some government officials had to be convinced; suitable women had to be recruited and trained; and facilities had to be tailored to women's needs. In addition, women were to be steered into some kinds of work but not others. Hoping to help construct a consistent and uniform policy for women's work during the war, Irish was ultimately frustrated and forced to make compromises, including some that accorded women a lower rate of pay.

Women's wages in munitions production were considered to be superior to most other occupations, but not all women munitions workers were content. Labour women and men consistently pointed out that female workers were not paid equally with their male counterparts in the industry. Helena Gutteridge, for example, brought up the topic at a Vancouver TLC meeting in July 1915 during a discussion of the visit of a British member of Parliament seeking skilled munitions workers. She urged the Vancouver TLC to press the issue of equality with the MP. Munitions workers in Victoria went on strike in May 1917 when a man was fired for trying to organize a union at the Victoria Machinery Depot. The company provided wage figures for its 85 women and 130 men, asserting that it paid good wages. The company claimed that the women earned an average wage of $48.90 per month, plus a bonus of $8.26, while the men earned an average of $118.38, plus a bonus of $11.12. Thus, according to the company's figures, women earned an average of 44 per cent of what men earned. While the men worked longer hours (eleven hours for twelve or thirteen hours pay at an average of 35 cents per hour), women supposedly worked eight hours a day at the new rate of twenty cents an hour. The company's figures suggest, however, that women munitions workers must have worked at least ten hours per week overtime to earn the sum claimed. Thus, the differences between the hours worked by women and men appear slight. Clearly the wartime emergency justified some stretching of the law's protective provisions for women workers (such as maximum hours legislation), but the crisis did not result in significant re-evaluations of wage work. In general, discussions of equal pay remained a vague hope supported by labour and women's groups, but not acted upon by government.[20]

The rhetoric of differences between men and women in muscular strength, skill levels, training, and other areas was accompanied by a discourse of protectionism aimed at women (both adult and adolescent). In munitions production, protective measures were relaxed in some areas but maintained in others. In the realm of women's work more broadly defined, protective measures such as factory and shop acts were augmented during the war and postwar era by gender-specific minimum wage legislation that promised to stem the flow of cheap female labour while at the same time buttressing the division of labour and the family wage.

III

While there were critics of minimum wage legislation from diverse sectors of economic life, including business and labour, minimum wage supporters argued that such legislation would benefit women workers by regulating rates of pay and by preventing the proliferation of sweated labour in industry. As McCallum has observed,

Between 1918 and the end of 1920, all provinces except Prince Edward Island, New Brunswick and Alberta had passed legislation providing for a three- or five-person minimum wage board to set wage rates for female wage-earners on an industry-by-industry basis after consultation with representative employers and employees. The western provinces and Ontario established functioning boards shortly after passage of the enabling legislation; Quebec did not appoint a board until 1925 and Nova Scotia not until 1930. Alberta had no minimum wage board until 1922, but it was the first province with minimum wage legislation, and the only province to enact a fixed statutory minimum for men and women. In 1917, in the legislative session before the provincial election, the Liberal government of A. L. Sifton passed the Factories Act which included provision for a minimum wage of $1.50 per shift for all adults and $1.00 per shift for all apprentices in any factory, shop or office building.

In no province did minimum wage legislation cover domestic servants or farm labourers. In some jurisdictions, the boards could regulate hotel, restaurant, shop, or office workers and some professionals, although the latter group was never actually affected by minimum wage legislation. Up until the Depression, with the lone exception of Alberta, these acts applied only to women and minors. In targeting women, Canada was more like the United States, where individual states enacted minimum wage laws beginning in 1912, than it was like Australia, New Zealand, or Great Britain, where men also could be regulated by such laws.[21]

Canadian jurisdictions applied a particular social policy model to women and minors, who were presumed to be single and without dependants, although not necessarily 'independent.' The minimum wage was based upon the idea that each person should be entitled to a 'living wage,' but the contours of that wage were determined by the presumption that women only needed enough to support themselves. Critics in many cases did not object to differential rates based on age, condition of apprenticeship, or infirmity, thus allowing young women under eighteen or disabled workers to be paid less than the 'living wage' determined by minimum wage boards. The clear assumption was that women under eighteen lived at home and therefore did not need the same minimum as older women. In addition, it was commonly assumed that women needed legislative protection where men did not, both because of their future roles as childbearers and because men could bargain for wages and conditions through unions. Certainly the trade union movement also argued for the unionization of women, but it primarily seemed to accept the minimum wage as a necessary alternative strategy for the vast majority of unorganized women.[22]

Judith Baer has noted several assumptions underlying the arguments for the minimum wage: the conditions justifying special laws for women were viewed as permanent; women's reproductive functions implied this primary commitment to children and home; and women's interests were almost always subordinate to family and society. Thus, increased state intervention in the form of protective legislation became acceptable by the war period, for this special category of worker, based on the recognition of sexual differences and the advocacy of social goals such as the protection of future generations. Furthermore, protective legislation could be easily restricted to women and juveniles on both biological and social grounds, without threatening to undermine the status quo for men.[23]

Minimum wage scales for male workers existed in Canada in this period, but under a different guise. Fair wage legislation had been passed at the federal level in 1900 in the wake of debates and revelations about sweated labour in the production of uniforms for the post office. Manitoba passed its Fair Wage Act in 1916, providing for a tripartite board to set rates and hours for construction trades workers employed on government public works. Fair wage boards set rates that reflected the prevailing wages in industry in order to prevent the use of sweated labour on government projects. Ironically, the original abuse it purported to correct, sweated female labour, faded into the background as fair wage legislation became identified with male construction work. Unlike minimum wage legislation, this type of state intervention was accepted as necessary and normal, and the potential parallel with minimum wage legislation ignored.[24]

In 1918 Manitoba became one of the first jurisdictions to pass and implement a Minimum Wage Act. The events leading up to the act and the subsequent practice of the provincial Minimum Wage Board are highlighted here as a case study. The impetus for the minimum wage arose from several sources – social reformers, the labour movement, and women's groups. Revelations from several investigative commissions detailed low wages and poor working conditions, while raising the spectre of moral degradation and prostitution. At the same time, the wartime boom produced more opportunity for labour organization among wage-earning women, and strikes of women workers publicized the inadequate wages, long hours, and unhealthy conditions of factories, shops, and stores. Heightened awareness, increased union activism among women, labour discontent, and criticisms mounted by reform and labour organizations put pressure on the provincial government to act. The provincial Liberals (who replaced the scandal-tainted Conservatives in 1915) derived considerable political mileage from association with the reform movement and some elements of the labour movement. Pressure from these movements and awareness of the political advantage that would accrue made support for the idea of minimum wage legislation quite attractive to the government.

The province's first female factory inspector, Ida Bauslaugh, lectured to the University Women's Club in June 1916 on the need for a minimum wage. At the end of that year at a meeting between the executives of the Trades and Labor Council and the Manitoba branch of the national Trades and Labor Congress, a resolution for a minimum wage bill for women was passed and subsequently sanctioned by the Winnipeg TLC. Its representatives met with the government to demand such legislation in early 1917. Since it was too late in the legislative session to introduce such a measure, a royal commission to examine women's work and wages was discussed as the 'next best thing.'[25]

Just after the appointment of the royal commission, strikes occurred among female salesclerks at Woolworth's and among telephone operators. While the Woolworth's strike only involved a few dozen female sales clerks, the telephone operators' action drew in approximately six hundred women. Both disputes highlighted the exploitative wages paid to women in the labour force.

In spring 1917, 350 Winnipeg sales clerks met in the Labour Temple under the auspices of the Trades and Labor Council to organize a union. The low wages paid to women and girls were noted by the speakers. Despite the rosy conclusions of a University Women's Club report on department stores in 1914, women employed in five-and-ten-cent stores like Woolworth's earned as little as six dollars per week. With the assistance of the Women's Labor League (WLL) of Winnipeg, led by Helen Armstrong, the Woolworth's employees demanded an eight dollar minimum, union recognition, and a half-day holiday. To back up their position they went on strike on 26 May. Woolworth's offered to meet their wage demands but refused to recognize the union.[26]

The WLL played a key role in this strike, as did the general labour movement of Winnipeg. Both helped to garner community support for the striking women, and the labour movement raised strike funds directly since the fledgling union had few resources. The strikers quickly faced an injunction against picketing and a $25,000 civil damages suit, although even the judge who granted the injunction noted that the civil suit would do little for the store's public image. Despite sympathy with the strikers, the injunction effectively broke the strike by allowing the hiring of scabs. The labour movement was outraged and demanded the immediate reinstatement of the striking workers. In the end, the union failed to get recognition, and most of the striking women lost their jobs. Still, an eight-dollar minimum was promised by the store after the strike ended on 11 June. More important, the strike had galvanized support for the plight of wage-earning women. At a public meeting called during the strike, the participants had resolved that 'we pledge ourselves to do everything in our power to secure a living wage for the women wage workers in this province.'[27]

A coincident strike by telephone operators also drove home the message that most women workers were inadequately remunerated for their labour. In February 1917 the 'Hello Girls' of Winnipeg had organized a union and applied to the International Brotherhood of Electrical

Workers for a charter. Half or more of the operators joined the union almost immediately. By March, reports were circulating about company spies within the union. In April the Manitoba Telephone Commission received a wage demand from the union requesting increases of 15 to 40 per cent. The commission in turn asked for a 10 per cent rate increase from the Public Utilities Commission. By then it was reported that nearly 100 per cent of the operators had joined the union and that sentiment for a strike was growing if the demands were refused. A three-hour strike by the operators on 1 May prompted an investigation, and the telephone workers agreed to remain on the job until the end of May when the investigatory board promised to report its findings. In the meantime the operators went back to work with an advance in wages. The government-run Telephone Commission promised to abide by the board's findings, although the workers refused to commit themselves to such a position. 'They possessed the power and they used it,' commented the *Voice* on the operators' stand.[28]

Insisting that their wages of thirty-five dollars per month were inadequate in the face of the rising cost of living during the war, the operators demanded a forty-dollar minimum and better hours and conditions. Women operators testified to the insufficiency of their wages before the board, which was headed by Ed McGrath, secretary of the Manitoba Bureau of Labor and chair of the royal commission investigating women's wages. Perhaps more influential, however, was the testimony of two large employers of women workers in banking and insurance. Both men testified that they paid their female employees a minimum of forty-five to fifty dollars per month. On the last day of May, the chair of the board delivered his report to the attorney general and met the operators in the Labour Temple to explain the terms of the settlement: $40 per month minimum; a $2.50 increase every six months up to a maximum of $60; and hours reduced to eight per day, with 203 hours constituting a month's work for the purpose of computing overtime pay.[29]

The settlement was regarded as a victory by most labour people. The success had resulted not only from public sympathy with the women but from the tactics adopted. The solidarity of operators throughout the province, the timing of an electrical workers strike the day after the three-hour strike by the operators, and the threat of other industrial disputes helped to put pressure on the government. A similar dispute in Regina in the fall pitted fifteen operators against the government telephone commission over inadequate wages and the discharge of three union operators. The Regina TLC supported the women, citing evidence from the Winnipeg investigation.[30]

Simultaneously with the strikes at Woolworth's and the telephone company, the minimum wage commission was getting down to work on a broad investigation of the wages, hours, and conditions of women workers, thus increasing the pressure for a minimum wage. The investigation was entrusted to Ed McGrath of the provincial Bureau of Labor. McGrath, a former TLC officer, hired Alice Blackburn as principal undercover investigator of the conditions and wages women workers faced in Winnipeg. From her expense accounts it appears that Blackburn began her work in summer 1917 by undertaking employment in various companies. While paid a salary by the Bureau of Labor, she worked for short periods at knit goods factories, laundries, confectionery manufacturers, and garment factories. The commission also interviewed women workers, completing a detailed interview schedule with over two hundred women. Unfortunately its report included only seven samples of these interview schedules, and the others have not survived. The commission also sought the opinions of two dozen prominent women drawn from many fields, including the labour movement, women's organizations, employers, social agencies, and the professions. The main body of the report consisted of statistical tables, industry by industry, with a survey of wage rates and number of employees. The companies were identified only by number. While the survey covered 9,354 women in 328 establishments, the final report gave information on only 2,960 women in 145 manufacturing establishments. The report was tabled with the understanding that much of it would remain confidential, perhaps because of the damaging nature of the evidence.[31]

The evidence of the report showed that most of the women (75 per cent) were over eighteen. A substantial number of surveyed employees (1,363) worked in retail stores. Of the 2,960 factory employees, the largest number worked in the garment trade (908), followed by laundries (369), confectioneries (313, almost half of whom were under the age of eighteen), and food stuffs (289). Despite the testimony of several prominent women that $500 per year was the minimum that a working woman could live on, the evidence showed that many women fell far below this level. A partial survey among sales clerks – retail stores were not compelled to answer the survey, and the results are incomplete – revealed that only 53 per cent earned more than ten dollars per week. Similarly, just over half the workers in the garment trade earned more than ten dollars per week, and some earned as little as three to five dollars. Results were even worse in other manufacturing sectors. Only 15 per cent of the women in the fifteen confectionery factories surveyed and 11 per cent of the women in the thirteen laundries included in the study earned more than ten dollars per week. The sample question-naires highlighted a few of the worst cases: a sixteen-year-old employed in a candy factory for five dollars per week; a twenty-two-year old, self-supporting Jewish woman who worked for eight dollars per week and who expected 'to be able to buy woollen underwear this winter for the first time;' a twenty-year-old Polish woman who worked in a bedding factory for $5.35 per week and as a result owed two months board and a doctor's bill.[32]

The undercover investigator also reported on her experiences work-ing in various factories. For the six positions she recorded she earned between five and seven dollars per week. While the stated work week was fifty hours in one case she worked sixty-three hours and in another fifty-three. By matching some of the expense accounts with her state-ments, it is possible to determine that investigator Blackburn earned seven dollars per week in a laundry, and six to seven dollars per week in three confectionery factories, thus supporting the general evidence of very low wages even for mature women.[33]

The commission's report was tabled in the legislature on 7 February 1918. Even before this official act, consultations were in progress between representatives of the TLC, the Manufacturers Association, and the Bureau of Labor. Meeting in early January, the groups engaged in confidential proceedings aimed at reaching an agreed-upon minimum wage figure. The *Voice* reported that a ten-dollar minimum wage would be suggested but noted that the manufacturers were expected to oppose 'not the amount of the minimum, but that it is impossible to put it into effect in this province first and that the matter should be taken in hand by the Dominion Government.'[34]

The WLL met with Ed McGrath on 15 January and urged all con-cerned women to be present. On the 18th the Winnipeg TLC debated the minimum wage question. While the TLC committee was complimented on its handling of the negotiations, one council member used the argu-ment of the family wage to take strong objection to a minimum wage for women. He was promptly answered by a woman delegate who pointed out that more and more women were entering the industrial labour force out of necessity, especially during wartime. The TLC took the posi-tion that it would support provincial legislation while recommending trade union organization to working women and campaigns for equal pay.[35]

As the negotiations continued between employers and labour over

the minimum wage, public pressure was brought to bear on the question through the churches and the People's Forum. At the request of the
WLL, a dozen pastors from different denominations gave sermons on
the minimum wage question. In the legislature, labourite F.J. Dixon
endorsed the ten-dollar minimum. Despite this pressure, no agreement
was reached, and a deputation of manufacturers approached the minister of public works in late January to propose an alternative. Despite the
fact that no bill had been introduced, hearings were held before the Law
Amendments Committee in early February to discuss the alternative
solution: a minimum wage board. The labour representatives proposed
a compromise measure when further discussions reached a stalemate.
They proposed a ten-dollar minimum for women seventeen and over,
seven to nine dollars for fourteen- to sixteen-year-olds, and a five-
person board with equal representation from labour and employers to
oversee the legislation. The manufacturers rejected this compromise,
and in the end two separate bills appeared before the Law Amendments
Committee, which chose the minimum wage board option. Curiously,
the vote was taken in the committee while most of the labour supporters
were absent. When the question was reopened after complaints about
the first vote, the labour supporters were voted down, ten to six. The
final Law Amendments Committee resolution recommended that two
of the five board members be women. Ed McGrath held out some hope
for the new legislation. There was, he said, 'no need to be downhearted
about the outcome of the minimum wage agitation. If the act passed by
the legislature is honestly and sympathetically administered, it will be
of immense benefit to the working girls. The legislature has very plainly
recognized the claim for a decent living wage for all grades of female
labor.'[36]

The Manitoba Minimum Wage Board (MWB) was appointed in April
1918 with Dr J.W. MacMillan, principal of Manitoba College, as chair.
Labour was represented by Lynn Flett, an activist in the WLL and the
Political Equality League, and by James Winning of the Winnipeg
Trades and Labor Council; the employers were represented by Mrs Edna
Nash and bakery owner Edward Parnell.[37]

Despite the appointment of Flett, some members of the WLL
remained dissatisfied with the board and its actions. In fall 1918 and
spring 1919, rumblings of discontent became loud protests that the
board was unreasonable in its awards. Helen Armstrong, outspoken
president of the WLL, was particularly vociferous in her criticisms. As
a supporter of the flat minimum wage rate, she objected to the board

as too weak and pointed out the difficulties of women trying to live on even $9.50 or $10 per week. The minimum, she argued, too often became the maximum wage rate. Some of her colleagues in the labour movement did not agree and wanted to give the board a 'longer trial.' They claimed that Armstrong misunderstood the purpose of the board, and her objections were dismissed by some as a tempest in a teapot.[38]

Undeterred, Armstrong continued to voice her objections to the MWB, particularly when the newly unionized government clerks protested their inclusion under MWB provisions in March 1919, evidently feeling they could achieve more through the union than through the board. This dispute fuelled further discussions in the press and at the Winnipeg Trades and Labor Council meetings in February and March. Eventually Armstrong was vindicated when the TLC voted to support the women's request that a flat twelve-dollar rate, irrespective of age, replace the board. This decision was forwarded to the premier, but with little result. Despite the vote in favour of the flat rate, dissension continued between the WLL and the TLC over the board. The crisis over the inclusion of government stenographers under the board's jurisdiction pinpointed the contradiction between a minimum wage strategy and unionization.[39]

In militating for minimum wage laws, the Women's Labor League was adhering to its goals 'to protect the women workers of Winnipeg from an inadequate wage and extreme working hours,' specifically through organization and 'through such legislation as the Minimum Wage and the Eight-Hour Day.' To accomplish these goals, the WLL participated in events that involved some of the members of the activist or feminist community based in the middle or upper-middle classes of Winnipeg. For example, league members were invited to listen to an address by journalist Lillian Beynon Thomas on laws affecting women. The WLL also sponsored a lecture by the socialist leader of the Women's Crusade, Gertrude Richardson of Swan River, Manitoba, as well as one by social gospel and labour activist Reverend William Ivens. While the WLL shared some of the concerns and goals of middle-class women's groups, tensions between the working-class organization and the wealthier women's groups grew, particularly after the Local Council of Women assumed a clear anti-labour stance during the 1917 Woolworth's strike and the 1918 civic workers' dispute. Thus while the WLL and the Political Equality League (PEL) might attempt to cooperate on a proposed convention on laws affecting women and children, ultimately the

PEL's association with the local council resulted in the WLL withdrawing its support for the meeting scheduled in October 1918.[40]

How did the Minimum Wage Board work and what were its decisions? In reflecting on the MWB, its first chair, Dr J.W. MacMillan, noted that the board operated in a unique fashion. Rather than using a dual structure of trade boards and a minimum wage board, the province devised in the MWB a structure that called all parties together to work out the regulations. MacMillan pointed out that this method was speedier and gave the MWB the balance of power in the meetings. Harmonious decision making was fostered by face-to-face meetings. MacMillan commented that in only two of thirty-five meetings held in the first fifteen months of the board's operations was he forced to cast a deciding ballot.[41]

A number of provinces adopted the Manitoba model of a five-person board, two each representing employer and employee, with an impartial chair. Consultation with representatives of both sides was built into the process of arriving at a minimum wage figure. In contrast, British Columbia's three-person board was chaired by the deputy minister of labour and operated at the pleasure of the lieutenant-governor-in-council. Furthermore, the BC legislation did not require employer or employee representation on the board, and a two-tiered structure of advisory conferences, which made recommendations to the board, complicated its operation. Structurally at least, the Manitoba model seemed to work best and represented both workers and employers. An additional feature required that two of the five members had to be women – one representing labour, the other management. Prior to 1921, the board handed down forty-four decisions affecting workers in a wide variety of manufacturing industries and in clerical, sales, and service work. These provisions applied only to the urban areas specified in the legislation, thus leaving rural women unprotected.[42]

In its first investigation the board tackled the laundry industry. Three representatives of the women laundry workers met with the board and three representatives of employers. A cost-of-living schedule was drawn up by the board and approved by the parties. The minimum wage of $9.50 per week was based on the estimate that a woman could live decently on just under $500 per annum. Inexperienced workers over eighteen and probationers, who were under eighteen, however, received less. In the latter case they might earn as little as $7 to start. Clearly the MWB assumed that these women lived at home. The *Labour Gazette* noted that the board granted these concessions to the industry 'because of the huge increase in the cost of doing business, also the competition of the Chinese laundries.' The board stipulated weekly pay, shorter hours, improvements in physical working conditions, and one week's notice of termination of employment.[43]

The same pattern was followed in subsequent board decisions in 1918, which covered the food industry, retail stores, and paper box and soap factories. Different minimums were established for learners and minors and, except for retail stores where the adult minimum was $12 per week, $9.50–$10 remained the usual award. Fourteen factory-based industries had been dealt with by the end of 1918. While the minimums awarded to adults matched the $12 minimum paid in retail stores, the probationary periods were considerably lengthened, usually to eighteen months in contrast to the MWB's first decisions, which specified periods of under twelve months. This pattern of a $12 minimum and longer probationary periods continued in the board's decisions in 1919, which covered knitting factories, tailoring and millinery establishments, ladies' wear factories, garment factories, ladies' hat manufacturing, mail order establishments, printing, dyeing, and dry cleaning establishments, hairdressing salons, and furrier and dressmaking establishments. In all of these decisions the MWB maintained differential wages for learners and minors, a $12 minimum for adults, hours limitations, regulations concerning light and ventilation, and a provision that no more than 25 per cent of the labour force could be classified as learners or minors.[44]

Perhaps most noteworthy in the later decisions were the provisions in June 1919 for hotel and restaurant employees that established a $12.50 minimum with no distinctions made by experience level. In hotels this scale applied to minors as well. In restaurants no one under sixteen could be hired, and in both hotels and restaurants night work was forbidden for those under eighteen. Café owners opposed the decision, according to board member Lynn Flett, not so much because of the wage level but because of the shorter hours: the board permitted a maximum of forty-eight hours a week and ten hours a day. Previously waitresses had worked as many as sixty-five to seventy hours a week. Meal breaks were also specified, and no work period could end between 12:30 AM and 7 AM. In addition, one full day off per week must be granted to each female employee. Flett also noted that tips were of no concern to the MWB, which felt that a basic living wage took priority. In this case, the board clearly took a more progressive stand than employers wished and rejected arguments that allowed for a lower minimum wage because of gratuities.[45]

In September 1919 the *Labour Gazette* reported on amending and supplementary orders as well as two new orders covering occupations that had not yet been included in MWB deliberations. Minimum wage rates were amended for workers in confectioneries and in biscuit, cigar, grocery, marcaroni and vermicelli, pickle, paper box, and soap factories as well as abattoirs and laundries. The old rates of $9.50–$10 per week were raised to $11, and minors and learners were to receive a flat increase of one dollar per week. Part-time workers in shops, stores and factories in Winnipeg, St Boniface, St James, and Brandon were to receive thirty cents per hour. A supplementary order provided that female employees in shops and stores in these cities, other than office staff or those engaged in manufacturing, were to be covered by MWB regulations.[46]

The most controversial regulation next to that applying to the waitresses was the order covering office workers. Office workers in Winnipeg, St James, and St Boniface were limited to eight hours per day and forty-four hours per week with one half-holiday, in addition to Sunday, each week. In stores and shops, hours of labour for clerical workers were to be the same as for the selling force. The minimum wages for learners were set at $10.50 for the first three months and $11.50 for the second three, after which the rate for experienced adults was to reach $12.50 per week. Minors' wages varied according to age, ranging from $8 for fifteen-year-olds to $10.50 for seventeen-and-a-half year-olds. In offices employing nine or more female workers, not more than 25 per cent of the total staff (male and female) could be learners or minors. Employees with business training were to be exempt from the six months' learning period, and casuals had to be paid the adult minimum rates.[47]

Setting rates was one thing; enforcement of the MWB's decisions was another matter. Labour troubles in the spring of 1919 indicated that employers were not necessarily following the rulings of the board. Candy makers struck at Dingle-Stewart over the discharge of a female employee. The one-day strike was settled with the reinstatement of the employee, but further trouble was expected because the women alleged that they were not receiving the minimum wage. Seventeen women employees at Blackwoods, a foodstuffs manufacturer, struck on 14 April for wage increases promised the previous September. In this case negotiation between union leaders and the company secured the women back pay up to the minimum wage level as well as an eight-hour day, a half-day holiday on Saturdays, and the promise of a lunch and dressing room, as specified in the Factory Act. Helen Armstrong reported that the union men had 'splendidly backed their efforts.' Union tailors also threatened to strike to back up the attempt of women employees at the Manitoba Clothing Company to receive the twelve-dollar minimum for a fifty-hour work week. At an April meeting of the Winnipeg TLC complaints were made that employers were not paying the minimum wage at Hitchings Box factory, where women with eight years of experience received only eight dollars per week and young women of sixteen were paid only six dollars.[48]

Manitoba's experience with the MWB during and immediately following the First World War suggests the contradictions implicit in the arenas of class and gender. Public concern with inequalities for workers, and particularly women workers, and anxiety over labour unrest focused on the minimum wage as a solution. The minimum wage promised to provide a living wage for exploited women workers whose labour was perceived to compete with skilled labour. At the same time it promised to establish a mechanism whereby the state, with the cooperation of employers and employees, could intervene in the labour market to forestall disputes and correct inequities. While for some women workers the MWB meant improvement, the obstacles to enforcement remained large.

In the arena of gender relations, the minimum wage appeared to provide a solution to the problem of competition between men and women in the labour market, and as a result the trade union movement supported this measure. Minimum wage provisions based on the standard of a single woman worker's needs left untouched the presumption that men should earn a family wage. That the trade union movement did not argue for a minimum wage for unskilled male labourers as well indicated the depths of the divisions between men and women workers and the acknowledgment of a gender-based division of labour. Furthermore this endorsement of the minimum wage also indicated the prevailing view of women as a transitory and low-skilled reserve of labour, a view also accepted by employers and the state.

Once the attempt to legislate a flat minimum failed, the labour movement was caught in a contradictory position and chose to support and participate in a mechanism that clearly favoured employers since it allowed them to make the case for industry-by-industry decisions and to plead special circumstances. The concession of allowing lower rates for learners and minors also gave employers some flexibility while ignoring the needs of women who had to support themselves. The dispute between the Winnipeg TLC and the WLL divided labour and high-lighted the tensions between men and women in the working class.

In terms of class relations, the acceptance of the MWB meant the par-ticipation of working-class representatives in a mechanism designed to defuse class conflict, as well as gender conflict. One of the state's func-tions is to smooth over class contradictions, 'conceal exploitation and manipulate relations among classes and sectors of the economy.' Although not entirely successful, the Manitoba MWB defused consider-able conflict up to spring 1919.[49]

## IV

One of the results of the war was the increasing mobilization of women workers into unions and other groups that addressed the needs of women as wage workers and sometimes as consumers. While the initial dislocations and the paralysed economy of the early war years damp-ened labour activity, the later years of the war and the immediate post-war era witnessed the highest number of labour disputes recorded in Canada in the period from 1891 to 1950. Only at the end of the Second World War did the number of strikes approximate the levels found in the earlier period. A similar pattern appears in strikes involving women, which more than doubled in number between 1915–16 and 1917–18. But the strike activity in the last year of the war pales in comparison to the event-filled year of 1919, which witnessed an explosion in the number of strikes involving women, in addition to various general and sympa-thetic strikes. Unlike the general pattern, however, the number of strikes involving women in 1920 dropped by almost half. Nevertheless, the more than two hundred strikes in the period 1915–20 equalled the num-ber of labour disputes traced for women in the entire earlier period from 1890 to 1914 (see Tables 2.1 and 2.2 for comparison). This suggests that women's labour activism, as measured by labour disputes, reached its heights during the late war and immediate postwar period.[50]

As in the prewar period, the garment trades dominated labour dis-putes involving women, representing approximately 30 per cent of the total. Textile disputes assumed less prominence during the war as other sectors emerged as the locus for strikes. Both the service category (res-taurants, hotels, and laundries) and the tobacco industry felt the effects of labour disputes. The presence of women in non-traditional work-places, such as munitions, engine plants, and occasionally in transporta-tion, also opened up disputes about equal pay. In industries such as

TABLE 5.1
Strikes Involving Women, 1915–1920 (by Industry)

| Year | Garment | Textile | Boot & Shoe | Tobacco | Service | Communication | Print | Food | Metal | Transport | Professional | Other* | Total |
|---|---|---|---|---|---|---|---|---|---|---|---|---|---|
| 1915 | 7 | — | — | — | 3 | — | 3 | — | — | — | — | — | 13 |
| 1916 | 6 | — | 1 | 7 | 1 | — | 1 | — | 1 | — | — | — | 17 |
| 1917 | 8(1) | 2 | 1 | 2 | 3 | 3 | — | 5 | 5(2) | — | 2 | 2 | 34 |
| 1918 | 6 | 4 | 3 | 3 | 5 | 4 | 3 | — | 4 | 2 | 2 | — | 36 |
| 1919** | 20 | 7 | 4 | 4 | 5 | 4 | 4 | 7 | 1 | 2 | 1(1) | 6 | 66 |
| 1920 | 12 | 3 | 4 | 3 | 1 | — | 3 | 3 | — | 1 | — | 8 | 38 |
| Total | 60 | 16 | 13 | 19 | 18 | 11 | 14 | 15 | 13 | 5 | 4 | 16 | 204 |

*Other: retail; musicians – 2; public utility; paper – 2; glass; paper box – 2; upholsterers, mining; logging; furniture; saw; carriage; electrical
( ) means strike details on women unclear
**Does not include general or sympathetic strikes of 1919
Source: Labour Gazette; Strikes and Lockouts Files (Department of Labour); newspapers

printing and bookbinding where women had already made inroads, the war provided some opportunities to challenge the status quo. For women in fields such as clerical work, which had recently become female-dominated, few labour disputes were found. While clerical workers in some areas did organize, others were brought under minimum wage guidlelines, as noted above. In general, the strikes of the war and postwar period reflect both the importance of traditional industries and also the widening out of women's work experience into new areas, some of them only temporarily. In addition, wartime shortages affected women as consumers and sometimes resulted in militant action in the community rather than the workplace.

*Garment Strikes*

Economic recession and in particular the outbreak of war brought a halt to a long Toronto strike that had begun in March 1914 over the issue of contracting out. The strike by employees of the Dominion Cloak Company was joined by the employees of Exclusive Cloak when the two companies merged in May. The ILGWU spent $9000 on the strike before it was called off without settlement at the outbreak of war. Two weeks later the company closed down. This long and acrimonious dispute was pursued by the union as part of its drive to organize the trade completely, particularly the estimated one thousand women in the cloak and suit trade and the two thousand women employed in making dresses and whitewear. While the Jewish women were said to be thoroughly organized, the union was eager to organize the Canadian women and had high hopes of accomplishing the task before the declaration of war cut short the drive.[51]

Improvements in conditions in the trade were slow to come, and by the beginning of 1917 a strike of fewer than two hundred women and men in Montreal mushroomed into a major dispute involving over fifty shops and five thousand garment workers. The original strike at Semi-Ready, a men's clothing manufacturer that also sewed uniforms, involved members of six locals of the relatively new and confrontational Amalgamated Clothing Workers of America (ACWA), which was seeking union recognition. In early 1917, while the vice-president of the company labelled the strikers as agitators and aliens and accused them of sabotaging the war effort, their ranks were increased by the spread of the strike to other members of the Clothing Manufacturers' Association and to many small independent shops. Increased wages and shorter hours were added to the strike demands. Eventually, a board of inquiry recommended a compromise settlement that gave some wage increase but fell short of union recognition. As the ACWA strike was building steam, over twelve hundred ILGWU women cloakmakers began a strike on 26 January in Montreal over higher wages and reduced hours. In their case, a joint arbitration board was established to settle the dispute, which ended on 19 March.[52]

The *Ladies' Garment Worker* reported in early 1917 that there was agitation for a general strike in both Montreal and Toronto, and noted that 95 per cent of the trade had been organized. Employers were cognizant of changing conditions and were offering better wages and shorter hours. In July the international president of the ILGWU, Benjamin Schlesinger, reported that in Toronto work weeks had been reduced to forty-six and one-half hours in most shops. In a few shops hours had been set at forty-four, which became the goal for the whole industry. Noting that Toronto's trade was concentrated in twenty shops employing twenty-three hundred workers, while Montreal's trade was scattered in smaller establishments, Schlesinger reported that unfavourable conditions in Toronto (where the Eaton factory alone employed twelve hundred) necessitated a shop-by-shop strike strategy. The wartime campaign had increased ILGWU membership from four hundred to fifteen hundred, and a growing number of 'Gentile' women were joining the union. During 1917 then, the garment workers made steady progress, particularly in Montreal and Toronto. Obstacles remained, especially in the larger manufacturing establishments such as Eaton's where a long history of conflict focused special attention on the need to crack open these fortresses of anti-union resistance. In April 1918, the vice-president of the ILGWU noted that a special fund had been created to organize the Eaton's shops.[53]

The half-dozen strikes in the garment trade in 1918 featured a number of failures, especially among the disputes involving small numbers of workers. One larger strike involved approximately 150 ACWA members at Toronto's Tip Top Tailors. Forty-five women were employed by the company, which produced made-to-measure men's clothing. The union charged discrimination against union members when the staff was reduced in January. The company responded with a shutdown of operations and reported that the ACWA wanted not only union recognition and consultation over layoffs, but also the retention of all workers on short-time during slow periods. Despite the pledges of clothing workers to stand by their fellow strikers, and the phenomenal growth of ACWA membership from two hundred to thirteen hundred in eighteen months, the strike was lost as the company refused to take back half of the strikers and tried to force some of the active unionists to agree to a fifty-dollar deposit guaranteeing no strikes. A much larger strike at the same firm just over a year later, however, produced a successful conclusion with the same coat-, pant-, and vestmakers winning a 25 per cent increase, union recognition, and time and a half for overtime. Indeed, the year 1919 proved to be a period of noticeable conflict in the garment trades, with at least twenty strikes taking place, over half of them in Montreal.[54]

A small strike in Winnipeg involving fifteen to twenty women and ten men at the Manitoba Clothing Company in April demonstrated the difficulty of enforcing the orders of the Manitoba Minimum Wage Board, which were supposed to protect vulnerable women workers. Despite a mandated minimum of twelve dollars per week, the 'girls' at this company were paid nine dollars for a fifty-hour week. The company claimed that the women were not experienced enough to warrant the minimum wage. The tailors warned of a general strike, while the police, firemen, and street railway workers threatened to demand the union label on all uniforms, promising to back up their threat with strike action if necessary. Within a few days of the 1 April strike, the company settled, granting a forty-seven-hour week and a 10 per cent increase, an amount still considerably below the minimum wage.[55]

In many cities, garment workers were supportive of the Winnipeg General Strike of 15 May to 26 June. In Winnipeg, Montreal, and Toronto, for example, garment workers voted to support the strike. The events surrounding the general strike mobilized thousands of garment workers. The largest confrontation developed in Toronto beginning on 2 July among members of the ILGWU. In the early spring, the ACWA had succeeded in winning the forty-four-hour-week, partly as a result of a major strike in New York City that set standards for the industry. The ILGWU's plans to campaign for the same goal had been sidetracked by the general strike, but in July, the union decided to push ahead with a major strike to win a new wage scale, end piecework, and obtain the forty-four-hour week, among other improvements. Garment workers were also concerned about abuses in overtime. They demanded time-and-a-half payment, limits on the amount of over-time, and the banning of overtime when there were unemployed workers needing jobs. The garment workers were scattered around dozens of shops and sewed various types of clothing, but the four locals worked together under a

joint board of cloak-, suit-, and dressmakers' locals for maximum leverage with employers.[56]

The garment workers remained solid, backed by the union, which
sent its international president to Toronto in July to bolster the strike.
Striker militancy resulted in a number of arrests on the picket line for
interfering with scabs. At least eight young women strikers appeared in
court in July and August for heckling or assaulting scabs. All the women
arrested were Jewish, and tensions in the union ranks surfaced during
the dispute between Jews and non-Jews. ILGWU official Sam Koldofsky
urged greater solidarity, reporting to the Toronto TLC that those who
refused to honour the strike were primarily 'gentiles.' Striker solidarity
faltered temporarily in mid-August, but resumed course after employers rejected a compromise settlement that would have replaced the original demand for an end to piecework with a new agreement on week
work and a minimum wage. The sticking point focused on recognition
of the union. Although the workers eventually failed to achieve full recognition of the union, the strike ended in September with considerable
gains and with the satisfaction that the employers had had to deal with
representatives of the cloakmakers as a body, rather than with individual shops.[57]

Not all garment trade strikes took place in large urban centres; small
towns were sometimes the site of militant activity among clothing trade
workers as well. Unlike urban strikes, however, small-town labour disputes could pit workers against the major source of employment in an
area, leaving strikers with few alternate sources of income.

In small towns with single employers or in larger centres where
employer associations functioned well, workers on strike could be
blacklisted and unable to find work to support their families. A major
strike in the hat industry in Montreal and in Marieville, a small town
east of that city, proved disastrous for the Marieville workers. Owner
E. Guillet, the self-styled 'King of Marieville,' blamed the hatmakers'
union for the 1919 strike among the straw-hat makers and the lockout of
the felt-hat workers who sympathized with the less-skilled and less
well-paid straw-hat workers. According to Mme Rosalinda Trudel's
memorandum to the Department of Labour on behalf of all the employees, Guillet's firm was the largest industry in the town, employing
approximately seventy workers, a few dozen of them women, some of
whom were married with children. Trudel's statement pointed out that
the workers were loyal and industrious and that their labour had created Guillet's wealth. The employers of Montreal and Marieville had

formed an association that specified a heavy fine for any manufacturer who employed a discharged worker, making it impossible for the hat workers to get alternate employment. Clearly, the hat workers felt that the employers were out to smash the union. Guillet had met with the workers and asked union members to stand on one side of the room and non-unionists on the other. He then proceeded to fire the unionists, 'many of them fathers of families and mothers of children.' Attempts to find other work and to convince Guillet to agree to Department of Labour or provincial government conciliation had been arrogantly refused, leaving the workers on the edge of starvation and hounded by company 'toadies.' The Marieville strike ended in January 1920, a total failure.[58]

By 1920, employers began to undermine workers' gains by attempting to reintroduce piecework among garment workers and by reducing wages or failing to pay union scale. In Montreal, for example, two hundred employees at H. Vineberg struck for a week in December against reduced hours and cuts in wages. As the company explained the situation, bad times meant that Vineberg could not pay as high a wage scale as it had during the wartime boom. When the 75 women and 125 men struck after promising to continue to fill special orders, the company advertised for workers in the newspaper, receiving hundreds of applications. In the meantime, the Department of Labour stepped in to arbitrate, and the strikers returned with the understanding that the company would accept a new agreement to be signed with the Clothing Manufacturers' Association. For sixty Toronto garment workers at J.H. Winter, a 1 December strike against reversion to piecework ended disastrously for the workers when the company decided to go out of business. For forty others who struck at A. Roth on 25 November, the result of the three-month battle was defeat: fifteen women and twenty-five men had to accept a return to the piecework system. The more favourable conditions accompanying the boom in the garment trade had come to an end.[59]

*Women in Male-Dominated Industries*

Just as women could be found in munitions performing work usually reserved for men, women also appeared in heavy industry during the war, although in small numbers and restricted jobs. Several strikes involving women in heavy industry occurred in Pictou County, Nova Scotia, in 1917 and 1918. Fifty to seventy-five women were counted as participants in a strike at the Eastern Car Company in Trenton when hundreds of workers struck, demanding the dismissal of an enemy alien in December 1917. The strike succeeded in forcing the dismissal of an American citizen born in Germany. Five months later, four thousand workers employed by Nova Scotia Steel and Coal (Scotia), Eastern Car, and two smaller firms, went on strike for wage increases and recognition of Federal Labour Union 14781. While several of the firms employed only men, Scotia and Eastern Car respectively employed 73 and 80 women strikers in munitions and car-building. A royal commission appointed to weigh the demands and determine a settlement proved to be disappointing, despite the presence of mine workers' leader, J.B. McLachlan, on the commission. Not satisfied with the partial increases and unhappy that the commission did not recommend recognition of the union, twenty-seven hundred employees at the steel works and the car company launched another strike in June. Workers' representative C.C. Dane noted in his report that two hundred women were among the strikers. Despite the second strike, union recognition failed to materialize and small wage increases remained the norm. Anti-strike sentiments were high at the time because of the war and the fact that the companies could not compete with technologically more sophisticated plants in other parts of Canada. For the women, however, the strike reportedly resulted in equal pay for equal work.[60]

The employment of women as specialists and inspectors at the Willys-Overland engine manufacturing plant in Toronto in 1918 caused some concern among the toolmakers and machinists who resisted what they viewed as attempts to lower wage scales generally by paying women less. The Toronto *World* stated that the employees walked out because they believed that the two hundred women taking men's places in factories should be paid men's wages. The union demanded forty-five cents an hour for specialists, both male and female, but only thirty-five cents for inspectors, who were mostly women. At the same time the company was trying to offer the women twenty to twenty-seven-and-one-half cents. T.A. Russell, a partner in the airplane engine plant, claimed that the women were unskilled and required weeks of instruction. Clearly Russell thought the average women's wage of $13.75 per week sufficient for their five-and-a-half-day week; men, however, averaged more than double this at $30.94. The week-long strike was settled by the acceptance of a wage schedule based on proficiency, thus undercutting the equal pay demand. A second strike at the Russell Car Company in June–July 1918 also illustrated the precarious position of women in non-traditional jobs. One hundred and thirty-five machinists and toolmakers, including seven women, struck against the dismissal of a man fired for trade union activity. The strike dragged on because the strikers insisted that the women be reinstated along with the men. A joint committee, however, ruled that the employment of women had never been the subject of an agreement. Moreover, it stated that the women's dismissal had been due to lack of work and promised that the women would be rehired as work became available.[61]

While American historian Maurine Greenwald has noted the obstacles faced by women who replaced men on streetcars, very little evidence exists of women actually substituting for men in Canada. One strike in Halifax in February 1918, however, revealed that twenty women worked as conductors for the Nova Scotia Tramways Company during the war. They were among 130 to 150 employees who objected to the dismissal and suspension of fellow workers over a refusal to follow orders regarding extra shift work. The issue for the strikers centred around extra shift work for regular conductors who were asked to act as relief motormen in addition to their regular work. Whether such extra shifts applied to women conductors is not clear. While the press pointed to male workers' opposition to the employment of women conductors, the company claimed that initial resistance to the female workers had ceased. Elsewhere in Canada, however, the replacement of men by women provoked labour resistance.[62]

Sectors associated with male craft skills, such as printing, also provided evidence of women's militancy during the war. While numerous women worked in binderies and a few as compositors, they were often found working as pressmen's assistants in large printing plants. Such was the case in Ottawa where women employees of the American Bank Note Company walked out five times during the war. Three disputes occurred in 1915, shortly after the women formed Federal Labour Union No. 20; one strike of less than a day occurred in 1916; and a long, drawn-out dispute occurred between November 1918 and February 1919. Four of the five incidents revolved around dismissals and charges of discrimination towards union members. Furthermore, three of these four clearly revealed conflict between workers and management about workplace discipline and implied standards of appropriate work behaviour. Eighty-five women walked out in February 1915, when the company dismissed members of a committee representing the women for refusing to say whether they had visited a local member of Parliament to obtain assistance in getting a laid-off woman rehired. Perhaps taken aback by the solidarity of the women, management quickly met with representatives and worked out a settlement to reinstate the woman who had objected to the company's refusal to abide by seniority in layoffs. In March, sixty women went out over wages and reached an equally quick settlement with management.[63]

In December, a week-long dispute at the same company involved sixty-three women alleging discriminatory treatment of a union woman who had been dismissed for hitting one of the printers. The company maintained that they had the right to discipline the woman by firing her. In the middle of the strike two young women employees and union members, Carrie O'Sullivan and Lola Winchester, visited the offices of the Department of Labour to relate a different story. According to the department's memo, the women reported that the dismissed employee had been molested by one of the men and had defended herself against his behaviour. In addition, they related that the strikers had been summoned to the superintendent's office and told they must sign anti-union pledges as a condition of reinstatement. O'Sullivan and Winchester had first consulted P.M. Draper of the Trades and Labor Congress, who sent them to the Department. Consultations between Draper and the Department resulted in officials promising both Draper and the women that their representations would be brought to the minister's attention, which it was, but only a month after the dispute had been settled. Despite the company's allegedly tough stand on the discipline issue, the suspended woman worker returned to her job and the parties agreed to set up a permanent conciliation committee representing both workers and management.[64]

With the exception of a short walkout over the dismissal of a foreman in 1916, no further labour disputes emerged at the American Bank Note Company until November 1918 when the women in the union again walked out in a dispute with management over a woman apparently engaging in 'inappropriate behaviour' during working hours. According to Tom Moore, president of the Trades and Labor Congress, the press feeders struck over a dispute that revolved around a woman laughing aloud. Unfortunately, except for a press report that indicated heated arguments at the Allied Trades and Labor Council, little more is known about the conflict, which resulted in a three-month strike and the replacement of the women. Sentiments were expressed that the men's union (presumably the Printing Pressmen) should have gone out in support of the women to help settle the strike. Moore was also criticized because he advised the women to ask the company for reinstatement.[65]

Despite the sketchy details, what is clear from the disputes at the American Bank Note Company is the relative independence of the women in the earlier strikes, which they waged alone. These women had a clear sense of themselves as workers and disputed the company's attempts to discipline and intimidate them. While they called upon the services of labour leaders, the Department of Labour, and at least one politician, they did so from a position of collective solidarity as women workers.

*Service Industries: Hotels, Restaurants, and Laundries*

While women had been employed in various service industries for decades, labour organization was slow to materialize and difficult to maintain among maids, waitresses, and laundry workers. Such jobs were often low-paid and described as unskilled, perhaps because of their resemblance to the domestic work performed by housewives. As a consequence of their low pay and unskilled label, these sectors attracted immigrant labour, and there were consistent attempts by workers and their unions to restrict or eliminate competition for service jobs from immigrants, most often Asian men. Unionization in the service sector was hampered not only by the nature of the work and the workplace, but also by the divided nature of the labour force as well as the assumption that unionization was tied to craft skill.

One of the most active unions of women restaurant workers was located in Vancouver. A large number of waitresses joined Local 28 of the Hotel and Restaurant Employees' Union when it was established in July 1900. The union was divided and weak, however, and experienced sharp ups and downs in its first decade of existence. The waitresses left to form their own local in June 1910, a trend towards autonomy that was also evident in American unions. Within four years, the waitresses had rejoined the cooks' and waiters' local. The recession, the failure to obtain shorter hours, and the loss of a strike at the Ritz Café in 1913, with the replacement of all ten or eleven waitresses, contributed to the failure of the waitresses' local. As in many other sectors, labour disputes in restaurants were more frequent and often more successful in the later war years. Most centred around changing the long hours (often ten to eleven hours a day, seven days a week) and raising the low wages. The union chose to adopt the tactic of the consumer boycott of non-union or unfair restaurants but found such methods difficult to enforce. The discharge of two union waitresses at McLeod's Café in October 1917 led to a prolonged strike with demands for the eight-hour day and six-day week, as well as minimum salaries. Despite months of maintaining a picket line, the aid of the Vancouver TLC and prominent women trade unionists such as Helena Gutteridge, and appeals to trade unionists and the public to avoid patronizing the restaurant, the strike fizzled out in December. At the December 21 meeting of Local 28, the strike committee reported on its decision to withdraw the 'girls' picketing McLeod's (because of cold weather!), and fraternal delegate Winch from the International Longshoreman's Association moved a vote of thanks to the waitresses 'for their determination, and by showing a good example to other Unions.'66

While it was difficult to win a strike in the hotel and restaurant trade, not all strikes produced such discouraging results. In Calgary in 1918, two strikes occurred in the first half of the year, the first involving forty waitresses and waiters at the Palliser Hotel (a Canadian Pacific hotel). The dismissal of unionist Mrs Marta Barber, employed as an extra in the dining room, caused the walkout of Local 597 of the Hotel and Restaurant Employees' Union in January. While the walkout prompted the manager to pay Barber's wages and give her a letter of recommendation, he would not agree to reinstate her. Two months later, approximately two hundred culinary workers in twenty-two establishments walked out for increased wages and union recognition. Such concerted action across the city meant more bargaining clout. While some workers were replaced, those in the larger establishments won a victory when their employers agreed to the union scale, six-day weeks, and eight-and-one-half-hour days. Limits were placed on apprenticeship, and wages were to be paid weekly instead of twice a month.67

The Canadian Pacific hotel in Vancouver also experienced a strike in 1918 by twenty-five chambermaids and an equal number of waiters, who were badly overworked and underpaid. Seven-day weeks of fifty-six hours for the waiters and sixty-six for the maids, both at extremely low pay, prompted a unanimous vote for the walkout. Threats by management to hire Japanese women at higher wages convinced the maids to join the union, according to one union source quoted in a Vancouver daily. In this industry, ethnic divisions and racial competition were directly experienced by white workers who often worked in the same establishment with Asians. The CPR maintained that the waiters received very high tips and refused to give into demands for a $15 a month raise to $50. The intervention of MLA Mary Ellen Smith on behalf of the maids failed to produce any results, but similar intervention by

Mrs Crothers, the wife of the federal minister of labour, produced some effect. Management agreed to increase wages by $3 to $22.50 per month, with a reduction in the work week to fifty hours, the latter a significant improvement. The corporation, however, threatened to replace members of the union as soon as it was convenient, thus underlining the hollow nature of the victory. What is striking here, nonetheless, is the solidarity between waiters and chambermaids; while the waiters went back to work under the old conditions, they agreed to end the strike 'in view of the fact the Chambermaids was [sic] granted concessions.' Cross-class gender solidarity, evidenced by the involvement of Smith and Crothers with the striking chambermaids, was also noteworthy, all the more because of its rarity.[68]

Prior to the general strikes of 1919, one of the most militant strikes in a service industry occurred in the laundry trade in Vancouver in the fall of 1918. Unlike the restaurant and hotel trade, the work process in laundries was factory-like and often dangerous. In addition, competition from Asian workers was indirect in that Chinese hand laundries were separate from the mechanized steam laundries employing whites. As in other sectors, the war boom provided encouraging conditions for unionizing. One participant recalled the decision to organize the union in May 1918 as stemming from the fact that 'we had one driver by the name of Victor Midgely,' a prominent figure in the Vancouver TLC. The fledgling union was also assisted by the engineers' union and by other unionists such as Helena Gutteridge.[69]

The strike, which began on Labour Day and ended at the close of 1918, involved primarily women workers (80 per cent of the 290 strikers were women) in a massive struggle to raise wages, lower hours, and obtain a union shop in the laundry trade. While two of the laundries granted the demands by the end of October, seven others refused. Financial assistance came from the union movement, and the public appeared sympathetic to the women's cause. The longshoremen's union was particularly supportive of the laundry workers. Ellen Barber, one of the strikers, recalled that it was common for longshoremen to buy meals for the women on strike and that they would rip the tires of the bosses' cars caught escorting scabs to the streetcar. Nonetheless the strike was doomed by employer intransigence, a decision by the Vancouver TLC not to call a general strike (on the advice of Helena Gutteridge, who reported that the strikers felt it would hurt their cause), and the Minimum Wage Board's investigation and eventual order that laundry workers be paid a minimum of $13.50 per week. Attempts to settle the strike through the provincial Labour Department and, through the mayor, by the invocation of federal Industrial Disputes Investigation Act, failed. While many lost their livelihoods, a few women like Barber found a position at the Excelsior Laundry, which started as a union laundry during the strike. Most of the strikers were not so fortunate, and some faced legal proceedings and jail terms as a result of strike incidents.[70]

This strike became a focal point for the labour movement in Vancouver in late 1918. The dispsute represented a massive face-off between organized labour and employers, one that gave added impetus to the labour revolt of 1919. This strike added incentive to the campaign for the One Big Union, which the Vancouver laundry workers supported when the time came. Less well known or understood is the class solidarity expressed by members of the Chinese and East Indian communities. While the Chinese promised not to scab, the Japanese refused, resulting in a boycott of Japanese laundries. The East Indian community helped finance the strike. These acts suggest that in times of crisis, at least, ethnic divisions within the working class might be overcome.[71]

*A Consumers' Strike*

Workplace strikes were not the only form of organized militancy among women during the war years. In addition to Women's Labor Leagues, trade union auxiliaries, anti-conscription groups, and labour churches, working-class women also organized against the high cost of living during the war. While public campaigns for thrift and consumer protection were most often associated with middle- or upper-middle-class Canadian or British-born women, working-class, ethnic women also protested the high cost of necessities such as food, shelter, and fuel. European historians have noted the importance of 'communal strikes' by neighbourhood women who, based on their sense of responsibility for the provision of subsistence to their families, demanded food, fuel, or moderately priced housing. Women testifying before the 1919 Royal Commission on Industrial Relations (Mathers Commission) also indicated that these issues were very much at the forefront of the minds of Canadian working-class and socialist women, as the commission travelled the country taking evidence about industrial unrest. A concrete example of women's militancy related to the cost of food occurred in Toronto's Jewish community in May 1917.[72]

Jewish women in Toronto organized a campaign against Jewish bakers in the city after learning of the bakers' decision to raise the price of

bread several cents, to twelve cents per loaf. Street-corner and synagogue meetings were held to condemn the 'bread trust,' and housewives urged their sisters to bake their own bread rather than buying it
from the fifteen Jewish bakeries in the city. A mass meeting held at the
McCaul Street synagogue on 24 May resulted in a resolution urging the
dominion government to appoint a food commissioner, a resolution echoed several days later at the Trades and Labor Council meeting. The
mass meeting also called on all housewives to refuse to patronize restaurants supplied by the bakers. The bakers responded by suggesting a
board of arbitration to settle the dispute, but the angry women refused
on the grounds that most of the bakers had an agreement with the mill-
ing firms to supply flour at a fixed price and that therefore the increases
were unnecessary.[73]

The bakers resolved to stand firm and most closed their shops. Baker
Harry Ruben stated in the press that his drivers were afraid to attempt
to deliver bread to his few remaining patrons. He also asserted that 'the
poorer classes of the Jewish community cannot afford to spend money
on coal to bake with and will have to pay such a high price for flour that
it will not pay them to bake their own bread.' Their only other alternative was to buy from Gentile bakeries charging the same price. The
women, however, were not deterred. According to Mrs Hanna Baker of
the Jewish women's strike committee, 'the women are not faltering but
standing together in an effort to force the bakeries to deliver bread at a
reasonable cost.'[74]

As the women grew more impatient with the bakers, street actions
resulted in broken windows, raids on bakeries and restaurants and
distribution of purloined bread to the poor. In addition, the women
appealed to non-Jewish bakers for support and also began to bake bread
for single men, as well as offering to bake for restaurants. Furthermore,
the women vowed to engage in similar actions for fish and meat once
the bread fight was won.[75]

Despite the women's appeal to Gentile bakers, the latter sided with
their Jewish counterparts, concerned that a successful campaign might
force them to reduce their own prices. While the Gentile bakeries had
dropped the price of bread to nine cents, they were only too aware of the
predicament of the Jewish bakers, who had been unable to sell their
bread since the strike began. As the strike dragged on, the bakers proposed various compromises, which were rejected. Even a compromise
supported by the women's committee was turned down at a mass
meeting of two thousand people on 10 June. A new committee was

appointed 'with instructions to secure bread at nine cents or not at all.' Ten days later a settlement was reached, which agreed to a price of ten cents per loaf until flour prices dropped, at which point a nine-cent loaf was mandated. Despite the compromise, the women strikers had waged a successful and impressive battle, mobilizing the Jewish community behind them.[76]

## V

The war presented women with new opportunities for organization and activism. The women's movement argued that women's services in the labour market and in the war effort should be recognized and taken as concrete proof that women were ready to assume the duties of citizenship, including the right to the franchise. Benevolent recognition of women's citizenship, however, was not the major factor in bringing about the franchise for women. At the federal level, wartime electoral politics were key.

At the same time the war period witnessed a heightened awareness of women's labour as evidenced by the investigations of women's work carried out by women's groups, other voluntary agencies, and government, the latter particularly through provincial inquiries and legislation to enact the minimum wage. Concern about the mobilization of labour power for the war effort became more intense by 1916, as the wartime boom absorbed previously unemployed men and women; conscription also added intensity to fears of labour shortages. At the federal level, the response was piecemeal, and the government remained reluctant to engage in sustained mobilization of women's labour power. While government encouraged the hiring of thousands of women in munitions production, labour policies stressed non-interference with the contractors who hired and paid the wages. While equal pay was much discussed, particularly as a means of allaying labour's fears that women would undercut men's hard-won gains, a clear-cut policy was lacking. Indeed, the relatively good wages initiated by Mark Irish for women munitions inspectors were subject to reduction for newly hired women without apparent discussion of whether women could live adequately on them. Just as Joseph Flavelle of the Imperial Munitions Board opposed any notion of a fair wage policy and eschewed interfering with men's wages, the bureaucracy under Irish steered away from taking any initiatives for women.

Despite lack of a clear-cut, positive policy on women's labour, women found wartime employment opportunities, not only in munitions and a few other non-traditional areas, but also in areas of traditional employment as well as in the newly expanding areas of sales, service, and clerical work. Trade unionists were particularly concerned about women replacing men and undercutting the boundaries of skilled work. While opposing the dilution of labour, male trade unionists also came to view equal pay as a trade-off in situations where women were employed at 'men's work.' Minimum wage legislation also received labour's support in many instances, often viewed as a substitute for the unionization of women. Nevertheless, some unions, also tried to organize women during the war, and women themselves found the prospect of unionization more attractive during the war boom and during the postwar period than they had in earlier years. Sectors previously unorganized or poorly organized, such as the garment trades, hotels and restaurants, sales, and professionals (teachers and civil servants) took advantage of favourable circumstances to organize women and to bargain collectively. The level of strike activity from 1917 through 1920 among women workers reflects these more favourable, if temporary, circumstances.

Labour and socialist women, like women identified with other political perspectives, were divided over the war itself. The outbreak of a worldwide conflict raised difficult issues for women who opposed armed conflict as a solution to international rivalries. For some socialist and labour women the war not only presented a personal, ethical crisis, but also a threat to those movements they so closely identified with in their search for a more just and equitable society for both women and men.

# 6

# 'This Crimson Storm of War':
# Women, War, and Socialism

For the women of the middle and ruling classes, generally speaking, war exists for them in conversations, military balls, reviews, anniversary banquets, organizing and raising patriotic funds, and kindred activities. Their husbands and sons go to war, but keep well away from the danger zones ... For the women of the masses, however, who supply 93 per cent of the army, the story is a different one. The women of the masses, during the war were used to do the meanest work ... While the blood of their men folk was being coined into profits on the battle fields, their labor, sex and necessities were the object of profit, extortion, and barter at home. In munition, garment and packing factories, they toiled incessantly, doing the work of men, but receiving 'woman's pay.' Ministers of the gospel grew wrathy and demanded that they 'do their duty to replenish the loss of war,' illegitimacy [sic] was winked at and excused as 'one of the inevitable results of war.' ... They were told to knit socks, scarfs and sweaters and other garments to keep the boys warm, but when they went to buy the yarn they found the price had soared.

Rose Henderson, *Woman and War*

Writing in 1924, Rose Henderson, a Montreal socialist, Federated Labor Party activist, juvenile court worker, and outspoken anti-war activist, captured the different impact of the First World War on women of various classes in Canada, a factor largely ignored in contemporary historical accounts. Socialist women, like the socialist and labour movements in general, were not united in their stance towards the war. A vocal minority of women such as Henderson, Violet McNaughton, Francis Marion Beynon, Laura Hughes, and Gertrude Richardson were outright pacifists. Most socialist women, while critical of war and keenly aware of its particular effects on the working class, did not adopt a pacifist position. Some actively worked to promote socialism either within socialist party structures or in more broadly based organizations; others worked for various reforms that would benefit the working class, especially women and children. A number of socialist women worked in organized groups like the people's forums, labour churches, leagues for soldiers' dependants, anti-conscription campaigns, or in organizations that focused on the problems of working women.[1]

These organizations were particularly active in the Prairie West, although efforts to fight conscription of manpower and to assist working women certainly existed in other parts of Canada as well. While the war divided socialist women (as well as men), both opponents and proponents of the conflict attempted to counter the effects of war on women and children and to challenge the imposition of compulsory military service, which promised to have a disproportionate effect on working-class men, women, and their families. Like Rose Henderson, many socialist women acknowledged the profound upheaval that the war represented. In 1918, Henderson wrote: 'Mighty are the changes wrought through war in the world of man, but mightier by far those taking place in the world of woman. It may not seem logical to separate the world of man and woman, but since woman bears, moulds and nurtures the race, and must continue to do so, what affects her and the unborn generations is basic and fundamental: a thousand times more important than man's mechanical inventions and material enterprises.' Not all socialist women focused on gender-related issues during the war. Women in the Socialist Party of Canada, for example, tended to emphasize the class dimensions of the war, as did prominent SPC men who maintained that the class struggle, not the sex struggle, was central to an agenda for social change.[2]

Despite these competing interpretations of the meaning of the war, some socialist women were able to raise women's issues in the context of class concerns and to integrate such issues into the socialist framework. Viewing working-class women as their particular, although by no means exclusive, constituency, women socialists tied specific gender issues, such as the impact of women's wage labour on her family responsibilities and inadequate allowances for soldiers' wives and dependent children, to the struggle for 'a world that is no longer ruled by fear and force, but guided and governed by reason and love with equal opportunities and a square deal for all,' as Harriet Dunlop Prenter wrote in 1917. In so doing, these women demonstrated the breadth of their vision and activities. As activists rather than ideologues, socialist women raised important issues that underlined the economic, political, and ideological restrictions on working-class women. Their creation of, and participation in, various socialist, labour, and progressive organizations during the war period also illuminates the interconnections between the members of these groups.[3]

What did socialist women expect the war to accomplish? Like their European counterparts they believed that war would increase the potential for class conflict, 'and that in the process the consciousness of proletarian women was bound to rise,' and they indeed found inspiration and opportunity for activism. The dislocations of the war gave plenty of scope for women socialists to utilize their organizational talents in ways that implicitly, if not explicitly, pushed the 'woman question' into the public arena. Explicit debate on the question never erupted with quite the same vehemence as it did in the prewar period, but the tensions surrounding gender and class issues continued to colour the socialist movement throughout the war.[4]

The activities of socialist women must be considered in the context of the initial enthusiasm for Canada's participation in the war. Widespread support for the war effort initially characterized communities, especially in the West, where recent English immigrants had settled. The provinces of Manitoba, British Columbia, and Alberta provided the highest enlistment rates in the country, while the Maritimes and Quebec demonstrated the lowest rates. The large wave of western enlistments meant that the problem of soldiers' families loomed larger in the West than elsewhere in the country. It is not surprising, then, that this is where significant activity around pensions and allowances for soldiers' dependants took place. In the West, the war specifically seemed to promise a way out from an economic slump that followed the slowdown in construction, particularly of railroad lines. The war promised the farmer higher prices for crops, but it also brought the West higher urban unemployment and tempted farmers to expand beyond their capabilities, while encouraging more and more reliance on the wheat economy.[5]

In the early stages of the war, hard times increased the attractiveness of enlistment to men without jobs. Later the conscription debate, the mounting casualties, and the hardships at home would dampen enthusiasm and lead to conflicts within communities. In Quebec, the war proved particularly divisive in an atmosphere of increasing discontent over language and national issues.

The war crisis energized women, who immediately responded by organizing support for the war effort through groups such as the Red Cross, the Patriotic Fund, the YWCA, the Women's Canadian Club, the Imperial Order Daughters of the Empire, and Local Councils of Women, among others. Activities ranged from promoting recruitment, knitting and sewing soldiers' comforts, and setting up employment bureaux for women to lobbying for mothers' pensions and improved pensions for soldier's dependants. Voluntary women's groups like the YWCA aided government by setting up hostels and canteens for women munitions workers. The director of the Department of Labour in the Imperial Munitions Board, Mark Irish, praised the efforts of YWCA women who repaid the IMB $2500 advanced to them to set up the hostel and canteen services, noting that these women were aiding the welfare work so necessary in the process of employing women in munitions production.[6]

In keeping with women's primary responsibility for the home, the high cost of living and food shortages drew the attention of women's groups like Calgary's Consumers' League, which sought to bring products in bulk to the city market to be sold at reduced prices. Food conservation and thrift campaigns were launched in many cities; in Toronto a women's convention on food conservation took place in July 1917 to discuss food substitutes and methods of preserving food. The demand for increased farm production for the war effort prompted some Ontario farmers to hire the services of young University of Toronto women as substitutes for scarce regular farm labour, but generally campaigns to recruit farm labour among women in urban areas met with limited success. Farm women as well as urban women, however, engaged in considerable war support activities, as the annual reports of prairie women's organizations demonstrate. On occasion, rural and urban women joined forces to discuss cooperation in the war effort.[7]

While most of this work occurred at the local level, the National Council of Women of Canada (NCWC), with its main strength in eastern Canada, endeavoured to promote coordination among its various local councils and affiliates scattered across the country. As a nationally organized body of middle-class women, the NCWC and its affiliates were sought out by government for information and advice in wartime, particularly in the areas of women's work and trade union organization. Hostile to pacifism and divided over conscription, the NCWC generally supported the war effort and cooperated with other organizations specifically concerned with war work.[8]

The suffrage movement in Canada was also divided over the war.

While the executive of Canadian Suffrage Association (CSA) 'kept an open mind on the whole issue of war and peace' and sponsored occasional lectures by pacifists, the rival and more conservative National Equal Franchise Union (NEFU) condemned any discussion of peace until the war ended and supported patriotic activities at the expense of continued suffrage activism. The CSA, on the other hand, maintained its campaign of pro-suffrage petitions and deputations throughout the war. When the Borden government passed the 1917 Wartime Elections Act, the CSA condemned it as a half-hearted, partisan measure while the NEFU enthusiastically supported the nativist and pro-conscription measure.[9]

The outbreak of war prompted Canadian socialist groups, fractured in the prewar period over various issues, including the commitment to internationalism, to react with anti-war pronouncements in the press. An SPC manifesto eschewed protest resolutions in favour of pointing out that the international capitalist class fomented wars for business reasons and that the result would be to divide the working class, which provided the capitalist class with its wealth. Thus, the working class had no stake or interest in this war: 'The only struggle that can be of vital interest to the working class of all nations is that which has for its object the wresting of this power from the hands of the master class.'[10]

The Social Democratic Party also opposed the war but was more divided within, largely along ethnic lines. The eastern European members of the SDP particularly stressed that the main enemy of the working class was at home, not in the trenches of Europe, while its English-Canadian leadership provided more abstract and sometimes pacifist-leaning responses to war. The SDP in particular broke into factions as the war continued. Members of both socialist parties abandoned the anti-war stance to speak out for Britain and against the 'Huns,' and some of the men enlisted in the armed services or encouraged others to do so. In the first years of the war, socialist party memberships declined as men enlisted and as anti-war positions came under attack. The ranks of immigrant members were also reduced as they became targets of arrest and internment as 'enemy aliens.' Interest in socialism revived in the last two years of the war as socialists emerged as front-line defenders of a working class hard-pressed by wartime inflation and repressive state policies that stifled protest and dissent.[11]

Anti-war sentiment among labour organizations before 1914 eventually gave way as workers enlisted during the early part of the war. Despite pronouncements of sympathy with the working class as the bearers of the war burden, and later opposition to registration, and conscription, labour councils and the national TLC backed off earlier proposals to stage general strikes to oppose the war, registration, and conscription. In 1914 the national TLC repudiated its 1911 resolution for a general strike in case of war and eventually urged support for the allies. Initially opposing both registration and conscription, the TLC backed the government once these measures were introduced.[12]

Despite these capitulations, the government did not reveal much readiness to cooperate with organized labour. In June 1917 TLC officials called a meeting to discuss the difficulties labour faced from the Imperial Munitions Board. Citing evidence of hostility to organized labour, the meeting noted the erosion of labour's position through the elimination of the eight-hour day, the introduction of female labour to replace skilled men, and the failure to preserve wage standards through equal pay. The meeting also opposed conscription of men and use of alien labour by the state, while condemning the high cost of living and suggesting measures to combat inflation through public ownership, food and fuel commissions with labour representation, and similar tactics. By January 1918, labour found the government more cooperative in the wake of the Unionist victory the previous month. A national conference between labour and government struck a bargain in which organized labour received some important concessions in return for its cooperation in the war effort. Socialists in the labour movement who had waged a vigorous fight against registration and conscription bitterly criticized the Trades and Labor Congress's moves, but were unable to muster enough support to succeed in changing policies. In the course of the struggle against registration and conscription and in the midst of spiralling prices and criticisms of war profiteers, socialist men and women began to find increasing sympathy among progressives. Socialist organizations began to recoup their losses, and their members surfaced as prominent leaders of a more militant union movement in the later war period.[13]

I

While it is difficult to discern any single approach to the war among socialist women, they were usually quick to point out that the conflict stemmed from rivalries among capitalist countries and to note the particular impact of war on women and children. The antipathy of women to war was a theme in both pacifist and non-pacifist commentary since motherhood was viewed as predisposing women to a critical view of war. To be sure, maternal ideology was also shared by supporters of the war effort, but the conclusions reached were quite different. While maternal feminist arguments stressed the importance of women's support for public activities geared to support the war, maternal feminism also shored up the arguments of socialist-pacifist women who appealed to women as mothers to stop the carnage on the battlefield.[14]

From the anonymous letters sent to socialist newspapers, to the columns written by women journalists such as Francis Marion Beynon and Gertrude Richardson, women socialists endeavoured to record their opposition to the war. Physical motherhood ('nine months of physical discomfort and suffering often culminating in hours of the most excruciating agony which mortals can have') made woman the 'natural conserver of life,' according to *Cotton's Weekly*. The war signified an 'awful moral cataclysm' for sons and brought heartbreak and anxiety to 'decent, well-ordered lives,' stated 'Mater Dolorosa.' Within a month of the start of the conflict, veteran journalist Francis Marion Beynon noted in her *Grain Growers' Guide* column the war's severe economic effects on single women workers. More importantly, for Beynon motherhood represented the potential source not only of opposition to the war, but also for social reform in general. Her columns thus argued for an expanded sphere for women in reform and political circles, encompassing temperance, suffrage, economic justice for farmers, improved rural health and schooling for children, and an emphasis on good citizenship. As Barbara Roberts has pointed out, for Beynon, 'politics was not something unrelated to family and work; daily life, family, community, national and international relationships all should be carried out in the same spirit.'[15]

With the outbreak of war, Beynon found her vision of women in the vanguard of social reform challenged as patriotic, nativist women in Canada rallied to the war effort and proclaimed that those who refused to assist were in league with the enemy. Despite the increasing pressure to support the war effort, Beynon maintained a principled pacifism and, in the process, became more radical and more critical of human progress. Her belief in the rationality of ordinary people, her respect for democratic principles, and her social gospel religious convictions were strengthened by the war experience. The war's 'intolerant and conformist' patriotism led Beynon to the position that 'patriotism and militarism were the ideological mask worn by the established, unjust order.' Her critique of war profiteering as individual and corporate greed was matched by an understanding of the wastefulness of war and the potential utility of putting funds used to buy military supplies into productive enterprises, such as health care and education. By 1916 Beynon urged a negotiated peace and the outlawing of war production profits, and by 1917 she both wrote against conscription and participated in anti-conscription activities in Winnipeg. She even proposed a plan to make future wars impossible. The unpopularity of such opinions and the harassment of war resisters, however, posed a serious threat to women like Beynon, whose views were considered dangerous. Her autobiographical novel, *Aleta Dey* (1919), provides a fictionized rendition of Beynon's views and the anxieties that accompanied such an unpopular position. The anti-war heroine of the novel actually dies from a beating administered by patriots.[16]

Criticized by her feminist colleagues and alienated by the increasing repression of dissent in Canada, Beynon resigned her position at the *Guide* in 1917 and moved to New York City to join her sister, Lillian Beynon Thomas, and her brother-in-law, A.V. Thomas, who had been fired from the Winnipeg *Free Press* in 1916 for his pacifist views and activities. From New York Beynon continued to write and worked in an Episcopal seamen's mission. While she was never a member of a socialist party, her views were radical in their condemnation of a system that exploited women's labour in the home and the workforce while amassing profits from this exploitation and from war production. Her critique of capitalism was sharpened by the war experience, and her feminism was altered by that critique. Having campaigned for woman suffrage for many years, she did not hesitate to attack Canadian feminists for their acquiescence in the Wartime Elections Act.[17]

Christian socialism, feminism, and pacifism underpinned the writings of another outspoken woman journalist in Canada, Gertrude Richardson of Swan River, Manitoba. Born in Leicester, England, Richardson had emigrated to Canada in 1911, married in 1912, and settled on a Manitoba farm with her pacifist-farmer husband where she continued to write columns for British socialist newspapers and later for the SDP's *Canadian Forward*. Like Beynon, with whom she established contact, Richardson was committed to anti-war positions, although she was more straightforwardly socialist in her beliefs. Critical of capitalism and religious institutions that ignored human suffering, Richardson opted for a Christian and feminist socialism that encompassed political rights for women, a commitment to the eradication of injustice and its replacement by real democracy, and opposition to war and militarism. Coming from a deeply religious and pacifist family background, she looked to

women's 'mother-hearts' to initiate and lead the struggle. For Richardson and others, physical motherhood was irrelevant; spiritual motherhood, 'a glorious self-giving longing to protect, conserve, guard and
save' formed the core of true womanhood and humanity. She was disap-
pointed that 'organized women' in Canada (members of women's organizations like the IODE or the NCWC) largely supported the war effort.
Richardson wrote to the *Leicester Pioneer* in 1917:

Something that repels me about many of the 'organized women' as they term
themselves here.
   There is a strange hardness – a callousness – a something that is neither manly
nor womanly. Something scarcely human.
   But there are some ... whose hearts are full of the mother-love that true
women all the world over are looking to, to heal the wounds of the rent and
broken world, when this crimson storm of war is past.

Richardson's best hope was that socialist women in particular promised
to take the lead in an international struggle for peace and justice. Her
international network of like-minded women correspondents was crucial in keeping her in touch with their activities and in extending the
network to wider circles.[18]
   Richardson's main organizing tactic was the Women's Peace Crusade,
which originated in Scotland and England, and a similar Australian
group, the Woman's Peace Army. Richardson distributed leaflets that
pledged the signer to the anti-war campaign. In a 1917 open letter 'To
the Women Crusaders,' she encouraged women not to lose heart and
reported on women's activities in the United States, Australia, and Great
Britain as a method of urging women to greater activism. Her letters and
columns often contained personal touches, reporting on chance meetings with strangers to demonstrate the widespread antipathy to war
among ordinary people. She frequently referred to letters from her
conscientious-objector brother in England who spent months in prison
for refusing to partake in the slaughter. Richardson's faith in ordinary
working men and women, although perhaps naive, sustained her as it
did Francis Marion Beynon. Her connections with like-minded women
in Canada, Great Britain, and elsewhere helped to ease her physical and
moral isolation. As she wrote to Saskatchewan's Violet McNaughton,
suffragist, pacifist, and farm women's champion, 'Here I have often felt
alone. There is Dear Mrs. Thomas and Miss Beynon and a few others but
we are all so far apart. There is Miss Laura Hughes of Toronto and a

number of socialist women there, and some in Vancouver – but, oh, there must be very many more – *if only I could find them.*'[19]

Gertrude Richardson continued to denounce the horrors of war throughout 1918, until the Canadian government banned the SDP and its newspaper. For her the war machine produced not only death and destruction on the battlefield, but also poverty, prostitution, and venereal disease as well as exploitation of women in the labour market. As human beings and mothers, women had twice as much to lose as the workers, she wrote in October 1917. Like Beynon and other socialist women, Richardson retained a firm belief that women's activism might make a difference. In the early 1920s, however, she suffered exhaustion and ill health complicated by anguish at the continued suffering of women and children in Europe during the postwar food blockade.[20]

The views and experiences of Violet McNaughton paralleled those of Richardson and Beynon in many ways. Like Richardson, she emigrated from England before the war, married a farmer, lived on a farm, and had been a pacifist since the Boer War. McNaughton wrote a column for the *Saturday Press and Prairie Farmer* during the war, in which she occasionally reprinted Beynon's columns and discussed the women's peace movement. Sharing the maternal feminism of Beynon and Richardson, McNaughton publicized the activities of the Women's International League for Peace and Freedom (WILPF) and urged Canadian women to become involved in efforts to promote a peace settlement. Introduced to the idea of a women's peace network by Laura Hughes and Elsie Charlton of Toronto, McNaughton used these contacts to obtain information on war profiteering in Canada. While her newspaper columns were usually mild in tone, reflecting the cooperative spirit of the farm movement, she occasionally used more forceful language to convey information on international arms manufacturing and war profiteering.[21]

While Winnipeg was the centre of western anti-war activities, especially during the conscription crisis of 1917, Toronto became the eastern stage for women socialist pacifists. Hughes attended the International Women's Peace Conference at the Hague in spring 1915. Working with Dr Margaret Gordon of the CSA and LCW, Flora MacDonald Denison of the CSA, Alice Chown, niece of the general superintendent of the Methodist Church, and Harriet Dunlop Prenter of the Toronto Political Equality League and writer for the SDP's *Canadian Forward*, Hughes set in motion the process that resulted in the founding of the Toronto branch of the WILPF. The organization apparently foundered in the rough seas of internal factionalism and external accusations of disloyalty. Laura

Hughes and Harriet Dunlop Prenter clashed in their views, and each accused the other of distortion and falsehood, indicating an intense rivalry over leadership of the Toronto women's peace group. Hughes doubted Prenter's commitment to pacifism, accusing her of being a climber and of trying to sell out the Labor Party to the Liberals in the 1917 election. The opposition of other women's groups to talk of peace in the midst of war also made peace activities difficult. Pacifist women nevertheless continued to express their desires for peace, their resistance to militarism, and their proposals for preventing future wars.[22]

## II

The outbreak of war and the enlistment of thousands of men in the military left many married women and their children to face the problem of earning a living to support their family. As Montreal's Rose Henderson noted in her postwar tract *Women and War*, the majority of men in the military came from working-class backgrounds, and their families were left in need. For the first few years of the war, the Canadian Patriotic Fund took on the task of disbursing supplementary allowances to needy soldiers' wives and widows, as well as assisting families in dealing with the government to obtain separation allowances and pensions. Staffed by volunteers, the local fund committees were often the source of discontent among soldiers' wives since they required a means test of applicants. The hardships imposed on these women were noted as early as October 1914 by the editor of the Winnipeg *Voice*. Local newspapers carried stories and letters detailing the difficulties soldiers' families faced on the meagre allowances provided.[23]

The economic hardships posed by the war vividly exposed the contradictory position of married working-class women. On the one hand these women were expected to shoulder the burden of maintaining the family without complaint and in a spirit of patriotism that complemented what their men were doing at the front. Working-class women were expected both to care for their children at home and, at the same time, provide the necessities of life for the family. On the other hand, they had to accept inadequate levels of assistance from the Patriotic Fund, from mothers' pensions, or from separation allowances provided by the military. In the first two cases women were subjected to scrutiny by middle-class boards that determined who deserved assistance and who did not. Mothers' pensions, intended for widows rather than wives without adequate support, were awarded on a very narrow basis, often at the whim of officials at the provincial or, sometimes, municipal level. Women were caught in a vicious circle. If they worked for wages, they were criticized for neglecting their children and their allowances were reduced; if they did not work outside the home, they found it extremely difficult to survive.[24]

The separation allowances and pensions provided by the military were frequently criticized as insufficient to allow soldiers' wives and dependants a decent level of income. Even these modest allowances drew criticism. 'A soldier's wife' wrote to the *Calgary Herald* in November 1916, objecting to cutting remarks made in the paper about the extravagance of soldiers' wives, noting her own struggle to pay the doctor's bills and funeral expenses for her child. The *Voice* also noted in 1916 the difficulties of one soldier's wife with three children trying to live on $39.19 per month. The actual separation allowances mandated for wives of privates in the regular army were indeed low: $20 per month until 30 November 1917. No additional allowance was granted for children, but a soldier had to assign a minimum of $15 of his pay each month to the recipient of the separation allowance. Privates received $1.10 per day throughout the war and thus $15 represented nearly half their pay. Separation allowances were raised to $25 in December 1917 and to $30 in September 1918. Thus a dependent spouse or relative might receive $35–$45 per month plus, occasionally, a small allowance for clothing. A memorandum from the accountant and paymaster general dated 17 November 1917 noted that a hundred thousand Canadian women were drawing the allowance, 85 per cent as the dependants of privates. In addition, around five thousand widowed mothers also relied on these allowances for their subsistence. The memorandum noted the increased agitation for pay raises and recommended the $5 per month increase to clamp the lid on growing dissatisfaction.[25]

Individuals and organizations of soldiers' dependants argued in the press and to government that women needed a minimum of $100 per month in order to survive. Others suggested a monthly rate of $40 plus $10 to $12 per child as the basic minimum. One correspondent to the *Nutcracker* in 1917 estimated that a mother and four children living without any comforts or luxuries would need $310 per year for housing, $470 for food, $225 for clothing, $30 for medical expenses, and $65 for miscellaneous items, a total of $1200 per year, or $23 per week. Various estimates of the cost of living were attempted during the war by government bodies as well as other groups such as trade unions. While these figures are fraught with difficulties, they do provide some indication of perceptions of the cost of living for a working-class family.[26]

In the Department of Labour's *Labour Gazette*, estimates of family budgets were based on an average family of five – husband, wife, and three children. Prices were collected across the country on specified items, and a cost of living based on these staple foods, fuel, lighting, and rent was derived from these figures. Weekly budget estimates used average prices in the cities of each province to arrive at a provincial figure. Separate computations based on prices in sixty cities provided a Canada-wide average for the same items. The figures show a steady rise: the average cost across the country for these basic items was $14.25 per week in December 1914, $16.33 in December 1916, $19.38 in December 1917, $21.64 in December 1918, and $23.49 in December 1919. Comparisons across provinces demonstrate some regional variations among the figures. Prices were lowest in the East and highest in the West, with Ontario occupying the middle range. For example, in October 1917, weekly figures in Alberta and British Columbia were $19.27 and $19.15, New Brunswick and Nova Scotia's costs were $18.05 and $18.62, while Ontario's estimate was $18.92. Two years later, the same pattern persisted. These figures did not include clothing, insurance, medical bills, and many other items necessary for a family. The absence of the soldier-husband from the family presumably meant some savings in food costs, but the expenses of the family for rent, fuel, and light would not significantly decrease. The United Mine Workers of America, District 18, estimated the weekly cost of living in Western mining districts (which probably were somewhat higher than in large urban cities) at the end of 1917 as $24.56 per week for a family of five. These scattered estimates suggest, however roughly, that the allowances and pensions for soldiers' families were extremely inadequate.[27]

When considered in the context of women's work and wages in this period, the economic implications for soldiers' wives are even clearer. Married women did not work outside the home unless necessity forced them to seek wage employment; some resorted to low-wage jobs as charwomen or took in boarders. The members of the female labour force, however, were predominantly young and single, and their wages reflected structural and ideological factors that presumed that they were not exclusively dependent on their wages for survival. Even the minimum wage campaigns so visible during the war period reflected this assumption.[28]

Married women who took on wage work when the family economy was threatened by a crisis, such as the loss of the breadwinner, were in many cases not covered by protective legislation. Labour such as taking in laundry or sewing, running a boarding house, or working as a domestic did not fall under the limited provisions of minimum wage acts. Thus married women could not rely on legislative protection, inadequate though it was. Even if married women found jobs covered by minimum wage legislation, the underlying assumptions of a single female labour force and the prevailing low wage rates for women workers would not enable them to maintain themselves and their children adequately. In addition the difficulty of finding and paying for childcare would reduce women's incomes even further.

Frustration with these conditions led to several strategies among women activists. Women's organizations lobbied for the establishment of mothers' pensions or for improvements in existing pensions, including larger allowances and wider coverage. Working-class women leaders sometimes joined middle-class organizations in this campaign, arguing that married women should be able to stay home with their children to provide proper care and upbringing. A second strategy emerged specifically from wartime needs and was pushed by organizations of soldiers' dependants, such as the Next-of-Kin Association, which had branches in many Canadian cities. The Next-of-Kin Association publicly lobbied for higher allowances and pensions for soldiers' families, a tactic that succeeded in a small increase in the allowances.[29]

In general, the Next-of-Kin Association was neither radical nor political but rather service-oriented. For the most part, it represented women relatives of privates, thus underlining the working-class nature of its membership. A few of the Next-of-Kin Associations, such as those in Winnipeg and Calgary, drew support from socialist and labour women and developed a set of demands that stressed economic justice for wives and widows of soldiers. Calgary's Next-of-Kin Association was founded by Scottish emigrant Jean McWilliam in 1916. Left to support herself and her two children during the war, McWilliam had worked as a cleaning woman and police matron to save enough money to buy a house, which provided her with income from boarders. Her boarders discussed socialism and perhaps contributed to her becoming a socialist later in the war. As a soldier's wife she experienced the difficulties of making ends meet and decided to organize a group for soldier's wives to pressure government into granting better allowances and pensions.[30]

In a letter to the *Voice* written by Unitarian pacifist Rachel Coutts, the Calgary organization outlined its concern with economic justice for soldiers' dependants. A series of resolutions to Prime Minister Borden

were included in Coutts's letter, asking for profit limits; higher taxes for
the rich and on land; removal of the tariff on necessities; price controls;
government controls on munitions, communications, and transport; and
demands for higher allowances and pensions for wives, widows, and
other dependants. The Calgary organization demanded equal pensions
for all, regardless of rank. Working-class privates should receive the
same benefits as officers from the more affluent social classes.[31]

In its formal platform the Calgary association also included demands
for free vocational education for soldiers' children, war funds to be
raised by taxation, internment of enemy aliens who were not employed,
and denial of the franchise to enemy aliens naturalized since the beginning of the war. After the war, the Calgary group demanded the eight-
hour day and equal pay for women and men, state hospitals and free
medical care, compulsory early closing and weekly half- holidays (for
stores), provision for income tax, government control of the liquor business, and the replacement of jails by houses of correction.[32]

The progressive approach of the Calgary Next-of-Kin Association
contrasted with the goals of more conservative groups in the province.
In March 1918 a confrontation developed between the Calgary organization and a group in Edmonton, with the latter seeking incorporation as a
Next-of-Kin Association through a private member's bill introduced in
the legislature by soldiers' representative Roberta MacAdams. The Calgary association loudly protested this move as usurping its prior claim
on the name. Mrs F.G. Grevette and Mrs Margaret Morley, the president
and secretary from Calgary, met with the premier and members of cabinet to present their case, arguing that their association was older and
represented a thousand members in the province, with branches in
Medicine Hat, Lethbridge, and MacLeod. These women pointed out that
the Edmonton organization, which was dominated by officers' wives
rather than working-class women, aimed at social and charitable activities, while the Calgary group sought economic justice, not charity. The
Calgary women were further aggrieved that the bill had been placed
before the legislature as a government measure. They demanded that
the bill be amended to recognize the Calgary group and be presented as
the bill of the Calgary organization or else be withdrawn, a demand that
the premier refused. Talks between the groups in Edmonton and Calgary reached a stalemate, with Calgary maintaining that its goals were
incompatible with those of Edmonton. Two months later, the *Alberta
Non-Partisan* editorialized on the conflict, asserting that the storm was
caused by the interference of the 'upper ten class of women' who

attempted to take over the working-class organization only after it had become established and influential. The editorial writer recommended that the officers' wives form their own organization: 'The Next-of-Kin is a working-class organization with the proletariat outlook, and will not be officered well by officers' wives.'[33]

This conflict was also fuelled by the demand of the Calgary organization for conscription of wealth as well as men, a demand of the labour movement across Canada. A motion for immediate conscription of wealth was amended at a May 1917 meeting to immediate conscription of both men and wealth, a compromise measure. When the 1918 conflict erupted, the loyalty of Calgary president Grevette to Borden's Union government was questioned. Grevette denied the accusation that she was hostile to the Union government, stating, 'My personal views are my own business but I have not brought them into the affairs of the association.'[34]

Calgary's Next-of-Kin Association featured strong leadership from prominent labour and socialist women such as Jean McWilliam; Rachel Coutts and her sister, Mrs Marion Carson; and Mrs. J.C. Bleaken, president of the Typographical Union's Women's Auxiliary. The group also developed ties with other progressive organizations. It held a joint meeting with the United Farm Women of Alberta and Women's Institutes in May 1918 to recruit women for agricultural work. Marion Carson volunteered to work as a 'servant girl' on a farm to aid the war effort in the summer of 1918, and recommended the experience as a means of increasing rural and urban women's understandings of each others' views and problems.[35]

The rival Edmonton organization flourished, attracting three hundred members to its monthly meetings in 1918–19. A provincial grant and donations from women's groups enabled this group to run a children's home that cared for forty children during 1918–19. On balance, the outlook and activities of the Edmonton organization were probably more typical of Next-of-Kin Associations across the country.[36]

## III

The conscription question was a political minefield that divided labour and socialist opinion from the mainstream of Canadian thought. Across the country, many trades and labour councils and socialist organizations fought conscription, adopting the position that conscription of wealth and property ought to be applied either in conjunction with, or as a replacement for, conscription of manpower. Socialist women added their voices to the demand. 'An Edmonton Mother' wrote the *Canadian Forward* in April 1917 asserting that wars were fought to preserve profits: 'If we must have conscription, let it be the food speculators, bond holders, war at any price capitalists' who are conscripted. Similarly, in Toronto, Harriet Dunlop Prenter suggested that 'a few thousand women armed with "thinking caps" – and votes – might insist upon and obtain a certain "conscription of wealth" ... which would make for some true "equality of sacrifice."'[37]

In Winnipeg as well as Calgary the conscription question was linked to the issue of inadequate pensions for disabled soldiers and soldiers' dependants. As a vocal anti-conscription advocate, Women's Labor League member Helen Armstrong argued in 1917 that 'had the government made ample pensions (as they have promised) the question of conscription would never have become the burning, all-important question that it has.' Enlistments, she postulated, would not have fallen off if adequate pensions had been mandated by the government, as had been suggested by the Winnipeg TLC. Armstrong and Mrs Queen, wife of socialist alderman John Queen, appeared at a mass meeting of women in Winnipeg in August 1917 and tried unsuccessfully to amend a pro-conscription resolution. Mrs Queen spoke of her own three dead brothers, who lost their lives at the front, and explained her seconding of the resolution to amend by saying, 'The men who make war have not suffered. You never touch the people who make wars. While you women have the chance to end war you do not take it.' Exactly one year later at a meeting of soldiers' dependants, the WLL proposed a poverty parade with a promise of support from both the Winnipeg TLC and WLL. The meeting, attended by over three hundred women, was chaired by Armstrong and addressed by three men: a returned soldier; J.G. Soltis, a socialist and TLC delegate; and John Queen. While the meeting passed a resolution for a revised scale of pay for dependants, subsequent press coverage noted that several leaders of the Next-of-Kin Association might not attend the parade because 'they object to the assistance "wished" upon them by members of the WLL and the element of socialism which permeated the meeting.' The Army and Navy Veterans Association played an active role in fostering the division within the Next-of-Kin Association and promised to pass a resolution condemning the parade. The poverty parade fizzled as a result, but a delegation, instructed by the WLL, proceeded to petition city council to pass a resolution in support of higher allowances and pensions for soldiers' dependants.[38]

Anti-conscription forces were particularly strong in Winnipeg and Vancouver, where the trade union movement took a militant stand against conscription, even in the face of the Trades and Labor Congress's failure to oppose it, once the Military Service Act became law in September 1917. Winnipeg's opposition first crystallized in the local Trades and Labor Council and the Anti-Conscription League, the latter founded by prominent socialist and labour leaders, including MLA Fred Dixon, the only pacifist in the Manitoba legislature. Gertrude Richardson noted the creation of a Workers' Council in Winnipeg in late 1917, which grew out of the Anti-Conscription League. The council aimed to 'resist the curtailment of the liberties we have been enjoying' and to 'further the cause of freedom by means of political action and education.' Freedom of speech and the press, as well as protection of citizenship rights and opposition to conscription formed the core of the council's platform. Organizations such as these kept the message of opposition to repression before the public.[39]

Public meetings opposing conscription sometimes elicited physical violence towards speakers and participants. Anti-conscription meetings in Winnipeg, Toronto, Kitchener, and Guelph were disrupted by returned soldiers and angry citizens. A Toronto meeting on 3 June 1917 erupted in pandemonium as three hundred returned soldiers filled the Labour Temple, unsuccessfully attempting to order the Finnish band to play 'God Save the King.' A similar occurrence in Winnipeg in fall 1917 resulted in the crowd roughing up MLA Fred Dixon and other speakers. When Helen Armstrong addressed a crowd in summer 1917, she was roughly handled by soldiers, receiving bruises from head to toe. Nevertheless thousands turned out for anti-conscription rallies in Vancouver, Toronto, and Montreal. Rebecca Buhay described the attendance of over six thousand people in Montreal and ordered two thousand copies of the special anti-conscription issue of the *Canadian Forward*. Harriet Dunlop Prenter shared an anti-conscription platform in Toronto in May 1917 with James Simpson and the *Forward*'s editor, Isaac Bainbridge. In her remarks she urged conscription of wealth to stop the war and stated that the majority of women opposed compulsory military service. Over one thousand listeners of various nationalities attended the meeting, where they heard denunciations of the rumoured disenfranchisement of the foreign-born. The *Canadian Forward*'s 24 May issue carried letters and telegrams from all over the country supporting its anti-conscription stand. One of these letters noted the importance of women in the movement: A.W. Bowles of Kitchener's SDP wrote, 'The women are with us and have resolved to go to prison with the rest.' The Toronto Women's Social Democratic League also sent a telegram of support as did other SDP organizations from British Columbia to Quebec. The SPC also opposed conscription and attracted large numbers to its meetings, particularly in Vancouver. Vancouver's labour movement, through the local Trades and Labor Council and the provincial Federation of Labor, strongly protested conscription by threatening a general strike.[40]

## IV

The conscription issue united socialists and labour supporters behind the anti-conscription campaign, although it did not lead to the eradication or softening of the differences between the major socialist parties. Differences between the SDP and the SPC remained too large, and the latter resisted any attempts at compromise. While individual SPC members might be found working on reformist issues, the party maintained a careful distance from official participation in organizations that drew on popular support. Continuing its prewar policy, the SPC rejected autonomous women's activities and groups and generally denied the legitimacy of gender-consciousness. If anything, the war intensified the SPC's concentration on class at the expense of gender.

Within the SPC, much of the published commentary on women and war came from the pens of a few prominent socialist men who criticized the maternalist arguments raised by social reformers and socialists alike. In 1915 W.W. LeFeaux criticized the maternalism espoused by British suffrage leader Emmeline Pankhurst. Noting that Pankhurst called the women of Germany enemies of women in England, he asked rhetorically: 'Have the much talked of female instincts and characteristics suddenly become nullified in Austrian and German women and accentuated in British women? If so, why?' He underlined the class interests of women of both sides as the overriding feature. Later in the war, prominent SPC leader W.A. Pritchard wrote a series of articles entitled 'After the War Problems' in which he postulated that the capitalists would push repopulation on women. Noting the dangers of widespread venereal disease as a result of the war, Pritchard concluded that women would not be able to produce healthy children. VD was a product of capitalism and the solution could only be found in a society which eliminated wage slavery. In these same articles Pritchard urged working-class women to put their energies into the class struggle rather than the sex struggle since denunciations of patriarchy would produce no lasting results. Women were being played off against men much as returned soldiers were played off against civilians, he suggested. Arguing that women as well as men had to sell their labour power, Pritchard stressed the common economic interests of the sexes. Pritchard's allusion to women as wage slaves with interests in common with working-class men notwithstanding, socialist organizations and publications continued to put most emphasis on women as wives and mothers.[41]

Women active in the socialist movement as speakers and propagandists for party positions were rarely visible. In Socialist Party of Canada circles, a few prominent women stood out. Helen Armstrong of Winnipeg devoted her energies to the Women's Labor League, organizing non-unionized women and conducting strike support activities and anti-conscription struggles, rather than working directly for the SPC. Sophie Mushkat devoted her energies during the early war period to socialist propaganda in Alberta. Mushkat, however, had her difficulties with the SPC and was expelled several times for not adhering to official policy.

A third outspoken woman, Sarah Johnston-Knight, emerged as a spokeswoman for the party in the later stages of the war. Johnston married British emigrant Joseph Knight in early summer 1914. Not much is known about her before her marriage. In 1914 Joseph Knight was a carpenter and well-known socialist and trade unionist, influential in the Edmonton Trades and Labor Council. Later in the war he was an outspoken critic of the Trades and Labor Congress's capitulation to registration and conscription and was a strong supporter of the One Big Union. Johnston-Knight became actively involved in party affairs as provincial secretary in 1915, and in early 1916 she was in charge of a special organizing fund for Alberta and Saskatchewan. When Knight ran in the conscription election in Red Deer, Johnston-Knight accompanied him and assisted in his campaign. She also joined him on other speaking tours. In October 1918 on her way to the United States, she spoke at a socialist meeting in Winnipeg's Rex Theatre. After her speech, which criticized American entry into the war, she was arrested for breaking the War Measures Act. Johnston-Knight stayed with Helen Armstrong while awaiting trial. Her case was dismissed on a technicality and she was warned not to speak about the war in her lectures. Her arrest coincided with a concerted move by the authorities to crack down on 'seditious' speech and literature. Seven raids occurred in Winnipeg at the same time, including the offices of *Robochyi Narod* (the Ukrainian socialist newspaper) and the Labour Temple.[42]

In January 1919 Johnston-Knight reported on the Alberta Federation of Labor convention in Medicine Hat where the socialists had swung the convention on a number of resolutions. In her letter to Winnipeg labour leader Bob Russell, Johnston-Knight claimed victory for the 'reds,' who had outmanoeuvred the more conservative executive of the federation, thus setting the stage for the Calgary Labour Conference in March 1919 and the creation of the One Big Union (OBU). The wrangle in the Edmonton TLC in spring 1919 over the OBU resulted in the expulsion of OBU supporters such as the Knights from that body. Johnston-Knight was defeated as Edmonton TLC delegate to the Calgary OBU meeting by moderate labour leader Alf Farmilo. In the aftermath of the 1919 general strike, the Knights eventually moved to Toronto where Johnston-Knight served as secretary of the Toronto branch of the SPC until her resignation in August 1920. Both Knights went on to become leading Communists in the 1920s.[43]

What is striking about these women activists is their lack of public articulation about gender questions. Of the three, only Helen Armstrong identified strongly with the problems faced by working-class women. Mushkat and Johnston-Knight rarely addressed women's issues, nor did they particularly identify with women as a constituency. While all three were critical of the war, they did not use 'maternalist' arguments to oppose it.

Mushkat's role as party organizer and link to the Slavic communities in rural Alberta demonstrate the relative rarity of ethnic women in leadership positions. While the multi-ethnic Social Democratic Party produced some ethnic women leaders of consequence, particularly among the Finns and the Jews, the leadership tended to be British- or Canadian born.

Women's participation in activist roles within the socialist movement varied by region across the country. Few women in the Maritimes, emerged as identifiable activists during the war. A few Maritime women's names appear in the socialist press. For example, the arrest of John Reid for sedition in Alberta prompted Mrs Zora Richardson of Amherst, Nova Scotia, to contribute to his defence fund, and Mary Currie of Saint John took on some organizing when her husband, long-time SPC activist Wilf Gribble, went to jail in early 1916. Sustained activity among working-class women in the Maritimes awaited the development of the Independent Labor Party and its women's auxiliaries in the postwar period. Rural women on the prairies and miners' wives proved a more fertile field for SPC organization. Many farm women in rural areas in Alberta helped the SPC organization drives, providing organizers such as John Reid and Sophie Mushkat with speaking engagements and acting as liaisons between the Provincial Executive Committee and the locals. Reid's arrest in August 1915 mobilized dozens of women to raise funds for his defence, as well as to assist itinerant SPC speakers. With the 1917 anti-conscription campaign, a number of women used their organizational and fundraising talents to provide financial support for this cause.[44]

Although many of these women were silent but effective supporters of the socialist movement, a few were more vocal, writing letters to newspapers such as the *Grain Growers' Guide* or *Cotton's Weekly*. Mary Nicolaeff of Morningside, Alberta, a small town on the railroad line, wrote to both papers on topics related to women and socialism, particularly on marriage, women's rights, and women's need for socialism. As a married woman with two married daughters, Nicolaeff condemned the economic thralldom of women caught in unequal and degrading marriages. 'The curse of woman's life will be abolished when this damned old system is swept away, not before,' she wrote in 1914. Disputing an anti-suffrage letter to the *Grain Growers' Guide*, Nicolaeff argued that women were equal partners with men and ought to use their intelligence to teach their children the higher ideals of socialism, so that their lives would be better. An emigrant from Russia, Nicolaeff came to Canada to find political freedom, 'but there is no more social justice than in the old country.' Farmers' wives 'do not toil less than the Russian peasant's wife,' although they now have comforts in life, she noted. For Nicolaeff, farm women were slaves, endlessly working, and without the time or motivation to study and read. 'We have no time to lose. We have to start at once the study of the social science called Socialism,' she concluded. An anonymous woman correspondent, commenting on another of Nicolaeff's letters in which she castigated Women's Institutes in New Brunswick for spending their meetings discussing jams and jellies, thoroughly approved of Nicolaeff's criticism, adding that the same criticism could be made of her own Grain Growers' Association. Women spent too much time binding and healing the wounds inflicted by society. Women are 'not satisfied with this endless healing and binding,' and want 'some real authority.' A number of rural socialist women must have agreed with these sentiments. Like Mary Nicolaeff, they threw their efforts into organizing meetings for the SPC as well as performing the more traditional roles of fundraising and contributing their domestic skills to socialist gatherings.[45]

Some women socialists also worked within the farm women's movement in the Prairies, but little explicit discussion of socialism appeared, at least among the identifiable leadership of the farm movement. One exceptional mention of the topic occurred in a letter from Erma Stocking of the Saskatchewan Women Grain Growers' Association (WGGA) who replied to farm women's leader Zoe Haight's query about the progress of socialism in the farmers' movement. In Stocking's opinion, more education was needed among farm women and men, and she cautioned that the executive 'not get too far ahead of their people.' The WGGA supported gradual disarmament and conscription of wealth and opposed military training in the schools. Both Haight and Violet and John McNaughton publicly spoke out against war and war profiteering. The United Farm Women of Alberta (UFWA) also opposed some aspects of the war although one of its most prominent leaders, Irene Parlby, believed the war to be necessary and justifiable. Parlby distrusted 'the political bunch' in the farmers' movement, referring to the 'Rootites' – Mrs George F. Root of Wetaskwin (near Edmonton) and Mrs Dowler – as opponents of farm leader Henry Wise Wood. Both women were active in the UFWA during the war and its aftermath. Root wrote occasional letters to the *Western Independent* as well, commenting in 1919 on inflation and the need for class struggle.[46]

The SPC dominated the socialist meovement in Edmonton. In Calgary, however, socialists rallied around the popular People's Forum sponsored by William Irvine's Unitarian congregation and the Non-Partisan League (NPL). Irvine's People's forum resembled J.S. Woodsworth's People's Forums in Winnipeg and drew mixed audiences of socialists and reformers to discuss major issues of the day. SDP organizer George Stirling reported favourably in 1917 on the forums in Calgary and noted that William Irvine felt the people were not yet ready for socialism. Stirling commented, however, that the NPL worked along SDP lines and that they were 'doing some good work.' Mary Nicolaeff, however, writing two years later, found the NPL 'all right as far as it goes,' but criticized the league for being too separate from the working-class movement and insufficiently class-conscious: 'There are two classes: *Toilers and Exploiters*. They are at war for the supremacy. *With whom will you side?*' Nicolaeff asked. Women with ties to the SPC, such as Nicolaeff, rejected social democratic-style politics with its emphasis on reforms and the ballot box. Nonetheless, Irvine's Christian socialism and work with the largely rural-based NPL attracted a number of women socialists and progressive reformers, including Rachel Coutts, Marion Carson, Jean McWilliam, Edith Patterson, and Amelia Turner.

These women were active in a variety of organizations including the Next-of-Kin Association. Later a number of these women would become involved in the strike events of 1919, the Calgary Defence League, Calgary's Labour Church, and the organization of a WLL.[47]

The Social Democratic Party had always been strongest in urban areas with large numbers of immigrants and in some mining and lumbering areas in British Columbia and Northern Ontario where the labour force was also drawn from immigrant groups. As the war dragged on, the strong connections to these ethnic groups provided a new challenge for the SDP. The length of the war and the increasing pressure upon, and prejudice towards, 'aliens' took its toll as more and more ethnic social-ists enlisted in the armed services, along with their British-born com-rades, or were interned or arrested. In Toronto the SDP lost many members to the military, including the Italian organizer of the SDP and the secretary of the dominion executive. Every local suffered numeri-cally and financially and several ethnic locals disappeared altogether. The conscription crisis, the labour organization upsurge of the late war, and the government's outlawing of foreign-language publications and various left-wing organizations increased domestic tensions about socialism and sharpened the contradictions between classes, as well as heightening resentment against foreigners.[48]

Despite these obstacles, women in the SDP continued their activities within the party and within the women's organizations. The heavy hand of government repression and the strike wave of the late war and postwar period would make new demands on socialist women who mounted a campaign to challenge restrictions on free speech and the right to association, as well as the right to bargain collectively. Even as the Canadian state geared up its campaign to suppress labour and socialist threats to the war effort, socialist women voiced their objections to the harsh treatment of those most closely associated with these move-ments – foreigners. While anonymous writers such as 'Contrary Mary' raised objections to the perpetuation of widespread hatred of Germans in general, other women such as Helen Armstrong and her colleagues in the Winnipeg WLL protested the treatment of imprisoned aliens and the neglect of their wives and children. Armstrong reported to the Trades and Labor Council in September 1917 that, despite assurances from civic charity organizations and a Winnipeg alderman, the wives and children of incarcerated foreigners were still hungry and 'being fed with crusts by the neighbours.' As was the case with other groups, such as conscien-tious objectors, Armstrong and the WLL championed the cause of those who were the victims of state repression and argued for community responsibility for their families who were left to fend for themselves.[49]

The achievement of provincial suffrage and the Wartime Elections Act also prompted some women socialists to defend the 'foreigner' against the threat of disenfranchisement. Commenting on women's enfranchisement in Ontario in 1917, Harriet Dunlop Prenter noted that 'one society lady' had urged the 'controlling of the foreigners' vote.' In response, Prenter wrote that it would be preferable for newly enfranchised and intelligent women to 'see to the "controlling" of these "patriotic pagans" [that is, wealthy women] since they and their ideals are a far greater menace to us than many legions of foreigners.' As an example, Prenter went on to point out that the wealthy class had already approached the legislature with a demand for the introduction of compulsory military training of boys in public schools, but not private ones, thus exempting the children of the upper class.[50]

The Wartime Elections Act of 1917 proved to be controversial in socialist as well as suffragist circles. When the Winnipeg WLL learned of the proposed bill in the fall of 1917, it wired both Prime Minister Borden and the leader of the opposition Liberals, Wilfrid Laurier, to protest the betrayal of democratic principles, labelling the bill 'more Prussian than British.' The WLL insisted on the full franchise for both women and men. Francis Marion Beynon also was quick to condemn the act and urge the electorate to repudiate it by refusing to elect candidates who supported 'that monstrous act of injustice' that 'has already roused bitter race hatreds.' Beynon, the former editor of the Country Homemakers' page in the Grain Growers' Guide argued that the act betrayed the confidence of the Canadian people, the soldiers who fought for Canada, and immigrants from other lands. The latter had accepted the invitation to come to Canada to build up the country, but now 'no foreign born citizen of any nationality will ever again set any real value on the naturalization papers issued at Ottawa,' she wrote. Thus, for a number of socialist and labour women, the Canadian government had betrayed basic democratic principles in the interests of militarism and winning the war.[51]

V

Socialist women found considerable opportunity to demonstrate their concerns with the class and gender issues so strikingly posed by wartime crisis. The war underlined the differential effects of mass mobilization on the bourgeois class and the working class but also on men and women. For those women prominent in socialist party circles, especially within the SPC, the former distinction assumed priority. For those women not tied so closely to party structures, the effect of war on working-class women and their families predominated. Lending their talents to popular organizations of various types, most of the socialist women discussed here campaigned for issues and aided organizations that would ameliorate conditions for working-class women and their families. Particularly striking were the campaigns that aided married women – wives and dependants of soldiers – and those that aided the predominantly single women workers discussed in the preceding chapter. While different strategies were utilized for the two, both were based on the fundamental acceptance of the family wage and the gendered division of labour. These campaigns nevertheless served to raise questions about the adequacy of a socio-economic system that ignored the interests of working-class women.

For socialist-pacifist women, capitalism profited from war and underpinned the war machine. Criticism of the government for allowing profits to be made from war production increased in 1917 as the threat of conscription became a reality. Socialist-pacifist women could not accept the patriotism of women who urged enlistment and conscription in the name of patriotic motherhood. Thus they joined with other women and men in the anti-conscription campaign.

For individual women activists against the war, whether pacifists, socialists, or labour supporters, there were personal repercussions as well. The war crisis meant individual sacrifices in an era of increasing suspicion towards radicals and critics. Some of the women lost members of their families to the slaughter or coped with the imprisonment of loved ones who refused to bear arms. Others found that the strain of war brought them illness and breakdown, both physical and mental, or, alternatively, the stress of leaving Canada for self-imposed exile. A few faced legal harassment or charges for their activities, particularly during the later stages of the war as opposition to conscription and, later, to the muzzling of free speech erupted. Labour unrest and renewed drives to organize workers after 1917, the Russian Revolution, and increasing government surveillance and repression all served to raise the stakes both for oppositional movements and the state.

While prevailing gender expectations and the material realities of most women's lives circumscribed and shaped women's activism into particular channels, those women who stood out as 'troublemakers' found that the state was no respecter of gender. Women such as Helen Armstrong, Sarah Johnston-Knight, Mrs R.P. Mendelssohn, and Sanna Kannasto, for example, experienced arrest and harassment for their activities. Even Rose Henderson, author of *Women and War*, social worker, socialist-pacifist, and widow of an accountant, found herself under suspicion, despite her respectable background. The deputy attorney general of Quebec, Charles Lanctot, wrote to the federal Minister of Justice in July 1919 noting seizures in Montreal carried out under search warrants issued in Winnipeg: 'Certain letters, documents and literature of a dangerous and suspicious character have been seized in possession of various persons, among others of Rose Henderson, probation officer of the Juvenile Court ... In view of the duties performed by Rose Henderson, we have an interest in taking communication of the documents seized at her residence and at the court.' Three of these letters later appeared in the materials gathered for the state's case against those arrested in the Winnipeg General Strike. As we shall see, the state's attitude towards women radicals and activists gave them 'no special protection – no sympathy,' since such women had clearly transgressed not only the boundaries of legitimate dissent in the eyes of the state, but also the boundaries of gender decorum.[52]

# 7

## 'No Special Protections ... No Sympathy': Postwar Militancy and Labour Politics

In these days when women are taking up special obligations and assuming equal privileges with men, it may be well for me to state now that women are just as liable to ill treatment in a riot as men and can claim no special protections and are entitled to no sympathy.

Judge Metcalfe, Winnipeg General Strike Trials, 1919

I shall continue to work for more protection for our girls and women workers, also for the enforcement of all laws relative to wages, better conditions and our social welfare problems.

Helen Armstrong, *Free Press* (Winnipeg), 19 November 1923

In postwar Canada, the authorities worried about civil unrest and labour strife. The end of the war in late 1918 did not signal the waning of labour and socialist activism, but rather a gathering momentum. The Winnipeg General Strike of spring 1919 threatened disruption and turmoil, and women activists were accused of transgressing normal expectations of feminine behaviour. Judge Metcalfe's warning during the general strike trials indicated the limits of tolerance for women who challenged gender boundaries. From the viewpoint of ruling elites, women as a group were expected to maintain a lady-like presence in public and certainly were not to take on active political roles. Even among working-class men, class conflict and class solidarity were considered masculine traits. While working-class women were applauded for their support in labour disputes, for their social and fundraising skills, and, above all, for their domestic abilities to stretch wages, it was not expected that women would be at the forefront of class politics. Workers' wives, daughters, and other female relatives played supportive roles in aiding working-class solidarity, but there was always a lingering anxiety or expectation that women lacked the capacity for such loyalty because they were either innately more conservative or more likely to be victims, traits that seem to have crossed class boundaries.

Despite these gender injunctions, some politically active women continued to contest the status quo through the ballot box and the podium. Four years after the dramatic confrontations of 1919, Helen Armstrong, the most prominent leader of women workers during the strike, ran for city council in Winnipeg, her second attempt in two years. Two other veterans of the labour revolt, Jessie Kirk and Edith Hancock, joined her on the hustings, seeking to become municipal representatives. While all three women were unsuccessful, their presence in the campaign was significant because it was still unusual for women to run as candidates and to take to the public platform. In the class-divided politics of the post-war and post–Winnipeg General Strike era, the turn to electoral politics was perceived as an important means of continuing the unfinished struggle. Yet, as the numbers of women candidates demonstrate, running for political office was still perceived as largely a masculine pursuit. In Winnipeg itself, Mary Kinnear has noted that only 4 to 7 per cent of municipal and school board candidates from 1918 to 1939 were women. Nevertheless, the presence of the women in Winnipeg and elsewhere in electoral campaigns marked a turning point.[1]

By the war's end, Canadian women in many jurisdictions possessed the franchise and intended to use it to accomplish social and economic change. Labour and socialist women organized to marshall their votes and candidacies to support measures that benefited working-class families and communities. In claiming political citizenship, women activists spoke not only for their class but also as women. As Jessie Kirk remarked during her successful 1920 campaign for city council, 'I am not here to do any antagonising whatever. I am here to stand on my merits as a woman.' Kirk's proclamation can be read as an affirmation both of women's citizenship and as an indication that the war crisis, the labour mobilization, and the expansion of women's political, economic, and social roles had challenged if not demolished accepted views of femininity and appropriate gender roles.[2]

For women like Kirk and Helen Armstrong, the move to electoral politics was a new phase of the struggle to improve women workers' conditions, a struggle begun years earlier in efforts to organize women workers into unions, Women's Labor Leagues, and labour political groups. These struggles, as well as wartime strikes, the defence of workers' rights to collective bargaining and free speech, and confrontations with the state provided a training ground for women political activists on the left, particularly during the late war and early postwar period. Women's political activism was affected by the momentum of labour unrest and the confrontation between the state and the labour and socialist movements, particularly in 1919 and 1920. The Winnipeg General Strike of May–June 1919 was symptomatic of larger labour unrest, which led to prosecutions and prison terms, the creation of the Royal Canadian Mounted Police, systematic surveillance of radicals, major government probes of industrial discontent, and a more interventionist state in general. On labour's side, the strike and its aftermath not only mobilized workers to defend themselves and their rights, but also divided the movement over the One Big Union and strategies for social and economic change. Electoral means were embraced by some activists, but others, inspired by developments abroad in the international socialist movement, chose to join the underground revolutionary movement that eventually emerged as the Communist Party of Canada.

If, unlike most historical accounts, we look at the events of the late war and early postwar period through the eyes of the women who participated, we can more fully appreciate the general outlines of the labour revolt as well as the context of women's political activism. The Winnipeg General Strike is the starting point for such a discussion. Revisionist accounts have established the national (rather than the local and western) dimensions of the strike, and the role played by ethnic tensions in the labour unrest of 1919. But not much consideration has been given to the gender dimensions of the strike, women's testimony before the Royal Commission on Industrial Relations, and the role of women in the nationwide campaign for collective bargaining and free speech, the OBU campaign, and more generally in labour political action.[3]

The intention here is not to recreate a militant golden age for women activists but to suggest that the twin crises of the war period – the war itself and the state's defence of capitalism against labour militancy and socialism – mobilized labour and socialist women as never before to defend working-class interests. These interests included protection of the family, women workers, and the democratic rights of organization, free speech, and collective bargaining. Women activists often continued to subsume their interests in broad labour or socialist concerns. Yet the suffering of the war period, the high cost of living, the enfranchisement of women, the development of a deeply felt concern for peace, and the formation of women's groups among working-class women, often based in local communities, contributed to an increased awareness of gender and a growing consciousness of working-class women's connections to the arenas of public debate and action. By and large, this awareness of a connection to economic, social, and political questions was suffused by a maternalism shared by middle-class women reformers and was hampered by the labour and socialist movements' acceptance of the breadwinner family ideal. The growth of the female waged labour force and unionization of previously unorganized women, as well as the public sector, in the years 1917–20, partially challenged labour and socialist notions that women, and the unskilled generally, were threatening and unorganizable, more conservative and unreliable. During the 1919 crisis, however, the state certainly viewed the increased militancy of unskilled women and immigrant workers as a threat requiring stern measures. The rank-and-file revolt of 1917–20 could not be controlled as easily as the moderate Trades and Labor Congress or its international union affiliates. Censorship, internment (mostly of men but also some women), suppression of the press and radical organizations, and the attack on democratic rights prompted women to utilize their resources to defend themselves and their families in whatever ways they could.[4]

By the late stage of the war, labour unrest and socialism, specifically 'bolshevism,' became an overriding concern to the Canadian state. Censorship and internment, used earlier in the war, were reinvigorated and expanded during 1918 and 1919 and specifically aimed at political dissidents. Internment had been used extensively at the war's beginning to remove 'enemy aliens' from the general population, although most of those interned were actually Ukrainians, not Germans. With the labour shortage after 1916, releases of aliens became commonplace. In 1918–19, the camps were once again used, but this time the internees were political radicals. Despite the end of the war in November 1918, these camps remained open until February 1920. Censorship also was stepped up. On 25 September 1918, PC 2381 banned publications in 'enemy languages.' Significantly, these languages also included Russian and Finnish, indicating that the target of the ban was radical political protest rather than wartime enemies. Accompanying the ban on publications, the government also banned freedom of association, assembly, and speech for many immigrant Canadians who belonged to the groups proscribed under another order-in-council, PC 2384. A fledgling security operation, first under the Dominion Police and later under the reorganized RCMP, provided the intelligence work necessary to enforce the orders-in-council covering censorship and internment. These wartime measures were reinforced by a third, PC 2525 (11 October 1918), which outlawed strikes for the duration of the war. While organized labour largely ignored the latter, it was more difficult to escape the repercussions of the other orders-in-council. Thus, by the end of the war, state repression helped set the stage for increasing militancy and concerted opposition among the labour and socialist movements to the erosion of political freedoms.[5]

## I

Winnipeg was the centre of the 1919 upheaval, brought on by a confrontation between the Metal Trades Council, consisting of six unions, and recalcitrant employers who refused to recognize or deal with the industrial-union-style council. Also involved in the dispute was the Building Trades Council representing various construction unions. Like the metal shop owners, the builders refused to meet with the building trades council. The result was a general strike, supported by a referendum of member unions of the Winnipeg TLC. At 7:00 AM on 15 May, four hours before the official starting point, five hundred women telephone operators began the general sympathetic strike by walking out. The official reason for the strike was the fight for collective bargaining. 'Beyond this, however, the strike soon became a struggle for a "living wage," a struggle in which women had good cause to be involved.' In addition, the strike provided an impetus to organize women workers in pursuit of the goal of a living wage. Later, the arrests and trials of strike leaders would add another dimension to the conflict: the defence of workers against the heavy hand of state repression.[6]

The day after the strike commenced, the Toronto *Globe* reported two thousand women among the thirty thousand strikers in Winnipeg. The precision of this estimate is unverifiable, although reports of votes for the strike indicate that those trades in which women worked voted overwhelmingly in favour of the strike. In addition to the telephone operators, the retail clerks, garment workers, waitresses, bookbinders, and confectionery workers voted strongly in favour of walking out. Women workers, both organized and unorganized, were urged to support the strike, largely through the efforts of Helen Armstrong, who assumed a crucial role in organizing the women for the duration of the strike and was a central figure in ensuring the well-being of women strikers. Armstrong kept the Winnipeg TLC informed of progress in organizing women during the early days of the strike and was arrested for disorderly conduct at the Canada Bread Company property shortly after the strike began. Described in the Toronto *Star* as 'business manager of the Women's Unions,' Armstrong was arrested several times in the course of the six-week strike. She organized innumerable meetings for working women, which aimed at organizing new unions and also served as information and strategy-planning sessions. Another of her noteworthy accomplishments was the implementation of a dining room to provide free meals for women strikers. Men who used the facilities were expected to pay or donate what they could, thus recognizing the fact that women workers were paid less. The dining room, which opened on 24 May, operated on the basis of donations from individuals and organizations. The Women's Labor League of Winnipeg provided the nucleus of support for the dining room, authorizing fundraising events as well as collecting money from the Labor Church, whose services were a major source of funds.[7]

The women on strike also found it difficult to pay rent without an income and turned to the WLL and the Strike Committee for financial assistance. The Relief Committee, under the direction of Mrs Webbs, helped to fund cash donations to women in need. Some citizens offered rooms to the women strikers, and the YWCA decided to take in any needy woman, striker or not.[8]

While the strike represented an opportunity to organize women workers, it also presented a chance to capitalize on existing grievances with employers. A strike of bakery and confectionery workers, for example, coincided with the general strike. These workers, mostly women and girls, struck because employers would not negotiate with their union. The strike had begun the day before the general walkout, but more candy and confectionery workers went out on 15 May to support the demands of the general strikers. Store clerks also quit work as part of the general strike, despite employer attempts to bribe them with a raise and, when that tactic failed, the stores' attempts to use strikebreakers. The T. Eaton Company sent scab labour from Toronto, but railway workers prevented them from reaching Winnipeg. Earlier investigations of women's work in department stores had led to a Minimum Wage Board ruling on salaries and hours, but not all employers had complied with the ruling, thus helping to set the stage for the clerks' participation in the strike. Helen Armstrong had organized clerks during the war, and in May 1919 she pushed the union drive further by concentrating on women employees in the smaller stores of Winnipeg, reporting considerable success on 26 May when a large number of women clerks were added to the strikers.[9]

Service workers also struck in 1919, many of them waitresses employed in the numerous cafés around Winnipeg. A revitalized Cooks', Waiters' and Waitresses' Union had been organized in 1914 before the outbreak of the war. The union had survived the war with considerable difficulty, and in the early days of 1919 efforts were renewed to attract new members, especially women. One day after the start of the general strike, it was reported to the TLC that the union had organized virtually all restaurants, with full support for the general strike among its members. Despite this show of strength, a number of cafés locked out their workers, according to one report. Conditions for waitresses were akin to slave labour in many restaurants. Evidence from men employed in six cafés showed that hours ranged from nine to fourteen and one-half hours a day, with one to three days off per month, for the sum of $15 per month, which, after deductions for laundry and tips to bus boys, left some women a grand total of $9 per month to spend. Despite the Minimum Wage Board's June order covering waitresses, reports from later in 1919 and 1920 indicate that employers got away with much lower rates than the mandated $12.50 per week minimum wage, often reducing the minimum by four dollars. Restaurateurs also continued to violate the restrictions on night work for women under eighteen. The Winnipeg *Tribune* reported twelve hundred members of the union still out on 27 June with demands for a $10 minimum for the waitresses and $15 for the men, even though the Minimum Wage Board had already ordered a higher sum for the women. By early July most of the members had returned to work, although the larger restaurants were still hostile to the union. Shaken by the strike, the union was reorganized several times in the latter part of 1919.[10]

Perhaps the most important group of women strikers was the telephone operators, whose reputation for militancy stemmed back to two earlier labour disputes in the city. The telephone operators had organized in February 1917 with the help of the International Brotherhood of Electrical Workers (IBEW) and had staged a three-hour walkout on 1 May 1917. The resulting investigatory board recommended wage increases and better hours and conditions. In May 1918, when the civic workers of Winnipeg staged a strike, the operators played a crucial role in tying up the city. In May 1919 they recalled some of the errors made in the 1918 strike and forestalled their replacement by 'volunteers' by pulling all the fuses on their equipment. Thus in the early days of the strike, communications were curtailed within the city and with the rest of the country. Within days operators all over the province had joined the strike. This militancy was remarkable, since in many small towns there were only a few women employed as operators. The pressure on these women to return to work was intense and intimidating. Some were informed that they would not be reinstated and others, from small centres, were replaced before the strike terminated. By the middle of June the commissioner of telephones announced that he had received 192 applications for permanent work. Forty-three of the women hired were former strikers who were reinstated after signing a pledge not to participate in sympathetic strikes. Despite the operators' actions, they were not able to prevent the use of volunteers completely, nor were they able to insist on the reinstatement of former operators without loss of seniority. Doris Meakin, an IBEW representative, stated at the end of June that only half of the operators were back at work, and those without seniority, and that they were forced to work overtime to maintain service. She also noted that the women demanded a protest strike but no action had been taken by the union.[11]

Employer refusal to reinstate women workers in many trades plagued those who had been looking after the women strikers. Helen Armstrong reported to the TLC in early July that she was unable to cope with all the demands for help, and she urged the TLC to employ a woman to help those desperate strikers who had been arrested for vagrancy or refused relief. A committee was appointed to secure reinstatement and raise relief funds, but, despite these efforts, however many women were not rehired.[12]

Women were militant participants in street actions during the general strike. Several weeks into the strike, newspapers began to report incidents that demonstrated the activities of women strike supporters. The Toronto *Star* noted the predominance of women and children in the crowds that gathered at the railroad shops to prevent male strikebreakers from going to work. The same story reported the hostility of crowds towards automobile drivers going into the Winnipeg's North End to pick up domestic help. In working-class areas such as Weston, women were observed pulling scab firemen out of the firehall and wrecking delivery trucks owned by local department stores. Three such trucks were destroyed, wheels and merchandise smashed. In addition, the women assaulted the drivers and special police trying to protect them. A few days later several women were charged with assaulting one of the drivers and were eventually fined twenty dollars and costs. Others were charged with offenses such as disorderly conduct and intimidation of shop girls. For their part in the riot of Bloody Saturday, several women were arrested for rioting and released on one thousand dollars bail. The mayor had banned parades and warned that 'Any women taking part in a parade do so at their own risk.'[13]

Strike leader Helen Armstrong faced several charges of inciting to disorder and counselling to commit an indictable offence when she appeared for trial in assize court. She was accused of telling girls on strike to take newspapers away from girls selling them on the street. Two young women, Ida Krantz and Margaret Steinhauer, testified that they asked Armstrong's permission to stop the selling of newspapers. The two received fines of five dollars and costs, but Helen Armstrong remained in jail for three days until bail was allowed after initially being refused by the judge. Armstrong, a feisty and dedicated leader, clearly posed a threat to the authorities. Her husband, George Armstrong, a prominent strike leader, was arrested along with other leaders a week before Helen was brought to trial. The Star's special correspondent reported that when officers appeared one night to arrest George, Helen refused to let them take him until she ran to the North End police station to telephone the chief of police to check on the federal warrant for his arrest. Only after his confirmation did she allow her husband to be taken away.[14]

The militant women of Winnipeg continued their activities after the strike finished. The repercussions of the six-week general strike were felt into summer and fall 1919 as the trials proceeded. In August at the trial of some women picketers from working-class Weston, witness Fred Gouldie commented: 'He would rather face the Huns than the women of Weston. He wanted to go to work at Eaton's, but they stopped him on the path and for nearly three weeks he did not try to pass their pickets. They were fierce – and then some. They didn't touch him but they were determined he shouldn't go to work.'[15]

With the strike leaders still in jail, women helped to mount protests against their continued incarceration and the refusal to grant bail. On Labour Day a giant parade filled the streets of Winnipeg with seven thousand protesters. The women's section, represented by the WLL, contributed two floats to the parade, one of them portraying the figures of Liberty, Equality, and Fraternity, certainly a pointed comment on the long incarceration of the strike leaders. A few days later, Helen Armstrong spoke to a mass meeting of women at the Winnipeg rink at which she announced WLL plans to present the visiting Prince of Wales with a petition for the release of the strike leaders. Winnipeg's chief of police threatened to prevent the WLL from parading in a body to greet the Prince of Wales. This did not daunt Helen Armstrong, who responded that the WLL would greet the prince as private citizens, although she added that they would carry a few signs to protest the refusal to grant bail to the strike leaders. For unknown reasons the women decided not to proceed with the demonstration, and a few days later the men were released on bail.[16]

When the strike trials began in late 1919 judicial authorities clearly revealed their attitudes towards women's militancy during the strike. Judge Metcalfe, in answer to defence arguments about undue force being used on crowds during the police charge on Bloody Saturday, responded with a statement of policy towards the presence of women on the streets. Implicitly the judge rendered judgment on those women who stepped outside accepted gender roles. Those women who behaved 'like men' and participated in protest actions would be 'cut down' by the strong arm of the law, thus losing their special 'privileges' and 'protections' as women. Class and gender expectations were intertwined; respectable middle-class or upper-class women would not participate in such unseemly behaviour.[17]

## II

Clearly, the Winnipeg General Strike occupied centre stage in spring and summer 1919. The industrial unrest of the period, however, extended across the country, in varying degrees and for local as well as national reasons. In most western cities, trades and labour councils were electing a more militant leadership with some convergence among labourist and socialist groups. During the war, key strikes, the conscription crisis, the boom in union membership, and the recruitment of new members into both older craft and newer industrial-type unions had demonstrated the potential for major upheaval. In Quebec, this new militancy was important in mobilizing women, the unskilled, and immigrants, whether in the socialist ranks of Jewish garment workers, among the metal trades workers, or among women employed in non-traditional industries such as rubber manufacturing. Despite the fractures within the union movement between Catholic, French-Canadian, and international organizations, the same kinds of forces as in Winnipeg threatened to explode on the labour scene, particularly in Montreal. As for Ontario, previously viewed as conservative and dominated by craft unions, while fewer dramatic confrontations occurred than in the rest of the country, the labour movement in the province also experienced growth within new sectors as well as old, and the conscription crisis of 1917 coupled with large-scale arrests of radicals in fall 1918 added fuel to the fire of labour's discontent. The war and surrounding events promised a bigger share for labour and changed priorities in the labour movement. Similarly, the Maritime provinces have also been characterized as conservative, but in some areas at least there was significant mobilization, some of it later than in other parts of the country. There, as elsewhere, union membership grew, labour disputes highlighted the presence of new recruits and competing unions, and, in the postwar years, labour turned increasingly to electoral politics to carry on the struggle.[18]

Activism among labour women, as workers, as union or socialist militants, and as working-class wives appeared to span the continent as well, although Winnipeg provides the most detailed evidence of concerted action. Working-class women testifying before the Royal Commission on Industrial Relations (Mathers Commission) detailed the conditions affecting women in their local areas. When this evidence is placed in context, it suggests the scope of women's activism in many urban centres. Outspoken women in Regina, Saskatoon, Calgary, and Montreal appeared before the commission to give their views.

In Saskatchewan two women testified on behalf their working-class sisters. Both were class-conscious activists with a definite sense of the inequalities faced by working-class women. Miss Francis of the Saskatoon Trades and Labor Council and the Citizen's Educational League advocated production for use rather than profit and warned that the comforts enjoyed by the few must be accessible to the masses or else the government courted disaster. While lacking precise statistics on average wages for women workers generally, Francis noted that female store clerks usually earned a minimum of nine dollars per week. Furthermore, she stated, because women were mothers responsible for the family economy, 'I am convinced that the women have a keener and more abiding interest in most problems than do men.' Mrs Resina Asals of Regina's WLL gave the commissioners considerable detail on conditions in Regina for women, based on her experience as a workingman's wife, a mother of four, and a wage earner. Asals cited examples of young inexperienced women earning seven to eight dollars or less per week and noted that given these wages it was no wonder that some women turned to prostitution. Organization of working women was difficult, she noted, referring to attempts to unionize the city's waitresses and waiters during the war. The workers could thank the capitalists, however, for 'awakening the worker up to the fact that he is the most important factor and that until we produce for use instead of profit this unrest will still prevail.' Worsening conditions affected women directly, often forcing married women to seek employment. In her own case, as the wife of a carpenter who returned from the war a disabled soldier, she had been forced to seek work to support the family. Her testimony also detailed Regina's poor housing and high rents, which consumed one-third of the wage packet of most workers. Most workers could not own their own homes because of high prices for housing, food, and clothing. 'Can you wonder why a woman would rather die than bring children into a world like this,' she asked. On the newly established provincial Minimum Wage Board, she noted that not only were there no workers on the board, there were three men and two women. When queried further, she asserted, 'I would advocate all women and no men at all, I do not suppose the men would come and ask the women what they want would they?'[19]

While Saskatoon's general sympathetic strike was larger and more successful than Regina's, very little evidence remains of the role played by women such as Francis in the conflict. Prominent in the strike were CPR shop workers, street railway men, freight handlers, postal workers, teamsters, and other unions. Evidence exists that some participated during the strike, which lasted from 27 May to 25 June. Waitresses joined the strike for better hours, conditions, and wages. Waitress Adela Blunt appeared before the Minimum Wage Board on 11 June and testified that, for ten- to twelve-hour days, restaurants paid $35 to $40 per month before the strike and $12.50 per week since the strike began.[20]

In Regina the previous fall, a strike similar to the Saskatoon waitresses' strike had been fought for a six-day week and a ten-hour day, but it had been broken by employer tactics, which included importing strikebreakers. Saskatchewan telephone operators, had also gone on a province-wide strike in October 1918 over the issue of low wages paid to women operators, with male union members waiving all other demands in order to achieve higher wages for women. In spite of this solidarity, the strikers were forced to return to work with only promises of a review of the wage schedule. These instances demonstrate the difficulty faced by women workers in the province, most of whom did not have the protection of a craft union like the IBEW to assist them. In the case of the 1919 strike, Saskatoon's lack of a women's labour organization might well have hindered more successful organization among women workers.[21]

Regina's labour women had organized a Women's Labor League in March 1917, with Mrs Ralph Heseltine as president. Supported by the Regina TLC, the WLL combined social events with efforts to investigate the conditions of working women and to organize them, as Asals's testimony to the Mathers Commission demonstrates. In May 1919 the WLL took a position in favour of the One Big Union and raised funds to send delegates to the conference of the OBU in Calgary that June. Ralph Heseltine represented the Regina TLC at the Calgary convention. Regina workers supported the general sympathetic strike in a vote, but only a small number eventually turned out, suggesting the existence of considerable tension within the labour movement over these questions which resulted in a purge of the leadership in August, including Heseltine and Joseph Sambrook, both OBU supporters. The WLL, however, continued to function and cooperated with the Regina TLC on the minimum wage issue. The league also continued to support the Winnipeg Defence Fund by raising money.[22]

Calgary's labour women were represented before the Mathers Commission by two outspoken defenders of working-class women, Mary Corse and Jean McWilliam. While Corse represented the Trades and Labor Council and played a direct role on Calgary's Central Strike Committee, McWilliam appeared before the commission as an individual. McWilliam, who had become increasingly radicalized during the war by her frustrations with government policies regarding soldiers' dependants, the high cost of living, and wage discrimination towards women workers, warned that revolt was imminent. She stated dramatically, 'If they ask us, "Are we in favor of a bloody revolution" why any kind of revolution would be better than conditions as they are now.' Like Mary Corse, McWilliam keenly felt class differences and criticized the Local Council of Women for its refusal to intervene in the firing of women laundry workers once they were unionized.[23]

Mary Corse's testimony before the Royal Commission documented the conditions of female labour in Calgary as well as commenting on a variety of other relevant issues, such as the cost of living, the need for a living wage, the housing shortage and inflationary rents, and unequal educational opportunities for working-class children. Speaking as a working woman, wife of a printing trades worker, and mother of six children, Corse pinpointed women's working conditions as one important cause of unrest among women. 'Almost every day, women are being added to the ranks of, shall I say, the socialist party or those with socialist inclinations,' she warned. The high cost of living and vast inequalities between the classes also helped to explain the unrest. As a labour representative on the Calgary School Board, Corse underlined her point about class inequality by asserting that because so many working-class children were needed as wage earners, only 6 per cent of Calgary's children reached high school. Moreover, married women had to leave home and children in order for the family to survive. Unlike many progressive women, Corse was not totally enamoured of mothers' pensions, insisting that decent wages for working women would help more. Corse was also more outspoken than any other women testifying before the commission on the need for birth control information, especially for working-class women. 'Birth control is a crime to the poor woman but the well-to-do woman who says she can only do justice to two or three children is commended for her intelligent outlook.' To illustrate her point, she gave the example of a pregnant woman who had advertised for someone to adopt her unborn child. Already the mother of four children, the woman could not afford to raise a fifth. McWilliam also commented on this case, noting that it was particularly this type of situation that led women to become activists.[24]

Within a few weeks of testifying before the commission, both women were deeply involved in a Women's Committee to aid the Calgary general sympathetic strike, which lasted from 26 May to 25 June. Mary Corse played a particularly prominent role on the Women's Committee and the Central Strike Committee. As in Winnipeg, the labour women circulated petitions, organized fundraising events and mass meetings for women, and provided food for strikers. The general strike also provided the opportunity to organize a Labour Women's Council (LWC) along the lines of Winnipeg's WLL. An OBU meeting in spring 1919 provided the opportunity for Corse to meet WLL activists, including Helen Armstrong, and directly inspired the creation of the LWC. Corse served as president, while McWilliam acted as vice-president. In addition to presenting petitions calling for the reinstatement of postal workers who had been fired by the government for taking part in sympathetic strikes, the LWC appointed a committee to appear before the school board to protest against teachers poisoning the minds of pupils in their comments in class that the strike was led by Bolshevists who should be shot. The school board agreed that teachers should not force their opinions on pupils. This concern with influences on children was a continuing feature of Calgary's LWC in the months that followed. No doubt Mary Corse's position on the school board influenced the group's activities. In November 1919 the LWC engaged in a controversy over child health and opposed a proposal that milk be distributed to needy children by the Associated Charities. McWilliam argued for universal distribution of milk to all children and for a policy of state assistance to needy children. The controversy over child malnutrition continued to surface occasionally in 1920. In addition to these activities, the Labour Women's Council, later renamed the Women's Labor League, was an active force in defending women workers and working-class concerns more generally.[25]

As the Mathers Commission moved from west to east, reaching Montreal by late May 1919, the labour situation had become critical. In Montreal labour unrest would peak in June, but would continue to trouble the city throughout the whole summer, with major strikes fought in the shipyards, in the textile, garment, and rubber industries, and in the building trades, among others. While the move towards a general strike failed, there was nevertheless a militant wave of labour and socialist activity in the city, which drew on the discontents of the war period and a strong reaction to the anti-labour policies of the municipal government. As elsewhere, the latter part of the war witnessed waves of organization among Montreal's workers, including women in clothing, rubber, and textile industries as well as clerical workers, salesclerks, and waitresses. Workers' clubs grew in numbers in the immediate postwar period, providing social and political bases for Montreal workers, some of whom affiliated with the Parti ouvrier, Quebec's labour party. The socialist movement in Montreal continued to draw on a multi-ethnic population, with strong representation from the Jewish, Russian, Ukrainian, Italian, Polish, French, and English communities. This socialist presence was particularly visible in May 1919 when three thousand May Day marchers confronted the police, who confiscated the red flags carried by marchers in defiance of police orders. Later in May, as the Mathers Commission gathered in Montreal, a large rally in support of the Winnipeg General Strike attracted several thousand people, who listened to speeches by several representatives of various labour and socialist groups, including 'socialist' Rebecca Buhay, the Social Democratic Party's Mrs R.P. Mendelssohn, and Rose Henderson of the Parti ouvrier. All three women were prominent in Montreal's left-wing politics.[26]

Henderson was the only one of the three to speak before the Mathers Commission. A few days after the rally she testified, not as a representative of the labour party, but in her official capacity as the non-Catholic probation officer for Montreal, a position she took on after her husband, an accountant at the MacDonald Tobacco company, died, leaving her a single mother with limited resources. Eventually, Henderson became a probation officer of the juvenile court, pursuing her abiding interest in children. In addition, as she testified before the Mathers Commission, she was an outspoken advocate for women, particularly working-class women who exhibited a clear interest in changing current conditions for themselves and their families. Her work at the juvenile court involved her in working-class family life, and she linked the economic difficulties experienced by the working class to the wartime increases in the case-load of the court. In the majority of homes, fathers earned twelve to fifteen dollars per week as unskilled labourers and were only seasonally employed. Both the mothers and children of such families often worked for low wages, especially when there were no other sources of income. The current labour unrest resulted, Henderson said, from two groups: the 'underdog' class three days away from starvation, whose children turned up in juvenile court, and the organized mass of labour who were determined not to return to prewar conditions. The latter group, especially the mothers, wanted a better life for their children. Her solutions included getting rid of profiteers, prohibiting the labour of children under the age of sixteen, securing the six-hour day, and introducing social welfare schemes, particularly mothers' pensions. Women were the source of social change, according to Henderson: 'In a great many houses that I visit, it is not the father who expresses himself; I find the real revolutionist is the mother – not the man. She says openly that there is nothing but Revolution.'[27]

Henderson's feminism, no doubt influenced by her Irish family's radical views, blended with her social democratic politics, which combined a keen concern for women and children with a social conscience shaped by her work among the working-class residents of Montreal. For Henderson, the women of the working class offered the greatest hope for change. Her viewpoint was strongly shaped by maternal feminist convictions shared by middle- and upper-class women reformers of the day who also found hope for change among women as a social group, rather than among working-class women in particular. Her class awareness, however, set her apart from these women and gave her the impetus to participate in the labour movement and later the peace movement as well. In spring and summer 1919 she found some common ground with more radical Montreal women in the promise of the One Big Union.

The Winnipeg General Strike rally in Montreal provided Henderson and others with a platform to support both the strike and the OBU. An undated letter from Henderson to R.B. Russell, Winnipeg's key figure in the general strike and the OBU campaign, indicates that Henderson was actively promoting the OBU in northern Ontario while on an organizing tour, possibly for the Independent Labor Party. She asked Russell to send her more OBU material: 'I am boosting it for all its worth, the idea is catching well.' The Montreal rally also featured a speech by Rebecca Buhay, who attacked craft unionism and the capitalist press while urging working-class support for the OBU. Buhay was an important figure in the radical movement in Montreal, along with her close colleague Annie Buller. Both were active in the OBU, as police surveillance reports indicate. An agent reported that on 13 November 1919, Buhay was elected organizer for the Montreal Local of the OBU and later was English recording secretary for the General Workers' Unit of the OBU, while Annie Buller filled the role of vice-president. Both women later played prominent roles in the Communist Party of Canada. Buller's reminiscences of Buhay, and surviving correspondence between them, indicate the close support these women gave each other in the earlier period and their shared commitment not only to socialism, but also to women's causes. Buller's first memory of Buhay was a lecture Becky gave to a group of socialist men shortly after her arrival from England in 1913. Her discussion of Ibsen's *The Doll House* stressed the need for the franchise, equal pay, and unions for exploited women workers. That event marked the beginning of a lasting friendship between the two women. While both women followed socialist orthodoxy on the woman question, they were keenly aware of the need to mobilize women as well as men.[28]

The issues brought to a head by the Winnipeg strike and the local strikes in Montreal – collective bargaining, freedom of speech, and the OBU – also brought Mrs R.P. Mendelssohn of the Social Democratic Party into the public debate. As secretary of the socialist committee planning the 1919 May Day parade in Montreal, Mendelssohn informed the press that if violence resulted, it would be the fault of the capitalists. Municipal authorities banned the use of public parks such as Fletcher's Field in Mount Royal Park unless express permission was granted. In early June, the police broke up a socialist gathering at the park and arrested Mendelssohn, who loudly protested against the police presence and the use of mounted officers. Insisting on her right as a citizen to use the park, at her trial Mendelssohn defended the use of the park by socialists, citing previous practice and the fact that she had written the mayor for permission, but had received no answer. The charge was dismissed, despite police testimony that her actions constituted incitement to rebellion. As well as defending free speech, Mendelssohn also actively worked for the OBU and the establishment of a rival trades and labour council, known as the Industrial Council, which was sympathetic to OBU goals. According to surveillance information, Mendelssohn was also a correspondent for the socialist paper the New York *Call* and was listed by the authorities as 'dangerous.'[29]

Thus in Montreal, as in Winnipeg, Regina, and Calgary, a nucleus of activist women played public roles in the labour unrest of 1919, through the labour and socialist movement. What about the rest of the country? While other major centres failed to provide the Mathers Commission with women witnesses who might provide the historian with first-hand glimpses of women's views and actions, labour unrest among women workers in specific industries was substantial in places like Amherst, Nova Scotia, Toronto, and Vancouver. As for recognizable female leadership in the general strikes in these cities, only Vancouver provides clear-cut evidence of specific women's organization.

## III

Toronto's general sympathetic strike of 30 May to 4 June resembled Winnipeg's in so far as the metal trades were at the centre of the crisis. The eight-hour day and forty-four-hour week, along with collective bargaining, provided the bone of contention that led to the sympathetic walkout of forty-four unions and twelve thousand workers. Approximately two thousand of those who went out were garment workers, half of them women. Their support of the metal trades workers proved to be a prelude to a summer-long garment workers' strike. The general sympathetic strike in Toronto signified, however, more widespread activities among the previously unorganized or weakly organized, largely 'unskilled' workers, including women. The Toronto District Labor Council (TDLC) had launched an organizing drive in spring 1919 and within two months had recruited ten thousand new members, many of them unskilled or semi-skilled workers, including candy and chocolate workers, rubber workers, and employees in meat-packing plants. A week-long strike of packinghouse workers included 'several hundred girls.' The conciliation board appointed to work out a settlement discussed the issue of equal pay, but failed to reach an agreement, apparently unable to find a mutually acceptable definition of what constituted 'equal work.' The only concession aimed at the women in the final settlement was an agreement that the companies would pay one-half the cost of necessary clothing worn by the women in the plants.[30]

Several groups of women workers, such as bookbinders, textile workers, telephone operators, and waitresses, increased their union membership in spring and summer 1919. Waitresses and domestics in Toronto as
elsewhere unionized in late 1918 and early 1919. Domestic workers were
assisted by the Toronto WLL under the guidance of Mrs Lucy Mac-
Gregor, president of the WLL and a member of the Women's Social
Democratic League. The Domestic Workers' Association's secretary,
Sarah Davies, pointed out that the domestics were affiliated with the
hotel and restaurant workers, but made their own decisions. Their goals
were an eight-hour day, no apprenticeship, one day off per week, and
$60 per month for 'live-outs' and $40 per month for 'live-ins.' As of 21
June, a hundred women had signed up for the union, which maintained
its willingness to discuss matters with employers.[31]

While local labour strife tended to occupy centre stage in Toronto, the
Winnipeg General Strike and the defence of the strikers were not
entirely forgotten in July and August, when several of the strike leaders
visited to address local audiences. A crowd of five thousand listened to
socialist aldermen John Queen and A.A. Heaps and veterans' representative T.H. Dunn when they spoke at Queen's Park in mid-July. Helen
Armstrong's visit in August, sponsored by the 'Women's Labor Union,'
probably the WLL, drew much smaller audiences, although on her
return to Winnipeg Armstrong herself commented favorably on the
strong committees in Toronto and Hamilton. When in Toronto, however,
she castigated the local labour council for its 'lukewarm' support of the
Winnipeg strike leaders, comments that apparently hit home because a
Defence Committee was appointed shortly after her remarks.[32]

Toronto's labour and socialist women did not emerge as strong figures in these events. The local WLL was active in organizing women
workers, as the example of the Domestic Workers' Association indicates.
Formed in late 1918 by Lucy MacGregor and Harriet Dunlop Prenter,
the WLL attracted left-wing and working-class women. Aside from the
domestics' union, there is little evidence of WLL participation in the
general sympathetic strike.

Two other general strikes occurred at opposite ends of the country. In
the east the labour unrest of 1919 produced a general strike in the small
industrial enclave of Amherst, Nova Scotia. Although no identifiable
female leadership emerged in Amherst during the three-week strike,
newspaper accounts suggest that women workers could be roused to
militant action in a climate of postwar expectations and insecurities.
Women workers were most prominent in the textile mills of Amherst,

which faced many of the same economic pressures as other industries in the town as the centralization of capital and the reorganization of business marginalized the workers. The Amherst Woollen Mills, taken over by the powerful Stanfields, witnessed three bitter strikes between 1918 and 1920. The 1919 confrontation coincided with the organization of a special unit of the Amherst Federation of Labor among the predominantly female workers. The Amherst federation operated along industrial lines and was popularly known as the 'one big union.' With strong participation from the carworks employees, the Amherst Federation of Labor led a three-week general strike beginning on 19 May. Women workers at the mills faced a recalcitrant employer who closed the mill down and refused to deal with demands. As a result, the mill workers strike continued after most of the others had been settled, ultimately resulting in defeat. Other workers fared better, as the unified tactics of the strike brought about wage and hour concessions, including some for women workers at the boot and shoe factory. The role of women in these events remains, however, shadowy.[33]

In the west, Vancouver's general sympathetic strike attracted support from approximately ten thousand workers, mostly from the metal trades, shipbuilding, and transport. As James Conley has argued, it was frontier labourers and craftsmen in crisis who formed the base for working-class radicalism in the first two decades of the twentieth century. Urban workers and factory operatives made poor material for radical politics, at least in Vancouver. Conley also suggests that gender and racial divisions tended to hamper the development of radicalism in the working class. While accepting the general thrust of these arguments, it is instructive to note that in Vancouver's general strike one particular group of women workers, the telephone operators, played a very visible and militant role, while other groups of women workers were exempted by the strike committee as essential workers. Many others were not unionized or belonged to unions that did not adequately protect their interests.[34]

Strike leaders called out the telephone operators in an attempt to force the city to outlaw the operation of jitneys that undercut the effectiveness of the street railway strike. The operators had a history of difficulties with the British Columbia Telephone Company, stemming back to the strikes in 1902 and 1906. During the war the IBEW had reorganized and chartered a new local for the operators. When the operators joined the general strike, they again confronted the problem of strikebreakers as they had in previous strikes. Company spokesman F. Helliwell claimed that 'Not one in fifty of the girls know what they are striking for,' and praised the company for its concern for the operators, citing the provision of a restaurant on company premises. The company's refusal to reinstate the operators at the end of the strike nearly prolonged the general strike and forced the operators and electrical workers to stay out until mid-July when they returned on company terms.[35]

Telephone operators played a prominent role in strike support meetings, such as the one held on 14 June, one day after the operators had gone out. Speaker Mrs Smith of the IBEW poured scorn on the company's offer of an 'association,' claiming 85 per cent of the operators were IBEW. Two days later at a meeting for women, operator and striker Mrs Yates spoke before over two hundred women along with Jack Kavanaugh and Dave Burge of the Central Strike Committee and Sarah Johnston-Knight, a well-known Edmonton socialist and OBU activist. On 18 June another mass meeting of close to five thousand people heard reports on the strike and contributed funds for needy families among the strikers. A week later a much smaller audience of women assembled to hear Sarah Johnston-Knight urge a 'spirited defence of the strike leaders' because 'as mothers, sisters and wives we are part and parcel of the working class.' She noted that, while the bourgeoisie never failed to use its women to fight the workers, referring to the 'volunteer' operators from the upper-middle class, no working-class women scabbed. Mrs H.G. Taylor of the Federated Labor Party (FLP) defended the strikers' claims, which she viewed as very mild. The organizing force behind such meetings is not clear. No doubt the women of the FLP were involved, and the presence of Helena Gutteridge on the Central Strike Committee also suggests that she may have organized the women during the general strike. As a well-known trade unionist who often represented women workers' concerns at the Vancouver TLC, Gutteridge was well placed to initiate such activity. She was also a member of the FLP.[36]

Despite the participation of the telephone operators and prominent labour activists such as Gutteridge, the relative dearth of organizing activities during the 1919 crisis in Vancouver stands in marked contrast to the more visible activities in centres such as Winnipeg, Calgary, and Montreal. The absence of a single focus, such as a Women's Labor League or some other women's group, might help to explain this phenomenon, and Vancouver was the headquarters of the Socialist Party of Canada, which frowned on separate women's organizations and activities.

## IV

This cross-country tour of women's activism has suggested that a wide variety of responses and levels of activity characterized the crisis of 1919. While the strikes themselves ended formally in the summer, the reverberations of the Winnipeg strike and the trials continued to be a concern of labour and socialist women. Like their male counterparts, women across the country felt a responsibility towards the strike leaders and their families as the trials were held in fall 1919, ultimately resulting in jail terms for most of the leaders. Winnipeg was the centre of organization for the Defence Committee, formed shortly after the strike ended. Its main purpose was to raise funds for legal costs and for the support of strike leaders' families, but it also used fundraising events to defend the right of collective bargaining and free speech. In Winnipeg, the committee consisted of representatives of various labour and socialist groups, including the Winnipeg TLC, the Central Labor Council of the OBU, the Ex-Soldiers' and Sailors' Labour Party, the Building Trades Council, the SPC, the Labour Church, the Dominion Labor Party, and the WLL. Despite the tensions between the TLC and the OBU, the Defence Committee received support even from those unions opposed to the OBU. Financial support from union locals, individuals, and women's organizations enabled the committee to send speakers all over the country, organize protests, and publish a bulletin. In Winnipeg, Women's Labor Leagues raised money through dances, concerts, bazaars, and picnics.[37]

Such efforts were repeated elsewhere across the country. Women speakers addressed local labour meetings and protest rallies on the subjects of the strike. Helen Armstrong made several trips to Ontario: in addition to her August trip, she accompanied her husband, George, to the Hamilton Trades and Labor Congress in October 1919, representing the WLL. 'The Wild Woman of the West,' as she was dubbed by eastern newspapers, found the East too quiet for her liking. Other women also spoke to audiences in support of the Winnipeg strikers. Winona Flett, wife of the labourite strike leader Fred Dixon, spoke on the strike at a farmers' picnic in Saskatchewan in July. Sarah Johnston-Knight and Joe Knight, SPC and OBU members, gathered support in Ontario, where they had moved after the purge of OBU supporters from the Edmonton TLC. Montreal's women socialists raised money for the Defence Committee, as did the WLL in Calgary. In the latter city, Jean McWilliam was instrumental in organizing the Calgary Defence Committee, with WLL initiative playing a key role. McWilliam reported that the outlying districts exhibited considerable interest in the Defence Committee. Mary Corse also threw her energies into several protest meetings in spring 1920. A meeting held in early April passed a resolution condemning the imprisonment of the strike leaders who were 'suffering in a just cause for the supposed rights of free speech.' A second meeting held a few days later featured Corse and A.A. Heaps of Winnipeg, with Corse urging the working class to stand together for the welfare of their children. Scenes such as these were repeated across the country, with women in the labour and socialist movement taking important if sometimes traditional roles to defend controversial working-class principles.[38]

For a number of these women activists the OBU provided some hope for women workers, as well as for men. An industrial-style union without distinctions of skill and gender seemed to promise a unified strategy and eradication of old divisions. In Winnipeg and Vancouver, the strongholds of the OBU, women joined units of the organizations. In Winnipeg they participated in the Needle Trades Council, which covered garment, textile, and glove workers, as well as tailors and tailoresses. At the beginning of 1920 a women's auxiliary of the OBU was formed in central Winnipeg, followed later by another for Weston/Brooklands and a Young Labor League which combined young women and men in one organization. The only requirement for joining the women's auxiliary was the signing of an application to demonstrate support for the OBU and its principles. In fact some of the old Women's Labor Leagues transformed themselves into OBU auxiliaries and then carried on many of the same activities with the same personnel. In Ontario, Port Arthur and Fort William labour women followed this example and created an auxiliary in late 1920, which included English and Finnish women. In Vancouver a General Workers' Unit brought together the skilled and unskilled, men and women. Unlike the trades that dominated the OBU in Winnipeg, in Vancouver it was waitresses, store clerks, mattress makers, stenographers, and barmaids who joined the glove workers in attending the first organizational meeting in April 1920. Some examples of women workers' involvement in the OBU can be found in the East, as well, but the strength of the organization lay in the West. Even there, it faced slow erosion as the international unions regained control.[39]

V

Labour and socialist women across the country responded to the post-war crisis and their newly won enfranchisement through active involvement in labour party politics and especially in election campaigns, mostly at the municipal and provincial level in 1919 and 1920. From Nova Scotia to British Columbia, women organized for, supported, and even ran as candidates for labour parties, which drew upon the ranks of socialists, labourites, and sometimes OBU supporters. A smaller number turned towards the nascent Communist movement and its aboveground Workers' Party.

The move towards the formation of labour parties in the late war and early postwar period signalled a renewed interest in a phenomenon that had attracted Canadian workers since at least the 1890s. The circumstances of the war and the labour conflict that characterized the period gave new impetus to local and provincial organizations that had appeared sporadically in the past. While earlier incarnations of labour parties had drawn on workers generally, by the war period a greater number of skilled workers became involved, and more women from the working class also took a direct interest in labour politics. As Craig Heron has noted, few labour party candidates were elected before the war, but by the end of the war local independent labour parties were successful in electing their members to school boards and municipal councils. While provinces like Manitoba and Ontario had provincial labour party organizations as early as 1907, it was only during the war that more coherent groups began to emerge in other provinces. No real national federation of labour parties existed, although the Canadian Labor Party, formed in 1917, was intended to provide a national framework. Unlike the SPC, for example, these labour formations espoused a practical philosophy of gradual change, based on radical liberalism, hatred of 'privilege,' and a commitment to equality, which included representation of labour's interests in politics. Thus, labour found a basis of cooperation with social democrats who more readily accepted electoral and gradualist politics. Between 1917 and 1920, socialists and labour political activists maintained an alliance, which began to disintegrate as conflicting interests clashed.[40]

Political activism was particularly noticeable in Winnipeg, where the fall 1919 municipal elections set the stage for a contest between labour and its opponents. With the Winnipeg strike trials about to begin, tensions were high, and the labour movement was determined to win political power through the ballot box. The question of women's votes was a highly contentious one in the city. Although women had the vote, property qualifications still limited the size of the electorate, effectively disqualifying those who did not own property, particularly women and the working class. Nevertheless, the women's vote in general was viewed as a weapon useful to labour. Helen Armstrong, at a mass protest meeting held on 7 September in the city stated, 'Women's vote had given us the club. Now we wanted women to use it.'[41]

Three women contested the school board elections as labour candidates in December 1919. Mrs Rose Alcin, a Jewish woman from Winnipeg's North End, successfully defeated her Jewish male opponent whose views were conservative. Alcin was attacked in the press as lacking in education, to which she responded that the contemporary educational system trained children to be 'obedient slaves to the existing capitalistic order and future good members of the Committee of 1,000.' Running with Alcin were two other prominent labour women, Jessie Kirk and Edith Hancock, both of whom were British-born and prominent members and speakers in various organizations, including the Labor Church, the WLL, and the Dominion Labor Party. Kirk had been fired from her job as a school teacher for her political activities, a factor that no doubt figured in her decision to run. All three women candidates ran on a program that advocated, among other things, equal pay for equal work, free text books, open school board meetings, collective bargaining rights for teachers, and the abolition of property qualifications for school trustees. Only Alcin was elected. Jessie Kirk ran successfully in 1920 for municipal council and continued to run for public office in the 1920s and 1930s. Kirk, along with WLL and Labor Church activist Mrs Rowe, was elected to the executive committee of the Dominion Labor Party (DLP) in March 1920, giving women two of the nine seats. Women were constantly urged to take public roles in the DLP by women activists and occasionally by the men. Speakers encouraged women to use their close connections with children and with life itself (as opposed to property) in the service of labour politics. Even before the Winnipeg General Strike, Winona Flett went so far as to urge women's participation in the DLP for the protection of men, although she pointed out that women needed relief from the drudgery of the household through cooperative schemes, if they were to increase their participation. When the provincial election campaign of 1920 began, women in the DLP had moved in a noticeably more feminist direction, planning to run several women candidates. While both Helen Armstrong and Jessie Kirk withdrew in favour of incarcerated strike leaders, Kirk expressed disappointment at what was clearly seen as a sacrifice for labour's cause. Winona Flett also urged women to support labour's candidates in the election, yet at an election meeting attended by two thousand people, she expressed regret that no labour women candidates would run. Furthermore, she urged more women to join the Labor Party to make it representative of both sexes: 'She served notice there and then that they (women) would demand nothing less than a 50/50 ticket.'[42]

Women were newcomers to many of these labour parties. Mobilized by the war, labour conflict, the campaigns to defend collective bargaining and free speech, and the search for new bases of organization, women formed Women's Labor Leagues, joined labour parties, and formed their own female branches of these parties, perhaps encouraged by specific promises of equality 'politically, socially and industrially.' In Hamilton, for example, women's interest in the Independent Labor Party was intertwined with union organization drives in industries such as garments and textiles, which employed significant numbers of women, as well as with the general thrust towards organization. Wives of labour movement leaders were prominent in the Hamilton branches of the Women's ILP, which took shape in April 1917 and featured speakers, study groups, election support, and attempts to elect women to the school board. While labour men's wives, such as Maude Cassidy and Maud Madden, were closely involved in the Women's ILP, a few single working women such as Janet Inman also took prominent roles. Inman was a middle-aged textile worker, spiritualist, and president of the Mount Hamilton ILP. Other prominent women participants included Mary McNab, a parson's daughter who became the first secretary and business agent of the newly organized Amalgamated Clothing Workers of America local formed in Hamilton in 1916. Reports in the labour press during 1917 indicated that the Women's ILP which rejected the status of auxiliary, attracted many new members.[43]

Two women's branches of the Ontario ILP were represented as part of the hundred-strong ILP delegation to the convention that met in Toronto to launch the Ontario section of the Canadian Labor Party at the end of March 1918. Both Cassidy and Madden took active roles, with the former on the resolutions committee and the latter speaking up for housewives as workers, a point that engendered some debate in convention. Other women also took a role in the convention, which included trade unionists, socialists (SDP and SPNA), farmers, and a miscellaneous group of cooperators, fabians, single taxers, and theosophists. Florence Custance of the Socialist Party of North America supported attempts to inject tougher, more class-conscious language into the wording of resolutions at the convention, attempts that met defeat in the face of opposition from ILP delegates and farmers. Unlike the SPNA, which denounced the British Labour Party as a branch of the Liberal Party, most of the delegates seemed to admire the British approach, although some, including many ILP delegates, thought it too radical for the majority of Canadian workers. These political differences divided the women as well as the men. Custance would eventually opt for the Communist Party of Canada, although most of the ILP women rejected that option.[44]

At the same time as the Hamilton Women's ILP was forming, other women in Ontario were also campaigning on behalf of labour organization and labour political action. Laura Hughes, niece of Militia Minister Sir Sam Hughes, had been a supporter of labour political action since at least 1915 and had spoken on the topic to the Trades and Labor Congress Convention in Toronto in September 1916. In November of that year, Hughes announced a lecture tour for Ontario's industrial centres. She stumped southern Ontario in spring 1917, lecturing in Guelph, Galt, and Kitchener to great acclaim for her speaking abilities, occasionally pushing suffrage and pacifist issues in addition to her labour message. In April Hughes became second vice-president of the Greater Toronto Labor Party. A proposed western tour was cancelled when Hughes married a conscientious objector and moved to Chicago, but she maintained many of her contacts among like-minded women in Canada.[45]

Activities such as these helped to encourage other women in Ontario to organize. In May 1917 Cobalt women were reported to be taking steps to organize under the Labor Party banner, and by early 1918 a women's auxiliary to the miners' union was reported by Toronto labour booster James Simpson. Women were also active in Brantford's ILP, which by spring 1918 featured a drive to organize women. One of the major figures in the campaign to organize women into the ranks of labour politics, particularly during 1919 and 1920, was long-time activist Minnie Singer, who had played a prominent role in the International Association of Machinists auxiliary movement since before the war. Singer frequently travelled and spoke at ILP meetings to assist in the organization of women's branches in Ontario. She assisted Rose Henderson, for example, in a February 1919 by-election campaign in St Catharines. Capitalizing on the interest created during the campaign, Singer assisted the St Catharines women in forming a branch of the Women's ILP. Another branch resulted from Singer's visit to Kitchener. She also travelled to Galt, London, Peterborough, and Ottawa in spring 1919 seeking to form new branches, although she was mainly unsuccessful in these locales. In the early part of 1920, Singer was reported as having organized a number of IAM auxiliaries in major American cities.[46]

'A New Departure Full of Promise' was the headline of the *Industrial Banner* in April 1919 when the newspaper featured a story on the initiatives of the Labor Educational Association (LEA) to organize a Provincial Women's Department of Work and Labour in Ontario. Minnie Singer was to organize and supervise the new department, which would be controlled by women and financed by the LEA, with assistance from labour organizations in the province. This initiative was timed to precede the LEA's annual convention in late May and the ILP's convention in mid-April. The announcement was accompanied by a flurry of activity in organizing new women's branches of the ILP, mostly under the auspices of Singer. As an umbrella group, the LEA counted the ILP as one of its strong supporters, and certainly overlapping memberships in both organizations were common, blending political and trade union interests.[47]

The ILP convention debated affiliation to the Ontario section of the Canadian Labor Party, passed resolutions against censorship and for the recall of Canadian troops from Siberia, and recommended a national minimum wage, a shorter work day, the guarantee to every child of life's necessities, and free hospital care for mothers. The convention also wrestled with the question of ILP affiliation to the NCWC. Despite the urgings of Mary McNab that working women's interests ought to be represented in the middle-class women's organization, the majority preferred to concentrate on their own class interests. Among the speakers was WLL representative and Christian socialist, Mrs Rose Hodgson, a former member of the British ILP who supported the strengthening of the labour movement through labour political action. Hodgson was elected second vice-president of the Ontario ILP, one of two women on the eight-person executive; Mary McNab of Hamilton became fourth vice-president.[48]

Hodgson, like Singer, was also very much involved in the May LEA meeting, which set up the committee to organize labour women. Six women were charged with this organizational work: Mrs Madden (Hamilton Women's ILP), Mrs Cook (Toronto, SDP), Mrs Singer (Toronto, Ladies' Auxiliary, IAM), Mrs Redford (Cobalt, Miners' Union Auxiliary), Miss O'Connor (Toronto, Textile Workers), and Mrs MacGregor (Toronto, WLL). While Hodgson was not on the organizing committee, she worked closely with MacGregor in the WLL, organizing women workers, including a union for domestics in Toronto. Indeed, a representative of the Domestic Workers Alliance also attended the LEA meeting. Among the resolutions proposed to the convention, Hodgson introduced one urging that no married woman be employed if her husband earned an adequate wage. The resolution passed unanimously. While a strong supporter of unionizing single women workers, Hodgson reflected a dominant strand among labour leaders, both male and female – that married, working-class women should not engage in paid labour.[49]

One of the major purposes for the broad labour women's organization in 1919 was to prepare for the fall elections and the mobilization of women in the electoral struggle. The ILP conducted an educational and organizational drive in the summer in preparation for the elections. The labour press carried stories of new successes in unionizing women workers during spring and summer 1919, noting successes among the bookbinders, textile workers, and boot and shoe workers, and the struggles of striking garment workers. A large Labour Day demonstration in Toronto featured a parade of seven thousand people, including representatives from feminized trades such as boot and shoe, glove, textile, and garment industries. The women's section of the parade highlighted recent organization among domestic workers – a float depicted the contrast between union domestics demanding the eight-hour day and a group of unorganized domestics working fourteen-hour days.[50]

After 1919 the OBU question posed a difficulty for labour women as well as men and threatened the uneasy alliances in labour politics. Minnie Singer undertook a westward trip in early 1920, seeking to counter divisions over industrial union strategies by organizing an IAM auxiliary in Edmonton. While failing to bring about the creation of a new auxiliary, she reported that, 'We have been able to do some real active work with good results considering the divisions in our ranks at this time.' Divisions over industrial strategy and the OBU were most keenly felt in the West where the OBU had more support among workers in resource extraction and transportation. Singer's mission reflected Ontario's economic base in manufacturing, where, as Heron has noted, skilled workers were more cautious politically and sometimes lined up with employers to protect fragile industrial growth, boost the union label, and fight against the large private utilities.[51]

Despite clouds of division on the horizon in 1920, women's labour political action continued to grow. By mid-1920, seven Women's ILP branches were active. At the Brantford meeting of the LEA, a reorganization of the 1919 effort took the form of the United Women's Educational Federation of Ontario, under the presidency of Minnie Singer, with the Hamilton ILP women providing the moving force. The intention was to unite all women's labour organizations to work for free state medical care for mothers, the full franchise for everyone over the age of twenty, meals and milk for school children, the eight-hour day, a minimum wage for men, and measures to curb unemployment and unrestricted immigration. Described as 'Labor's National Council of Women,' the federation was open to all women's groups 'who are interested in the welfare and uplift of women workers on both the industrial and political fields.' The trade union movement was asked to provide names of eligible women's organizations. This group maintained its existence at least until the late 1920s, absorbing the Women's ILP of Hamilton in 1924 as a branch. Some of the original members, such as Janet Inman and OBU supporter and textile worker Jean Ingles, moved into the Hamilton WLL, which had a close relationship with the communist movement.[52]

Labour's alliance with the left, always contingent and insecure, foundered in the postwar period as labour's attention receded from industrial struggles and focused on the political arena of the legislature, especially in central Canada. Labourism lost ground among workers in the 1920s after a brief period of success in the wake of 1919. Socialism increasingly became identified with the Workers' Party and communism, which in its early days tried to work with the trade union movement. Another factor in the polarization of labour and the left was the rising prominence of middle-class spokespersons within the Labor Party and at the polls. While speaking for and to working-class women, for example, Labor Party activists such as Laura Hughes, Dorothy Glen, and Rose Henderson were not working class. Both Glen and Henderson worked in the juvenile court system and both had married professional men. Later, both would become involved in the CCF, as would Beatrice Brigden of Brandon, Manitoba, who also involved herself in social work for the Methodist Church's Department of Social Service and Evangelism. Brigden came from a farm family but eventually her father set up business as a druggist in Brandon. With the events of 1919, Brigden became embroiled in more explicit political activities, joining the Dominion Labor Party and its successor the ILP, and serving as a vice-president of the DLP in 1920. For Brigden, labour politics complemented her involvement in A.E. Smith's Peoples' Church, and her energies were increasingly directed towards these ends rather than the Methodist Church, which she felt paid too little attention to movements among the 'common people.' Like other labour political activists, she shared a sense of mission towards the working class and supported the cause of labour political activism.[53]

Social service work also provided Rose Henderson a path into politics, in part. Family background, widowhood, and single parenting may also have contributed to her interest in working-class politics and women's issues. In 1920 she undertook a cross-country tour for the ILP, first in Ontario in the spring and Nova Scotia in the summer. In addition to bringing the ILP message to labour groups, she also met with groups of women, urging them to become involved in labour politics. The Labor Party had met with considerable success in Nova Scotia from 1917 on, but few women appeared to have taken a leading role, as Gertrude Steckler of Sydney noted in 1918 in one of several articles contributed to the *Canadian Labor Leader*. A Russian Jew by birth, Steckler decried the secondary role played by women in labour and politics and urged women to make time for reading, thinking, and politics. Two years later, Rose Henderson's message was very similar, urging women to use their potential and their recently won vote to work for reform and justice. While touring the province, Henderson assisted in organizing Ladies' Auxiliaries of the ILP as well as campaigning for a July provincial election.[54]

One of the candidates in that election was Bertha M. Donaldson, wife of a retired steelworker and president of the New Glasgow Ladies' Auxiliary of the ILP. She was chosen unanimously as a candidate along with H.D. Fraser, president of the steelworkers' union, and the Pictou County TLC and farmer candidate, Allen D. McKay. Donaldson ran as the Great War Veterans' Association candidate, having had three sons who fought in the war and a daughter who worked on munitions in the steel plant. The local newspaper commented that Donaldson was very familiar with soldiers' views, and noted that she had grown up on a farm, giving her an understanding of farmers' problems. In addition, she was a good speaker, according to the press. Despite the excitement and interest generated by a woman candidate, Donaldson lost. Still, she garnered nearly three thousand votes, about half of what her male colleagues received. While the newspaper congratulated her for doing so well, it also had doubts about the wisdom of nominating a woman: 'Evidently we will have to travel a considerable distance yet, before a woman candidate will be acceptable. The woman candidate in Cumberland (Conservative) also met with defeat. Hard luck, Mrs Donaldson!' The number of votes Donaldson received was not insignificant given the fact that she 'was never seen or heard on the public platform in Trenton yet her friends polled hundreds of votes for her.' Seemingly undaunted by her defeat, Donaldson proceeded to assist Truro women in a fall election campaign.[55]

While labour politics clearly provided an opening for some women, they remained in the minority and faced considerable obstacles to full participation. While a few women representing labour, farmer, or farmer-labour constituencies succeeded in formal politics, most politically active women played far different roles at the local community level in the aftermath of the war and the postwar crisis.

Socialist women further to the left rejected labour politics, as did their male colleagues. Events at home and abroad helped to convince many that a new political formation was needed in Canada, one that was in line with developments in the Soviet Union and the international communist movement. Whether one dates this activity from the founding meeting of the underground Communist Party of Canada (CPC) in 1921 or earlier in 1919–20, left-wing dissidents were active in launching new initiatives aimed at a more revolutionary approach to restructuring capitalism. Among the more prominent women involved in these activities were Florence Custance, Becky Buhay, and Annie Buller. As was noted above, Buhay and Buller were very active in socialist politics and the OBU from 1919 on. Both Buller and Bella Gauld, another future Communist, attended the Rand School of Social Science in New York, where they met and became friends. On their return to Montreal in the aftermath of the general strike, the two linked up with Buhay and became part of the founding group of the Montreal Labour College, which conducted classes for workers and provided space and offices for a variety of labour and political groups. A similar undertaking earlier in 1920 in Toronto was the Ontario Labour College, one of whose founders was Florence Custance, a founder of the SPNA and a participant in the formative stages of the CPC. A somewhat shadowy figure, Custance was more of an intellectual, trained as a school teacher in England. Joan Sangster notes that she was married to a carpenter and was active in the women's auxiliary of the carpenters' union. In the early days of the CPC she was the only woman in the party's central leadership and played a central role in the women's organizations within the CPC until her death in 1929.[56]

While these women have figured to some extent in accounts of the early communist movement, other women, less well-known and outside of the leadership circles, have not. One colourful and eccentric figure was Sophie Mushkat McClusky. Outspoken in her views, McClusky appeared to have had a very stormy relationship with all the political organizations she joined, and in the 1920s she re-emerged on the political scene after several years of homesteading and the birth of her daughter. RCMP reports in 1921 indicated that she had joined the OBU women's auxiliary and participated in SPC debates in Edmonton on affiliation with the Third International, a position she favoured. The RCMP agent noted in his report, 'She got very bitter at some objections that were taken to affiliation and stated that we should not hesitate to make the party an underground organization and work for the overthrow of the present government as hard as possible ... we would have to show whither were [sic] were real revolutionists or just a party of social democrats ... SHE is a real menace.' In fall 1921 McClusky moved to Calgary, where she made her living teaching English to immigrants. Despite her previous experience in that city teaching English, the Calgary School Board was wary of her political views and refused her a position, forcing her to teach privately. That same fall she applied for reinstatement in the SPC, six years after she had been expelled for partaking in a prohibition campaign. Although she was readmitted by the Edmonton local, the RCMP records are silent on her subsequent activities until 1924–25 when they noted her presence in Calgary and her continued public support for the Soviet Union at radical forums and unemployed meetings. In the mid-1920s McClusky was also reported as a former SPC member and activist in the Women's Labor League, the Labour Women's Social and Economic Conference, and the Ukrainian Labour Temple Association. Again, she disappears from the RCMP files until 1929, when she moved to Halifax where she remained until her death in 1954.[57]

Unlike Custance, Buhay, Buller, and others, Sophie McClusky never found a niche in left-wing political circles. Too outspoken and too much of a maverick, she often found herself at odds with party discipline and on the outs with the various political formations she was associated with, whether the SPC, the Workers' Party, the CPC, the CCF, or, during the Second World War, the Labour-Progressive Party, which replaced the banned CPC. There must have been other women like McClusky who did not fit easily into left-wing politics, as defined in the early postwar period by the underground communist movement and its aboveground Workers' Party. Nevertheless, for some women activists in the postwar period, the communist movement promised to provide economic and class equality.

Clearly the postwar period offered women political activists some important ground for new initiatives in labour and left-wing movements. The crisis of 1919 evoked labour and political activism among women of the working class and among middle-class progressive women who identified with their struggle for collective bargaining, free speech, and a new political agenda. Women's needs and their quest for a voice in these struggles were acknowledged on occasion by contemporary political movements. Still, women activists had to contend with gender-based ideologies and political practices that continued to assign women lesser roles within these movements or separate responsibilities, usually for women's issues, within the larger framework. A few women played central roles, but most were marginalized from centres of power.

# Conclusion

Writing the history of labour and left-wing women in late-nineteenth- and early-twentieth-century Canada has not been an easy task. Whether searching for 'ordinary' working women who expressed their belief in honest womanhood, women who took active roles in organizing female wage earners, or women who participated in various forms of left-wing, oppositional politics, the challenge has been daunting. Few of them left behind written evidence in the form of personal papers or organizational records, and thus their stories are, of necessity, partial and incomplete. This book began with a look at 'working girls' and efforts to study and regulate the problem of women's work at the turn of the century. While those observing the problem of working women focused on the negative – competition in the labour market, immorality and promiscuity, the necessity of protective legislation – the working women whose voices were not completely muted defended their honest toil, most turned their backs on domestic service where possible, and sometimes expressed publicly their own sense of self-worth, as individuals or as a group. Attempts to regulate working women's lives presumed knowledge and understanding based on a set of class, ethnic, and gender-related assumptions about these women's lives. Such assumptions included the belief that young working-class women were vulnerable to exploitation not only by employers but also by fellow workers. The reverse side of this vulnerable femininity was working-class masculinity, which promised to protect. Middle- and upper-class responses also recognized class- and gender-based vulnerability, but the solutions proposed were regulatory: factory and shop acts; domestic service training or clean, white-collar work; and minimum wage acts and other legislative attempts to control conditions and hours for women (and children).

Whether analysing the labour market, the labour movement, or left-wing organizations in this period, there is clear evidence that a gender division of labour prevailed. Despite worries that women would compete with men in the job market, women's work remained for the most part distinguishable from men's. Similarly in the labour movement there existed a tension between the need and desire to organize women workers and the officially held views and practices that declared women difficult to organize because they worked in isolation, because their work lives were episodic, or, as some believed, because of an inherent conservatism in women's nature.[1] Gender divisions within the working class suggested, furthermore, that women's waged labour, especially for married women, was undesirable. Under the rubric of manliness based on notions of protection and kinship, male trade unionists sought to protect their wives and daughters from demeaning and demoralizing waged labour. The notion of women's wage work threatened to undermine the very masculinity working men identified with their ability to provide for as well as to protect their families. Under these assumptions, it is not surprising that trade unionists were less than enthusiastic about organizing women workers and favoured the family wage. Garment workers' organizer Sam Landers, for example, deplored that women were entering non-traditional areas of work such as typesetting and core-making. Indeed the whole idea of women working outside the home seemed problematic to him. Landers suggested that 'if some of our "women's rights" opponents who use the now stereotyped phrase, "Women should remain in the homes," were to get down to business and grapple with some of the political and economic problems that drive women out of the homes, they would be doing a practical service instead of theorizing without relief.' The implicit message was that, in more ideal circumstances, women would stay home and tend to their proper sphere. The language of protection and kinship suggests that women were characterized by, and understood to be primarily concerned with, domestic life and the household, where their primary allegiances lay, thus identifying true womanhood not with honest toil in the labour force, but with hard work within the family.[2]

Despite these messages, the mostly young, single female wage earners sometimes found opportunities to defend their need to work and to obtain decent wages and conditions. Their attempts to organize and to contest their conditions were often brief flashes, as in the short-lived Working Women's Protective Association or in brief walkouts in garment and textile strikes, but in other instances women workers settled in for long, contentious strikes, sometimes in less traditional areas of women's work. Labour women also created Women's Labor Leagues, label leagues, and women's auxiliaries. The latter groups provided women activists with an entrance into the union movement, especially for the wives of trade unionists, who often did not participate in wage labour. These groups provided women with a setting in which to support their men but also gave women opportunities to learn organizational and speaking skills. Practical advantages might also be gained in the form of insurance benefits as well as social contacts with other working-class women. Women's activism then, was in part linked with their kinship roles as wives, mothers, sisters, and daughters of working men. In boosting the union label, joining auxiliaries, and participating in workers' cooperatives, working-class women acted within their roles as consumers rather than producers. Some women, however, were not content to sit back and accept the limits such a role implied. Particularly during the war and in the postwar period, efforts were made by women activists to move beyond these boundaries into the public world of labour organization and labour politics. Rather than accept the limited definition of kinship and its protections, politically active women tried to forge their own organizations parallel to those formed by men.

The turn-of-the-century socialist movement did not escape gender divisions either. Despite early pronouncements that a socialism without women could not live, the movement rarely practised what it preached. Ethical or Christian socialism drew adherents from a broad spectrum of 'progressive' reformers, including those who supported women's right to the franchise. This sort of socialism promised more equitable relationships between women and men not only by supporting suffrage, but also by providing a milieu in which women's issues were discussed and women's potential debated. As more women were thinking about larger issues such as politics and the economy, noted Mary Cotton Wisdom in 1909, 'they are no longer looking on man as a little tin god.' No longer was it necessary for women to look to men to run their affairs. For the early pioneers, such as Bertha Merrill Burns or Dora F. Kerr, socialism promised women more control over their personal and public lives. Envisioning a politically active sisterhood, women socialists urged like-minded women to organize themselves, cautioning that only women would attend to women's needs and perspectives, even in a changed society. Thus Mila Tupper Maynard, writing for the women's page of *Cotton's Weekly*, encouraged the socialist movement to gain the sympathy of women by educating them. She was amazed to see the indifference of the Socialist Party of Canada that not one in ten members was a woman.[3]

Gender divisions became more pronounced with the emergence of avowedly scientific socialist parties in Canada, particularly the SPC. Women 'full of the spirit of revolt' were stymied within the party by its insistence on a restrictive and orthodox understanding of class-consciousness, a position that left little room for gender-based activism. Gender divisions were also reinforced by a pervasive adherence to beliefs in biological and social differences between women and men. Prominent male socialists continued to claim that the differences between the sexes were primarily based in biology and thus difficult to change. From this perspective it was difficult to see how women could take active and important roles when socialism itself was identified with masculine traits and characteristics while femininity was viewed as the antithesis of change. Furthermore, women's activism was tainted by the suspicion that feminism was inherently bourgeois and had little to offer working-class and socialist women while threatening to divide such women from their obvious political allies, working-class men. As the Western Clarion asserted in 1911, 'there is absolutely no foundation in fact to the sex equality upon which the feminists insist and no reality to the sex war as some of them proclaim. The normal functions and characteristics of the two sexes do not compete or clash. They dovetail into and complete one another.' In practical as well as political terms, socialism in Canada was associated with manliness, and women's work within socialism officially excluded roles associated with masculine pursuits, such as party organizer or soapbox orator. The effect of such exclusions was to assign women secondary and supportive roles, punctuated occasionally by an 'unusual' woman who might transcend her feminine limitations.[4]

For the few women who challenged these gender boundaries, there were obstacles and substantial personal costs. The handful of women organizers from the first two decades of the century suffered scathing remarks, isolation, marriage breakdown, and other privations. The peripatetic lifestyle of an organizer was at odds with the demands of most women's lives where family obligations were most often paramount. While women's familial roles were utilized to assist and support the labour and socialist movements, there were profound ambiguities and boundaries that circumscribed what women were encouraged to do.

While few women risked roles as public as that of organizer, women in the socialist movement created their own spaces, forming their own groups or joining ones that welcomed their contributions. Women in Toronto formed the Women's Social Democratic League, for example, and several study groups emerged before the First World War. Ethnic women favoured sewing circles and cultural groups where women could learn skills in public speaking, debating, and other accomplishments, sometimes in women-only venues. There they could freely discuss socialist tracts, controversial literature, politics, and women's problems as well as domestic and community concerns. Women's Labor Leagues drew in many socialist and labour women who were specifically concerned about women workers' lives. Winnipeg's WLL was a particularly active and visible group, expecially during the war boom in the context of women's strikes and also in the debates about proposed minimum wage legislation.

Unprecedented opportunities for women's activism came with the war as the unemployment of the early war years was eased by the boom beginning in 1916. In the years 1917–20, strike activity among women workers reached new heights. In traditional areas of women's employment, such as garments, the push to organize the entire industry and to raise wages and reduce hours afforded women workers opportunities to demonstrate their willingness to engage in contestative and even militant action. Buoyed by the war and union drives to organize as many shops as possible, garment workers fought many strikes. Women strikers were favourably commented upon in many wartime garment worker disputes. Mary McNab, Hamilton organizer for the Amalgamated Clothing Workers in 1917 and prominent member of the Women's ILP, praised militant garment workers in nearby Dundas during a strike: 'When I think of the splendid spirit of these girls, I am proud I am a woman.'[5]

Manpower shortages resulted in a grudging acceptance of women in some non-traditional areas of employment but also revealed, despite the war crisis, persistent beliefs that women were cheap labour who competed with male workers, and were in need of protection. Even progressives such as the Reverend William Ivens noted that 'the result of women in industry will of necessity be to throw the men out of employment.' While equal pay for equal labour would provide some 'balm' for workmen, it might also encourage women to continue to work and to eschew marriage, Ivens warned. Some unions, such as the International Association of Machinists, for example, reluctantly began to accept women, in a bid to preserve jobs for men once the war concluded. Legislative initiatives, such as the minimum wage, were speeded up by the war and growing uneasiness about the actual conditions of women workers and the accompanying worry that young, single women faced grave moral dangers as a result of low wages. Here too, gender assumptions were important in shaping legislators' and reformers' exclusive focus on young, single female workers who were labelled as family dependants living at home and thus not in need of a 'living wage.' Minimum wage legislation, which applied only to women and was based on highly protective notions about women's condition, promised to help regulate women's labour, remove some of the worst abuses of female wage labour, and defuse working men's anxieties about women's wage work.[6]

The First World War meant crisis for socialists and pacifists as well as trade unionists. While the trade union movement opposed war in principle, the catastrophe of the war split union ranks. Initial opposition to registration and conscription gradually diminished, although not without significant resistance that came particularly from committed pacifists and socialists. Activist women were struck by the class differences observed among their gender: while women's patriotic organizations, largely composed of upper- and middle-class women, rolled bandages, knit socks, and chastised young men not in uniform, working-class women faced the prospect of intensified wage labour, inadequate soldiers' pensions and allowances, and critical reception of married women's work – work that in itself was necessary because of the absence of the 'breadwinner' and the limits on other forms of support. Women pacifists with journalistic skills decried war and its effects on women as mothers of soon-to-be-slaughtered sons and on the decimated ranks of mostly working-class soldiers. Thus, at the height of the war, Gertrude Richardson could write to her 'mother-hearts' to oppose the killing and to join her Women's Peace Crusade. Her organization pledged to support those who worked for peace and freedom and the suppression of militarism, and was committed to 'social and political purity, the world for the workers (to whom it belongs), the true religion, that is the fulfillment of the Golden Rule, and the creation of a safe and happy world for the unborn.' Such women worked hard to convince the public to oppose conscription of manpower and to insist on the need to conscript wealth first. For activists, such opposition might mean physical violence from angry citizens and returned soldiers or arrest for unpatriotic activities.[7]

These wartime developments set the stage for women's activism at various levels. The most dramatic developments culminated in 1919 with the full-scale labour revolt and the Winnipeg General Strike. Under the leadership of Helen Armstrong, women activists threw their energies into strike-support activities that utilized women's domestic skills, but they also called upon women to organize into unions and take more public roles defending the strikers, free speech, and collective bargaining. As participants in civil disturbances, Winnipeg women harassed strikebreakers, participated in protest marches, and faced a state authority that clearly warned them that their gender would not protect them from state reprisals. Elsewhere in Canada, women activists also challenged gender expectations with similar collective actions. The distemper of the times encouraged working-class women to form new groups, to provide evidence to the 1919 Mathers Commission, and to increase their participation in the labour movement.

The war crisis and the achievement of women's suffrage federally and in most provinces helped to illustrate women's connections to the public and the political. The wartime labour crisis and state repression highlighted, in a particularly vivid fashion, the importance of labour political action in the defence of working-class families and values. Women activists discussed the importance of using their votes to benefit their class; a minority went as far as offering themselves as candidates. Labour political women, however, also had their own agendas – free medical care, especially for mothers and children, access to education for workers' children, protective legislation for women workers, equal pay, and social welfare measures – which drew on maternalist arguments shared with middle-class reformers. While political office was one way to effect such changes, there were other important grass-roots structures to be created or influenced. Political women created, for example, women's auxiliaries to labour parties and unions. In Ontario, they also created a women's umbrella group to coordinate the activities of members from a number of labour, progressive, and socialist organizations. Not all politically minded women chose these paths. Others, dissatisfied with reformist labour politics, chose to follow the direction of new organizations spawned by the socialist revolution in Russia. Opting to throw their lot in with the above-ground Workers' Party or the underground Communist Party of Canada, women on the revolutionary left participated in a new departure in Canadian political life in much changed historical circumstances.

What the women of the pre-1920s labour and socialist movements achieved was to make visible not only the public work women performed in the factories, offices, and shops, but also the political work they could do. To accomplish this, they had to contest the boundary lines drawn around their gender and to insist that women's public and political work was vital to the well-being of their families, communities, and society in general. In the process these activist women, though divided by ethnicity, region, and political predilections, created new spaces in which women could challenge, albeit in fragmented ways, the structures and attitudes that denied them agency in building what they hoped would be a more just and humane future. That they were able to accomplish so much is worth remembering, pondering, and celebrating.

# Notes

## Introduction

1 Carolyn Strange, *Toronto's Girl Problem: The Perils and Pleasures of the City, 1880–1930* (Toronto, 1995), 32 and 39

2 Veronica Strong-Boag, *The New Day Recalled: Lives of Girls and Women in English Canada, 1919–1939* (Toronto, 1988), 42

3 Susan Levine, 'Workers' Wives: Gender, Class, and Consumerism in the 1920s United States,' *Gender and History* 3, 1 (1991): 45–64; Sylvie Murray, 'Quand les ménagères se font militantes: La Ligue auxiliaire de l'Association internationale des machinistes, 1905–1980,' *Labour/Le Travail* 29 (Spring 1992): 157–86

4 Dana Frank, *Purchasing Power: Seattle Labor and the Politics of Consumption, 1919–1929* (Cambridge, 1994)

5 Ardis Cameron, *Radicals of the Worst Sort: Laboring Women in Lawrence, Massachusetts, 1860–1912* (Urbana, 1993)

6 Steven Penfold, '"Have You No Manhood in You?": Gender and Class in the Cape Breton Coal Towns, 1920–1926' in *Gender and History in Canada*, ed. Joy Parr and Mark Rosenfeld (Toronto, 1996), 270–7

7 David Frank, 'The Miner's Financier: Women in the Cape Breton Coal Towns, 1917,' *Atlantis* 8, 2 (Spring 1983): 137–43

8 Mark Pittenger, *American Socialists and Evolutionary Thought, 1870–1920* (Madison, 1993), 8 and 188

9 For a recent examination of racial and gender oppression among the Chinese, see Madge Pon, 'Like a Chinese Puzzle: The Construction of Chinese Masculinity in *Jack Canuck*' in *Gender and History*, ed. Parr and Rosenfeld, 88–100.

10 Ruth Frager, *Sweatshop Strife: Class, Ethnicity, and Gender in the Jewish Labour Movement of Toronto, 1900–1939* (Toronto, 1992), chap. 3; Gerald Tulchinsky,

*Taking Root: The Origins of the Canadian Jewish Community* (Toronto, 1992), chap. 11

11 *Cotton's Weekly,* 17 Aug. 1911; Frager, *Sweatshop Strife,* 92–3.
12 Agnes Calliste, 'Race, Gender, and Canadian Immigration Policy: Blacks from the Caribbean, 1900–1932' in *Gender and History,* ed. Parr and Rosenfeld, 70–87
13 *Western Clarion,* 22 June 1907
14 My most immediate debt is to Mari Jo Buhle whose *Women and American Socialism, 1870–1920* (Urbana, 1981) first inspired me to contemplate a similar study for Canada. Joan Sangster's *Dreams of Equality: Women on the Canadian Left, 1920–1950* (Toronto, 1989) and Barbara Taylor's *Eve and the New Jerusalem: Socialism and Feminism in the Nineteenth Century* (London, 1984) were also influential. More recent literature, including previously cited works by Cameron, Frank, Frager and others, has raised questions about neighbourhood, community, and culture that pushed women's historians to think about activism beyond the workplace, union, and party. See also the introduction in Linda Kealey and Joan Sangster, eds., *Beyond the Vote: Canadian Women and Politics* (Toronto, 1989).
15 Janice Newton, *The Feminist Challenge to the Canadian Left, 1900–1918* (Montreal, 1995)
16 While Winnipeg radicals Helen Armstrong and George Armstrong, for example, were under surveillance, their RCMP files have not survived. The necessity to prove death dates to obtain access through CSIS to RCMP surveillance files has also presented problems since it is not always possible to trace dates of death of individuals. See National Archives of Canada, Department of Justice, RG 18, vol. 2448, Register of Bolsheviks and Agitators, for a numbered list of radicals; the Armstrongs are numbers one and two in the file. Yet access requests failed to turn up their security files.
17 Barbara Taylor, *Eve and the New Jerusalem,* chap. 9

## 1: 'Only a Working Girl'

1 Carole Gerson, 'Marie Joussaye Fotheringham: Canada's First Woman Labour Poet,' *Canadian Notes and Queries* 44 (Spring 1991): 21–3
2 Bettina Bradbury, *Working Families: Age, Gender, and Daily Survival in Industrializing Montreal* (Toronto, 1993); Joy Parr, *The Gender of Breadwinners: Women, Men, and Change in Two Industrial Towns, 1880–1950* (Toronto, 1990)
3 Suzanne Morton, 'Separate Spheres in a Separate World: African–Nova Scotian Women in Late Nineteenth-Century Halifax County' in *Separate Spheres: Women's Worlds in the Nineteenth-Century Maritimes,* ed. Janet Guild-

ford and Suzanne Morton (Fredericton, 1994), 185–210; Ruth Frager, *Sweat-shop Strife: Class, Ethnicity, and Gender in the Jewish Labour Movement of Toronto, 1900–1939* (Toronto, 1992); Varpu Lindström-Best, *Defiant Sisters: A Social History of the Finnish Immigrant Women in Canada, 1890–1930* (Toronto, 1988)

4 Sarah Eisenstein, *Give Us Bread but Give Us Roses: Working Women's Consciousness in the United States to the First World War* (London, 1983), 88; Mariana Valverde, 'Love of Finery: Fashion and the Fallen Woman in Nineteenth-Century Social Discourse,' *Victorian Studies* 32 (Winter 1989): 169–88. See also Carolyn Strange, *Toronto's Girl Problem: The Perils and Pleasures of the City, 1880–1930* (Toronto, 1995), chap. 2.

5 On child labour see, for example, John Bullen, 'Hidden Workers: Child Labour and the Family Economy in Late-Nineteenth-Century Urban Ontario,' *Labour/Le Travail* 18 (Fall 1986): 163–87; see also Dominique Jean, 'Le Recul du travail des enfants au Québec entre 1940 et 1960: une explication des conflits entre les familles pauvres et l'État providence,' *Labour/Le Travail* 24 (Fall 1989): 91–129, on the later period.

6 Constance Backhouse, *Petticoats and Prejudice: Women and Law in Nineteenth-Century Canada* (Toronto, 1992), 269–70

7 See, for example, Eric Tucker, 'Making the Workplace "Safe" in Capitalism: The Enforcement of Factory Legislation in Nineteenth-Century Ontario,' *Labour/Le Travail* 21 (Spring 1988): 45–85. Tucker notes that the first Ontario inspectors were carefully chosen to represent the interests of both capital and labour: Robert Barber was a manufacturer from Toronto; James R. Brown was a mechanic from Oshawa and former Knights of Labor activist; and O.A. Rocque was an ex-alderman from Ottawa with political connections to the Liberal Party. Brown also had Liberal connections through D.J. O'Donoghue and acted as the Oshawa correspondent for the Ontario Bureau of Industries. See also Eric Tucker, *Administering Danger in the Workplace: The Law and Politics of Occupational Health and Safety Regulation in Ontario, 1850–1914* (Toronto, 1990). Mariana Valverde argues for the ongoing importance of the voluntary sector in social welfare measures and examines their relationship to the state in *The Age of Light, Soap, and Water: Moral Reform in English Canada, 1885–1925* (Toronto, 1991), especially chap. 7.

8 On Toronto, see Gregory S. Kealey, *Toronto Workers Respond to Industrial Capitalism, 1867–1892*, 2nd ed. (Toronto, 1991), chaps. 1–2; on Montreal, see Bradbury, *Working Families*, 29–30.

9 Susan Mann Trofimenkoff, 'One Hundred and Two Muffled Voices: Canada's Industrial Women in the 1880s,' *Atlantis* 3, 1 (Fall 1977): 66–72. See also Gregory Kealey, ed., *Canada Investigates Industrialism* (Toronto, 1973), for an edited version of the royal commission, and Strange, *Toronto's Girl Problem*, 29.

10 Trofimenkoff, 'One Hundred and Two Muffled Voices,' 66–72
11 Jean Thomson Scott, 'The Conditions of Female Labour in Ontario,' *Toronto University Studies in Political Science* 1 (1892): 102–6, 111
12 Robert McIntosh, 'Sweated Labour: Female Needleworkers in Industrializing Canada,' *Labour/Le Travail* 32 (Fall 1993): 117
13 See Valverde, *The Age of Light, Soap, and Water.* For a critical sketch of A.W. Wright, see G.S. Kealey and Bryan Palmer, *Dreaming of What Might Be: The Knights of Labor in Ontario, 1880–1900* (New York, 1982), 178–9. *Report upon the Sweating System in Canada* (Ottawa, 1896), 15–19 (Wright's recommendations).
14 *Report upon the Sweating System in Canada*, 21–6.
15 Ibid., 26–8, 38–40, 42
16 Ibid., 42–4. Information on the strike comes from Doug Cruickshank's research for G.S. Kealey for the *Historical Atlas of Canada*, vol. 3 (Toronto, 1990).
17 Sweated labour is discussed in *Citizen and Country,* 17 June 1899, 2, 9 Sept. 1899; *Cotton's Weekly,* 28 July 1910; *Toiler,* 22 Jan. 1904; *B.C. Federationist,* 31 Dec. 1915 (re militia contracts in Toronto). See also McIntosh, 'Sweated Labour,' 136.
18 Scott, 'The Conditions of Female Labour,' 107–10, 112. On women in the Knights, see Susan Levine, *Labor's True Woman: Carpet Weavers, Industrialization, and Labor Reform in the Gilded Age* (Philadelphia, 1984), and Karen Dubinsky, '"The Modern Chivalry": Women and the Knights of Labor in Ontario, 1880–1891' (MA thesis, Carleton University, 1985).
19 Scott, 'The Conditions of Female Labour,' 91–100
20 Ibid.
21 See Veronica Strong-Boag, *The Parliament of Women: The National Council of Women of Canada, 1893–1929* (Ottawa, 1976), 195–9; discussion and debates at NCWC meetings are recorded in the council's publication, *Women Workers of Canada* (April 1894), 61–4, 110–11. The WWPA is also referred to as the Women's Protective Union.
22 *Women Workers of Canada* (April 1895), 173–84 (Machar resolution), and 222–5. Lady Julia Drummond was the wife of Senator G.A. Drummond, who was also the president of the Bank of Montreal. See Backhouse, *Petticoats and Prejudice,* 276–88. See also Henry J. Morgan, *The Canadian Men and Women of the Time* (Toronto, 1912), 319, 345–6.
23 Alison Prentice, et al., *Canadian Women: A History* (Toronto, 1988), 126. In 1904 the NCWC passed a resolution for the appointment of a second woman inspector, *Toiler,* 22 April 1904; Michael Piva, *The Condition of the Working Class in Toronto 1900–1921* (Ottawa, 1979), 88, 91 (on Carlyle). See also Tucker, 'Making the Workplace "Safe,"' especially 76–7, on Margaret Carlyle, who

had worked in manufacturing in Glasgow and advocated equalizing male and female wages to counter the downward trend in wages when women performed work formerly done by men. See Ontario, Department of Agriculture, Report of the Inspectors of Factories (1898), 31. Carlyle's salary was half that of male inspectors, and even after nearly twenty years of service her salary was below that paid the most junior male inspector (Tucker, 'Making the Workplace "Safe,"' 76n 128). Elsewhere, Tucker notes that Carlyle put her male colleagues to shame in terms of the number of factories visited (60n 54).

24 William Y. Smith, 'Axis of Administration: Saint John Reformers and Bureaucratic Centralization in New Brunswick, 1911–1925' (MA thesis, University of New Brunswick, 1984), chap. 3; Margaret J. Strople (Campbell), 'Prohibition and Movements of Social Reform in Nova Scotia, 1894–1920' (MA thesis, Dalhousie University, 1974); Peter D. Lambly, 'Toward a "Living Wage": The Minimum Wage Campaign for Women in Nova Scotia, 1920–1935' (Honours BA thesis, Dalhousie University, 1977), for general background. See also D.A. Muise, 'The Industrial Context of Inequality: Female Participation in Nova Scotia's Paid Labour Force, 1871–1921,' *Acadiensis* 20, 2 (Spring 1991): 3–31.

25 *Daily Sun* 20 March, 4 Dec. 1903 (for discussion of factories visited); see also 20 Nov. 1903 for Fabian League meeting attended by members of the 'Women's Council' to discuss need for legislation. Hatheway was a grocer and former president of the Board of Trade.

26 *Daily Sun*, 25, 26, and 31 March, 2, 6, and 7 April 1904

27 New Brunswick, House of Assembly, *Journals*, Appendix (1905), 137–53; *Daily Sun*, 13, 18–20, 23, and 25 August 1904 (clip from *Newcastle Advocate*); 3, 6 Jan., 3 Feb., 17, 30, and 31 March 1905

28 See *Daily Sun*, 5 April 1905 for amendments to final legislation.

29 Ibid., 1, 7, and 8 September 1905; 28 Jan. 1910 (LCW's request for a woman inspector); 23 Feb. 1910 (Inspector John Kenny's report); R. Philip Campbell, *Challenging Years, 1894–1979: Eighty-five Years of the Council of Women of Saint John* (Saint John, 1979?), 47, notes the 1918 nomination.

30 Lambly, 'Toward a "Living Wage"' 61–3. On the LCW in Halifax, see also Rebecca Veinott, 'A Call to Mother: The Halifax Local Council of Women, 1910–1921' (Honours BA thesis, Dalhousie University, 1985), chap. 1.

31 *Revised Statutes of Nova Scotia, 1923*, vol. 2 (Halifax, 1923), 1420–2; Nova Scotia, *Statutes, 1909* (Halifax, 1909), 129–30; *Herald* (Halifax), 14, 15, and 18 April 1910; Nova Scotia *Statutes, 1910* (Halifax, 1910), 158. The *Eastern Labor News*, 30 April 1910, reported that the cotton manufacturers had initiated the move to amend the Factory Act regarding child labour and had been defeated by the combined opposition of the unions and religious societies.

32 Nova Scotia, House of Assembly, *Journals* (1909), pt. 2, 'Report of Factories Inspector' (hereafter Factories Inspector's Report); *Herald*, 26 Oct., 7 Nov. 1910, 1 February 1911. See the prosecution of Louis Miller, lumber mill owner, for employing an underage boy killed in an accident. *Herald*, 23 Nov. 1912.

33 See Factories Inspector's Report, 1909, 9, for the case of Maggie Farrell, whose hand had been crushed at the Windsor Steam Laundry. Factories Inspector's Report, 1910, 1914. The 1920 *Report of Commission on Hours of Labour, Wages, and Working Conditions of Women Employed in Industrial Occupations* (Halifax, 1920) is discussed in Lambly, 'Toward a "Living Wage."'

34 Christine Smillie, 'The Invisible Workforce: Women Workers in Saskatchewan from 1905 to World War II,' *Saskatchewan History* 39, 2 (Spring 86): 63

35 Ibid., 63–4

36 Bryce M. Stewart, *Canadian Labor Laws and the Treaty* (New York, 1926), 439–41; Doug Smith, *Let Us Rise* (Winnipeg, 1985), 40; *Voice*, 26 June 1914. On the 1915 scandal, see W.L. Morton, *Manitoba: A History*, 2nd ed. (Toronto, 1973), chap. 14.

37 *Voice*, 18 Dec. 1914; 12 Feb. 1915; 11, and 18 Feb. 1916

38 J.S. Woodsworth, *Report of a Preliminary and General Social Survey of Regina*, (Department of Temperance and Moral Reform of the Methodist Church, Sept. 1913), 20; *Saskatchewan's Labor's Realm*, 1 May 1908; *Lance*, 26 Feb. 1910; Saskatchewan, Department of Agriculture, *Report of the Bureau of Labour* (1914), 20–2; Saskatchewan Archives Board, Regina, Regina Trades and Labour Council Minutes, 7 March 1914 (re laundry workers earning one dollar per day and motion requesting the government to investigate wages and hours of women workers). See also Smillie, 'The Invisible Workforce,' 62–79.

39 Stewart, *Canadian Labor Laws*, 443–5, 450–1; British Columbia, *Sessional Papers*, vol. 2 (1914), 'Report of the Royal Commission on Labour,' M7, M19–20, M1; *Vancouver World*, 19 June 1909 (YWCA report); *BC Federationist*, 28 Sept. 1912 (city refuses to investigate women's work)

40 Vancouver LCW, Minute Books, 1914–15, 17 Sept. 1914, 59; Vancouver Trades and Labor Council, Minutes, 20 Feb. 1913; BC *Sessional Papers* (1914), 'Report,' M19; Provincial Archives of British Columbia (hereafter PABC), Royal Commission on Labour, GR 684, vol. 4, box 2, file 1, 1–13 (LCW testimony)

41 PABC, Royal Commission on Labour, GR 684, vol. 7, box 3, file 4, 427–41

42 Graham Lowe, *Women in the Administrative Revolution* (Toronto, 1987), 1–2

43 Wayne Roberts, *Honest Womanhood: Feminism, Femininity, and Class Consciousness among Toronto Working Women, 1893–1914* (Toronto, 1976), 27–8

44 University Women's Club of Winnipeg, *The Work of Women and Girls in the Department Stores of Winnipeg* (Winnipeg, 1914); Manitoba, *Report of the Royal Commission on Technical Education and Industrial Training*, Sessional Paper No. 3 (1912), transcripts of the testimony held by the Provincial Archives of Manitoba. G.R. Coldwell, KC, was the chair of the commission and minister of education at the time.

45 *Report of the Royal Commission on Technical Education*, transcripts, 867–74 (Rue), 875–81 (Tweedy)

46 Ibid., 839–56 (Lillian Mason, All Peoples' Mission), 922–31 (Grace Tonkin, All Peoples' Mission). See also Alan F.J. Artibise, *Winnipeg: A Social History of Urban Growth, 1874–1914* (Montreal, 1975), especially chaps. 10 and 11.

47 *Report of the Royal Commission on Technical Education*, 192–7 (Muir); see also Carol Lee Bacchi, *Liberation Deferred? The Ideas of the English-Canadian Suffragists, 1877–1918* (Toronto, 1983), 121, for mention of Muir. Bacchi notes Muir's suspicion of professional, middle-class state interventionism.

48 Canada, *Royal Commission on Industrial Training and Technical Education*, Sessional Paper 191d, part 4 (1913), 1746–50; quote on 1749

49 Ibid., 1974–80

50 See Roberts, *Honest Womanhood*, for an early discussion of working women's culture in Toronto.

51 The debate on Halifax working women is found in the *Herald* (Halifax), 6 Dec. 1912 (the original letter is found in the *Mail* (Halifax), 27 Nov. 1912); see also *Herald* (Halifax), 13 Dec. 1912.

52 *Garment Worker*, 6 Nov. 1914.

## 2: Gender Divisions

1 *Voice*, 6 June 1902 ('Paulin-Chambers Co'y Declared Unfair,' editorial)

2 Ibid., 6 June 1902

3 Ian McKay, 'Strikes in the Maritimes, 1901–14' in *Atlantic Canada after Confederation: The Acadiensis Reader*, vol. 2, ed. Phillip A. Buckner and David Frank (Fredericton, 1985), 216–59

4 *Labor Advocate* (hereafter *LA*), 23 Jan. 1891, 61. On the difficulties of using the courts for remedies in labour disputes in Ontario, see Eric Tucker, *Administering Danger in the Workplace: The Law and Politics of Occupational Health and Safety Regulation in Ontario, 1850–1914* (Toronto, 1990), chap. 3

5 *LA*, 13 May 1891, 113, 115, 116; 10 April 1891, 149, 152; 17 April 1891, 153; 1 May 1891, 176. On the telephone controversy, see *LA*, 12 June 1891, 219; 19 June 1891, 228, 229; 26 June 1891, 235; 24 July 1891, 265, 267, 268

6 *LA*, 2 Aug. 1891, 299

7 *Voice*, 25 Sept. 1897; 23 Sept. 1898; Wayne Roberts, *Honest Womanhood: Feminism, Femininity, and Class Consciousness among Toronto Working Women, 1893–1914* (Toronto 1976), 42. The glovemakers' strike is covered in the *Globe*, 24 Jan. 1893, 25 Jan. 1893, 7 April 1893. The role of the Working Women's Protective Association is noted in the *Mail* (Toronto), 8 April 1893

8 Data on strikes in the 1890s are taken from newspaper research and the strike files compiled by Douglas Cruickshank for Plate 39 of volume 3 of the *Historical Atlas of Canada* (Toronto, 1990)

9 *Gazette*, 9, 10 May 1899

10 Strike data are from research materials of D. Cruickshank and G.S. Kealey for the *Historical Atlas of Canada*, vol. 3; see also *Amherst Evening News*, 27 April 1894.

11 Kealey and Cruickshank strike data

12 *Globe*, 25–8 Sept. 1899. The scale provided twenty to twenty-one cents per hour in King Street shops and eighteen to nineteen in Queen and Yonge Street shops. Strike pay of $1.50 per day was paid by the International.

13 For the 1893 strike, see Kealey and Cruickshank, strike files, and the ample press coverage in the *Manitoba Daily Free Press*, 2–3 Feb., 4, 7, 21 March, 13 April 1893, and in the *Manitoba Free Press*, 25 Feb., 22, 25, 28, 30 March, 7, 11, 24 April 1893.

14 See, for example, *Voice*, 13 Feb. 1899, Special Strike Issue; see also *Free Press*, 17, 23 Feb. 1899 (resolution of UGWA urging girls not to accept positions at Emerson and Hague), and 24 Feb. 1899 (resolution of sympathy from the ILP); *Tribune* (Winnipeg), 18 Feb. 1899 (coverage of first women delegates at TLC meeting), and 21 Feb. 1899 (resolution of Tinsmiths union re union label buying and WCTU meeting); *Free Press*, 1 March 1899 (letter to the editor – 'Experience of a Striker'); 6 March 1899, 8 (announcement of new overall factory); 'The Garment Workers' Strike of 1899,' *Voice*, 6 June 1902 (report on the strike and comments on the success of the Hoover Manufacturing Company).

15 *Voice*, 13 Feb. 1899

16 See Cruickshank and Kealey, Strike Files, 1894 and 1895; see also *Daily Examiner*, 11 April, 3 May 1895

17 See Cruickshank and Kealey, Strike Files, 1892 (Kingston); 1891 (Montreal), Merchants Manufacturing Cotton Company struck by 200, mostly female, workers over new overseer; 1893 (Montreal), Dominion Cotton Mills, 12 workers, mostly female, objected to new foreman; 1896 (Hamilton), Canadian Colored Cotton Company, ill treatment of foreman; 1899 (London), Laidlaw and Watson Shoe Company, 40 men and women struck against tyrannical forewoman; 1894 (Toronto), J.D. King Company, 125 men and

women on strike. See also *Mail*, 19 Jan. 1894; 22 Feb. 1894 (WPU entertained striking women); 27 Feb. 1894 (settlement). See also *Toronto World*, 16 Jan. 1894.

18 The strike is covered in detail in the *Daily Mail*, 9, 11, 13, 17, 19, 22, 24, and 25 Jan. 1894; for a report of the trial, see 6 Feb. 1894; 12, 14 Feb. 1894 (union support); 24 Feb. 1894 (men's statement that they will not settle until the company settles with the women); 27 Feb. 1894 (settlement).

19 In the absence of complete strike data, the information presented here probably undercounts the extent of women's strike activity. The creation of a federal Department of Labour in 1900 inaugurated the collection of information on strikes published in the *Labour Gazette* and collected in the Strikes and Lockouts files. In many cases the reportage does not specify clearly whether the strikers are men or women, and in some cases observers assumed, without clear confirmation, that strikers were men. The Strikes and Lockouts files, which contain correspondents' reports, occasional letters, and newspaper clippings, often provide more detailed information with clues to the identities of the strikers. By themselves these government-generated sources are not sufficient since they tend to be less complete about labour disputes in regions such as the Maritimes or the West. The labour press and targeted research into the daily press supplement government sources.

20 *Lance*, 26 Aug. 1911; see also *Ladies' Garment Worker*, Feb. 1911. *Lance*, 9 Sept. 1911

21 Jacques Rouillard, *Les Travailleurs du coton au Québec, 1900–1915* (Quebec, 1974), 53; see also Jacques Ferland, '"In Search of the Unbound Prometheia": A Comparative View of Women's Activism in Two Quebec Industries, 1869–1908,' *Labour/Le Travail* 24 (Fall 1989): 11–44. For the royal commission, see *Labour Gazette* (hereafter *LG*), Feb. 1909, 850–61.

22 *LG*, Nov. 1900, 101–3. See also James Thwaites, 'La Grève au Québec: Une analyse quantitative exploratoire portant sur la période 1896–1915,' *Labour/Le Travail* 14 (Fall 1984): 196–8.

23 *LG*, Nov. 1900, 101–3; Thwaites, 'La Grève au Québec,' 68–9

24 *LG*, Sept. 1900, 68–9

25 Ibid., May 1903, 904–7. See also accounts carried in the *Saint John Semi-Weekly Sun*, 12 Jan., 11 Feb., 18, 21 March 1903. On Maritimes strike activities, see McKay, 'Strikes in the Maritimes,' 216–59. The Milltown strike was resolved after a series of meetings between Mackenzie King and the employers and employees. A drop in wages and, to a lesser extent, conflict with the overseer had precipitated the strike. The overseer apologized, the employees accepted the wage cut after it was explained to them, and the company agreed not to discriminate against the strikers.

26 Joy Parr, *The Gender of Breadwinners: Women, Men, and Change in Two Industrial Towns, 1880–1950* (Toronto, 1990), only briefly discusses the 1907 strike; see also National Archives of Canada (hereafter NAC), Department of Labour, RG 27, Strikes and Lockouts files, vol. 294, nos. 3010 and 2925.

27 For the 1908 St Hyacinthe strike, see *LG*, March 1908, 1147, and April 1908, 1247. For the Almonte strike in 1909, see NAC, RG 27, vol. 297, no. 3208

28 NAC, RG 27, vol. 296, no. 3131, and vol. 299, no. 3424

29 Ibid., vol. 297, no. 3251

30 Ibid., vol. 301, no. 18

31 Mercedes Steedman, 'Skill and Gender in the Canadian Clothing Industry, 1890–1940' in *On the Job: Confronting the Labour Process in Canada*, ed. Craig Heron and Robert Storey (Kingston, 1986), 169n. 3.

32 Ibid., 161 and 53n. See also John E. Hample, 'In the Buzzard's Shadow: Craft Subculture, Working-Class Activism, and Winnipeg's Custom Tailoring Trade, c. 1882–1921' (MA thesis, University of Winnipeg, 1989). *LG*, April 1904, 1031.

33 *LG*, Jan. 1906, 802, 804; April 1907, 1127

34 NAC, RG 27, vol. 294, nos. 2979 and 2981; the union was identified as the Clothing Cutters and Trimmers, Local 80.

35 Ibid., vol. 297, no. 3218; both the Clothing Cutters and Trimmers, Local 80, and the UGWA, Local 134, were reported as involved. *Voice*, 10 June and 25–6 Feb., 1910

36 NAC, RG 27, vol. 297, no. 3221

37 On the Eaton's strike, see Steedman, 'Skill and Gender'; see also Charlene Gannage, *Double Day, Double Bind: Women Garment Workers* (Toronto, 1986); Ruth Frager, 'The Eaton's Strike of 1912,' *Canadian Woman Studies* 7, 3 (Fall 1986): 96, and Frager, 'Class, Ethnicity, and Gender in the Eaton Strikes of 1912 and 1934' in *Gender Conflicts: New Essays in Women's History*, ed. Franca Iacovetta and Mariana Valverde (Toronto, 1992), 189–228. See also NAC, RG 27, vol. 299, no. 3446 (Toronto), no. 3453 (Montreal), no. 3455 (Toronto, JTU strike).

38 Frager, 'Class, Ethnicity, and Gender,' 193–4

39 Information on the ITU auxiliary found in Henry Trachtenberg, 'The Eaton Strike of 1912' (unpublished ms), 19. My thanks to Mr Trachtenberg for allowing me to read his manuscript.

40 Ibid., 34–6. Barnum wrote fiction as well as essays for the labour press. For examples of her fiction, see *Ladies' Garment Worker*, April, May, July 1910; Feb., Nov., Dec. 1911; Feb., March, April 1912. See also NAC RG 27, vol. 299, no. 3446, for various newspaper clippings on the strike

41 Alice A. Chown, *The Stairway* (Boston, 1921), 151–3. A labour newspaper

column entitled 'A Fund for Displaced Working Girls' was authored by Chown and sought donations for the striking women and their families. See *Lance*, 30 March 1912.

42  Trachtenberg 'Eaton Strike,' 38–42; *Lance*, 12, 30 March 1912 (strikebreakers). See also reports in *Ladies' Garment Worker*, March, April, May 1912. *Lance*, 13 April 1912 (anti-begging by-law used against strikers)

43  While a national boycott failed to achieve much support outside the Jewish community, some opposition to the Eaton's company did garner general support. See especially discussions in *Jack Canuck* during February and March 1912.

44  NAC, RG 27, vol. 299, no. 3455; *Lance*, 13 April 1912

45  NAC, RG 27, vol. 301, no. 26

46  Ibid., vol. 300, no. 3509. According to the press, the manufacturers stated that the demands were: a forty-nine-hour week, week work, overtime pay, one apprentice for every ten cutters, and a 10 per cent increase for pantmakers (usually a woman's job), and abolition of subcontracting. The file does not indicate whether the strikers were successful in all these demands. The quote is from Gerald Tulchinsky, *Taking Root: The Origins of the Canadian Jewish Community* (Toronto, 1992) 207–13

47  NAC, RG 27, vol. 301, nos. 26 and 37; see also Steedman, 'Skill and Gender,' 162.

48  NAC, RG 27, vol. 301, no. 37

49  NAC, RG 27, vol. 303, no. 112. The third company, Shulman's, took over Vineberg's work, and the union pulled out 150 men and 20 women on strike as a result. In mid-November, a small strike also erupted at Queen's Cloak and Skirt Factory, which employed twelve men and women. The manager claimed the UGWA wanted to exclude French-Canadian workers and only have Jews; the employees insisted that the issue was the closed shop.

50  Jacques Ferland, 'Syndicalisme "parcellaire" et syndicalisme "collectif": Une interprétation socio-technique des conflits ouvriers dans deux industries québécoises, 1880–1914,' *Labour/Le Travail* 19 (Spring 1987): 49–88; see also Ferland, '"In Search of the Unbound Prometheia,"' 11–44.

51  *LG*, Nov. 1900, 134–5; Dec. 1900, 155–9; Jan. 1901, 229ff; Feb. 1901, 294–7. See also Jean Claude Dupont and Jacques Mathieu, *Les Metiers du cuir* (Quebec, 1981), 353–7. Quote from Ferland, '"In Search of the Unbound Prometheia,"' 16. The 1913 strike appears in NAC, RG 27, vol. 303, no. 118. See also *LG*, Jan. 1914, 825, and March 1914, 1076, and M.A. Bluteau et al., *Les Cordonniers, artisans du cuir* (Montreal, 1980), 123.

52  NAC, RG 27, vol. 294, no. 3014. For other shoe strikes see vol. 297, no. 3233: vol. 298, no. 3329; vol. 301, no. 50.

53 Ibid., vol. 300, no. 3628
54 These strikes are discussed in detail by Elaine Bernard, *The Long Distance Feeling* (Vancouver, 1982).
55 See Joan Sangster, 'The 1907 Bell Telephone Strike: Organizing Women Workers,' *Labour/Le Travailleur* 3 (1978): 109–31. See *Canadian Labor Leader*, 24 Aug. 1918, for a report on the unionization of Toronto's five hundred telephone operators. For labour commentary see *Lance*, 22 July 1911 (on difficulty in obtaining operators for long hours, short pay); 9 March 1912 (report of discontent among operators); 24 May 1913 (raise of two dollars per week). The royal commission's influence on American investigations is noted by Stephen H. Norwood, *Labor's Flaming Youth: Telephone Operators and Worker Militancy, 1878–1923* (Urbana, 1990), 61.
56 *Tribune* (Toronto), 14 Oct. 1905 (Galt); NAC, RG 27, vol. 294, no. 2980; vol. 296, no. 3171
57 *Lance*, 2 Sept. 1911
58 Shirley Tillotson, 'Canadian Telegraphers, 1900–1930: A Case Study in Gender and Skill Hierarchies' (MA thesis, Queen's University, 1988); *Toiler*, 8 April, 6 May 1904
59 Ava Baron, 'On Looking at Men: Masculinity and the Making of a Gendered Working Class History' in *Feminists Revision History*, ed. Ann-Louise Shapiro (New Brunswick, NJ, 1994), 146–71
60 In Canada, see Sara Diamond, 'A Union Man's Wife: The Ladies' Auxiliary Movement in the IWA, the Lake Cowichan Experience' in *Not Just Pin Money: Selected Essays on the History of Women's Work in British Columbia*, ed. Barbara K. Latham and Roberta J. Pazdro (Victoria, 1984), 287–96, and more recently, Sylvie Murray, *A la Junction du mouvement ouvrier et du mouvement des femmes: La Ligue Auxiliaire de l'Association Internationale des Machinistes, Canada, 1903–1980* (Montreal, 1990), especially chap. 3. In the United States, see Marjorie Penn Lasky, '"Where I Was a Person": The Ladies' Auxiliary in the 1934 Minneapolis Teamsters' Strikes' in *Women, Work and Protest: A Century of U.S. Women's Labor History*, ed. Ruth Milkman (Boston, 1985), 181–205.
61 *Vancouver World*, 12 Dec. 1908, 28; 6 Feb. 1909; for Chenoweth's letter see University of British Columbia, Special Collections, WFM/Mine-Mill Papers, box 152, H. Chenoweth to the Officers and Members of Local No. 81, 21 Nov. 1911; box 159–16, A. Shilland, Secretary-Treasurer, WFM to Officers and Members (various locals), 10 July 1911. Little is known about the women's auxiliary; see BC *Federationist*, 16 Jan. 1914, for a brief mention.
62 For an example of women's militancy at Springhill, see *Voice*, 13 May 1910, 3, and *Cotton's Weekly*, 11 Aug. 1910. Ladies' Auxiliaries of the UMWA were noted in the *Western Clarion*'s coverage of the Vancouver Island strikes,

6 Dec. 1913. See also Provincial Archives of British Columbia (hereafter PABC), Women's Labour History Collection, Interview with Richard and Phyllis Whisker (by Sara Diamond), 3598-1, and PABC, Attorney General's Correspondence Inward re Nanaimo Strike 1913, GR 429, box 19.

63 For Toronto, see *Tribune* (Toronto), 9 Sept. 1905, for the railroad conductors, trainmen, and locomotive engineers auxiliaries; for the street railway auxiliary, see *Lance*, 26 Feb. 1910. On 5 March 1910 *Lance* reported on the annual social for the BLFE in Toronto. For St Thomas, see *Industrial Banner*, 12 June 1914, 22 Jan. and 26 March 1915. For Calgary, see Glenbow-Alberta Institute (Hereafter GAI), BRT, Mountain View Lodge, no. 333, Ladies' Auxiliary, Membership and Policy Register, M 7068, c. 1908–42; *Locomotive Firemen and Enginemen's Magazine*, various issues, 1913–20; see, for example, June 1913, 876, for report on the death of Hannah Hayden, Lodge 37, St Thomas, Ontario, and notice of two hundred dollars insurance. Halifax's Brotherhood of Railway Carmen also featured an active Ladies' Auxiliary, which participated in the Labour Day parade in 1909, the first women to do so; see *Eastern Labor News* (hereafter *ELN*), 4 Sept. 1909. A women's auxiliary to the BLFE was founded in Moncton with forty charter members, according to *ELN*, 30 April 1910, but this group did not correspond with the union's magazine during the years surveyed (1913–14, 1918–19).

64 See *Locomotive Firemen and Enginemen's Magazine*, Aug. 1913, 325–32, for an extensive report on the Eleventh Annual (First Triennial) Convention; 1 Aug. 1919, 17–18, for Moore's presidential report.

65 *Lance*, 26 Feb. 1910

66 *Voice*, 1 June and 3 Aug. 1917; 28 June 1918; *Western Labor News* (hereafter *WLN*), 11, 25 Oct. 1918

67 For Winnipeg, see *Voice*, 8 June 1917; activities of the Winnipeg auxiliary are discussed on 15 Feb. 1918; *WLN*, 6 Sept. and 4 Oct. 1918 (request for use of 'women's auxiliary' and reply); on the same issue see *Voice*, 12 July 1918, 19 Oct. and 5 Dec. 1917. On the Alberta Federation of Labor's acceptance of women's auxiliary delegates, see *Voice*, 18 Jan. 1918. For the Cooperative Society, see note 74.

68 For Toronto, see *Toiler*, 26 Dec. 1902, 23 Jan. 1903, 18 Nov. 1904; *Tribune*, 9 Sept. 1905 (Mrs Crawford, secretary, later ran for political office in Toronto for the Social Democratic Party); on the aims of the IAM auxiliary see IAM *Bulletin*, Dec. 1913; on the early history of the Toronto local, see *Bulletin*, June 1914; on membership and history of the internaional organization, *Bulletin*, Oct. 1914, which also mentions that women relatives of specialists and helpers would be able to join the auxiliary after 1 Oct. 1914. Moncton, New Brunswick, had an active auxiliary to the IAM, founded in 1908; for its activities,

see *ELN*, 13 Feb. 1909 (bean supper); 6 March and 5 June 1909 (officers elected); 8 Jan. 1910 (pending election of officers for thirty-member auxiliary). Murray suggests that Stratford formed one of the earliest locals in 1903, along with Toronto; see *A la Junction*, 57.

69  *Bulletin*, June, Aug., and March 1914, April 1915; quote appeared in 'A.L.'s' report, June 1914. According to Murray, *A la Junction*, 63, Singer was Canadian vice-president of the Grand Lodge from 1913 to 1942. She also remarks on Singer's frustration at the lack of an organizer for the women's auxiliaries

70  *Tribune*, 18 Nov. 1905; for activities in Winnipeg related to the war, see *Voice*, 19 May 1916, and IAM *Bulletin*, May and June 1916; for Toronto, see *Bulletin*, July 1915; membership drives, see *Bulletin*, June and Dec. 1916. Logan's report on the Baltimore convention of the IAM is contained in *Bulletin*, Sept. 1916.

71  Minnie Singer's leadership of the Canadian IAM Auxiliaries may have been key in the auxiliary's interest in working women. Singer herself was a garment worker, beginning work at age fifteen. Whether she continued wage work during her marriage is not known, but widowhood in 1925 probably necessitated wage work in the later years of her life; see Murray, *A la Junction*, 75n. 50. For McKelleher's visit, see *Bulletin*, April 1917; formation of the Winnipeg WLL is also noted in this issue. Helen Armstrong's address on working women is mentioned in the *Bulletin*, June 1917; for Bauslaugh, see *Bulletin*, Dec. 1917. Opposition from husbands to women joining the auxiliary is mentioned in Calgary's report, *Bulletin*, Feb. 1917. Russell's report on the Angus shops, *Bulletin*, Jan. 1917 (Calgary's Lodge 457 wired Winnipeg to say they would strike if women were not removed within fifteen days). See also 'Women Labor,' *Bulletin*, July 1918, which includes the agreement between the western executive of the IAM and the superintendent of Motive Power for the western rail lines, 1 July 1918; quote from 'Ogden Scribe' appears in the same issue. By October 1918 women and men of the federated rail trades were on strike against the CPR; see *Bulletin*, Oct. 1918. As early as December 1917 the IAM had declared in favour of bringing all machinists, male and female, into the organization. See *Bulletin*, Dec. 1917.

72  *Globe*, 30 Oct. 1902; *Toiler*, 19 June, 21 Aug., and 18 Dec. 1903. For Labour Temple subscriptions, see *Toiler*, 15 April, 6, 20, 27 May, and 3 June 1904.

73  *Toiler*, 7 Oct. 1904; *Tribune* (formerly *Toiler*), 16 Sept. and 18 Nov. 1905, 3 Feb. 1906, 27 Jan. 1906

74  *Voice*, 23 Jan. 1914, notes the first meeting of the Cooperative Society and the formation of the women's committee; the WCG was formally launched in November 1914; see *Voice*, 27 Nov. 1914 for the speeches by Rigg and Iveson. The WCG sent delegates to the TLC; see *Voice*, 8 Jan. and 15 Feb. 1915.

Speakers to the WCG included Alderman Rigg on trade unionism (*Voice*, 9 April 1915); Mr Mackenzie, Grain Growers' Association (*Voice*, 7 May 1915); and Lillian Beynon Thomas on the women's movement (*Voice*, 5 Feb. 1915). The WCG continued to meet until at least 1920.

### 3: 'A Socialist Movement Which Does Not Attract the Women Cannot Live'

1 *Western Socialist* (formerly *Canadian Socialist*), 20 Sept. 1902.
2 Several small socialist organizations developed in the Maritimes in this period, and Martin Butler published a small newspaper that addressed some of the major reform issues of the day (1895–1915?), but with the exception of the Fabian Society of Saint John and the Women's Enfranchisement Association, also of that city, few women appear to have played an active role. See David Frank and Nolan Reilly, 'The Emergence of the Socialist Movement in the Maritimes, 1899–1916,' *Labour/Le Travailleur* 4 (Fall 1979).
3 See Ramsay Cook, *The Regenerators: Social Criticism in Late Victorian English Canada* (Toronto, 1985), 167. On the social gospel see Richard Allen, *The Social Passion* (Toronto, 1971). See also Brian J. Fraser, *The Social Uplifters: Presbyterian Progressives and the Social Gospel in Canada, 1875–1915* (Waterloo, 1988), which argues that, among Presbyterians, the leadership expressed considerable distrust of socialism and trade unions
4 Edward Bellamy, *Looking Backward* (1888). See also Cook, *The Regenerators*, especially 261–2n 21, which provides a discussion of Bellamy's influence in Canada, and Mary Jo Buhle, *Women and American Socialism, 1870–1920* (Urbana, 1981), 75–82. Quote on Blatchford from Stanley Pierson, *British Socialists: The Journey from Fantasy to Politics* (Cambridge, 1979), 35. Pierson notes that in the first decade of this century Blatchford became explicitly anti-Christian; 72–8. On William Morris, see E.P. Thompson, *William Morris* (London, 1977).
5 See Friedrich Engels, *The Origin of the Family, Private Property, and the State* (1884; reprint, New York, 1970); August Bebel, *Woman and Socialism* (New York, 1910). Published works on American women and socialism include the major studies by Buhle, *Women and American Socialism*, and Sally Miller, ed., *Flawed Liberation* (Westport, CT, 1981). For recent works on women and European socialism, see Marie Kennedy and Chris Tilly, 'Socialism, Feminism, and the Stillbirth of Socialist Feminism in Europe, 1890–1920,' *Science and Society* 51, 1 (Spring 1987): 6–42.
6 For Toronto, see Archer Wallace, 'The History of Socialism in Toronto' (typescript, University of Western Ontario Library, London); for Thompson, see Ramsay Cook, *The Regenerators*, chap. 9, and Gregory S. Kealey and Bryan D.

Palmer, *Dreaming of What Might Be: The Knights of Labor in Ontario, 1880–1900* (Cambridge, 1982), chap. 8. In the late nineteeth century, Thompson was well known for his journalism and labour reform efforts in the Knights of Labor.

7 For information on early socialism in Canada, see G. Weston Wrigley, 'Socialism in Canada,' *International Socialist Review* 1 (1900–1): 685–9; J.M. Conner, 'The Canadian Socialist Movement' in Conner Papers, J.S. Woodsworth Collection, University of Toronto Rare Books and Special Collections; Archer Wallace, 'History of Socialism.' In its 15 April 1899 edition, *Citizen and Country*, published a list of 'progressive organizations' that included the Socialist Club, Galt; Social Progress Club, St Thomas; Social Progress League, Collingwood; Social Science Club, Ottawa; Canadian Direct Legislation League, Social Reform League, Proportional Representation Committee of Ontario, Single Tax Association, and Henry George Club, all located in Toronto. The list also named a number of trades and labour councils and four branches of the SLP in Toronto, London, Brantford, and Hamilton. Only one organization outside of Ontario appeared on the list: the Reform and Labor Association in Revelstoke, BC. Founded in 1877, the SLP was a small vanguard party attractive to European immigrants to North America. In the 1890s, the SLP was increasingly identified with Daniel de Leon (1852–1914) socialist lawyer, orator, and writer. On Colin McKay and the early CSL in Montreal see Ian McKay, ed., *For a Working-Class Culture in Canada: A Selection of Colin McKay's Writings on Sociology and Political Economy, 1897–1939* (St John's, 1996), xxvii–xxx.

8 *Citizen and Country* (hereafter *C&C*), 15 July 1899, 4 May 1900; quote from Wrigley appears in *C&C*, 11 March 1899; OSL platform appears in *Canadian Socialist* (hereafter *CS*), 6 June 1902. The *CS* replaced *C&C* on 6 June 1902. The editor of *C&C* and *CS* moved the newspaper from Toronto to Vancouver in 1902 where it became the *Western Socialist* (hereafter *WS*). See *WS*, 20 Sept. 1902, for the report of sixty-eight locals.

9 Phillips Thompson was a British emigrant, as was J.H. Beever, a leader of the Social Reform League and member of the CSL; Beever was a British Fabian from Halifax. George Pursey, president of the Social Reform League in the late 1890s, later emerged as a leader of the CSL. A shoemaker by trade, he was also a member of the Toronto Astronomical and Physical Society and credited his boyhood reading of Robert Owen as an important influence. See *C&C*, 12 Aug. 1899, on Beever and Thompson; see Cook, *The Regenerators*, chap. 9 on Thompson generally; for Pursey, see *C&C*, 17 June 1899 and 4 May 1900. The Social Reform League amalgamated with the CSL in Oct. 1899, according to *C&C*, 4 May 1900. The WCTU connection with *C&C* is difficult to gauge. Sarah Wrigley was well-known as the WCTU Ontario superinten-

dent for temperance in Sunday schools; Mrs Thornley, Ontario provincial president of the WCTU in the 1890s, was described by *C&C* as a Christian socialist, having been influenced by Frances Willard; Mrs Rounds, president of the Illinois WCTU commented at Hamilton on her Canadian sisters: 'Why cannot a greater number of our Canadian WCTU sisters develop an interest in other social problems than those of prohibition and woman's suffrage? We are with them in our battle and we deserve their cooperation in the broader sphere of Social Reform.' *C&C*, 29 April 1899.

10  *C&C*, 13, 27 April 1900 (thanks to Christina Burr for drawing this to my attention). On the WCTU and tobacco, see letter in *C&C*, 13 May 1900.

11  *C&C*, 4 May 1900; Wrigley, 'Socialism in Canada'; *CS*, 6 June, 9 Aug., 20 and 27 Sept. 1902; *WS*, 8 Nov. 1902, 17 Jan. 1903; *Western Clarion* (hereafter *WC*) 4 Feb., 20 May, 10 June 1905. For the women's column dispute, see chapter 4.

12  See, for example, *Social Justice* (hereafter *SJ*), 5 March and 1 Oct. 1903, re donations to the Socialist Propaganda Fund; *WS*, 27 Sept. 1902; *C&C*, 13 April 1900.

13  See *C&C*, 4 May, 14 Sept. and 5 Oct. 1900 (Mrs King is re-elected treasurer), 30 May 1902; *SJ*, 5 March 1903. Youmans's name had appeared in the 1890s as secretary of a Socialist League of Canada. Miss Maxine Simpson was vice-president and Miss E. Adams, librarian. These references appear in *The Lamp*, 1 (15 Aug. 1894) and 2 (15 Sept. 1894) (references provided by Russell Hann). *CS*, 23 Aug. 1902

14  *C&C*, 16, 23, 30 May 1902; Haile's activities in the United States are mentioned by Buhle, *Women and American Socialism*, 94, 105, 117.

15  *Globe*, 9 Nov. 1901; *Tribune* (Toronto), 18 Nov. 1905; *CS*, 20 June 1902; *SJ*, 5 March 1903

16  An unpublished, revised version of Wayne Roberts, *Honest Womanhood*, has been of immense help on May Darwin; see also *Globe*, 30 Oct. 1902; *Tribune* (Toronto), 18 Nov. 1905. *SJ*, 5 March 1903, noted that Darwin accepted the secretary's post with no salary; see also *SJ*, 6 Aug., 3 Sept., and 1 Oct. 1903 for information on the socialist tent at the exhibition. The latter issue noted that the furnishings of the tent had been supplied by Mr and Mrs George Robinson. Darwin's brothers – Robert and William Glocking – were labour movement activists.

17  See Ross McCormack, *Reformers, Rebels, and Revolutionaries: The Western Canadian Radical Movement, 1899–1919* (Toronto, 1977), 20–6, and Carlos A. Schwantes, *Radical Heritage: Labor, Socialism, and Reform in Washington and British Columbia, 1885–1917* (Seattle, 1979), especially chap. 6, for a discussion of this period in the development of BC socialism. Wrigley's western trip is noted in *C&C*, 2 Sept. 1899. The Ruskin Colony is described in detail in *C&C*,

8 July 1899, and information can be found in the Ormand Lee Charlton
Papers, University of British Columbia Special Collections.

18  H.M. (Annie) Charlton's reminiscences in typescript can be found in the Dorothy Steeves Collection, UBC Special Collections. Annie Charlton's obituary
appeared in the *Times* (Victoria), 31 Jan. 1940, 15. O.L. Charlton, born in New
Brunswick in 1865, lived until 1962; information found in Provincial
Archives of British Columbia, Clipping files.

19  *WS*, 14 Feb., 10 April 1903; *C&C*, 8, 15 July 1899, 12 Aug. 1899

20  A brief obituary appeared in the *Province* on 17 April 1944, which noted that
Ada Oliver Clayton was born in London, married Edward Clayton in 1891,
and that Edward was a well-known general merchant in the early days. His
obituary in the *Province*, 15 June 1955, noted that he had come to Vancouver
in 1891 after marrying Ada Oliver in Toronto. Born in Hereford, England,
Edward Clayton ran a grocery business in Vancouver before his retirement in
1930. No mention is made in the obituaries of either one's roles in the socialist movement. See also *C&C*, 30 May 1902; *SJ*, 4 June 1903. The demise of the
Victoria local is reported in *WC*, 27 Jan. 1906; *WC*, 23 June 1906. *WC*, 9 Nov.
1907 contains a letter from Ada Clayton as secretary of Local 2, Victoria. In
*WC*, 30 Nov. 1907, she comments on the even sex division among the local's
membership

21  See Schwantes, *Radical Heritage*, chaps. 7 and 8, for a more detailed discussion of these events; see also McCormack, *Reformers, Rebels, and Revolutionaries*, 25–6; *WS*, 8 Nov. 1902. *WS*, 15 Nov. 1902, carried a letter from W.T. Horn,
Port Renfrew, BC, which made a plea for tolerance of differences of opinion.
*WS*, 22 Nov. 1902, reported nearly four hundred members in the SPBC.

22  See *WS*, 8, 22 Nov. 1902, for nominations. The vote count is given in *WS*,
17 Jan. 1903; Dora F. Kerr and Ada Clayton finished near the bottom of the
list. McCormack, *Reformers, Rebels, and Revolutionaries*, 42, cites Merrill as
involved in the ALU. An article written by Miss B.E. Merrill, of Nelson,
appeared in the *ALU Journal*, 6 Aug. 1903, entitled 'Why Women Should Be
Socialists.' Toronto's *Social Justice* reported that the *Western Clarion* was
booming with R.P. Pettipiece and Bertha Merrill in charge (6 Aug. 1903).
After 1903, Bertha Merrill became Bertha Merrill Burns. For Ernest Burns, see
a letter he wrote reminiscing on the occasion of his eighty-fourth birthday in
March 1955; in it he recalls his youthful enthusiasm for the British Social
Democratic Federation and his involvement in the Knights of Labor and later
the populist movement in Washington state. O.L. Charlton Collection, UBC
Special Collections, box 1. A short transcript of an interview done with Burns
can be found in the Dorothy Steeves Collection, Early Socialist Reminiscences, UBC Special Collections. See also *WS*, 22 Nov. 1902 and 3 Jan. 1903.

23 Merrill's comments appeared in *WS*, 31 Jan. 1903. Ernest Burns also had sympathies with the Christian socialist position; in *WS*, 24 Jan. 1903, he wrote 'A
   Plea for Toleration' in which he objected to the disparagement of Blatchford
   and Bellamy and noted that it took time to become a socialist. These positions eventually led Ernest Burns and Bertha Merrill Burns to leave the SPC.
24 *CS*, 5 July, 20 Sept. 1902
25 *CS*, 5 July 1902; *WS*, 27 Sept., 18 Oct. 1902
26 *WS*, 8 Nov. 1902, contains the letter and Dorothy Drew's response.
27 On Burns's experience working at a newspaper, see National Archives of
   Canada, MG 30, A 109, Bertha Burns to Mrs MacDonald, 29 April 1907; *CS*,
   16, 2 Aug. 1902; *WS*, 27 Sept. 1902.
28 *CS*, 26 July 1902; *WS*, 7 Feb. 1903; *CS*, 19 July 1902; *WS*, 15 Nov. 1902; *CS*,
   2 Aug. 1902
29 For a more detailed discussion of socialist attitudes and actions on the
   woman suffrage question, see chapter 4.
30 *WS*, 25 Oct. 1902; 13 Aug. 1904
31 *American Labor Union Journal*, 6 Aug. 1903
32 Ibid.
33 On maternalism, see Linda Kealey, ed., *A Not Unreasonable Claim: Women and
   Reform in Canada, 1880s–1920s* (Toronto, 1979); *WS*, 20 Sept. 1902; on Frances
   Willard's role as a Christian socialist see Buhle, *Women and American Socialism*, chap. 2.
34 *WS*, 14 Feb. 1903, 4 Oct. 1902, and 3 Jan. 1903
35 For a discussion of Robert Kerr and Dora Forster, see Angus McLaren and
   Arlene Tigar McLaren, *The Bedroom and the State: The Changing Practices and
   Politics of Contraception and Abortion in Canada, 1880–1980* (Toronto, 1986), 73–
   5, and Angus McLaren, *Our Own Master Race: Eugenics in Canada, 1885–1945*
   (Toronto, 1990), 86 (quote). Both Forster and Kerr supported women's suffrage. See also Dora Forster, *Sex Radicalism as Seen by an Emancipated Woman
   of the New Time* (Chicago, 1905), especially 26, 21–2. The book was published
   by Moses Harman, a leading libertarian sex reformer and eugenicist. See also
   *Lucifer, the Light Bearer* (hereafter, *Lucifer*), 3 Dec. 1903, 369; *Lucifer* was published by Harman as well. Forster, *Sex Radicalism*, 46–7, 20, 39, 11, 44, 41, 47.
36 For Forster's comments on women's work, see *Cotton's Weekly* (hereafter
   *CW*), 15 April 1909; the quote on women and socialism comes from *CW*,
   11 March 1909
37 Information on Kurikka and Sointula can be found in several articles by J.
   Donald Wilson, especially 'Matti Kurikka: Finnish-Canadian Intellectual,' *BC
   Studies* 20 (Winter 1973–4): 50–65, and '"Never Believe What You Have Never
   Doubted": Matti Kurikka's Dream for a New World Utopia' in *Finnish*

*Diaspora,* vol. 1, *Canada, South America, Africa, Australia, and Sweden,* ed.
Michael G. Karni (Toronto, 1981), 131–53. Most of the information for this
section comes from these articles, but see also J. Donald Wilson, 'Matti
Kurikka and A.B. Makela: Socialist Thought among Finns in Canada, 1900–
1932,' *Canadian Ethnic Studies* 10, 2 (1978): 9–21. Malcolm Island is two hundred miles north of Vancouver, and its population in 1903 was 238, including
88 children. Men outnumbered women at least two to one, and there were
few single women in the colony, which may explain the interest in free love.
Kurikka envisioned the colony as attracting about two thousand people but
its location so far north and its limited agricultural possibilities reduced its
viability. See Wilson, 'Matti Kurikka,' 58 and 51. Wilson also comments on
the contradictions in Kurikka's attitudes towards male/female roles: he portrayed men as stereotypically positive and active and women as negative
and passive. Kurikka also commented on the squabbling among the women
at both colonies, yet later suggested that women would do a better job of law
making. See '"Never Believe,"' 143–4, 146.
38 Wilson, 'Matti Kurikka,' '"Never Believe,"' and 'Matti Kurikka and A.B.
Makela'
39 *CS,* 23 Aug. 1902; *WS,* 27 Sept. and 1 Nov. 1902
40 'The Recent Canadian Elections,' *International Socialist Review* 5 (1904–5): 401

## 4: 'Full of the Spirit of Revolt'

1 Phillip Foner, ed., *Clara Zetkin: Selected Writings* (New York, 1984), 98.
2 On impossibilism and the SPC platform, see Ross McCormack, *Reformers,
Rebels, and Revolutionaries: The Western Canadian Radical Movement, 1899–1919*
(Toronto, 1977), 54–5. Impossibilism, according to McCormack, involved
three related propositions: 1) capitalism could not be reformed; 2) trade
unions had limited benefits; and 3) capitalism could only be destroyed by
class-conscious political action. Recently, Peter Campbell has argued that a
'Marxism of the third way' existed within the SPC, stressing education as key
to socialist visions of change. Education and propaganda work would prepare the workers for the overthrow of capitalism and the eradication of the
wage system. While Campbell makes a good case for a more nuanced view
of the SPC, these Marxists differed little from other SPC members in their
views of women. See J. Peter Campbell, '"Stalwarts of the Struggle": Canadian Marxists of the Third Way, 1879–1939' (PhD thesis, Queen's University,
1991). On BC radicals in general, see Mark Leier, *Red Flags and Red Tape: The
Making of a Labour Bureaucracy* (Toronto, 1995).
3 Mari Jo Buhle, *Women and American Socialism, 1870–1920* (Urbana, 1981)

4 Karen Honeycut, 'Clara Zetkin: A Socialist Approach to the Problem of Women's Oppression' in *European Women on the Left: Socialism, Feminism and the Problems Faced by Political Women, 1880 to the Present*, ed. Jane Slaughter and Robert Kern (Westport, CT, 1981) 29–49

5 Most of this information is drawn from the *Western Clarion* (hereafter *WC*); see 5 Oct. 1907; 8 Aug. 1908; for Manitoba, see 1 April 1905; Dawson figures appear in 15 April 1905.

6 On Montreal, see ibid., 7 Oct. 1905, 12 May 1906, and 18 May 1907. In subsequent years, Montreal socialists fought with police over the May Day parades and carrying the red flag. On the church see *Cotton's Weekly* (hereafter *CW*), 4 Feb. 1909, and *WC*, 2 July 1910; on ethnic groups, see *CW*, 7 Oct. 1909, and *WC*, 21 June 1913.

7 Sanna Kallio, later Kannasto, was employed as the Finnish organizer; Comrade Tomashavsky was sent to Alberta to organize Ukrainians, see *WC*, 22 Feb. 1908. On Winnipeg see *WC*, 26 Oct. 1907, 11 July, 19 Sept. 1908, and 16 Jan. 1909 (lists 154 members for Manitoba); for Vancouver see *Vancouver World*, 9 Jan. 1909 (Wage Earners' page).

8 There are no documented membership figures for the SPC; see McCormack, *Reformers, Rebels, and Revolutionaries*, 68, where he estimates the membership at three thousand. Carlos Schwantes, *Radical Heritage: Labor, Socialism, and Reform in Washington and British Columbia, 1887–1917* (Seattle, 1979), 180; National Archives of Canada (hereafter NAC), J.R. MacDonald Papers, Bertha M. Burns to Mrs Ramsay MacDonald, 26 July 1906 and 29 April 1907

9 *WC*, 26 Sept. 1908; the vote was eighteen to seventeen.

10 *WC*, 29 Aug. 1908; *CW*, 27 May 1909; *WC*, 17 July, 7 Aug. 1909, *CW*, 26 Aug., 2 Sept. 1909; 20 Aug., 29 Oct. 1910

11 *WC*, 30 Oct. 1909, 6 Aug. 1910. The pamphlet, 'Facts for Ontario Socialists,' was reprinted in *WC*, 22 Jan. 1910.

12 See *WC*, 9 April 1910, for Local 24's resolution to dissolve Ontario's PEC; see also 22 April 1910. The 1910 Ontario convention proceedings are reported in *WC*, 19 June 1910, and *CW*, 16 June 1910. By August 1910, Local Berlin's charter was revoked by the DEC, see *WC*, 6 Aug. 1910. For the 1911 Ontario convention, see *CW*, 4 May 1911. Still using the name the Socialist Party (of Ontario), the dissidents reported a membership of twenty locals with 625 dues-paying members. H. Martin of Berlin was the new provincial secretary; *CW*, 9 Feb. 1911.

13 See Ian Angus, *Canadian Bolsheviks* (Montreal, 1981), 6–7; *The Worker*, 5 April 1926, contained an article by 'F.C.' (Florence Custance) on the history of the SPNA. *The Worker* was a publication of the Communist Party of Canada

14 *WC*, 27 May 1911. Lena Mortimer was married to Scottish trade unionist and socialist activist John Mortimer, a tailor by trade who was blacklisted in Winnipeg after the 1899 tailors' strike, according to the *Western Socialist*, 7 March 1903. Epplett and Kerr's remarks, *CW*, 8, 22 April 1909.

15 On Hawthornthwaite, see *WC*, 20 Jan., 10 Feb., and 7 July 1906, 20 March 1909. See *WC*, 22 April 1911, for response to the PEL. 'A Lady's View' appeared in *WC*, 2 Dec. 1911.

16 Later SPC views of suffrage were much like those of C.M. Christiansen, author of 'The Suffragettes,' in *WC*, June 1917, 12.

17 *CW*, 25 Feb., 1 April, and 23 Sept. 1909

18 See K. Marianne Wargelin Brown, 'Trailblazers in Finland for Women's Rights: A Brief History of Feminism in Finland' in *Women Who Dared: The History of Finnish American Women*, ed. Carl Ross and K. Marianne Wargelin Brown (St Paul, MN, 1986), 11; *CW*, 14 Nov. 1912 (public meeting on votes for women held by the Vancouver SDP); on Mary Norton, see 'Great-grandma Still Does Battle,' *Sun*, 24 Nov. 1969, and Mary Norton interview transcript, 21 Feb. 1973, Provincial Archives of British Columbia (Tape 141–1).

19 On Helena Gutteridge, see Susan Wade, 'Helena Gutteridge: Votes for Women and Trade Unions' in *In Her Own Right: Selected Essays on Women's History in BC*, ed. Barbara Latham and Cathy Kess (Victoria, 1981), 187–203, and see also Irene Howard, *The Struggle for Social Justice in British Columbia: Helena Gutteridge, the Unknown Reformer* (Vancouver, 1992). 'Helena Gutteridge's Story,' *Pacific Tribune*, 8 March 1957, and Gutteridge's column, 'Woman Suffrage,' *BC Federationist* (1914–15). The column disappeared in 1915, as did discussion of the suffrage issue from the newspaper.

20 On the Winnipeg SDP's support for equal suffrage, see the *Voice*, 21 Sept. 1917. On the PEL, see Catherine Cleverdon, *The Woman Suffrage Movement in Canada*, 2nd ed. (Toronto, 1974), 55–6; Provincial Archives of Manitoba, Political Equality League, Minute Books, 1912–14 (on Winnipeg). On Dixon's 1914 and 1915 campaigns, see various issues of the *Voice*, including 6 March 1914, (platform). Nellie McClung campaigned vigorously for Dixon as well; see, for example, the *Voice*, 24 April 1914. For Winona Flett's marriage and a brief biography, see the *Voice*, 14, 16 Oct., 1914. Dixon's election was reported in the *Voice*, 17 July 1914. See chapter 7 for Winona Flett's later activities. On Francis Marion Beynon, see Ramsay Cook, 'Francis Marion Beynon and the Crisis of Christian Reformism' in *The West and the Nation*, ed. Carl Berger and R. Cook (Toronto, 1976); Barbara Roberts, '"Why Do Women Do Nothing to End War?": Canadian Feminist-Pacifists and the Great War,' CRIAW Paper No. 13 (1985); Ann Hicks, 'Francis Beynon and *The Guide*' in *First Days, Fighting Days: Women in Manitoba History*, ed. Mary Kinnear (Regina, 1987), 41–52.

See also Susan Jackel, 'First Days, Fighting Days: Prairie Presswomen and Suffrage Activism, 1906–1916' in ibid., 53–75.

21  On Toronto's SPC, see *WC*, 3 April 1909; *CW*, 29 Dec. 1910. *Labor Advocate* (hereafter *LA*), 2, 16 Jan., 17, 24 April 1891. For LCW resolution, see *LA*, 6 Feb. 1891.

22  On Denison, see Deborah Gorham, 'Flora MacDonald Denison: Canadian Feminist' in *A Not Unreasonable Claim: Women and Reform in Canada, 1880s–1920s*, ed. Linda Kealey (Toronto, 1979), 47–70, and especially 57, for Denison's role as columnist for the Toronto *World*; see also Wayne Roberts, '"Rocking the Cradle for the World": The New Woman and Maternal Feminism, Toronto, 1877–1914' in ibid., 24, 37. The *Lance*, 30 Oct. 1909, noted coverage of increasing suffrage agitation in the *World*. The *Voice*, 3 June 1910, noted that suffragists in Toronto were becoming interested in organizing women workers: 'Some of the leaders are very friendly to organized labour,' noted the *Voice*, 28 Oct. 1910. The 1914 referendum is covered in *Industrial Banner* (hereafter *IB*), 2, 9, and 16 Jan. 1914. James Simpson presented labour's case for woman suffrage at a meeting with the government; see *IB*, 4 Feb. 1916.

23  On WSDL support for the franchise, see *IB*, 18 Dec. 1914, 2 March 1917. For early ILP support of suffrage, see the *Lance*, 10 June, 16 Sept. 1911. On Mendelssohn see *CW*, 9 Jan. 1913.

24  *WC*, 22 Aug., 12 Sept. 1908

25  Ibid., 12 Sept. 1908

26  Ibid., 12 and 28 Sept. 1908. *Socialist Woman* was begun by Josephine Conger-Kaneko in 1907 and changed its name to *Progressive Woman* in 1909; see Buhle, *Women and American Socialism*, 148.

27  *Cotton's Weekly* began as the *Observer* on 17 Sept. 1908. The name was changed in Dec. and the paper shifted from local news to the discussion of ideas. In the issue dated 21 Jan. 1909, Cotton described the editor and manager of the paper as members of the SPC. See the *Observer*, 17 Sept. 1908, *CW*, 3 Dec. 1908; 27 May 1909. For a more detailed look at Wisdom and her column, see Janice Newton, *The Feminist Challenge to the Canadian Left, 1900–1918* (Montreal and Kingston, 1995), and her article, 'The Alchemy of Politicization: Socialist Women and the Early Canadian Left' in *Gender Conflicts: New Essays in Women's History*, ed. Franca Iacovetta and Mariana Valverde (Toronto, 1992), 135–9. *Cotton's Weekly* became the *Canadian Forward* (*CF*), organ of the SDP in the early years of the war

28  Peter Krawchuk, *The Ukrainian Socialist Movement in Canada, 1907–1918* (Toronto, 1979), gives an overview of the movement and discusses centres of activity; see also Frances Swyripa, 'Outside the Bloc Settlement: Ukrainian Women in Ontario during the Formative Years of Community Conscious-

ness' in *Looking into My Sister's Eyes: An Exploration in Women's History*, ed. Jean Burnet (Toronto, 1986), 155–78, especially 157. Swyripa notes that even as late as 1931, the Prairies claimed 85.7 per cent of Ukrainians in Canada. The standard history of early Ukrainian settlement is Orest T. Martynowych, *Ukrainians in Canada: The Formative Period, 1891–1924* (Edmonton, 1991)

29 *Chervonyi Prapor* (hereafter *CP*), 12 Dec., 26 Dec. 1907; on suffrage see *CP*, 6 Feb. 1908. *CP* folded in 1908 after eighteen issues. In 1909, *Robochyi Narod* (hereafter *RN*) began to publish from Winnipeg, lasting until 1918.

30 The letter from 'H. R-kivna' appeared in *CP*, 5 Jan. 1908; Osadchuk's letter appeared in *CP*, 13 Feb. 1908. Hanna Stechyshyn's activities are noted in Krawchuk, *Ukrainian Socialist Movement*, 11, and in *RN*, 2 June 1909, 9 Feb. 1910. Membership figures with sex breakdown appear in various issues of *RN* from 1912 on. See *RN*, 1 March 1911, on morality; 1 May 1911, on children. On minimum wage laws and protective legislation, see *RN*, 15 Oct. and 10 Dec. 1913. The FUSD emerged in 1909–10 to unite all Ukrainian socialists in a new organization distinct from the SPC, which took a negative view of the language groupings and also opposed trade unionism and the equality of women. See Krawchuk, *Ukrainian Socialist Movement*, 13–19.

31 *RN*, 22 Jan. 1914

32 Women members of the FUSD in Ontario and Quebec benefited from a lower membership fee after a convention in January 1914. Because women earned less, their fees were half the men's; see *RN*, 11 February 1914. *RN*, 28 January 1914, reported 821 members of the Ukrainian SDP (the new name for the FUSD after April 1914 when the nearly defunct western FUSD was revitalized under the new name). Ten of the 28 locals, accounting for 312 members, were located in Ontario and Quebec; Alberta led the West with 9 locals and 242 members. For the amateur theatre circle, see *RN*, 29 April 1914, 14 April 1915; Anne B. Woywitka, 'A Pioneer Woman in the Labour Movement,' *Alberta History* 26, 1 (Winter 1978): 11–12. See also Martynowych, *Ukrainians in Canada*, 285–98.

33 The Canadian Census reported the numbers of Canadians of Finnish, Jewish, or Ukrainian origin as follows: in 1911, 15,500 Finns, 76,199 Jews, and 75,432 Ukrainians; in 1921, 21,494 Finns, 126,196 Jews, and 106,721 Ukrainians. See F.H. Leacy, ed., *Historical Statistics of Canada*, 2nd ed. (Ottawa: Statistics Canada, 1983), A125–63. On unions in the clothing trade, see Mercedes Steedman, 'Skill and Gender in the Canadian Clothing Industry, 1890–1940' in *On the Job: Confronting the Labour Process in Canada*, ed. Craig Heron and Robert Storey (Kingston, 1986), 161.

34 *WC*, 9 Dec. 1905, reports the formation of a Jewish branch of the SPC; Gribble's comments appear in *WC*, 22 June 1907. A general history of Toronto's

Jewish community can be found in Stephen A. Speisman, *The Jews of Toronto: A History to 1937* (Toronto, 1979), although he does not address the question of the Jewish socialist movement in the book. See also Gerald Tulchinsky, *Taking Root: The Origins of the Canadian Jewish Community* (Toronto, 1992), chap. 11. On Jewish women's participation in the WSDL, see *CF*, 2, 27 Dec. 1916, 10 Sept. 1917. The socialist Sunday school is described in the *International Socialist Review* 12 (1911–12), 884. Elizabeth Crockett, a member of the SDP and later the WSDL, conducted the school. The Young Workers' Club (also known as the Young Jewish Club) is mentioned in *CF*, 10 April, 24 Oct. 1917, 25 Jan. 1918.

35 A photograph of the Young Jewish Literary Association, 1915–18, Winnipeg, at the Provincial Archives of Ontario (hereafter PAO), Max Dolgoy Collection, MSR-0900-25, includes photos of Annie Dolgoy and Clara Cooperstock, both active in left-wing circles. Other photos in this collection include Freda Usiskin and Clara Cooperstock, 1915–16 (Number 21), and a left-wing picnic in Winnipeg, 1923 (Number 7) which includes prominent members of Winnipeg's Jewish left. For the Young Socialist Club, see *RN*, 26 Feb. 1913, which describes the club for children ten to fifteen years old. Gonevitch is mentioned in the *Voice*, 13 March 1914. See also *CF*, 24 March 1917, on the fourth anniversary. The suggestion to start a similar English club is contained in the *Voice*, 23 March 1917.

36 On Alcin, see Roseline Usiskin, 'Toward a Theoretical Reformulation of the Relationship between Political Ideology, Social Class, and Ethnicity: A Case Study of the Winnipeg Jewish Radical Community, 1905–1920' (MA thesis, University of Manitoba, 1978), especially 181–7, on the Jewish Radical School and the socialist Sunday school; see also Henry Trachtenberg, '"The Old Clo Move": Anti-Semitism, Politics, and the Jews of Winnipeg, 1882–1921' (PhD diss., York University, 1984), 804–33, on Alcin's election to the school board, and 490 for mention of several women in the SDP, including Zeimanovich, Rose Victor, Sarah Winick, and Belke Chafetz. The *Canadian Israelite* (Yiddish), 2 April, 8 May 1914, mentions the radical school; on the Sunday school see also the *Voice*, 27 Oct. 1916, 4 May 1917. Articles on suffrage appeared in various issues of the *Canadian Israelite* (hereafter *CI*); see, for example, 30 May 1912, 26 Feb., 18 March, and 21 April 1914; Nellie McClung spoke on suffrage at the Talmud Torah Hall, see *CI*, 10 March 1914.

37 Ruth Frager, *Sweatshop Strife: Class, Ethnicity, and Gender in the Jewish Labour Movement of Toronto, 1900–1939* (Toronto, 1992), chap. 7

38 Buhle, *Women and American Socialism*, 302; Varpu Lindström-Best, *Defiant Sisters: A Social History of Finnish Women in Canada* (Toronto, 1987)

39 Varpu Lindström-Best, 'The Socialist Party of Canada and the Finnish Con-

nection' in *Ethnicity, Power, and Politics in Canada*, ed. Jorgen Dahlie and Tissa
Fernando (Toronto, 1981), 113–19; Moses Hahl, 'Suomalaiset Kanadassa' in
*Airue I* (Port Arthur, 1910), 74–90, surveys Finns in Canada in 1910; on p.
90, Hahl estimates 9,000 to 9,350 settled Finns and 6,000 to 7,000 itinerant workers in Canada. Fewer women than men emigrated from Finland in this
period; on this point and domestic service, see Joan Sangster, 'Finnish
Women in Ontario, 1890–1930,' *Polyphony* 3, 2 (Fall 1981): 46–54. For the 1910
survey in Toronto, see Hahl, 'Suomalaiset,' 75.
40 On Finnish women's activism in the SPC, see *WC*, 22 June 1907, and *Toveritar*,
29 Sept. 1925; the latter gives the Toronto female membership of thirty-eight.
Sanna Kallio Kannasto was born in Finland on 26 September 1878, came to
the United States around the turn of the century, went to the Finnish Workers' College in Hancock, Michigan, became involved in socialist politics, was
elected Eastern organizer for the United States and Canada in 1907 for sixteen months. Operating out of Port Arthur, Ontario, she continued to organize Finns for the SPC and later, the SDP. See below for more detail.
41 See Hahl, 'Suomalaiset,' 86–90; see also Aku Paivio, ed., *Canadan Suomalaisen
Sosialistijarjeston Ensimaisen Edustajakokouksen Poytakirja: Kokous pidetty Port
Arthurissa, Ont., 19–23, p:na maaliskuuta 1914* (Port Arthur, 1914), 28 for a 1914
survey that reported 2,829 Finns in the Finnish Socialist Organization, with
565 (20 per cent) women. On the fist press, see Varpu Lindström-Best, 'Fist
Press: A Study of the Finnish Canadian Handwritten Newspapers' in *Roots
and Realities Among Eastern and Central Europeans*, ed. Martin Kovacs (Edmonton, 1983), 129–34. The Edmonton publication *Moukari* can be found in PAO,
Multicultural History Society of Ontario Collection, Oct. 1979, MU 3351,
Series D28, Finnish People's Library, Edmonton, file 4, drawer 4, item 28, file
4, no. 3
42 For Sointula's sewing circle, see *Toveritar*, 6 March 1928; minutes of this sewing circle were cited as existing from 1911 to 1918; on Rossland, see *Tyomies*,
9 Feb. 1909. For Toronto see *Toveritar*, 29 Feb. 1916 (Lehto), and 20 June 1916
(Autio); on Sault Ste Marie, see *Toveritar*, 14 Nov. 1916.
43 See *Toveritar kymmenvuotias, 1911–1921; Muistojulkaisu (Toveritar, Ten Years of
Age, 1911–1921: A Commemorative Publication)* (Astoria, OR 1921); Hulda
Anderson is mentioned on p. 7.
44 See, for example, issues of *WC* and *CW* between 1909 and 1914 for mention of
women subscription hustlers; some, such as Mrs M.A. Owen of Fernie BC,
sent in scores of subscriptions. For social events see, for example, *WC*,
18 June 1904, 21 Oct. 1905, 27 Jan. 1906, 15 Feb., 9 May 1908, 20 Feb. 1909. Visiting lecturers included Charlotte Perkins Gilman, *WC*, 24 June 1905; May
Wood Simons, *WC*, 30 Sept. 1905, 23 May 1908, and *CW*, 26 Jan. 1911; Lena

Morrow Lewis, *WC*, 18, 25 Nov. 1905; Irene Smith, *WC*, 3 Feb. 1906; and Elizabeth Gurley Flynn, *WC*, 24 April 1909. British women leaders such as Sylvia Pankhurst also sometimes visited Canada.

45 On the study club, see *CW*, 4 Feb. 1909, and *WC*, 20 Feb. 1909; see also B.O. Robinson's letter on the study club in *WC*, 15 May 1909. Whether the Vancouver study group materialized is not clear; see *WC*, 29 Aug. 1908 for a mention of the planned study group. Buhle, *Women and American Socialism*, 111–12, notes the popularity of educational study groups in the United States.

46 *CW*, 4 May 1911; see Nesbitt's report in the *International Socialist Review* 12 (1911–12), 884. For Crockett, see *Globe*, 28 Nov. 1912; *CW*, 26 Nov. 1914. On British Columbia see *CW*, 6 Nov. 1913. *The Social Democrat*, 1914 (fragment) provides a directory with names of secretaries. Winnipeg also had a women's branch of the SDP, which is mentioned in *CF*, 27 Dec. 1916; when it was founded is not clear.

47 For activities of the WSDL, see *IB*, 11 Sept., 2 Oct. 1914; *CW*, 15 Oct. 1914 (James's speech); *IB*, 6 Aug., 28 May 1915; quote from *CW*, 12 Nov. 1914; *CF*, 28 Oct. 1916; *IB*, 1 Dec. 1916.

48 For the Knights' activities, see also chapter 6. Both Lestors were British emigrants; originally a blacksmith, Charles Lestor also worked as a solicitor, labourer, actor, and waterworks manager. A tour between Vancouver and Quebec is mentioned in *CW*, 5 Jan. 1911, along with the biographical details. Ruth Lestor's speech in 1909 is covered in *WC*, 10 July 1909; *WC*, July 1911; Ruth Lestor's illness is mentioned in *CW*, 5 Jan. 1911; *WC*, 20 June 1914 reported the birth of a daughter; *WC*, Aug. 1915 reported Lestor's departure from the SPC. See *WC*, Sept. 1917, for Charles Lestor's prison term and the mention of his wife and children. Other speeches by Ruth Lestor are found reported in *WC*, 19 June, 11 Dec. 1909; *CW*, 24 June 1909, 19 Jan. 1911.

49 Information on Sanna Kannasto was obtained from the press and from Finnish materials held by NAC, Finnish Organization of Canada (hereafter FOC), MG 28, translated by Mauri A. Jalava; some translation of Finnish materials was also done by Eeva Rose. Varpu Lindström has also greatly assisted this research by generously sharing her research on Finnish radical women. Information on Sophie Mushkat was found in the socialist press up to 1915. Pat Roome, Mt Royal College, Calgary, alerted me to Mushkat's marriage and activities in Alberta in the early 1920s. The Canadian Security Intelligence Service provided the RCMP Personal History File on Sophie McClusky, which dates from 1921 to 1968, when the file was reviewed and deactivated; McClusky died in 1954. See also chapter 7. Kannasto's death date is unknown; she was still alive in 1960 when she was eighty-two years old. See University of Toronto, Rare Books, Kenny Collection, box 41.

50 A brief biographical sketch of Sanna Kannasto appeared in *Koyhaliston Juija* (1910), n.p., in NAC, FOC, MG 28, V 46, vol. 90, file 17. On the 1908 convention, see *WC*, 26 Sept. 1908; her illness and trip to Michigan is discussed in *Tyomies*, 6 April 1909, 13 May 1909, 29 May 1909; issues of *Tyomies* are found in NAC, FOC, MG 28, V 46, vol. 291.

51 The 1914 meeting of the representatives of the FSOC and the discussions of Kannasto's role in 1913–14 appear in Paivio, ed., *Canadan Suomalaisen*, 19, 21, 28, 85.

52 Letters from S. Kannasto to J.W. Ahlqvist, 1914, in NAC, FOC, MG 28, V 46, vol. 3; 16 April 1914; letter and accounts, S. Kannasto to J.W. Ahlqvist for period 1–30 April 1914, n.d.; 2 June 1914, Worthington, ON

53 See letters, S. Kannasto to J. W. Ahlqvist, in NAC, FOC, MG 28, V 46, vol. 3, various files: 10 June 1914, Naughton, ON, (file 24); 21 Nov. 1914, Finland, ON, (file 25); 3 Dec. 1914, Winnipeg (file 24); 1 Jan. 1915, n.p. (file 26); 9 Jan. 1915, Makama, ON (file 26); 27 Jan. 1915, Port Arthur (file 26); 3 July 1916, Monnessen (file 27).

54 On her husband's opposition to Sanna's organizing trips, see Paivio, *Canadan Suomalaisen*, 28, which records that as an organizer and speaker 'Sanna Kannasto was used formerly more but Mr. Kannasto sharply forbade it.'

55 See letter, n.d., University of Toronto Rare Books Room, Kenny Collection, box 41, 'Dear Bert ...,' signed by 'Taimi.' For the attempt to deport Sanna Kannasto, see NAC, Canada, Immigration Branch, RG 76, vols. 625–7. Microfilm reel no. C10,442, File 961162, Agitators, 1919–20, Part 1, Item 12190, F.C. Blair to Mr Ireland, 27 April 1920. For Kannasto's post-1920 activities, see Lindström-Best, *Defiant Sisters*, 151–2.

56 Biographical information on Sophie Mushkat comes from the socialist press and the Canadian Security Intelligence Service, RCMP Personal History Files, Sophia Lindsay (McClusky), 1921–68. Sophie married twice, the first time to William McClusky in 1916 and the second time in 1944, ten years before her death. On p. 169 of the RCMP file, dated Halifax, 2 Nov. 1943, a report on Sophie's remarks at a meeting of the Canadian Friends of the USSR quoted her as making reference to her entry to Canada in 1904. An earlier report in this file (p. 96, 13 Sept. 1933) dated her arrival in 1903 and gave her birthplace as Warsaw. As Sophie Mushkat, her activities were first noted by Roscoe Fillmore in a letter to H.H. Stuart in July 1909. See University of New Brunswick, Harriet Irving Library, Henry Harvey Stuart Collection, MG H25, file 3a, Fillmore to Stuart, 22 July 1909. The letter indicates that the Mushkats and Fanny Levy ran a dry goods store in Moncton. See also *CW*, 29 July 1909, for Fillmore's comments on Mushkat as a revolutionist. Fillmore's Aug. comments are in *WC*, 7 Aug. 1909. Wilf Gribble reported on Mushkat's visit to

Saint John to organize in *CW*, 12, 19 Aug. 1909. For Gribble's comments on the Jewish comrades, see *CW*, 26 Aug. 1909. See also *CW*, 2 Sept. 1909. The trial is reported in *CW*, 30 Sept. 1909, and *Eastern Labor News* (hereafter *ELN*), 4 Dec. 1909. Clipping of the Newcastle meeting and Stuart's note about Mushkat are found in H.H. Stuart Collection, scrapbook.

57  On Springhill see *WC*, 12 March 1910, and *ELN*, 5 March 1910; *CW*, 24 March, 28 July 1910.

58  Mushkat's presence is recorded at a Winnipeg WLL meeting in 1910. On her activities in Alberta, see *WC*, 5 April, 15 March 1913 (report of the Alberta executive of the SPC for 1912 states there are 21 locals and 362 members); 2 Aug., 27 Sept., 11 Oct. 1913; 28 Feb., 11 April, 10 Oct. 1914. *CW*, 11, 25 Sept. 1913, notes her speeches in New Brunswick in late August and September.

59  Information on the unemployment conference is found in the Provincial Archives of Alberta, Warren Caragata Collection, 80.218, 59, box 2.

60  On 1915 see *WC*, 16, 30 Jan.; 1 March, July–Aug., Sept. 1915. John Reid, SPC candidate for Red Deer, was arrested in the summer of 1915 for sedition. See *WC*, Feb. 1916, for a report of his sentencing to fifteen months. Mushkat's marriage is mentioned in her Personal History File, 92, Oscar Coderre to the Commissioner, RCMP, 19 Sept. 1933. For her activities in the early 1920s, see the Personal History File, 1–32, Jan.–Nov. 1921. On her unemployed activities in the 1920s, see Glenbow-Alberta Institute, 'McClusky, Sophie,' Clipping Files. These clippings also reveal that sometime in the 1920s, she separated from McClusky.

61  The letter to Tim Buck can be found in the RCMP, Personal History File, 'Sophia Lindsay (McClusky),' 66–8, dated 9–6–31. The reference to Kannasto's brother is in NAC, FOC, MG 28, V 46, vol. 3, file 27, Sanna Kannasto to J.W. Ahlqvist, 10 June 1916, Port Arthur. For more on Anna Louise Strong, see Barbara Sicherman and Carol Hurd Green, eds., *Notable American Women: The Modern Period* (Cambridge, 1980), 664–6.

62  For Alf Budden, see *WC*, 10 Dec. 1910, 1 April 1911.

63  'Sex Equality,' *WC*, Aug., 1911; for Lefeaux, see W.W.L., 'Morality,' *WC*, July 1911. At this time the *WC* published only monthly.

64  *CW*, 1 April 1909, 19 May 1910, 2 Jan. 1913, and 10 Dec. 1914; *BC Federationist*, 28 Sept. 1912; 18, 25 April, 3 July, 13 June, and 29 Aug. 1913; 13 March, 9, 16 Oct., 20 Nov., and 4 Dec. 1914. For an estimate of trade union membership, see McCormack, *Reformers, Rebels, and Revolutionaries*, 56, where he estimates that 60 to 90 per cent trade of SPC members were trade unionists.

65  *WC*, 4 Nov. 1905; *CW*, 17 June, 1 July, 23 Sept. 1909

66  Comments on married women's freedom to choose a partner appear in *WC*, 14 Dec. 1907, 26 Dec. 1908, 19 April 1913; *CW*, 11 Feb., 8 April 1909, 30 June

1910, 13 Nov. 1913. While Janice Newton is correct to point out that the socialist movement failed to deal seriously with the domestic realm, and that some women recognized this, the point that I make is that the source of much of this failure lies in acceptance of the family wage ideal, which permeated the labour and socialist movements of the period. See Newton, *The Feminist Challenge*, 54–5.

67 On the family wage, see Michèle Barrett and Mary McIntosh, 'The "Family Wage": Some Problems for Socialists and Feminists,' *Capital and Class* 11 (1980), and Michèle Barrett, *Women's Oppression Today* (London, 1980); Sonya Rose, '"Gender at Work": Sex, Class, and Industrial Capitalism,' *History Workshop* 21 (Spring 1986): 113–31; WC, 26 Dec. 1908; CW, 17 June 1909; WC, 14 Dec. 1907, 19 April 1913; CW, 11 Feb. 1909, 30 June 1910, and 19 Jan. 1911.

68 CW, 19 Jan., 4 May 1911; WC, 13 Jan. 1906; CW, 13 May, 11 Nov. 1909, 3 April 1913.

69 On middle-class reform efforts directed at child labour, see Neil Sutherland, *Children in English-Canadian Society: Framing the Twentieth-Century Consensus* (Toronto, 1976), and Joy Parr, *Labouring Children: British Immigrant Apprentices to Canada, 1869–1924* (London, 1980). *Labour Advocate*, 26 June 1891, editorial comment; CW, 27 May, 30 Dec., 18 Nov. 1909.

70 WC, 30 May 1908, reports rejection of the resolution on working with children at the Interprovincial Convention between British Columbia and Alberta; see earlier discussion of the SDP's youth groups; CW, 11 Feb. 1909 (pensions for children); Local 1, Toronto (the breakaway from the SPC), passed a resolution on free medical care for school children, including inspection, dentistry, and medical staff hired by the school board to provide free care; see CW, 20 Oct. 1910. For Beynon's column, see *Grain Growers' Guide*, 28 Aug. 1912.

71 On Springhill, see CW, 29 Sept. 1910, 6, 20 April, 11 May 1911; the moving force behind the SYG was a Belgian socialist miner, Jules Lavenne.

72 CW, 28 Jan., 9 Sept. 1909; 8 Dec. 1910; WC, 20 Feb., 19 June 1909, 30 April 1910; CW, 13 Nov. 1913, 19 May 1910. See also Janice Newton, 'From Wage Slave to White Slave: The Prostitution Controversy and the Early Canadian Left,' in *Beyond the Vote: Canadian Women and Politics*, ed. Linda Kealey and Joan Sangster (Toronto, 1989), 217–36.

73 For the prostitution controversy and the women's comments, see CW, 28 Jan., 11 Feb., 4 March 1909. While the attention here was on Montreal, similar discussions of prostitution and the need for reform of urban policies towards 'red light districts,' as well as efforts to redeem individual fallen women, occurred in most major Canadian cities. Official surveys of the problem were commissioned in many North American cities, including Toronto. See Social

Survey Commission of Toronto, *Report* (Toronto, 1915). While the latter report strongly disavowed the theory that insufficient wages alone could explain why women turned to prostitution, the commission did venture that a minimum wage policy might be necessary, although beyond its scope. See also Newton, 'From Wage Slave to White Slave.'

74 On Gutteridge, see footnote 19 and *BC Federationist*, 16 Jan., 9 Oct., 16 Oct., 20 Nov., 27 Nov., 4 Dec. 1914.

75 The Women's Employment League, organized in Sept. 1914, focused on women's unemployment. See chapter 6 below.

## 5: 'Wanted – Women to Take the Place of Men'

1 *Telegram*, 19 Nov. 1915; *Star*, 19 Nov. 1915

2 *Voice*, 14 Jan. 1916

3 *BC Federationist*, 15 Oct. 1915

4 *Labour Gazette* (hereafter *LG*) 14 (Aug. 1913), 149–51 (Toronto) 152 (Vancouver). For Winnipeg, see *LG* 14 (Dec. 1913), 681. See also *LG* 14 (Oct. 1913), 423, for Toronto, where unemployment in the building trades resulted in an increase in women seeking day work and childcare. For an example of a municipal employment bureau, see reports on Winnipeg in *LG* 14 (Dec. 1913), 681, and 14 (April 1914), 1162; on Toronto, see *LG* 15 (Aug. 1914), 186–8; on Winnipeg, ibid., 188–9.

5 On the war's effect, see *LG* 15 (Sept. 1914), 368–72, (Oct. 1914), 464–6. For the Trades and Labor Council estimates, see *LG* 15 (Nov. 1914), 574, (Dec. 1914), 678. The first women correspondents to the *LG* were: Miss Gabrielle R. des Isles (Montreal); Miss Edith Elwood, Evangelia Settlement (Toronto); Miss Harriet J. Williams, secretary, Grace Church (Winnipeg); and Mrs Rose Carson (Vancouver). See *BC Federationist*, 25 April 1913, which also contains Carson's first report on Vancouver. See also Sheila Lewenhak, *Women and Trade Unions* (London, 1977), chap. 10, for a discussion of similar unemployment trends among British women workers at the start of the war.

6 University of British Columbia, Special Collections, Vancouver (Local) Council of Women, Minutes, 1914–15, box 4, 17, 22 Sept., 5 Oct. 1914. Quote and statistics from 22 Sept. 1914 minutes. On Vancouver's social welfare system, see Diane L. Matters, 'Public Welfare Vancouver Style, 1910–1920,' *Journal of Canadian Studies* 14, 1 (Spring 1979): 3–15. On Calgary see Judith B. Bedford, 'Social Justice in Calgary: A Study of Urban Poverty and Welfare Development in the 1920s' (MA thesis, University of Calgary, 1981).

7 *BC Federationist*, 9, 23 Oct., 20 Nov., and 4 Dec. 1914, 19 Feb. and 18 June 1915.

8 The Toronto toy factory is mentioned in *LG*, 15 (Dec. 1914), 678–80; on Win-

nipeg, see ibid. (Oct. 1914), 466–7; see also *Voice*, 11 Dec. 1914. *Grain Growers' Guide*, 16, 2 Sept. 1914. On Calgary and Moose Jaw, see Glenbow-Alberta Institute, Calgary City Clerk Papers, file 779, G.D. Mackie to J. Millar, 26 May 1915; Minutes of 'Meeting of the Special Labor Bureau Committee ... Jan. 5, 1915' (Calgary). Matters, 'Public Welfare Vancouver Style,' also notes municipal attempts to restrict the provision of work to married men with families. Single homeless men were looked after by various missions, some of which received municipal grants. During the 1913–15 crisis, the city was forced by circumstance to hire both single and married men under its relief programs. See ibid., 4–5.

9  *LG* 16 (Feb. 1916), 889 (Winnipeg); ibid. (March 1916), 994–5 (Winnipeg); and ibid. (April 1916), 1091–2 (Montreal), and 1093–4 (Vancouver). On Vancouver domestics, *LG* 16 (July 1916), 1358. On the railways, Toronto, see ibid. (Aug. 1916), 1446. On women conductors in Vancouver, see *BC Federationist*, 24 Nov. 1916.

10  See Enid M. Price, *Changes in the Industrial Occupations of Women in the Environment of Montreal during the Period of the War, 1914–1918* (Montreal, 1919), for a contemporary survey of women in munitions work and other fields, both traditional and non-traditional. See also one of the first attempts to encapsulate women's war experience in Canada: Ceta Ramkhalawansingh, 'Women during the Great War' in *Women at Work: Ontario, 1850–1930*, ed. Janice Acton, Penny Goldsmith, and Bonnie Shepard (Toronto 1974), 261–307. *BC Federationist*, 26 Jan. 1917

11  *Voice*, 15 June 1917. Among the unions that began to organize women during the war was the IAM, which held a referendum on admitting women in Feb. 1917. See *BC Federationist*, 16 Feb. 1917.

12  *Industrial Banner* (hereafter *IB*), 26 May, 23 June 1916. As several British authors have noted, equal pay for British women workers was not often achieved and was the subject of repeated campaigns by women trade unionists during the war. See Lewenhak, *Women and Trade Unions*, chap. 10, and Norbert Soldon, *Women in British Trade Unions, 1874–1976* (Dublin, 1978), chap. 4.

13  National Archives of Canada (NAC), Flavelle Papers, MG 30, A 16, vol. 38, Circular, 'To Manufacturers Who Are Engaged in the Production of Munitions and Component Parts,' 1 Sept. 1916 (announcement of Irish's appointment). See also two circulars sent by Irish to 'All Contractors,' 30 April 1917 and 23 April 1918, on labour shortages and women's labour.

14  NAC, Flavelle Papers, MG 30, A 16, vol. 38, Irish to Flavelle, 12 Oct. 1916

15  Ibid., Irish to Flavelle, 14 Feb. 1917; 17 Feb. 1917 (draft letter to Bennett); Flavelle to Irish, 20 Feb. 1917 (advice to Irish to rewrite the letter, leaving out personal feeling); Irish to Bennett, 24 Feb. 1917.

16 On the badges, see ibid., Irish to Flavelle, 4 April 1917, where he notes that he is merely unburdening himself to Flavelle and won't intervene.

17 Ibid., vol. 11, Irish to Flavelle, 21 Jan. 1918

18 Ibid., vol. 38, Irish to Flavelle, 18 Sept. 1918; Flavelle to Irish, 21 Sept. 1918. Mary Irving Fenton succeeded Miss Winnifred Wiseman, the first supervisor of female labour in the Department of Labour, IMB, who moved on to the British Consul's office in Washington. Fenton was associated with Wiseman from the beginning of the work and was the widow of Frederick Fenton, MD. See Irish to Flavelle, 14 Jan. 1918.

19 Ibid., vol. 9, Rollo to Flavelle, 29 March 1917; Montreal Women Inspectors to Flavelle, 31 March 1917; T.S. Griffiths (president, Canadian Inspection and Testing Laboratories) to Edwards, 31 March 1917; Edwards to Mr Fitzgerald, 31 March 1917 (on arrangements made by Irish); on the savings made by wage reductions, see W. Dalziel (Inspector of Shell Components) to Edwards, 5 Feb. 1917; see also Irish to Edwards, 5 March 1917 (on changes in hiring).

20 See Vancouver TLC, Minutes, 2 July 1915. On the Victoria strike, see NAC Department of Labour, Strikes and Lockouts Files, RG 27, vol. 306, strike 59 (1917) (hereafter RG 27).

21 Margaret E. McCallum, 'Keeping Women in Their Place: The Minimum Wage in Canada, 1910–25,' Labour/Le Travail 16 (Spring 1986); 30–32. See also Dennis Guest, The Emergence of Social Security in Canada (Vancouver, 1980), 73–4.

22 Philip Snowden, The Living Wage (London, n.d.), 7–8; 16–17; 22–3.

23 Judith A. Baer, The Chains of Protection: The Judicial Response to Women's Labor Legislation (Westport, CT, 1978), chaps. 2 and 3

24 On the origins of the federal legislation, see R.M. Dawson, William Lyon Mackenzie King: A Political Biography, 1874–1923 (Toronto, 1958), 65–70. Manitoba's Fair Wage Act, Statutes of Manitoba, 1916, section 10, chap. 121; a list of wage rates for 1916–19 can be found in the Provincial Archives of Manitoba (hereafter PAM), Minister of Public Works, RG 18, B2, box 9, file labelled Fair Wage Board, 1916–20.

25 Ibid., 2 June, 8 Dec. 1916; 5, 19 Jan., 9 March 1917

26 Voice, 25, 4 May, 1 June 1917

27 Ibid., 8, 22 June 1917

28 Ibid., 9, 16, and 23 Feb., 16 March, 6 and 13 April, 4 May, 1 and 22 June 1917.

29 Testimony was also given by an operator and supported by Ed McGrath that women turned to prostitution because of low wages. The operator testified that she personally knew fifty women who had left the telephone company in the last nine years for 'the profits of an immoral life.' Voice, 18 May 1917

30 Ibid., 28 Sept. 1917

31 Blackburn's expense accounts are located in PAM, Manitoba, Department of

Public Works, Deputy Minister's Files, RG 18 B2 (box 5), 1917. See also the Minimum Wage Commission's Report, 1918, n.p. in the PAM. The main findings of the Minimum Wage Commission are summarized in the *Voice*, 8 Feb. 1918.

32 *Voice*, 8 Feb. 1918; Minimum Wage Commission, Report, 1918, n.p.
33 Ibid.
34 *Voice*, 7 Dec. 1917, 4, 13 Jan. 1918
35 Ibid., 13, 18 Jan. 1918
36 Ibid., 25 Jan., 1, 8, 15, and 22 Feb., 1, 8 March 1918
37 The Winnipeg TLC and the WLL nominated members for the MWB. See ibid., 22 March, 12 April 1918.
38 *Tribune* (Winnipeg), 11, 13 Sept. 1918; *Western Labor News* (hereafter *WLN*), 7 Feb. 1919
39 *WLN*, 7, 14 Feb., 14 March 1919
40 *Voice*, 23 March 1917, 15 March, 12 April, 17 May 1918; *WLN*, 4 Oct. 1918
41 *LG* 19 (Dec. 1919), 1454
42 Kathleen Derry and Paul H. Douglas, 'The Minimum Wage in Canada,' *Journal of Political Economy* (April 1922): 156–74. See also Marie Campbell, 'Sexism in British Columbia Trade Unions, 1900–1920,' in *In Her Own Right: Selected Essays on Women's History in BC*, ed. Barbara Latham and Cathy Kess (Victoria, 1981), 179–80. *LG*, 19 (Dec. 1919), 1453–4.
43 *LG* 18 (July 1918), 537
44 See the tabular summary, published in *LG* 20 (April 1920), 466–8.
45 *LG* 19 (July 1919), 846; *WLN*, 22 Aug. 1919
46 *LG* 19 (Sept. 1919), 1093–4.
47 Ibid.
48 *Tribune* (Winnipeg), 1, 15, 2 April 1919. *WLN*, 18, 4 April 1919
49 E.J. Campbell, '"The Balance Wheel of the Industrial System": Maximum Hours, Minimum Wage, and Workmen's Compensation Legislation in Ontario, 1900–1939' (PhD diss., McMaster University, 1980), 23
50 On the overall strike pattern, see Douglas Cruickshank and Gregory S. Kealey, 'Strikes in Canada, 1891–1950,' *Labour/Le Travail* 20 (Fall 1987): Table A, 134.
51 RG 27, vol. 303, strike 9 (1914); *Ladies' Garment Worker* (hereafter *LGW*), July 1914 (resolution for a general strike in Montreal and Toronto)
52 RG 27, vol. 304, strike 18a (1917); vol. 306, strike 34 (ACWA) and strike 35 (ILGWU) both 1917
53 *LGW*, Jan., Feb., and July 1917, April 1918
54 RG 27, vol. 308, strike 52 (1918); *Globe*, 18 Jan. 1918 (report of six men arrested); RG 27, vol. 311, strike 65 (1919)

55  RG 27, vol. 311, strike 51 (1919)
56  On the garment workers' plans to present new demands in June, see *Star*, 4 June 1919; on the events of the strike, see also *IB*, 4 July 1919; *Star*, 8, 10, 12 July 1919 (visit of ILGWU president Schlesinger and meeting with workers).
57  See *Star*, 4 July 1919, for Koldofsky's comments on Gentiles. Arrests and trials of women strikers appear in *Star*, 15, 17, 30 July 1919, and in clippings contained in RG 27, vol. 316, strike 254 (1919). The strikers had decided to abandon the strike in mid-Aug. but renewed the struggle soon after; see *Daily Star*, 21 Aug. 1919. The settlement and criticisms of the strikers for almost abandoning the strike appeared in *Justice*, 13, 20 Sept. 1919.
58  RG 27, vol. 318, no. 423 (Marieville) and no. 410 (Montreal), 1919–20. Three of four Montreal companies 'agreed to union conditions,' according to the millinery workers' union representative. The Marieville workers belonged to the United Cloth Hat and Cap Makers of America, Local 48.
59  RG 27, vol. 324, strikes 395, 396, and 396a (1920–1)
60  RG 27, vol. 306, strike 71 (1917); vol. 308, strikes 77 and 85 (1918); see also L. Anders Sandberg, 'Dependent Development, Labour, and the Trenton Steel Works, Nova Scotia, c.1900–1943,' *Labour/Le Travail* 27 (Spring 1991): 127–62.
61  RG 27, vol. 308, strike 84 (1918); RG 27, vol. 308, strike 87 (1918). Note also that these two strikes prompted Mark Irish to telegraph the minister of labour to suggest arbitration in such cases to avoid disruption in production. To Irish's disgust, the order-in-council that resulted was permissive rather than mandatory, in suggesting the use of conciliation boards prior to strikes and lockouts. Irish wrote to Flavelle in August: 'For spineless cowardice and double-faced action can this be excelled? Oh you fearless Union Government!' See NAC, Flavelle Papers, MG 30, A 16, vol. 38, 27 June 1918 and 24 Aug. 1918.
62  See Maurine Weiner Greenwald, *Women, War, and Work: The Impact of World War I on Women Workers in the United States* (Westport, CT, 1980). RG 27, vol. 309, strike 140 (1918); see also *BC Federationist*, 24 Nov. 1916 (union men will not object as long as women receive equal pay); *Canadian Labor Leader*, 22 June 1918 (story on the Brantford, Ontario, TLC's condemnation of a proposal to employ girls or returned men since the present employees do not receive a living wage); NAC, Flavelle Papers, MG 30, A 16, vol. 38, Irish to Fitzgerald, 28 June 1918, commenting on his pessimism about labour unrest, cited the opposition of the Toronto Street Railway men to putting women on cars, noting that the men might go out as threatened. Two strikes in Moose Jaw in 1919 also reveal the employment of some women as conductors; the strikes occurred over wages, hours, and conditions. See RG 27, vol. 315, strike 210 (1919) and vol. 317, strike 296 (1919).

63 *Ottawa Citizen*, 9, 10 Feb., 26 March, 1915. The vast majority of women earned seven dollars per week.

64 *Ottawa Citizen*, 16 Dec. 1915; see also RG 27, vol. 304, no. 46 (1915).

65 RG 27, vol. 308, no. 71a (1918)

66 *LG*, 17 (Nov. 1917); RG 27, vol. 307, strike 133 (1917). See also University of British Columbia, Special Collections, Hotel, Restaurant and Culinary Employees and Bartenders Union, Local 28, Minutes, box 4 (6 Jan. 1910 to 21 Jan. 1921), 5, 19 Oct., 16, 23 Nov. and 21 Dec. 1917. James Robert Conley, 'Class Conflict and Collective Action in the Working Class of Vancouver, BC, 1900–1919' (PhD diss., Carleton University, 1986), 650–5. See also Dorothy Sue Cobble, *Dishing It Out: Waitresses and Their Unions in the Twentieth Century* (Chicago, 1991), which argues that separate female locals helped stimulate union membership and leadership among American waitresses.

67 RG 27, vol. 310, strike 178 and 179 (1918)

68 Ibid., strike 180 (1918); Local 28, Minutes, 31 July, 1, 5, 6 August, no date (7 Aug.?) 1918. Smith was a prominent club woman and reformer who was elected to the provincial legislature as an independent, after the death of her husband, Ralph Smith, left his Vancouver constituency vacant. She was re-elected as a Liberal in 1920, 1924, and 1930 and became the first woman cabinet member in the British Empire (1921) and first woman speaker of the provincial legislature (1928). See Linda L. Hale, 'Appendix. Votes for Women: Profiles of Prominent BC Suffragists and Social Reformers' in *In Her Own Right*, ed. Latham and Kass, 299–300.

69 RG 27, vol. 310, strike 182 (1918)

70 Provincial Archives of British Columbia, Ellen Barber interview, tape 3607 (interviewed by Sara Diamond). See also Star Rosenthal, 'Union Maids: Organized Women Workers in Vancouver, 1900–1915,' *BC Studies* 41 (Spring 1979): 36–55. On race and gender in the province, see Alicja Muszynski, *Cheap Wage Labour: Race and Gender in the Fisheries of British Columbia* (Montreal and Kingston, 1996).

71 Conley, 'Class Conflict and Collective Action,' 664–5; Barber tape, 3607–2, side one

72 See, for example, Linda Kealey, '"No Special Protection – No Sympathy": Women's Activism in the Canadian Labour Revolt of 1919' in *Class, Community, and the Labour Movement: Wales and Canada, 1850–1930*, ed. Deian R. Hopkin and Gregory S. Kealey (Aberystwyth, 1989), 134–59, on the WLL and testimony from women at Mathers's Commission hearings. See also Temma Kaplan, 'Women and Communal Strikes in the Crisis of 1917–1922' in *Becoming Visible: Women in European History*, 2nd ed., eds. Renate Bridenthal, Claudia Koonz, and Susan Stuard (Boston, 1987), 429–49.

73  *Globe*, 24, 25, 26, and 28 May 1917
74  Ibid., 26 May 1917
75  Ibid., 29 May 1917; see also Stephen Speisman, *The Jews of Toronto: A History to 1937* (Toronto, 1979), 195–6, for a brief discussion that draws upon other newspaper sources. Speisman also reports several incidents of damaging bread or flour and the storming of Goldenberg's restaurant by one hundred women who confiscated the bread and distributed it to the poor. Speisman claims that these actions were led by 'respectable' citizens since the meetings occurred in the McCaul Street Synagogue and the Zionist Institute; commentary in the press, however, notes the absence of 'the better class of Jew and Jewess,' *Globe*, 29 May 1917.
76  *Globe*, 30 May, 2, 11, and 20 June 1917. While research into the Yiddish press would undoubtedly shed further light on the possibility of frictions within the Jewish community between old and new immigrants, the leadership of women in this dispute remains key.

**6: 'This Crimson Storm of War'**

1  For a detailed look at Beynon, McNaughton, Hughes, and Richardson see Barbara Roberts, '"Why Do Women Do Nothing to End the War?": Canadian Feminist-Pacifists and the Great War' CRIAW Paper no. 13 (1985).
2  *BC Federationist*, 27 Sept. 1918
3  *Canadian Forward* (hereafter *CF*), 24 March 1917
4  Jane Slaughter and Robert Kern, eds., *European Women on the Left: Socialism, Feminism and the Problems Faced by Political Women, 1880 to the Present* (Westport, CT, 1981), 5; for the prewar period's debates see Linda Kealey, 'Canadian Socialism and the Woman Question, 1900–1914,' *Labour/Le Travail* 13 (Spring 1984): 77–100, and chapter 4 in this volume.
5  An attempt to estimate enlistment rates, based on the available pool of men, can be found in C.A. Sharpe, 'Enlistment in the Canadian Expeditionary Force, 1914–1918: A Regional Analysis,' *Journal of Canadian Studies* 18, 4 (Winter 1983–4): 15–29. See also John Herd Thompson, *The Harvests of War: The Prairie West, 1914–1918* (Toronto, 1978), chap. 3. For a general history of conscription in Canada see J.L. Granatstein and J.M. Hitsman, *Broken Promises: A History of Conscription in Canada* (Toronto, 1977).
6  See the discussion of women's war-related activities in Veronica Strong-Boag, *The Parliament of Women: The National Council of Women of Canada, 1893–1929* (Ottawa, 1976), chap. 7; National Archives of Canada (NAC), Flavelle Papers, MG 30 A16, file 38, Mark Irish to George Edwards, Comptroller, IMB, 1 June 1917.

7 For the Calgary Consumers' League, see Strong-Boag, *Parliament of Women*, 317. For farm women's activities see, for example, the Manitoba Grain Growers' *Yearbook* (1919), 51, in the Provincial Archives of Manitoba (hereafter PAM), MG10 E1, box 15, for a report of 1918 activities of the Women's Section of the Manitoba Grain Growers' Association. Mrs J.S. Wood notes in her address the amount of money raised by farm women in her district of Oakville as well as the number of items of clothing and packages sent overseas. Similar accounts can be found in the minutes and annual reports of farm women's organizations in Alberta and Saskatchewan. On thrift campaigns, see Barbara M. Wilson, *Ontario and the First World War, 1914–1918* (Toronto, 1977), xcii–xciii. On rural-urban cooperation see the Saskatoon meeting on food conservation in Saskatchewan Archives Board (hereafter SAB) (Saskatoon), Local Council of Women, Minutes, 4 Sept. 1917. Violet McNaughton spoke on food conservation and the need for price controls.

8 Strong-Boag, *Parliament of Women*, chap. 7; NAC, Employment for Women File, MG 28 I25 V.66, F.A. Acland to Mrs Cummings, 19 Aug. 1916; B.M. McKenna to Mrs Huestis, 7 Feb. 1917, and other letters in the same file.

9 Roberts, 'Why Do Women,' 2, and Carol Lee Bacchi, *Liberation Deferred? The Ideas of the English-Canadian Suffragists, 1877–1918* (Toronto, 1983), 139–41. This 1917 act gave the vote to women relatives of soldiers and disenfranchised all citizens of enemy alien birth if they had been naturalized after 31 March 1902. Members of pacifist religious groups and other conscientious objectors were also deprived of the vote.

10 Ian Angus, *Canadian Bolsheviks: The Early Years of the Communist Party of Canada* (Montreal, 1981), 8; *Western Clarion* (hereafter *WC*), 1 March 1915

11 Angus, *Canadian Bolsheviks*, 12–14, and chap. 1 in general. On Ukrainians who were interned as Austrians, see Orest T. Martynowych and Nadia Kazymyra, 'Political Activity in Western Canada, 1896–1923' in *A Heritage in Transition*, ed. Manoly R. Lupul (Toronto, 1982), 96–100. See also chap. 7 below.

12 Angus, *Canadian Bolsheviks*, 16–18; Warren Caragata, *Alberta Labour: A Heritage Untold* (Toronto, 1979), 55–60; Thompson, *Harvests of War*, chap. 6.

13 *Voice*, 15 June 1917, 8 Feb. 1918; Caragata, *Alberta Labour*, 58–60; David Bercuson, *Confrontation at Winnipeg: Labour, Industrial Relations, and the General Strike* (Montreal, 1974), 40–4. See also J.M. Bliss, *A Canadian Millionaire: The Life and Business Times of Sir Joseph Flavelle, Bart., 1858–1939* (Toronto, 1978), 320–5.

14 See, for example, articles in the *Grain Grower's Guide* (hereafter *GGG*), 9 Dec., 30 Dec. 1914; *WC*, 1 March 1915, carried a notice of Sophie Mushkat's speech in Alberta, 'War and Its Effects on Humanity'; *Cotton's Weekly* (hereafter *CW*),

15 Oct. 1914; see Roberts, 'Why Do Women,' for comments on maternal ideology. On the women's peace movement in Canada generally, see Barbara Roberts, 'Women's Peace Activism in Canada' in *Beyond the Vote: Canadian Women and Politics* ed. Linda Kealey and Joan Sangsten (Toronto, 1989), 276–308.

15 *CW*, 15 Oct. 1914; *Nutcracker* (hereafter *NC*), 3 Feb. 1916; *GGG*, 2 Sept. 1914; Roberts, 'Why Do Women,' 7. Much of the following discussion on women socialist pacifists is directly inspired by Barbara Roberts's article.

16 Roberts, 'Why Do Women,' 11. Roberts makes the point that Beynon was a radical although not a member of any socialist organization; on this point see also the different interpretation of Ramsay Cook, 'Francis Marion Beynon and the Crisis of Christian Reformism' in *The West and the Nation*, eds. Carl Berger and Ramsay Cook (Toronto, 1976), 187–208.

17 See Beynon's editorial 'Democracy' in *CF*, 10 Dec. 1917. The Wartime Elections Act was heavily criticized by the Winnipeg WLL and by some LCW branches as well as other groups.

18 See Roberts, 'Why Do Women,' 20–6 on Richardson; *Leicester Pioneer*, 31 Aug. 1917 (thanks to Barbara Roberts for this reference). See also Barbara Roberts, *A Reconstructed World: A Feminist Biography of Gertrude Richardson* (Montreal and Kingston, 1996).

19 *CF*, 24 Oct. 1917; other letters can be found in *CF*, 10 July, 24 Sept., 24 Nov. 1917; 10 March, 10 April, 10 July 1918. See also a biographical sketch of Richardson in *CF*, 10 Sept. 1917 and her poem 'A Call to Women,' *CF*, 24 Aug. 1918. *CF*, 24 Nov. 1917, contains a letter from Mrs R.C. Maxwell of Corner Clarke Harbour, New Brunswick, justifying pacifism. The *Voice* also carried letters by Richardson on the Women's Crusade; see especially 19 Oct., 30 Nov. 1917, 22 Feb. 1918. Letter to Violet McNaughton as cited in Roberts, 'Why Do Women,' 25

20 *Voice*, 19 Oct. 1917; on Richardson's breakdown, see Roberts, 'Women's Peace Activism,' 285.

21 Roberts, 'Why Do Women,' 15–20

22 The founding meeting of Toronto's WILPF in June 1915 appears in Frances Early, 'The Historic Roots of the Women's Peace Movement in North America,' *Canadian Woman Studies* 7, 4 (Winter 1986): 45. See also Roberts, 'Why Do Women' 3, and her 'Women's Peace Activism,' 280–1. Thomas Socknat, *Witness Against War: Pacifism in Canada, 1900–1945* (Toronto, 1987), 55–9, discusses the Toronto pacifist women as well. The rivalries between Hughes and Prenter are evident in correspondence contained in the University of Colorado Libraries, Western Historical Collections (Boulder), WILPF Records, 1915–66. See in particular II 1–23, 25 Feb. 1920, Laura Hughes

Lunde to Emily Balch. Xeroxes of Canadian materials provided by Barbara Roberts. Opposition to discussion of the Hague Congress appear in the *Voice*, 30 April, 7 May 1915; the latter issue noted the Winnipeg LCW's resolution condemning the Hague Congress.

23 *Voice*, 16 Oct. 1914. See also Maine socialist Grace Silver's comments on the Patriotic Fund in *International Socialist Review* 15 (1914–15): 479–80.

24 On Canadian patriotic activities during the war see Robert M. Bray, 'The Canadian Patriotic Response to the Great War' (PhD diss., York University, 1976); *NC*, 10 May 1917. For general information on mothers' pensions see Veronica Strong-Boag, 'Wages for Housework: Mothers' Allowances and the Beginnings of Social Security in Canada,' *Journal of Canadian Studies* 14, 1 (Spring 1979): 24–34.

25 *Calgary Herald* (hereafter *CH*), 22 Nov. 1916; *Voice*, 13 Oct. 1916. See Thompson, *Harvest of War*, 165–6, for evidence cited of the hardships faced by next-of-kin; see also Desmond Morton and Glenn Wright, 'The Bonus Campaign, 1919–1921: Veterans and the Campaign for Re-establishment,' *Canadian Historical Review* 64, 2 (June 1983): 154. For separation allowances see the Department of National Defence papers at the NAC, RG 24, vol. 1252–4, which contain the substantial correspondence relating to these allowances. PC 2266, 4 Sept. 1914, established the separation allowance level by rank: the rank and file received $20 per month, sergeants received $25, and the highest rank of colonels or lieutenant-colonels received $60 per month for dependants. Subsequent orders-in-council modified or revised the amounts and the regulations pertaining to them. For increases in 1917 and 1918 see PC 3257 (29 Nov. 1917) and PC 2573 (7 Nov. 1918). The memorandum from the accountant and paymaster general can be found in RG 24, vol. 1253, 7 Nov. 1917. This same memorandum noted that a private's widow without children received a pension of $40 per month, an increase of $8. An increase of $5 per month in the separation allowance (to $25 per month) plus $15 from the soldier's pay would give the soldier's wife $40 per month, and thus a woman without children should not have to depend on the Patriotic Fund for assistance. Thanks to Glenn Wright for leading me to these materials.

26 *NC*, 13 April 1917. For critical assessment of the budgets and indexes used by the Department of Labour, see Gordon Bertram and Michael Percy, 'Real Wage Trends in Canada, 1900–1926' *Canadian Journal of Economics* 12 (1979): 299–312.

27 *Labour Gazette* (hereafter *LG*) 20 (Jan. 1920), 79; *LG* 18 (Jan. 1918), 49; *LG* 19 (Aug. 1919), 1005; Glenbow-Alberta Institute, UMWA, District 18 Collection, Convention Proceedings, 1919, typescript, 105

28 For a discussion of the minimum wage campaign in Manitoba, see Linda

Kealey, 'Women and Labour during World War I: Women Workers and the Minimum Wage in Manitoba' in *First Days, Fighting Days: Women in Manitoba History,* ed. Mary Kinnear (Regina, 1987), 76–99, and chapter 5 above.

29 See, for example, the *Lance,* 14 Sept. 1912, 1, for Rose Henderson's activities on behalf of mothers' pensions (speech given at the Guelph meeting of the TLC). Henderson also spoke on this topic at the 1914 Social Service Congress of Canada meeting. See Social Service Council of Canada, *The Social Service Congress of Canada, 1914* (Toronto, 1914), 89–115. See also discussions in the *BC Federationist,* 26 Feb., 30 April 1915. On Manitoba, see the *Voice,* 3 July 1914, 12 March, 20 Aug. 1915, 3 March 1916 (act passed by the Manitoba legislature). For a general overview, see Strong-Boag, 'Wages for Housework.'

30 Jean McWilliam McDonald, 'Memoir' (typescript), Provincial Archives of Alberta (72.338 SE); McWilliam McDonald Collection, Glenbow-Alberta Institute (M724, file 7); *CH,* 25 July 1981 (clipping in McWilliam McDonald Collection). Jean McWilliam (later McDonald) was born in Ireland in 1877 and raised in Scotland. Her father was a pig-iron lifter and a staunch defender of the working class. With the death of her mother she became a domestic and eventually received training in butter and cheese making. After their marriage she and her husband worked as hired hands on a dairy farm before moving to Canada in 1907 with their two surviving children. Both worked as hired hands in Ontario before moving west. While her husband attempted to homestead, McWilliam rented a house in Calgary and worked as a cleaning woman until she had enough money to open a boarding house. The war and the Russian Revolution converted her to socialism. Her second husband, William A. McDonald, was a painter by trade who died in 1950. McWilliam died in 1969.

31 *Voice,* 7 Sept 1917; on Coutts, see note 35 below.

32 *Voice,* 7 Sept 1917; see also 27 July 1917, for an account of the passing of a resolution for a general strike to bring the concerns of the working class, including conscription of wealth and higher pensions for soldiers' dependants, to the attention of government. This resolution was passed at a meeting of the Unity Club, an organization of women in the Unitarian Church, and sent in by Rachel Coutts.

33 *Alberta Non-Partisan* (hereafter *ANP*), 15 March 1918; *CH,* 4, 5, 8 March 1918; *ANP,* 10 May 1918

34 *CH,* 25 May 1917, 6 March 1918. Mrs Grevette (sometimes Grevett) was also a long-time member of the LCW, which she joined in 1919; later, she was president of the WLL. Her husband was a clerk at the CPR. See Pat Roome 'Amelia Turner and Calgary Labour Women, 1919–1935' in *Beyond the Vote,* ed. Kealey and Sangster, 112n 26.

35 Anthony Mardiros, *William Irvine: The Life of a Prairie Radical* (Toronto, 1979),

36–8. See the obituary of Mrs William Carson in *CH*, 15 July 1950. Rachel Coutts and her sister, Marion Carson (1861–1950), came from an Ontario family in Kent County. Carson moved to Manitoba as a child and in 1898 moved to Calgary with her husband, William Carson, who became a grain merchant. Rachel Coutts lived with the Carsons while she taught school in Calgary. Both Marion and Rachel were pacifists; the former became a pacifist after her son's death in 1917. Carson's obituary lists three surviving daughters and two sons. The date of Rachel Coutts's death is not known, but she seems to have died before her sister. Information obtained from *CH*, 15 July 1950, and *Henderson's City Directory*, Calgary, 1910–19. The organization of the Next-of-Kin Association in Calgary is covered in *NC*, 10 May 1917; the organizational meeting is described in the *Voice*, 18 May 1917; the joint meeting of the association with the UFWA and Women's Institutes appears in *CH*, 1 May 1918. Carson's farm experiences are discussed in *ANP*, 12 Aug. 1918.

36  On the Edmonton Next-of-Kin, see Edmonton *Journal*, 2, 4, 7 July 1919. On Carson and Coutts, see also Pat Roome, 'Amelia Turner.'

37  *CF*, 10 April, 24 March 1917

38  *Voice*, 10 Aug., 31 Aug. 1917; *Tribune* (Winnipeg), 3, 5, 6, 7 Aug. 1918

39  Socknat, *Witness to War*, chap. 3; Gertrude Richardson, 'The Workers' Council of Canada,' *Leicester Pioneer*, 7 Dec. 1917

40  Disturbances were reported for Kitchener, Ontario, in *CF*, 12 June 1917; in Guelph, Ontario, and Toronto in *CF*, 25 June 1917. For Winnipeg, see the *Voice*, 30 Nov. 1917, and *Leicester Pioneer*, 14 Dec. 1917, for Helen Armstrong's activities as reported by Richardson. For Montreal and Toronto, see *CF*, 24 May 1917; this entire issue is filled with comments on conscription. For Vancouver anti-conscription meetings, see *CF*, 12 June (threat of general strike), and 25 June 1917 (report of five large meetings that attracted twelve hundred to five thousand people or more). One of these was SPC-sponsored and attended by two thousand people. See *WC*, June 1917.

41  *WC*, June 1915; for Pritchard's series see *WC*, April, May, June, Sept. 1918. See also comments in the *Voice*, 10, 17 Aug. 1917, by John Gabriel Soltis. On 10 August, Soltis wrote concerning the socialist future: 'The work of the world will be performed by men and not by children, maidens and old women.' On 17 Aug. he noted that the war enabled capitalists to replace men with cheap female labour, and he prophesied that even in the postwar period, women and children would continue to supply the labour power for industry. The theme of women's competition with men's labour can also be found in Pritchard's 'After the War' article in *WC*, April 1918, and 'Women's Emancipation,' 16 May 1920.

42  *WC*, 6 June 1914; Caragata, *Alberta Labour*, 58; David Bercuson, *Fools and Wise-*

*men: The Rise and Fall of the One Big Union* (Toronto, 1978), 109–11. Johnston-Knight is listed as secretary of the Alberta Provincial Executive in *WC*, Aug. 1915, Feb. 1916, Jan. and Sept. 1918. For Johnston-Knight's arrest and trial see Winnipeg *Tribune*, 3, 5, 12 Oct. 1918; *Western Labor News* (hereafter *WLN*) 4, 18 Oct. 1918; *WC*, 15 Oct. 1918.

43 PAM, R.B. Russell Collection, MG16 A14/1, box 3, file 7, Johnston-Knight to Russell, 13 Jan. 1919. *WC*, 16 Aug. 1920, notes Johnston-Knight's resignation as secretary of Local Toronto. See Angus, *Canadian Bolsheviks*, 70, for information on the Knights in the CP.

44 On contributors to the John Reid fund, *WC*, Oct., 1915; on Gribble and Currie, see *WC*, March 1916. For John Reid's Alberta organizing tour, involving Mrs Nickeleff [*sic*], from Ponoka, and Mrs Schunerman, from Evarts, see *WC*, 27 March 1915; Reid's arrest is noted in *WC*, Aug. 1915, which also lists Mrs J.R. Macdonald, from Flowerdale, and Sophie Mushkat, of Hillcrest, as on the executive. Joseph R. Knight's organizing tour was aided by Mrs Charles Myers, Lacombe, and Mrs E. Thorburn, Sundial; see *WC*, Nov. 1915. Women contributors to the Reid fund were listed in *WC*, Sept. 1915 (ten women); Oct. 1915 (six women), March 1916 (Mrs Hitchcox, Edmonton), May 1916 (seven women). *WC*, Jan. 1918, reported Mrs Hitchcox and Mrs J.R. Macdonald as contributors to the anti-conscription fund.

45 *CW*, 4 June, 29 April 1914; *GGG*, 30, 16 Sept., 7 Oct. 1914

46 SAB (Saskatoon), Mrs S.V. Haight Papers, GS 8, A5, file 3, Erma Stocking to Mrs Haight, 26 Jan. 1916. 'The Women Grain Growers' Association and Its Objects,' ibid., file 7 (speeches); see Haight's speech, 'Women's Work in the Legislation of the Future' in Glenbow-Alberta Institute, Tom Williams Collection, M 1718. Parlby's letter to McNaughton is found at the SAB (Saskatoon), Violet McNaughton Papers, A1 D 54, Parlby to McNaughton, 14 Dec. 1919; Mrs Root's letter appeared in the *Western Independent*, 1 Oct. 1919; she and Mrs Dowler were elected to the board of directors of the UFWA in 1917; see United Farmers of Alberta, *Annual Report and Year Book* (Calgary, 1918), 319; during 1918, Mrs Root organized nineteen of the fifty-five new UFWA locals; see UFA, *Annual Report, 1918* (Calgary, 1919), 78.

47 On Irvine and his activities, see Mardiros, *William Irvine*. A more thorough treatment of Amelia Turner and Edith Patterson is found in Roome, 'Amelia Turner,' in *Beyond the Vote*, ed. Kealey and Sangster, 89–117. Patterson and Turner became involved in the Unitarian Church and the People's Forum; Turner also worked at the NPL office and later the UFA office and ran for office as a CCF candidate in the 1930s. All these women became involved in the WLL and labour party politics after the war. *CF*, 10 Nov. 1917; *ANP*, 19 June 1919

48 On the threat of the foreigner, see Donald Avery, *'Dangerous Foreigners': European Immigrant Workers and Labour Radicalism in Canada, 1896–1932* (Toronto, 1979); Gregory S. Kealey, 'The State, the Foreign Language Press, and the Canadian Labour Revolt of 1917–1920' in *The Press of Labor Migrants in Europe and North America, 1880s to 1930s*, ed. Christiane Harzig and Dirk Hoerder, (Bremen, 1985), 311–45.
49 *Voice*, 7 Sept. 1917
50 *CF*, 24 March 1917
51 *Voice*, 14, 21 Sept., 7 Dec. 1917
52 Helen Armstrong was arrested several times during the 1919 Winnipeg General Strike: see chapter 7 below. Mendelssohn was arrested in Montreal in June 1919 for failing to get the city's permission to hold a rally: see chapter 5 above. Varpu Lindström-Best discusses Sanna Kannasto's arrest in Alberta in early 1920 in *Defiant Sisters: A Social History of Finnish Immigrant Women in Canada* (Toronto, 1988), 150–1. On Henderson, see NAC, RG 13 A2, vol. 239, file 1877, Charles Lanctot to the Minister of Justice, 15 July 1919. The seized letters are found in PAM, King vs. Ivens, RG4 A1, box 3.

## 7: 'No Special Protections ... No Sympathy'

1 See Mary Kinnear, 'Post-Suffrage Prairie Politics: Women Candidates in Winnipeg Municipal Elections, 1918–1939,' *Prairie Forum* 16, 1 (Spring 1991): 41–57.
2 Quoted in ibid., 48
3 Contrary to David Bercuson's claim that recent literature on 1919 does not substantially alter his interpretation, it should be evident by now that this work has significantly altered the historical view he presents. See David Bercuson, *Confrontation at Winnipeg: Labour, Industrial Relations, and the General Strike*, 2nd ed. (Montreal and Kingston, 1990), especially the new section, 'A Longer View,' 196–205.
4 Ruth Milkman, ed., *Women, Work, and Protest: A Century of Women's Labor History* (Boston, 1985), usefully cautions against substituting a new myth of militancy for old myths of passivity among women workers. She notes that we need to know which historical circumstances encourage or impede women's militancy and suggests that effective mobilization utilizes forms rooted in women's culture and experience. Furthermore, she notes that it is instructive to examine the structural characteristics of unionism as well as the impact of the broader gender ideology. See also James Naylor, *The New Democracy: Challenging the Social Order in Industrial Ontario, 1914–1925*, chap. 5, for the influence of maternalism on working-class women.

5  Gregory S. Kealey, 'The State, the Foreign Language Press and the Canadian Labour Revolt of 1917–1920' in *The Press of Labor Migrants in Europe and North America, 1880s to 1930s*, ed. Christiane Harzig and Dirk Hoerder (Bremen, 1985), 311–45; see also Donald Avery, *'Dangerous Foreigners': European Immigrant Workers and Labour Radicalism in Canada, 1896–1932* (Toronto, 1979).

6  Quote from Mary Horodyski, 'Women and the Winnipeg General Strike of 1919,' *Manitoba History* 11 (Spring 1986): 29

7  *Globe*, 16 May 1919; *Western Labor News* (hereafter *WLN*), 16 May 1919; Armstrong reported that knitting and laundry women were organized. *WLN*, 20 May 1919, announced a day-long meeting for the purpose of organizing all women workers. Organizing meetings for specific groups of women workers were reported in the *WLN* throughout the course of the strike. Armstrong's arrest was reported in the *Globe*, and the *Star*, 17 May 1919. The dining room was mentioned in *WLN*, 23 May 1919, under the auspices of the WLL and the administration of Helen Armstrong. Donations of food were requested in the same edition of the *WLN*. The opening of the dining room is reported in the *WLN*, 24 May 1919. Examples of Labour Church collections for the dining room appear in *WLN*, 26, 27 May, and 2 June 1919. The WLL authorized fundraising events for the dining room, as fragmentary evidence from the exhibits collected for the trial of the Winnipeg General Strike leaders shows. See Provincial Archives of Manitoba (hereafter PAM), RG 4 A1, King vs. William Ivens, Exhibit 175, 11 June 1919.

8  For the Relief Committee's role, see Horodyski, 'Women and the Winnipeg General Strike,' 30, and *WLN*, 23 May 1919. For the YWCA's role, see Horodyski, 'Women and the Winnipeg General Strike,' 30. Offers of rooms for striking women appear in *WLN*, 27 May 1919.

9  See Horodyski, 'Women and the Winnipeg General Strike,' 31, and *WLN*, 16 May 1919, for confectionery workers; for store clerks, see Horodyski, 'Women, and the Winnipeg General Strike,' 32, and *WLN*, 19 May 1919. Investigations of women's work in department stores occurred in 1914 under the auspices of the University Women's Club and in early 1919 by the Minimum Wage Board. See Linda Kealey, 'Women and Labour during World War I: Women Workers and the Minimum Wage in Manitoba' in *First Days, Fighting Days: Women in Manitoba History*, ed. Mary Kinnear (Regina, 1987). On Armstrong's campaign among clerks in small stores, see the *Tribune* (Winnipeg), 26 May 1919.

10  On the organization of waitresses, see Kealey, 'Women and Labour during World War I.' See *WLN*, 3, 10, 24, and 31 Jan. 1919, for the drive to increase the membership of the union. *WLN*, 16 May 1919, reported the union as nearly 100 per cent organized and showed that culinary workers supported

the general strike. Lockouts are listed in *WLN*, 27 May 1919. For a report on the evasions of the minimum wage, see *WLN*, 10, and 17 Oct. 1919; *Tribune* (Winnipeg), 27 June 1919; *WLN*, 28 June, 9 July 1919. Reorganization of the union is discussed in *WLN*, 29 Aug. 1919, 7 Nov. 1919. The international organizer, Mackenzie, in *WLN*, 24 Sept. 1920, noted that the union was 'badly shaken' during the 1919 strike but was recovering.

11 For a discussion of the telephone operators activities in 1917 and 1918, see Kealey, 'Women and Labour during World War I' and Horodyski, 'Women and the Winnipeg General Strike' 32–3. *WLN*, 19, 20, 21, 24, 26 May 1919. Intimidation is reported in *WLN*, 3 June 1919. *WLN*, 14 June 1919, reported the arrival in Winnipeg of six operators from Carman who had been replaced. The statement of Telephone Commissioner George A. Watson is reprinted in the *Star*, 19 June 1919. The *Tribune* (Winnipeg), 27 June 1919, reported 225 vacancies, 350 applications, and the loss of seniority as well as the 'no strike' pledge. Doris Meakin's statement is found in the Toronto *Star*, 30 June 1919.

12 Helen Armstrong's report to the Winnipeg TLC is in *WLN*, 3 July 1919. The *WLN*, 10 July 1919, reported 119 operators had been refused reinstatement.

13 *Star*, 4 June 1919. *WLN*, 5 June 1919. *Tribune* (Winnipeg), 6 June 1919; *Star*, 7 June 1919; *Tribune* (Winnipeg), 10 June 1919; the *Star* noted that Mrs J. McCrom was fined twenty dollars and costs for assaulting a delivery truck driver; see *Star*, 13 June 1919. On 19 June 1919, the *Star* reported twenty women and men strikers has been fined or imprisoned on charges of intimidation. Bloody Saturday, 21 June, followed the arrest of the strike leaders late in the evening of 16 June and in the early hours of 17 June. A silent parade to protest these arrests turned into a riot when special police and the RNWMP attacked the protesters, killing one person and injuring others. Mayor Gray's statement was quoted in the *Star*, 24 June 1919.

14 The arrests of Armstrong, Krantz, and Steinhauer were reported in the *Tribune* (Winnipeg), 13 June 1919. Armstrong was committed for trial on 27 June, and the other two were tried on the same day. See the *Tribune* (Winnipeg), 24 June 1919; *Star*, 25 June 1919; *Tribune* (Winnipeg), 27, 28 June 1919; *WLN*, 27 June 1919; *Star*, 28 June 1919; *WLN*, 28 June 1919. For the account of Helen Armstrong's actions regarding her husband's arrest, see the *Star*, 19 June 1919.

15 See *WLN*, 15 Aug. 1919, for the quote from Gouldie.

16 The protest parade is described in *WLN*, 5 Sept. 1919, and in the One Big Union *Bulletin*, 6 Sept. 1919. Helen Armstrong's speech at the rink and the petition campaign are covered in the *Tribune* (Winnipeg), 8, 9 Sept. 1919. *WLN*, 12 Sept. 1919, reports the release of George Armstrong on bail. Strike

leaders were officially welcomed at a reception sponsored by the WLL and others; one thousand people turned out according to *WLN*, 19 Sept. 1919.

17  *WLN*, 19 Dec. 1919

18  For Montreal, see Geoffrey Ewen, 'La Contestation à Montréal en 1919,' *Histoire de Travailleurs Québécois* (Bulletin de RCHTQ) 36 (Automne 1986): 40–1.

19  Royal Commission on Industrial Relations, Evidence, Saskatoon, 7 May 1919, 1035–7; Regina, 8 May 1919, 1189–96

20  Gregory S. Kealey, '1919: The Canadian Labour Revolt,' *Labour/Le Travail* 13 (Spring 1984): 30; Saskatchewan Archives Board (Saskatoon), Minimum Wage Board, Minute Book, 1919–29, 11 June 1919.

21  For a discussion of the 1918 strikes, see Christine Smillie, 'The Invisible Workforce: Women Workers in Saskatchewan from 1905 to World War II,' *Saskatchewan History* 39, 2 (Spring 1986): 73–4.

22  The *Voice*, 16 March 1917, noted the creation of the Regina WLL; WLL activities reported in the Regina TLC Minutes, of 13 Aug. 1917, 28 April 1919, 8 Sept. 1919; the OBU support appears in *WLN*, 8 May 1919; on the general outlines of the Saskatchewan labour movement, see W.J.C. Cherwinski, 'Organized Labour in Saskatchewan, 1905–1945' (PhD diss., University of Alberta, 1972), especially chap. 2. For tensions within the Regina TLC, see Minutes of 2 June 1919 and 25 Aug. 1919. On the minimum wage issue see Regina TLC Minutes, 8 Sept. 1919.

23  On McWilliam's activities during the First World War and the class-conscious nature of Calgary's Next-of-Kin Association, see Linda Kealey, 'Prairie Socialist Women and WWI: The Urban West' (unpublished paper, 1986), and chapter 6 above; Royal Commission on Industrial Relations, Evidence, Calgary, 2 May 1919, 782–93 (McWilliam)

24  Royal Commission on Industrial Relations, Evidence, Calgary, 2 May 1919, 635–50 (Corse)

25  The United Brotherhood of Carpenters and Joiners, Local 1779 (Calgary), Minutes, 29 May 1919, Glenbow-Alberta Institute, record Mary Corse's presence as a representative of the Central Strike Committee. For more information on Corse, see Kealey, 'Prairie Socialist Women' and *Woman's Century*, April 1920, 25. The activities of the Women's Committee during the general sympathetic strike are covered in the Calgary *Strike Bulletin*, no. 2, 31 May 1919; no. 6, 7 June 1919; no. 8, 14 June 1919; no. 9, 16 June 1919; no. 10, 18 June 1919. The controversy over child health appears in the *Calgary Herald*, 24, 26 Nov. 1919, and in the *Searchlight*, 28 Nov. 1919, 20 Feb. 1920. The LWC also protested working conditions for waitresses at the CPR lunch counter and lobbied for changes to Alberta's Factory Act to benefit women workers. See *Edmonton Free Press*, 27 Dec. 1919, and *Searchlight*, 3 Sept. 1920. In 1920 the

LWC also took part in the Calgary Defence Committee, established to defend the Winnipeg General Strike leaders and the principles of collective bargaining and free speech.

26 See *Chronologie des mouvements politiques ouvriers au Québec de la fin du XIXe siècle à 1919*, Mai 1976, 258–93, published by the Regroupement de chercheurs en histoire des travailleurs québécois; Ewen, 'La contestation'; Gregory S. Kealey, '1919,' 22–3; The May Day parade is described by J. Lanch, 'May First in Montreal,' *Justice* (publication of the ILGWU), 10 May 1919. The rally in support of the Winnipeg General Strike is covered in the *Gazette*, 28 May 1919; it was sponsored by the IAM and the Amalgamated Society of Engineers. For Buhay and Mendelssohn see below note 28.

27 Royal Commission on Industrial Relations, Evidence, Montreal, 29 May 1919, 3147–68. As a widow with a daughter to bring up, Henderson moved from volunteer work to the juvenile court. She also had worked in factories, laundries, and restaurants, living and working with the young women employed there, according to a biographical note in the *Workers Weekly* 6 Aug. 1920. By 1920 she had joined the ILP, organizing in Ontario and the Maritimes. She also was a member of the WILPF. Later in her life she joined the CCF, and in 1935 she ran for a seat in Toronto where she lived in the last years of her life. She died in Toronto on 30 Jan. 1937. Many of the details of Henderson's life are missing, but see Richard Allen, *The Social Passion: Religion and Social Reform in Canada* (Toronto, 1971), 20. Her obituary appeared in the *Globe and Mail*, 4 Feb. 1937, and notes that the memorial service involved both the Quakers and the Theosophical Society.

28 *Gazette*, 28 May 1919; PAM, RG 4 A1, box 3, King vs. Ivens, Rose Henderson to R.B. Russell, no date; Royal Canadian Mounted Police (RCMP), Personal History File, Rebecca Buhay, 17 Nov. 1919, 1 July 1920; Annie Buller, 'In Memory of Becky Buhay,' *Marxist Quarterly* (Dec. 1957–Jan. 1958): 18–22. Buhay was born in London's East End in 1896, emigrated to Canada in 1913, and died in 1953. For more information on women in the Communist Party of Canada, see Joan Sangster, 'Canadian Women in Radical Politics and Labour, 1920–1950' (PhD diss., McMaster University, 1984), and her *Dreams of Equality: Women on the Canadian Left, 1920–1950* (Toronto, 1989). Two biographies published by the CP pay tribute to two prominent Montreal Communist women: Louise Watson, *She Never Was Afraid: The Biography of Annie Buller* (Toronto, 1976), provides glimpses of Buhay as well; Catherine Vance, *Not by Gods but by People: The Story of Bella Hall Gauld* (Toronto, 1968), also provides information on the other women. Bella Hall also testified before the Mathers Commission as a resident of the University Settlement on her work with immigrants. Her brief testimony underlined the poor health of immi-

grant children and the miserable living conditions in general. Hall came from Winnipeg where she worked at J.S. Woodsworth's All Peoples' Mission before moving to Montreal to work at the settlement.

29 *Daily Star*, 1 May, 2, 10 June 1919. The *Star*, 21 July 1919, commented on the split in the Montreal labour movement and listed Mendelssohn as actively working for the OBU; the *Daily Star*, 21 July 1919, carried a similar story on the OBU. National Archives of Canada (hereafter NAC), Records of the Post Office, RG 13, A 2, vol. 237, file 1537, J.N. Carter to A.J. Cawdron, 26 June 1919. A search of the *Call* has not turned up Mendelssohn's name.

30 *Star*, 29, 30 May 1919; see 22 May 1919, for a report on the general organizing drive led by H. Lewis of the TDLC, also a socialist. For the meat-packing strike, see *Star*, 5, 22, 23 May 1919. Three days before the meat-packing strike began on 5 May, several hundred women from the Cowan Chocolate and Cocoa Company struck for half a day for increases in wages and a reduction of hours, which they negotiated, despite the fact they were not unionized; by 22 May they had been unionized with the assistance of the TDLC. See *Eastern Federationist* (hereafter *EF*), 10 May 1919.

31 See reports in the *Edmonton Free Press*, 17 May, 21 June 1919; *Star*, 4, 21 July 1919; the *Star*, 3 July 1919, reported on a meeting of the Domestic Workers' Association that discussed a nine-hour day and a ten-dollar minimum, indicating that they had perhaps been unsuccessful in pushing the shorter day and higher wage. See also James Naylor, 'Toronto, 1919,' Canadian Historical Association *Historical Papers* (1986): 33–55.

32 The *Star*, 15 July 1919, reported on the address by Queen, Heaps, and Dunn. Armstrong's visit was reported in the *Daily Star*, 12, 19 Aug. 1919; see also the *Industrial Banner* (hereafter *IB*), 15, 29 Aug. 1919. The latter edition carried the critical remarks made by Armstrong. Armstrong's positive remarks appeared in *WLN*, 12 Sept. 1919.

33 See J. Nolan Reilly, 'The Emergence of Class Consciousness in Industrial Nova Scotia: A Study of Amherst, 1891–1925' (PhD diss., Dalhousie University, 1983), especially chap. 5 on the general strike. Newspapers, such as the *Eastern Federationist* occasionally reported on women's work and wages; see, for example, 10 May 1919; clerks in stores commonly received five to eight dollars per week. In other places like Windsor, near Amherst, the Nova Scotia Underwear Company exercised paternalist measures to keep its young female workforce unorganized and uncomplaining. The *EF*, 7 June 1919, accounted for the lack of labour unrest in the preceding seven years by the provision of company boarding houses for the women, who were largely from out of town. Other sporadic attempts at organizing are reported in the *EF*, 26 April 1919 (unorganized strike by women houseworkers in Sydney)

26 April 1919 (entertainment organized by the Keddy Textile Workers Union, Truro – this Stanfield operation was not recognized by the employer as a union); 10 May 1919 (women at Halifax chocolate factory owned by Moir went on strike for an eight-hour day and won, although not unionized). Women's activities in the mining communities of Pictou County and Cape Breton remain largely unreported in the newspapers surveyed, although occasional glimpses do emerge, as in the prewar Springhill strikes.

34 This argument is made by James R. Conley, 'Class Conflict and Collective Action in the Working Class of Vancouver, British Columbia, 1900–1919,' (PhD diss., Carleton University, 1986). On page 10, Conley provides a table listing the participants (by industry) in the general strike; among the exemptions are hotel and restaurant workers, hospital employees, laundry workers, and retail clerks. These groups all included large numbers of women. The surviving minutes of Local 28, Hotel, Restaurant and Culinary Employees and Bartenders' Union, 1910–21, University of British Columbia Special Collections, 1 June 1919, record a vote in favour of the sympathy strike, with 149 voting for and 75 against. While laundry workers were exempt, those in the union voted unanimously for the OBU. See Conley, 'Class Conflict,' 19. The laundry workers' strike of 9 Sept. to 31 Dec. 1918, which ended in defeat for most of the strikers who were replaced, is discussed in chapter 5 above.

35 Details of the telephone operators' history can be found in Elaine Bernard, *The Long Distance Feeling: A History of the Telecommunications Workers Union* (Vancouver, 1982), chaps. 1–3; see also Conley, 'Class Conflict' 552–59; quote from *Daily World*, 13 June 1919.

36 Strike support meetings are covered in the daily press. See *Daily World*, 16, 17 June 1919 (the twenty-four-person strike committee is also listed here) 19, 25 June 1919. Helena Gutteridge (1879?–1960) emigrated to Canada from England in 1911, already a suffragist and Labour Party member. She became active in the Vancouver TLC around 1913 and organized laundry and garment workers, as well as assisting other groups of women workers. In later years she joined the CCF and was active in Vancouver city politics, as well as pursuing her concern for peace in the WILPF. For more biographical information, see Susan Wade, 'Helena Gutteridge: Votes for Women and Trade Unions' in *In Her Own Right: Selected Essays on Women's History in BC*, ed. Barbara Latham and Cathy Kess (Victoria, 1980), 187–201. See also Irene Howard, *The Struggle for Social Justice in British Columbia: Helena Gutteridge, the Unknown Reformer* (Vancouver, 1992). On the SPC's attitudes towards women, see Linda Kealey, 'Canadian Socialism and the Woman Question, 1900–1914,' *Labour/Le Travail* 13 (Spring 1984): 77–100, and chapter 4 above. There had been a very active, if small, Social Democratic Party in Vancouver

before the war, but it seems to have dissipated during the later years of the
First World War.

37 David J. Bercuson, *Fools and Wise Men: The Rise and Fall of the One Big Union*
(Toronto 1978), especially chap. 6, 'Labour's Civil War.' Reports of fundraising by women appear in the OBU *Bulletin*, especially 13 Dec. 1919; 21 Feb.,
6 March, 27 Feb. (composition of the Defence Committee); 3, 9, 10 April 1920
(bazaar and dance raised almost $2500, attended by four thousand).

38 OBU *Bulletin*, 24 April 1920 (Labour Church Women's Auxiliary and Calgary
WLL). *WLN*, 7 May 1920 (May Day protest parade with one thousand
women and children, carried banner that read 'Labor's Boys of Today are the
Men of Tomorrow'), OBU *Bulletin*, 22 May, 5 June, 24 July 1920. Donations
were received from Mrs Mendelssohn, Montreal, Sarah Johnston-Knight,
Toronto, Mr and Mrs A.V. Thomas, New York. Funds also came from Winnipeg's Houseworkers' Association and individual Jewish women. On Helen
Armstrong's Ontario trip, see *WLN*, 12 Sept. and 3 Oct. 1919. Mrs Dixon's
speech in Saskatchewan: *WLN*, 18 July 1919. Sarah Johnston-Knight's activities, OBU *Bulletin*, 25 Oct. 1919. For Calgary, see *Searchlight*, 28 Nov. 1919,
2, 9 April, 28 May 1920; the *Calgary Herald*, 5 April 1920, covered the first
protest meeting.

39 OBU *Bulletin*, 22 Nov. 1919, 21 Feb. 1920, discusses the formation of the Needle Trades Council. Scattered references to specific groups of needle trades
workers are found in *Bulletin* issues throughout the fall of 1919 and in 1920.
For the Women's Auxiliary, see *Bulletin*, 10, 17 Jan., 6 March 1920. The *Bulletin* also reported on 17 April 1920 that the Weston/Brooklands WLL had
unanimously voted to change its name to the OBU Women's Auxiliary. The
Young Labor League in the North End of Winnipeg is reported in the *Bulletin*, 19 June 1920. Scattered issues of the paper give more detail on the
Women's Auxiliary. While Helen Armstrong did not take a public role in the
Central Women's Auxiliary, many of the names are familiar WLL names,
such as Mrs W. Logan and Mrs Watts. For Port Arthur and Fort William, see
*Bulletin*, 27 Nov. 1920, 4, 18, 25 Dec. 1920. For Vancouver, see *Searchlight*,
2 April 1920, and *Bulletin*, 18 Oct. 1919. Toronto women also showed some
interest in the OBU; see the *Bulletin*, 1 Nov. 1919 (textile and laundry workers). Women textile workers in small-town Ontario (i.e., Carleton Place and
Pembroke) also joined the OBU. See the *Bulletin*, 19 June 1920.

40 Craig Heron, 'Labourism and the Canadian Working Class,' *Labour/Le Travail*
13 (Spring 1984), 45–75; see also Alvin Finkel, 'The Rise and Fall of the
Labour Party in Alberta, 1917–1942,' *Labour/Le Travail* 16 (Fall 1985): 61–96.

41 The DLP was formed in 1918; candidates for school trustee were nominated at
a labour convention on 6 Oct. 1919. See *WLN*, 10 Oct. 1919. A Miss McBeth,

school teacher, was also endorsed by labour for the West Kildonan area. The debate on abolition of property qualifications raged in early 1920. See *WLN*, 16, 23 Jan., 27 Feb., 5, 26 March 1920. Armstrong is quoted in *WLN*, 12 Sept. 1919.

42 Alcin was attacked in the *Free Press* (hereafter *FP*), 21 Nov. 1919. For information on Kirk, see *FP*, 27 Nov. 1919; her firing is noted in *WLN*, 4 Oct. 1918. On Hancock, see *FP*, 28 Nov. 1919. The vote is reported in *WLN*, 5 Dec. 1919; Alcin beat Max Steinkoff 1,728 to 1,049. On Kirk's 1920 victory, see *WLN*, 10 Dec. 1920. For Kirk and Rowe's election to the DLP executive, see *WLN*, 12 March 1920. For examples of appeals to women to become active in labour politics, see *WLN*, 6 Sept. 1918 (Ivens); *WLN*, 5 Sept. 1919 (Bland); *WLN*, 7 March 1919 (Winona Flett [Mrs Dixon]); *WLN*, 27 Feb. 1920 (Rowe). On the provincial election of 1920, see Armstrong and Kirk's withdrawal in *WLN*, 16 April 1920, and Winona Flett's remarks at the labour rally in *WLN*, 25 June 1920. On Winnipeg's post-strike municipal elections, see J.E. Rea, 'The Politics of Conscience: Winnipeg after the Strike,' Canadian Historical Association *Historical Papers* (1971): 276–88, and his 'The Politics of Class: Winnipeg City Council, 1919–1945' in *The West and the Nation*, ed. Carl Berger and Ramsay Cook (Toronto, 1976), 232–49. Neither article notes women candidates.

43 W. Craig Heron, 'Working Class Hamilton, 1895–1930' (PhD diss., Dalhousie University, 1981), vol. 2, 437–69. *IB* 20 April, 4, 11 May, 6 July, 5 Oct. 1917, for discussions of the Women's ILP.

44 The convention launching the Ontario section of the Canadian Labor Party is reported in *IB*, 5 April 1918, and lists 400 delegates in total, including 100 from the ILP, 3 each from the SPNA and the Russian Revolutionary Party, 56 from the SDP, 7 miscellaneous, 7 from the United Farmers of Ontario and 34 trade unionists. The SPNA was a small, Toronto-based breakaway party from the SPC, formed in 1911. Most of its members became Communists in the 1920s. See Joan Sangster, *Dreams of Equality*, chap. 2 on Custance.

45 *IB*, 30 March 1917, 20 April 1917, 13 Oct. 1916 (TLC speech), 10 Nov. 1916 (lecture tour announced), 23 Feb. 1917 (suffrage). The western lecture tour is mentioned in the *Voice*, 19 Oct. 1917. See the *Voice*, 1 March 1918, for a letter of congratulation from Hughes to the Manitoba branch of the Labor Party. It also indicates her marriage and change of citizenship. Note the comments of socialist writer and intellectual T. Phillips Thompson, on Hughes in *Canadian Forward* (hereafter *CF*), 24 May 1917: 'Miss Laura Hughes has come so far already that she will probably go farther. It won't take such a brainy and progressive woman long to find out the futility of a so-called "Labor" movement that ignores Socialism.' Later in *CF*, 10 Aug. 1917, he predicts that Hughes will not stay with the ILP because of her anti-conscription views.

46 *IB*, 22 March, 12 April 1918. See *IB*, 22 Feb. 1918, and *Canadian Labor Leader*, 23 March 1918, for mention of Bessie Knight's activities in the London ILP.

Singer's speaking tour in 1919 is found in *IB*, 4 April, 2 May 1919; see also University of Toronto, Rare Books, Woodsworth Memorial Collection, MS 35, box 6, Thomas Tooms Papers, for the minutes of a public ILP meeting in Peterborough, 6 May, at which Singer spoke; Tooms was MPP for Peterborough. See also Naylor, *The New Democracy*, 148–9.

47  *IB*, 4 April 1919 (announcement of LEA initiative), 25 April 1919 (convention report of ILP)

48  *IB*, 25 April 1919; see the same issue for a letter from Rose Hodgson on 'Modern Christianity and the Socialistic Movement.' Curiously, the ILP meeting decided that women's branches should be represented on non-political bodies.

49  *IB*, 30 May 1919

50  *IB*, 4 July 1919, 5 Sept. 1919. On 20 Oct., the United Farmers of Ontario won forty seats at Queen's Park and formed the new government with the cooperation of eleven labour members.

51  For Singer's organizing tour, see the *Edmonton Free Press*, 8, 22 May 1920 (reprint of extract from the *Machinists' Monthly Journal*). See also, Heron, 'Labourism,' 68–71.

52  *Edmonton Free Press*, 10 July 1920, 5. Heron, 'Working Class Hamilton,' vol. 2, 466–9. See also Joan Sangster, *Dreams of Equality*, chap. 2, especially 28–31, 44–52, and Naylor, *The New Democracy*, 149.

53  See Dorothy Glen Papers, Metropolitan Toronto Public Library, for information on her personal and political background. She ran in Toronto for the Board of Education in 1920 and served as a vice-president of the ILP. On Brigden, see her 'One Woman's Campaign for Social Purity and Social Reform' in *The Social Gospel in Canada*, ed. Richard Allen (Ottawa, 1975), 36–62; see also PAM, Beatrice Brigden Collection, MG 14 C 19, General Correspondence, file 9, Brigden to Rev. T.A. Moore, 12 July 1920, where she declines further speaking engagements because of her health and her waning enthusiasm for the orthodox church: 'My work this spring was rather shockingly "radical" ... I am not very heroic and think it well to withdraw before "dismissal" comes "forthwith."'

54  *Workers' Weekly* 4, 25 June, 2 July, 6 Aug. 1920; see also *Edmonton Free Press*, 24 July 1920.

55  *Workers' Weekly*, 18 June 1920 (organization of the auxiliary in New Glasgow), 25 June 1920 (Henderson and Donaldson speak at organizational meeting of the Thorburn auxiliary), 9 July 1920 (nomination of Donaldson), 16 July 1920; 30 July 1920 (election results), 27 Aug. and 17 Sept. 1920 (Truro). See also 20 Aug. 1920, which reports Donaldson's presence among the new officers of the Farmer-Labor Party.

56  See note 28 above on Buhay and Buller; see also Joan Sangster, *Dreams of*

*Equality,* for detailed information on these early Communist women. See Ian Angus, *Canadian Bolsheviks: The Early Years of the Communist Party of Canada* (Montreal, 1981), which argues that an underground Communist Party existed by 1919. William Rodney, *Soldiers of the International: A History of the Communist Party of Canada, 1919–1929* (Toronto, 1968), provides one of the standard accounts.

57 Canadian Security and Intelligence Service, RCMP Records, Mrs Sophia Lindsay (McClusky), Personal History File, 1921–68, 10 (24 Feb. 1921); 32 (30 Nov. 1921); 33 (30 Jan. 1924); 34 (n.d.); 37 (9 Feb. 1925); 39–40 (25 June 1925); 41 (23 Aug. 1929, Halifax). Her remarriage was noted on page 187 (2 Feb. 1945); in the mid-1920s McClusky had separated from her husband, Wallace McClusky. See Glenbow-Alberta Institute, clipping file, 'Sophie McClusky,' which contains an undated newspaper clipping recording McClusky's appearance before Magistrate Sanders to prosecute a charge of non-support against her husband; Sanders used the opportunity to berate Mrs McClusky for her 'Communist ideas.' On McClusky's conflict with the Calgary School Board in 1921, see Glenbow-Alberta Institute, Calgary Protestant School Board Papers, box 40 B, Dept. of Education, Correspondence File, 1921, L–Z, letters dated 27 Oct., 1, 3 Nov. 1921, and clipping file, 'Sophie McClusky,' no date. (Thanks to Pat Roome for the clipping file and school board references.) On McClusky's Halifax period, see Linda Kealey, 'Sophie,' *New Maritimes,* Nov. 1987, 12–13.

## Conclusion

1 See Ruth Frager, *Sweatshop Strife: Class, Ethnicity, and Gender in the Jewish Labour Movement of Toronto, 1900–1939* (Toronto, 1992), 99, for evidence of this view among Toronto's Jewish community.
2 Ibid., 111. The emphasis on male breadwinning was key to both the labour and socialist movements' views of women's work and potential within political movements. For an attempt to contest this view, see Janice Newton, *The Feminist Challenge to the Canadian Left, 1900–1918* (Montreal and Kingston, 1995), 54–5 and 82–4.
3 *Cotton's Weekly,* 21 Jan. 1909; ibid., 1 April 1909
4 *Western Clarion,* Aug., 1911, 18
5 Quoted in Frager, *Sweatshop Strife,* 135
6 *Voice,* 1 Feb. 1918
7 *Canadian Forward,* 24 June 1918

# Selected Bibliography

ARCHIVAL SOURCES

**Canada**

*Canadian Security Intelligence Service (CSIS)*

RCMP Personal History Files. Rebecca Buhay
RCMP Personal History Files. Florence Custance
RCMP Personal History Files. Sophia Lindsay (McClusky)
Subject Files. Women's Labour League

*National Archives of Canada*

Manuscript Groups
 Finnish Organization of Canada Collection
 Sir Joseph Flavelle Papers
 J. Ramsay MacDonald Collection
 National Council of Women of Canada Papers
 Toronto Trades and Labor Council. Minutes
 J.S. Woodsworth Collection

Records Groups
 Department of Immigration and Colonization Papers
 Department of Justice Files
 Department of Labour. 'Evidence Taken Before the Royal Commission on
  Industrial Relations, Justice T.G. Mathers, Commissioner' (1919)

Department of Labour. Strikes and Lockouts Files
Department of National Defence. Papers
Secretary of State. Chief Press Censor's files

**Alberta**

Edmonton City Archives, Edmonton. Board of Public Welfare Papers

*Glenbow–Alberta Institute*

Brotherhood of Railway Trainmen, Mountain View Lodge, No. 333, Ladies'
   Auxiliary. Membership and Policy Register, c. 1908–42.
Calgary City Clerk Papers
Calgary Protestant School Board Papers
Calgary Trades and Labor Council Minutes, 1914–20
Clipping Files (McClusky, Sophie)
IBEW Local 348 (Calgary). Papers
Jean McWilliam McDonald. Papers
Irene Parlby Papers
United Brotherhood of Carpenters and Joiners, Local 1779 (Calgary)
   Minutes
United Mine Workers of America, District 18 Collection
WCTU Papers
Tom Williams Collection

*Provincial Archives of Alberta*

Attorney General's Files
Brotherhood of Locomotive Firemen and Engineers. Papers
Warren Carragata Papers
Alf. Farmilo Papers
Jean McWilliam McDonald Collection. 'Memoir' (typescript)

**British Columbia**

*Provincial Archives of British Columbia*

Attorney General. Correspondence. Inward, 1872–1937
Royal Commission on Labour, 1912–14
Women's Labour History Project Collection

*University of British Columbia, Special Collections*

William Bennett Memorial Collection
Colleen Bourke Collection (oral histories)
Ormond Lee Charlton Papers
Hotel, Restaurant and Culinary Employees and Bartenders Union, Local 28.
    Minutes 1910–21
Angus MacInnis Collection
Grace MacInnis Collection
Dorothy Steeves Collection
Vancouver Trades and Labor Council Minutes
Vancouver (Local) Council of Women. Minute Books, 1914–18
Western Federation of Miners/Mine-Mill Papers
E.E. Winch Papers

**Manitoba**

*Legislative Library of Manitoba*

Clipping Files. Obituaries
University Women's Club of Winnipeg. 'The Work of Women and Girls in the
    Department Stores of Winnipeg' (Winnipeg, 1914)
J.S. Woodsworth Pamphlet Collection

*Manitoba Museum of Man and Nature*

Oral History Collection

*Provincial Archives of Manitoba*

Attorney General. King vs. Ivens
Beatrice Brigden Papers
Department of Public Works. Fair Wage Board Papers
Department of Public Works. Minister of Public Works. Files
Deputy Minister's Files
Fred Dixon Papers
Manitoba Grain Growers' Association
R.A.C. Manning Papers
T.C. Norris Papers
Political Equality League. Minute Books

R.B. Russell Collection
Lillian Beynon Thomas Papers
United Farmers of Manitoba Papers
Winnipeg Construction Association Papers
Winnipeg Local Council of Women Papers

**New Brunswick**

University of New Brunswick. Harriet Irving Library. Henry Harvey Stuart
   Collection

**Nova Scotia**

*Provincial Archives of Nova Scotia*

E.H. Armstrong Papers
Halifax Local Council of Women. Papers, 1911–19
Halifax Typographical Union, Local 130. Minute Books

**Ontario**

*Metropolitan Toronto Public Library*

Dorothy Glen Papers
James Simpson Papers
Archer Wallace. 'History of Socialism in Toronto' (typescript)

*Provincial Archives of Ontario*

Max Dolgoy Collection
Solomon Eisen. Diary, Scrapbooks
Multicultural History Society of Ontario Collection
Abraham Nisnevitz Collection
Phillips Thompson Collection

*United Church Archives (Toronto)*

Samuel D. Chown Papers
A.E. Smith Papers

*University of Toronto, Rare Books and Special Collections*

Flora MacDonald Denison Papers
Kenny Collection
Thomas Tooms Papers
J.S. Woodsworth Memorial Collection

**Saskatchewan**

*Saskatchewan Archives Board, Regina*

Oral History Collections
Provincial Equal Franchise Board. Minute Book, 1915–18
Provincial Secretary. Correspondence of the Lieutenant-Governor
Regina Council of Women. Papers
Regina Trades and Labor Council. Minutes

*Saskatchewan Archives Board, Saskatoon*

Department of Agriculture. Bureau of Labor. Annual Reports 1911–20
Mrs S.V. Haight Papers
Local Council of Women. Minute Books
W.M. Martin Papers
Violet McNaughton Papers
Minimum Wage Board. Minute Book, 1919–29
Women Grain Growers' Association. Papers

NEWSPAPERS

*Alberta Non-Partisan* (Calgary)
*American Labor Union Journal* (Butte, MT)
*Amherst Evening News* (Amherst, NS)
*BC Federationist* (Vancouver)
*Bulletin* (International Association of Machinists, Winnipeg)
*Calgary Herald*
*Canadian Forward* (formerly *Cotton's Weekly*) (Toronto)
*Canadian Israelite* (Winnipeg)
*Canadian Labor Leader* (Sydney, NS)
*Canadian Socialist* (Toronto)

*Chervonyi Prapor (Red Flag)* (Winnipeg)
*Citizen and Country* (Toronto)
*Cotton's Weekly* (Cowansville, QC)
*Daily Examiner* (Peterborough, ON)
*Daily Mail* (Toronto)
*Daily Star* (Montreal)
*Daily Sun* (Saint John)
*Daily World* (Vancouver)
*Eastern Federationist* (New Glasgow, NS)
*Eastern Labor News* (Moncton, NB)
*Edmonton Free Press*
*Free Press* (Winnipeg)
*Garment Worker* (New York)
*Gazette* (Montreal)
*Globe* (Toronto)
*Globe and Mail* (Toronto)
*Grain Growers' Guide* (Winnipeg)
*Herald* (Halifax)
*Independent* (Vancouver)
*Industrial Banner* (London, ON, later Toronto)
*International Socialist Review* (Chicago)
*Jack Canuck* (Toronto)
*Journal* (Edmonton)
*Justice* (New York)
*Labor Advocate* (Toronto)
*Ladies' Garment Worker* (New York)
*Lance* (Toronto)
*Leicester Pioneer* (Leicester, England)
*Machinist Monthly Journal* (Washington, DC)
*Mail* (Halifax)
*Mail* (Toronto)
*Newcastle Advocate* (Newcastle, NB)
*Nutcracker* (Calgary)
*One Big Union Bulletin* (Winnipeg)
*Ottawa Citizen*
*Pacific Tribune* (Vancouver)
*Progressive Woman* (Chicago)
*Province* (Vancouver)
*Red Flag* (Vancouver)

*Robochyi Narod* (*Working People*) (Winnipeg)
*Saint John Semi-Weekly Sun*
*Saskatchewan's Labor's Realm* (Regina)
*Searchlight* (Calgary)
*Star* (Toronto)
*Strike Bulletin* (Calgary)
*Sun* (Vancouver)
*Social Justice* (Toronto)
*The Tailor* (Bloomington, IL)
*Telegram* (Toronto)
*Times* (Victoria)
*Toiler* (Toronto)
*Toronto World*
*Toveritar* (*Woman Comrade*) (Astoria, OR)
*Tribune* (Toronto)
*Tribune* (Winnipeg)
*Tyomies* (Hancock, MI)
*Vancouver World*
*Voice* (Winnipeg)
*Western Clarion* (Vancouver)
*Western Labor News* (Winnipeg)
*Western Socialist* (Vancouver)
*The Worker* (Toronto)
*Workers Weekly* (Stellarton, NS)
*Women's Century* (Toronto)
*Women Workers of Canada* (Montreal)

GOVERNMENT REPORTS AND PUBLICATIONS

British Columbia. Sessional Papers vol. 2. 1914. 'Report of the Royal Commis-
    sion on Labour'
Canada. 'Royal Commission on Industrial Training and Technical Education.'
    Sessional Paper 191d, Part IV. 1913
*Labour Gazette*. Ottawa.
Manitoba. 'Report of the Royal Commission on Technical Education and Indus-
    trial Training.' Sessional Paper No. 3. 1912
Nova Scotia. House of Assembly. *Journals* 1908–18.
*Report of the Ontario Commission on Unemployment*. Toronto, 1916
Wright, Alexander W. *Report of the Sweating System in Canada*. Ottawa, 1896

322   Selected Bibliography

PUBLISHED SOURCES

Allen, Richard. *The Social Passion: Religion and Social Reform in Canada, 1914–1928*. Toronto: University of Toronto Press, 1971

Angus, Ian. *Canadian Bolsheviks: The Early Years of the Communist Party of Canada*. Montreal: Vanguard, 1981

Avery, Donald. *'Dangerous Foreigners': European Immigrant Workers and Labour Radicalism in Canada, 1896–1932*. Toronto: McClelland and Stewart, 1979

Baron, Ava. 'On Looking at Men: Masculinity and the Making of a Gendered Working-Class History.' In *Feminists Revision History*, ed. Ann-Louise Shapiro, 146–71. New Brunswick, NJ: Rutgers University Press, 1994

Bernard, Elaine. *The Long Distance Feeling: A History of the Telecommunications Workers Union*. Vancouver: New Star Books, 1982

Bercuson, David. *Confrontation at Winnipeg: Labour, Industrial Relations, and the General Strike*. Montreal and Kingston: McGill-Queen's University Press, 1990

– *Fools and Wisemen: The Rise and Fall of the One Big Union*. Toronto: McGraw-Hill Ryerson, 1978

Bradbury, Bettina. *Working Families: Age, Gender, and Daily Survival in Industrializing Montreal*. Toronto: McClelland and Stewart, 1993

Buhle, Mari Jo. *Women and American Socialism, 1870–1920*. Urbana: University of Illinois Press, 1981

Burnet, Jean, ed. *Looking into My Sisters Eyes: An Exploration in Women's History*. Toronto: Multicultural History Society of Ontario, 1986

Calliste, Agnes. 'Race, Gender, and Canadian Immigration Policy: Blacks from the Caribbean, 1900–1932.' In *Gender and History in Canada*, ed. Joy Parr and Mark Rosenfeld, 70–87. Toronto: Copp Clark, 1996

Cameron, Ardis. *Radicals of the Worst Sort: Laboring Women in Lawrence, Massachusetts, 1860–1912*. Urbana: University of Illinois Press, 1993

Chown, Alice A. *The Stairway*. Boston, 1921

Cook, Ramsay. 'Francis Marion Beynon and the Crisis of Christian Reformism.' In *The West and the Nation*, ed. Carl Berger and Ramsay Cook, 187–208. Toronto: McClelland and Stewart, 1976

– *The Regenerators: Social Criticism in Late Victorian English Canada*. Toronto: University of Toronto Press, 1985

Derry, Kathleen, and Paul H. Douglas. 'The Minimum Wage in Canada.' *Journal of Political Economy* (April 1922): 156–74

Ewen, Geoffrey. 'La Contestation ouvrière à Montréal en 1919.' *Histoire de travailleurs Québécois* (Bulletin de RCHTQ) 36 (Automne 1986): 37–62.

Ferland, Jacques. '"In Search of the Unbound Prometheia": A Comparative View of Women's Activism in Two Quebec Industries, 1869–1908.' *Labour/Le Travail* 24 (Fall 1989): 11–44

Forster, Dora. *Sex Radicalism as Seen by an Emancipated Woman of the New Time.* Chicago: M. Harman, 1905

Frager, Ruth. *Sweatshop Strife: Class, Ethnicity, and Gender in the Jewish Labour Movement of Toronto, 1900–1939.* Toronto: University of Toronto Press, 1992

Frank, Dana. *Purchasing Power: Seattle Labor and the Politics of Consumption, 1919–1929.* Cambridge: Cambridge University Press, 1994

Frank, David, and Nolan Reilly. 'The Emergence of the Socialist Movement in the Maritimes, 1899–1916.' *Labour/Le Travailleur* 4 (Fall 1979): 85–113

Granatstein, J.L., and J.M. Hitsman. *Broken Promises: A History of Conscription in Canada.* Toronto: Oxford University Press, 1977

Greenwald, Maurine Weiner. *Women, War, and Work: The Impact of World War I on Women Workers in the United States.* Westport, CT: Greenwood Press, 1980

Guildford, Janet, and Suzanne Morton, eds. *Separate Spheres: Women's Worlds in the Nineteenth-Century Maritimes.* Fredericton: Acadiensis Press, 1994

Henderson, Rose. *Woman and War.* N.p., 1924

Heron, Craig, and Robert Storey, eds. *On the Job: Confronting the Labour Process in Canada.* Kingston: McGill-Queen's University Press, 1986

Howard, Irene. *The Struggle for Social Justice in British Columbia: Helena Gutteridge, the Unknown Reformer.* Vancouver: UBC Press, 1992

Iacovetta, Franca, and Mariana Valverde, eds. *Gender Conflicts: New Essays in Women's History.* Toronto: University of Toronto Press, 1992

Joussaye, Marie. *Songs that Quinte Sang.* Belleville, ON: n.p., 1895

Kealey, Greg. *Canada Investigates Industrialism.* Toronto: University of Toronto Press, 1973

– *Toronto Workers Respond to Industrial Capitalism, 1867–1892*, rev. ed. Toronto: University of Toronto Press, 1991

Kealey, Gregory S., and Bryan D. Palmer, *Dreaming of What Might Be: The Knights of Labor in Ontario, 1880–1900.* New York: Cambridge University Press, 1982

Kealey, Linda, and Joan Sangster, eds. *Beyond the Vote: Canadian Women and Politics.* Toronto: University of Toronto Press, 1989

Kerr, Donald, and D.W. Holdsworth, eds. *Historical Atlas of Canada.* Vol. 3. *Addressing the Twentieth Century, 1891–1961.* Toronto: University of Toronto Press, 1990

Kinnear, Mary. 'Post-Suffrage Prairie Politics: Women Candidates in Winnipeg Municipal Elections, 1918–1939.' *Prairie Forum* 16, 1 (Spring 1991): 41–57

– , ed. *First Days, Fighting Days: Women in Manitoba History.* Regina: Canadian Plains Research Center, 1987

Krawchuk, Peter. *The Ukrainian Socialist Movement in Canada, 1907–1918*. Toronto: Progress Books, 1979

Latham, Barbara, and Cathy Kess, eds. *In Her Own Right: Selected Essays on Women's History in BC*. Victoria: Camosun College, 1981

Levine, Susan. 'Workers' Wives: Gender, Class, and Consumerism in the 1920s United States.' *Gender and History* 3, 1 (1991): 45–64

Lindström-Best, Varpu. *Defiant Sisters: A Social History of the Finnish Immigrant Women in Canada, 1890–1930*. Toronto: Multicultural History Society of Ontario, 1988

Mardiros, Anthony. *William Irvine: The Life of a Prairie Radical*. Toronto: Lorimer, 1979

Martynowych, Orest T. *Ukrainians in Canada: The Formative Period, 1891–1924*. Edmonton: Canadian Institute of Ukrainian Studies Press, 1991

McCallum, Margaret E. 'Keeping Women in Their Place: The Minimum Wage in Canada, 1910–1925.' *Labour/Le Travail* 17 (Spring 1986): 29–56

McCormack, Ross. *Reformers, Rebels, and Revolutionaries: The Western Canadian Radical Movement, 1899–1919*. Toronto: University of Toronto Press, 1977

McIntosh, Robert. 'Sweated Labour: Female Needleworkers in Industrializing Canada.' *Labour/Le Travail* 32 (Fall 1993): 105–38

McKay, Ian, ed. *For a Working-Class Culture in Canada: A Selection of Colin McKay's Writings on Sociology and Political Economy, 1897–1939*. St John's: Canadian Committee on Labour History, 1996

McLaren, Angus. *Our Own Master Race: Eugenics in Canada, 1885–1945*. Toronto: McClelland and Stewart, 1990

Milkman, Ruth, ed. *Women, Work, and Protest: A Century of Women's Labor History*. Boston: Routledge and Kegan Paul, 1985

Morgan, Henry J. *The Canadian Men and Women of the Time*. Toronto: William Briggs, 1912.

Muise, D.A. 'The Industrial Context of Inequality: Female Participation in Nova Scotia's Paid Labour Force, 1871–1921.' *Acadiensis* 20, 2 (Spring 1991): 3–31

Murray, Sylvie. *A la Junction du mouvement ouvrier et du mouvement des femmes: La Ligue Auxiliaire de l'Association Internationale des Machinistes, Canada, 1903–1980*. Montreal: RCHTQ, 1990

Naylor, James. *The New Democracy: Challenging the Social Order in Industrial Ontario, 1914–1925*. Toronto: University of Toronto Press, 1991

Newton, Janice. *The Feminist Challenge to the Canadian Left, 1900–1918*. Montreal and Kingston: McGill-Queen's University Press, 1995

Parr, Joy. *The Gender of Breadwinners: Women, Men, and Change in Two Industrial Towns, 1880–1950*. Toronto: University of Toronto Press, 1990

Penfold, Steven. '"Have You No Manhood in You?": Gender and Class in the

Cape Breton Coal Towns, 1920–1926.' In *Gender and History in Canada*, ed. Joy Parr and Mark Rosenfeld, 270–93. Toronto: Copp Clark, 1996

Pittenger, Mark. *American Socialists and Evolutionary Thought, 1870–1920*. Madison: University of Wisconsin Press, 1993

Piva, Michael. *The Condition of the Working Class in Toronto, 1900–1921*. Ottawa: University of Ottawa Press, 1979

Pon, Madge. 'Like a Chinese Puzzle: The Construction of Chinese Masculinity in *Jack Canuck*.' In *Gender and History in Canada*, ed. Joy Parr and Mark Rosenfeld, 88–100. Toronto: Copp Clark, 1996

Price, Enid M. 'Changes in the Industrial Occupations of Women in the Environment of Montreal during the Period of the War, 1914–1918' (MA thesis, McGill University, 1919)

Roberts, Barbara. *A Reconstructed World: A Feminist Biography of Gertrude Richardson*. Montreal and Kingston: McGill-Queen's University Press, 1996

– '"Why Do Women Do Nothing to End War?": Canadian Feminist Pacifists and the Great War.' CRIAW Paper No. 13 (Ottawa: CRIAW, 1985)

Roberts, Wayne. *Honest Womanhood: Feminism, Femininity, and Class Consciousness among Toronto Working Women, 1893–1914*. Toronto: New Hogtown Press, 1976

Rodney, William. *Soldiers of the International: A History of the Communist Party of Canada, 1919–1929*. Toronto: University of Toronto Press, 1968

Ross, Carl, and K. Marianne Wargelin Brown, eds. *Women Who Dared: The History of Finnish American Women*. St Paul: Immigration History Research Center, University of Minnesota, 1986

Rouillard, Jacques. *Les Travailleurs du coton au Québec, 1900–1915*. Montreal: Presses de l'Université du Québec, 1974

Sangster, Joan. *Dreams of Equality: Women on the Canadian Left, 1920–1950*. Toronto: McClelland and Stewart, 1989

– 'The 1907 Bell Telephone Strike: Organizing Women Workers.' *Labour/Le Travailleur* 3 (1978): 109–31

Schwantes, Carlos. *Radical Heritage: Labor, Socialism, and Reform in Washington and British Columbia, 1887–1917*. Seattle: University of Washington Press, 1979

Scott, Jean Thomson. 'The Conditions of Female Labour in Ontario.' *Toronto University Studies in Political Science* 1 (1892)

Social Survey Commission of Toronto. *Report*. Toronto, 1915

Stewart, Bryce M. *Canadian Labor Laws and the Treaty*. New York: Columbia University Press, 1926

Strange, Carolyn. *Toronto's Girl Problem: The Perils and Pleasures of the City, 1880–1930*. Toronto: University of Toronto Press, 1995

Strong-Boag, Veronica. *The New Day Recalled: Lives of Girls and Women in English Canada, 1919–1939*. Toronto: Copp Clark Pitman, 1988

- *The Parliament of Women: The National Council of Women of Canada, 1893–1929.* Ottawa: National Museum of Man, 1976

Taylor, Barbara. *Eve and the New Jerusalem: Socialism and Feminism in the Nineteenth Century.* London: Virago Press, 1984

Thompson, John Herd. *The Harvests of War: The Prairie West, 1914–1918.* Toronto: McClelland and Stewart, 1978

Tucker, Eric. *Administering Danger in the Workplace: The Law and Politics of Occupational Health and Safety Regulation in Ontario, 1850–1914.* Toronto: University of Toronto Press, 1990

Tulchinsky, Gerald. *Taking Root: The Origins of the Canadian Jewish Community.* Toronto: Lester, 1992

Valverde, Mariana. *The Age of Light, Soap, and Water: Moral Reform in English Canada, 1885–1925.* Toronto: McClelland and Stewart, 1991

# Index

domestic service 10, 22–3, 27, 32, 130, 144, 156, 163, 237, 247
Domestic Workers' Association (Toronto) 237, 246
Dominion Labor Party 243, 248
Donaldson, Bertha M. 249
Draper, P.M. 184
Drummond, Lady Julia 27
Dunn, T.H. 237

T. Eaton Company 38, 178, 224. *See also* strikes: garments, Toronto
Edmonton Trades and Labor Council 211–12
Elwood, Edith 69–70
Engels, Friedrich 92, 101, 133
enlistments, First World War 194, 202, 208
Epplett, E.M. 118, 133
equal pay 22, 148, 153, 156, 162, 175, 182, 190–1, 197, 206, 235–6, 238, 257
ethnicity/race 8–10, 17, 68–9, 114, 185–6, 188, 216, 222, 233, 257

Fabian League 29–31
factory acts: British Columbia 35–6; Manitoba 34, 174; New Brunswick 29–32; Nova Scotia 29, 32–3; Ontario 26–7
fair wage legislation 164. *See also* minimum wage legislation
family wage 4–5, 16, 43, 48, 144–5, 148, 168, 174, 217, 247, 254
Farmilo, Alf 212
Federated Labor Party 239
Federation of Ukrainian Social Democrats (FUSD) 126
femininity 7, 78, 253, 256
feminism 12, 125, 142, 170, 192, 199, 201, 234, 256

Fenton, Mary 160
Ferland, Jacques 73
Fillmore, Roscoe 139, 141, 145
Finnish Socialist Organization of Canada (FSOC) 137
Fiske, Emma 30
Flavelle, Sir Joseph 157–61, 190
Flett, Lynn 121, 169, 172
Flett, Winona (later Dixon) 121, 240, 243
Frager, Ruth 9, 66–7, 130
Francis, Miss 229–30
Frank, Dana 6
Fraser, Florence 134
Fraser, H.D. 249

garment trade, organization of 63
Gauld, Bella 250
general strikes (1919): Amherst, NS 237–8; Toronto 236–7
general sympathetic strikes (1919): Calgary 232; Regina 231; Saskatoon 230; Vancouver 238–9
German Social Democratic Party (SPD) 113–14
Glen, Dorothy 248
Gonevitch, Rose 129
Gordon, Dr Margaret 122, 201
Gouldie, Fred 227
Greenwald, Maurine 183
Grevette, Mrs F.G. 206–7
Gribble, Wilf 112, 129, 139, 212
Gurofsky, Louis 24–5
Gutteridge, Helena 120–1, 147–8, 153, 154–5, 161, 186–7, 239

Haight, Zoe 214
Haile, Margaret 97, 101
Hancock, Edith 220, 243
Hatheway, W.F. 29–30

_retail sales 3 6-39_

Women Shoe Fitters' Association 53, 73

women's auxiliaries 79–85; New Glasgow, ILP 249; of the OBU 241

Women's Cooperative Guild 86–7. *See also* Winnipeg Cooperative Society

Women's Employment League (Vancouver) 147–8, 154–5

Women's Independent Labor Party: Hamilton 244, 248; St Catharines 245, 247–8

Women's Institutes 207, 213

Women's International League for Peace and Freedom (WILPF) 201

Women's International Union Label League (WIULL) 85–6

Women's Labor League: Calgary 215; Cape Breton 7; Hamilton 248; Regina 229, 231; Toronto 134, 237; Winnipeg 7, 38–9, 82, 121, 165, 168–71, 211, 215–16, 224, 227–8, 240, 243

women's paid work, socialist views of 143–4, 146–8

Women's Peace Crusade 200, 258

Women's Social Democratic League (WSDL) 122, 129, 133–5, 210, 237, 257

women's strike activity 47, 49, 54–5, 175–7, 191, 254–5, 257. *See also* strikes

women's wages 35–7, 42, 53, 55, 59–60, 64, 69–72, 74, 76, 151, 156,

167–8, 179, 182, 186–7, 229–30, 232, 237; in munitions, 160–1. *See also* minimum wage legislation

women's work; non-traditional 84, 152–3, 181–5, 191, 197; in munitions, 156–62

Woodsworth, J.S. 35, 38

Woolworth's strike 165, 170

Workers' Council 209

Workers' Party 141, 248, 251

Working Women's Protective Association (Women's Protective Union) 3, 27–8, 49, 53, 73, 254

Woywitka, Anne 128

Wright, A.W. 23

Wrigley, George 94, 98

Wrigley, George Weston 95–6, 109–10, 117, 123–4

Wrigley, Sarah 94–5

Youmans, Miss M.E. 96

Young, May 134

Young Jewish Literary Association 129

Young Jewish Workers' Club 129

Young Peoples' Socialist League 134

Young Socialist Club 129

Young Women's Christian Association (YWCA) 38, 195, 224

Zeimanovich, Sara 130

Zetkin, Clara 113–14

# STUDIES IN GENDER AND HISTORY

General editors: Franca Iacovetta and Karen Dubinsky

# STUDIES IN GENDER AND HISTORY

General editors: Franca Iacovetta and Karen Dubinsky

1 Suzanne Morton, *Ideal Surroundings: Domestic Life in a Working-Class Suburb in the 1920s*

2 Joan Sangster, *Earning Respect: The Lives of Working Women in Small-Town Ontario, 1920–1960*

3 Cecilia Morgan, *Public Men and Virtuous Women: The Gendered Languages of Religion and Politics in Upper Canada, 1791–1850*

4 Mona Gleason, *Normalizing the Ideal: Psychology, Schooling, and the Family in Postwar Canada*

5 Cynthia Comacchio, *The Infinite Bonds of Family: Domesticity in Canada, 1850–1940*

6 Kathryn McPherson, Cecilia Morgan, and Nancy M. Forestell, eds., *Gendered Pasts: Historical Essays in Femininity and Masculinity in Canada*

7 Linda Kealey, *Enlisting Women for the Cause: Women, Labour, and the Left in Canada, 1890–1920*

8 Joy Parr and Mark Rosenfeld, eds., *Gender and History in Canada*

9 Veronica Strong-Boag, *The New Day Recalled: Lives of Girls and Women in English Canada, 1919–1939*